ACCESS AFRICA

SAFARIS FOR PEOPLE WITH LIMITED MOBILITY

Gordon Rattray

With foreword by John Carter

edition 1

www.bradtguides.com

Bradt Travel Guides Ltd, UK
The Globe Pequot Press Inc, USA

Gulf of Aden

Equator

500km
500 miles
0
0

ATLANTIC
OCEAN

Lake Nakuru National Park
Kenya
Page 137

Amboseli National Park
Kenya
Page 151

Zanzibar
Tanzania
Page 203

The Maasai Mara/ Serengeti ecosystem
Tanzania & Kenya
Pages 145 & 195

Ngorongoro Crater Conservation Area
Tanzania
Page 192

Moyale

Lodwar

Lake
Turkana

K E N Y A

▲ Mt. Kenya

NAIROBI

Lamu Island

Amboseli
NP

Mt. Kilimanjaro

MOMBASA

Maasai Mara
NP

Lake
Victoria

Serengeti
NP

MWANZA

Ngorongoro
Crater NP

ARUSHA

Zanzibar
DAR ES

DODOMA

Lake
Tanganyika

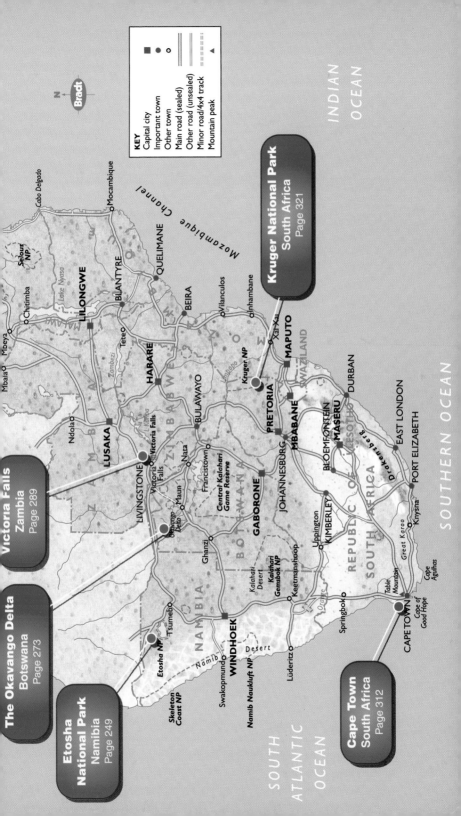

KEY
■ Capital city
● Important town
○ Other town
━━━ Main road (sealed)
═══ Other road (unsealed)
┅┅┅ Minor road/4x4 track
▲ Mountain peak

N
Bradt

INDIAN OCEAN

Kruger National Park
South Africa
Page 321

Victoria Falls
Zambia
Page 289

The Okavango Delta
Botswana
Page 273

Etosha National Park
Namibia
Page 249

Cape Town
South Africa
Page 312

Mozambique Channel

SOUTH ATLANTIC OCEAN

SOUTHERN OCEAN

Cabo Delgado
Mocambique
QUELIMANE
BLANTYRE
LILONGWE
Chitimba
Mbala
Mbeya
Lake Nyasa
Selous NP
Tete
BEIRA
Vilanculos
Inhambane
QUELIMANE
Zambezi
HARARE
BULAWAYO
LUSAKA
Ndola
ZIMBABWE
ZAMBIA
MOZAMBIQUE
Kariba
Kafue
Victoria Falls
LIVINGSTONE
Victoria Falls
Nata
Francistown
Maun
Okavango Delta
Okavango NP
Ghanzi
Central Kalahari Game Reserve
GABORONE
BOTSWANA
JOHANNESBURG
PRETORIA
Kruger NP
MAPUTO
Xai-Xai
MBABANE
SWAZILAND
MASERU
LESOTHO
BLOEMFONTEIN
Drakensberg
DURBAN
EAST LONDON
PORT ELIZABETH
Great Karoo
Knysna
KIMBERLEY
Uppington
Keetmanshoop
Kalahari Gemsbok NP
Kalahari Desert
NAMIBIA
WINDHOEK
Tsumeb
Etosha NP
Namib Desert
Swakopmund
Namib Naukluft NP
Skeleton Coast NP
Lüderitz
Springbok
Orange
Cape of Good Hope
Cape Agulhas
Table Mountain
CAPE TOWN
REPUBLIC OF SOUTH AFRICA

Access
Africa

Don't
miss...

The Great Migration
A timeworn traipse through the
Serengeti and Maasai Mara (TI)
pages 145–51 & 195–202

Zanzibar
East Africa's tropical
'spice island' (AVZ/FLPA)
pages 203–18

The Okavango Delta
A pristine wilderness surrounded by desert
(FL/FLPA) pages 273–80

Victoria Falls
The largest sheet of falling water in the world
(IV) pages 289–305

Kruger National Park
One of Africa's largest and most accessible national parks
(JCS/FLPA)
pages 321–9

left **Craft market in Windhoek, Namibia**
(J&SH) pages 223–33

below **Stone Town, Zanzibar** (IV) page 203

bottom **Cape Town and Table Mountain, South Africa** (IB/FLPA) pages 312–21

right **Roadside shop, Kenya** (IV) pages 115–69

below **On the way to work, Zanzibar** (IV) pages 203–18

bottom **Swakopmund, Namibia** (J&SH) pages 233–40

top left **Samburu girl, Kenya** (IV)

top right **Maasai children, Tanzania** (IV)

above left **Man from the Kapoko Tribe Cultural Group, Katima Mulilo, Caprivi** (J&SH)

above right **Two Nama ladies, Solitaire near Sesriem** (J&SH)

below **Man fishing in the Okavango Delta, Botswana** (TI)

FOREWORD *John Carter*

More years ago than I care to remember, I broadcast once a month on Radio 2's *Jimmy Young Programme*, dealing with listeners' travel and holiday questions.

One came from a middle-aged single man in (I think) Nottingham. Following the death of his mother, he wanted to fulfil his ambition of travelling around the world. The only 'fly in the ointment' – to use his phrase – was that childhood polio had confined him to a wheelchair. What did I advise?

After a lot of thought, I said he should go for it. If he didn't, he would spend the rest of his life wondering what might have been. There would be obvious difficulties and hazards, but it was possible.

During the course of the live broadcast we got a lot of telephone calls saying this was very bad advice – and a bare handful agreeing with me.

Either way it was a tough call, for this was a time when most people referred to 'the handicapped' and thought they should be kept out of mainstream activities for their own good.

I subsequently spent some time talking with a couple of disability organisations and the London tourist offices of the countries the Nottingham chap planned to visit. They, and the airlines, went out of their way to help.

He made that trip. And returned to England with a wife. Like him, she was in a wheelchair, and they met through an organisation in Bangkok that had agreed – like so many others along his route – to look out for him.

It is because of that memory and my opinion that, with determination, most obstacles can be overcome, that I was both pleased and honoured to be asked to write these words, commending Gordon Rattray's book to you.

Like me, you may be fortunate enough to have suffered no illness or injury that affects your mobility. However, none of us can escape the effects of the passing years and the wear and tear of time on our bodies. That might have slowed us down, but it is no reason to stop travelling. Nor should disability be a reason to give up the wonderful experiences the world has to offer – destinations to enjoy and fascinating people to meet along the way.

Gordon Rattray has done us all a favour by producing this book. Go for it!

John Carter was for many years a lead writer and presenter on BBC's *Holiday*, ITV's *Wish You Were Here...?* and was former Travel Editor for *The Times*.

PRAISE FOR THIS BOOK

"This unique book is an inspiring and invaluable resource for those with a can-do attitude and a sense of adventure. With thorough firsthand research, Gordon Rattray opens up safari holidays to those who may have thought them an impossibility. This book is a must for those who refuse to let limited mobility stop them exploring the world's most exciting places."
Ade Adepitan, Paralympian and television presenter

"An excellent guidebook offering practical and comprehensive advice to the less-mobile traveller. It is not uncommon to find journals offering this level of detail and advice to able-bodied travellers, but regrettably, it is a rarity to find such wide ranging, firsthand knowledge and experience, offered in a well-respected publication, for the disabled traveller."
Andy Wright, MD of Accessible Travel

"I have waited eagerly for the release of this guide which fills a gaping hole in travel resources on Africa for the world's 500 million persons with disabilities.
   Gordon Rattray is well-respected for his work among African tour operators who offer accessible safaris. *Access Africa* is carefully researched by an author with intimate knowledge of African tourism as well as the unique travel priorities of persons with disabilities. If you plan to safari in Africa, buy this book!"
Dr Scott Rains, international advisor on disability travel and owner of The Rolling Rains Report

"Before discovering this guidebook, I would have considered an organised African safari or – bolder yet – independent travel in east and southern Africa to be among the most challenging holiday options any person with limited mobility could undertake. *Access Africa* argues convincingly against such perceptions, even for wheelchair users. Speaking from the heart as well as from personal experience, the author offers plenty of travel tips for people with special needs as well as detailed action plans for independent exploration. [...] He marries inspiration and strategic reality within every page of this path-breaking book."
Alison Gardner, Editor of Travel with a Challenge *web magazine,* www.travelwithachallenge.com

"As a wheelchair user, I know how difficult and stressful it can be to travel abroad. I've travelled all over the world and have experienced the problems people with limited mobility can face. There are so many unknowns and options are often limited, which is why this book is such a fantastic resource and will be a great help for people who would like more adventurous holidays."
Stephen Miller, three times Paralympic champion

AUTHOR

Gordon Rattray graduated in Botany from Glasgow University, but itchy feet led him from the lab to travel through Australia and New Zealand. Truck driving and a passion for adventure eventually brought him to Africa where he had the good fortune to explore more than 20 countries as an overland driver. A diving accident cut this short and rendered him a wheelchair user, but Gordon soon returned to the continent and discovered how possible adventurous travel with a disability can be. He is a regular contributor to Bradt guides and runs ⌂ www.able-travel.com, an information service for travellers with disabilities.

AUTHOR'S STORY

I first went to Africa in the mid 1990s, yearning adventure. The continent has long been synonymous with some of the greatest tales of exploration, so excitement was not hard to find. Fast forward to 2000 when, after becoming quadriplegic, I was hankering to return. The potential for problems appeared huge and what had previously been challenges now looked more like insurmountable barriers. As many people with disabilities will know, the mere thought of leaving the security of home can be stomach churning. For me, doubts about access (specifically bathroom issues) were the first to arise, then worries such as how my body would respond to the heat and how Africans would react to my disability were quick to follow. One friend suggested that it might be good to go back 'if only to get Africa out of your system'. But although he meant well, he was mistaken. That trip became the first of many.

I soon realised that safaris were quite feasible for less-mobile travellers, but a lack of information meant that many people were missing out. Bradt were easily persuaded of the need for this guide and very soon I had the dubious pleasure of counting steps and measuring toilets throughout the safari circuit. Virtually everywhere I went, owners, management and staff were enthusiastic, desperate to show where they'd made efforts to cater to disabled guests and eager to learn how they could do more. I carried guidelines with me and not only have I received emails since, with images showing where adaptations have been made, but some changes were even made during my visit!

If the idea of a safari appeals, then read on, but be warned – Africa is addictive. Far from 'getting it out of my system', each return trip I make now just accentuates how much more is possible. Accommodation is becoming inclusive and I notice increasingly that I'm not the only traveller using the disability services in African airports. The most exciting continent on earth has taken its time, but it is now opening its doors to everyone.

First published August 2009

Bradt Travel Guides Ltd,
23 High Street, Chalfont St Peter, Bucks SL9 9QE, England; www.bradtguides.com
Published in the USA by The Globe Pequot Press Inc, 246 Goose Lane,
PO Box 480, Guilford, Connecticut 06437-0480
Text copyright © 2009 Gordon Rattray
Maps copyright © 2009 Bradt Travel Guides Ltd
Photographs copyright © 2009 Individual photographers
Editorial Project Manager: Anna Moores

ISBN-13: 978 1 84162 286 6
British Library Cataloguing in Publication Data
A catalogue record for this book is available from the British Library

Photographs Asbl Décalage (AD); David Delmage (DD); Endeavour Safaris (ES); FLPA:
ImageBroker (IB/FLPA), Jurgen & Christine Sohns (JCS/FLPA), Frans Lanting (FL/FLPA),
Ariadne Van Zandbergen (AVZ/FLPA); Go Africa Safaris & Travel (GS); Judy & Scott Hurd
(J&SH); MalaMala Game Reserve (MM); Ngepi Camp (NG); Riz Jiwa (RJ); Tips Images (TI);
Ingrid Vekemans (IV)
Front cover Design by James Nunn. Images: Reticulated giraffes in Etosha National Park,
Bull African Elephant near Victoria Falls (both IV), Birdwatching in Tsavo National Park,
Kenya (Mark Boulton/Alamy)
Title page Lilac-breasted roller, Springbok, Diani Beach, Mombasa, Kenya (all IV)
Back cover Lion (IV), Man in Namibia (J&SH) & Burchell's zebras (IV)
Page i John Carter © www.travelguru.tv
Maps Dave Priestley (with Tanzania maps based on source material from Philip Briggs;
Namibia, Botswana & Livingstone maps based on source material from Chris McIntyre;
Kruger, Addo and the Cape Peninsula maps based on source material from SANParks; Cape
Town map based on source material from SA Venues (*www.sa-venues.com*))

Typeset from the author's disc by Artinfusion
Printed and bound in India by Nutech Print Services

Acknowledgements

This guide would never have been completed without the help of a large number of people. Some I knew before I began but most I've met – to my great pleasure – along the way. I thank them all and apologise now to any I may have forgotten to mention.

The vast majority of the research was done in Africa. For Kenya and Tanzania, the organisation and support of Yvonne Matiba and Esther Nthemba of Go Africa Safaris was invaluable at every stage. Bedan Mbui not only drove but was happy to assist with transfers, and George Egondi also helped for part of the journey. Maria Luijten of Southern Cross Safaris, Faith Mbaya of Sarova Hotels and Mutua Kivuitu, John Kinyua and George Kiama of Guerba Kenya also provided vital support for the mainland section of this trip, while Salma Salum and Kheir Kombo at Sama Tours ensured Zanzibar was equally problem-free. In Namibia, Zambia and Botswana, Martin Webb-Bowen of SandyAcre Safaris provided faultless logistical support while his team – expert driver Rodney Katuutja and superb assistant Nyathi Mwariombande – made sure the journey went exactly to plan. Karin Coetzee contributed detailed information for much of the South Africa content, especially Kruger National Park where Chris Patton of SANParks provided the essential planning advice.

Within Africa there is a growing band of operators who genuinely cater to the needs of less mobile travellers, all of whom selflessly offered information and advice. In no particular order, and not forgetting the aforementioned Yvonne and Esther of Go Africa Safaris, these include Pam and Jeff Taylor of Flamingo Tours, Jennae Bezuidenhout of Access2Africa Safaris, Sabine and Alfie Smith of Epic Enabled, Pete and Annabel Hemingway of Hemingways and Mike and Silvia Hill of Endeavour Safaris. Thanks especially to the latter couple for their kind hospitality in Maun.

I am also in debt to several experts in various fields. Thoughts from Chris McIntyre and Bruce Cameron helped me plan the research strategy and book format, while Philip Briggs was always forthcoming with advice and information. Dr Jane Wilson-Howarth patiently checked and corrected the health information (several times!) and I am also very grateful to Mr David Allen of Scotland's National Spinal Injuries Unit for reading that text through and giving his suggestions.

Many travellers and travel professionals furnished me with access reports, advice and general information. Again, in no particular order, these include Tricia Hayne, Marius Barnard, Martin Webb-Bowen, Scott Rains, Tracy Lederer, Michael Sweeney, Candy Harrington, Colin Javens, Chris Campbell-Rodgers, Graham Teager, Jane Stuckey, Daryl Flint, David and Kay Delmage, Keith Somerville, Jaap Smith, Sheena Nicolson (who also proofread much of the text), Sue Mitchell, David Roberts, Xavier Thirionet, Scott Hurd, Janet and Allan Bimson at the Sedia Hotel in Maun, Ari Sierlis and Carla-Jane Haines from QASA, Tony and Clover King at Safpar, and Riz Jiwa, Annette Bulman and Ron Beaton in the Maasai

Mara. As well as these, I received tips on how to cope with mobility difficulties from, amongst others, Amanda Salas, Sue Mack, Eric Doran, Lieke Scheewe, Angela Mundt, Margit Schäfer, Colin Stewart, Yvonne Tollan, Hefina Sunderland, Lauren Meisner, Kyran Geraghty, Anya Clowers, Katja Stokley, John Cook, Jane Brymer, Helen McGowan, Frank Gardner, Karin Broske, David Egan, Debra Berry, Jean Davis, Dammy Vermeers, Brian Schiner, Kendall Artz and Hilton Purvis.

I am equally grateful to everyone in Africa who helped with accommodation and to those who assisted with air travel. Without that, none of the rest would have been possible.

The whole Bradt team was superb throughout, but Anna Moores' meticulous management and Adrian Phillips' unwavering support deserve special mention; they complemented Hilary's initial enthusiasm for the project perfectly. In the latter stages, Dave Priestley, who patiently redrew my maps, and the designers at Artinfusion have done a marvellous job – thank you all.

Finally, I am most in debt to Ingrid, who not only provided the bulk of the photographs for the book and accompanying website, but has (arguably) kept me sane throughout.

KEY TO STANDARD SYMBOLS Bradt

■	Capital city	•	Other attraction
•	City/town	✈	Airport – international/domestic
○	Village	✛	Airstrip
⌂	Hotel/guesthouse		Ferry – car/passenger
⊠	Post office	↘	Beach
$	Bank	✳	Scenic viewpoint
✕	Restaurant	⑂	Waterfall
⚇	Museum/art gallery	⚑	Golf course
⊞	Hospital	▲	Campsite
✚	Clinic/pharmacy	⠶	Historic site
ⓘ	Tourist information		Urban park
▢	Railway station		National park
🚐	Bus station/taxi rank	ᵜ	Marsh
✝	Church/cathedral	▲	Mountain peak
ς	Mosque	→	One-way arrow
🐘	Zoo	⋯	International boundary
⛽	Petrol station	⋯	State boundary
Ⓟ	Parking	═══	Main roads – paved/unpaved
⤫	Border/entrance gate	══	Other roads – paved/unpaved

vi

MAP LIST

Contents

Introduction

Taken from Swahili (the lingua franca in east Africa), the word 'safari' translates as 'journey'. In English it has evolved to mean 'travel of an adventurous nature', specifically game viewing in Africa. However, the best description of safaris I have heard (from a visitor to Tanzania) is 'complete sensory overload'. From the sweet smell of dry grass at dawn to the paralysing roar of a lion declaring his territory, the senses are jolted awake. Visual delights also await; apart from being set in stunning scenery – towering mountains, endless plains and oceanic lakes – wild areas abound with colourful birds, extravagant flora, and – the highlight of the trip for most – a unique array of animals. Beyond this, and at risk of sounding slightly airy-fairy, we apparently have a sixth sense that only Africa can reach. Whether it is because our species evolved from this continent, or due to something more basic (feeling closer to nature and the elements), there is, for many people, a deep feeling of homecoming when they first touch African soil.

This book is aimed not just at people with disabilities, but also many older travellers and those with knee or hip problems, breathing difficulties or temporary injuries. It describes the access details of nearly 300 camps, lodges and hotels spread through the six most commonly visited safari countries, some of which may require a degree of compromise but many are accessible to Western standards. Not only is a safari physically undemanding (a lot of the time is spent sitting in vehicles), but visiting Africa is much more possible than most people with reduced mobility dare to imagine. Airlines generally provide excellent assistance, communications are rapidly improving and good medical services are widespread. There are knowledgeable agents who can arrange suitable itineraries, while the advent of the internet has made it easy to book tours directly with specialist disability operators on the ground.

For Africa first-timers information is included that explains all the basics, from health issues to flight procedure, while for those who have been before and are looking for new destinations, the countries covered should provide enough choice to tempt even the most experienced traveller. The style of safari you choose will depend largely on your budget and desired level of comfort, but everything is possible from self-drive in a 2wd car to a tailor-made, all-inclusive adventure that flies into the most refined and remote luxury camps.

Access, and especially access in bathrooms, is usually the first concern of anyone with mobility limitations. Once secure in the knowledge that ablutions can be done in comfort and privacy, then most will be prepared to put up with some degree of difficulty in other zones of their life. This may mean taking a slightly scenic route to the swimming pool or avoiding steps to the dining room by taking the goods entrance through the kitchen, but these inconveniences are commonplace anywhere in the world. If there's no room for compromise, then accommodation with facilities for all abilities can be found, but as one contributor told me, these small detours should be looked upon as an opportunity to see somewhere no other tourist gets to!

Transport is also a common worry. Minibuses and 4x4 vehicles are usually used on game drives, and although it is true that they are higher than standard cars, this can actually suit people who struggle to stand from a sitting position. For anyone who is happy to be helped, there is never a shortage of willing – and very able – hands, but if this is also out of the question then wheelchair-adapted vehicles can be found in all the areas covered. Travelling between game parks and reserves is usually done by road, which gives an 'up-close' view of the country, but many reserves also contain airstrips and, if getting in and out of light aircraft is possible for you, then a more suitable – and faster – option might be to fly. This may be a worthwhile consideration. Boat, canoe, balloon and elephant-back safaris provide yet more methods of getting close to the wildlife, each with its own limitations and advantages.

Whatever style and standard of trip is preferred, making sure your itinerary is unhurried is the key to completely appreciating the wild places. It is essential to plan enough days in each place and not to squeeze too many highlights in – this is especially true if mobility is an issue, where more time is often required for the mundane daily tasks. Journeys and activities are normally scheduled in the mornings and afternoons, avoiding higher midday temperatures, but if this sounds problematic, operators are usually flexible. And do remember that this is Africa; nature's rhythms come to the fore here, meaning you often want to eat and sleep according to the sun rather than having these routines dictated by unnatural factors. Late nights are rare. Everyone looks forward to the evening campfire, where sipping a hot (or strong) drink warms the stories of the day's escapades. But the truth is that few people last long at these; most drift off to bed, lulled by sleep, not long after dark.

Safaris began as the luxury escape of the wealthy minority. They have since become an affordable mainstream holiday destination for adventurous travellers, honeymoon couples and, more recently, families with young children. The current focus in this process of inclusion is people with mobility difficulties. Whether you want a holiday with complete access and no surprises, or you prefer a trip left more to chance and escapade, Africa won't disappoint. Visit now – the continent awaits!

How to Use this Book

GENERAL STRUCTURE

Chapter 1 (*Planning and Preparation*) deals with the process of researching and booking a safari. It points out the essentials, giving contacts to follow up, and makes suggestions about various other aspects of the trip. When working through this, reference should continually be made to *Chapter 3* (*The Trip*), which gives a more in-depth portrayal of what to expect on your trip, from the international flight to types of accommodation and transport available in Africa.

Chapter 2 (*Health*) should be considered from an early stage in the planning process and is also organised chronologically. It deals first with preparatory issues, then discusses health on safari and finishes by talking about what to do on your return.

The chapters in *Part Two* give the 'on-the-ground' information about the countries themselves, including brief descriptions of the regions covered and more detail about access in the accommodation available.

Where appropriate, I have included contact details and references for further information in the text. The *Appendix* lists various other resources and further reading.

Images relating to this book can be seen at ⊕ www.access-africa.co.uk. These are mainly photographs of access routes, doorways and bathrooms in the properties listed in *Part Two* and should help to create a clearer visual image of their access. For further information about any of these properties or any other issues raised, contact **e** info@access-africa.co.uk.

ACCESS

There is no globally recognised standard method of describing access in tourist accommodation. Even if there was, it would be difficult to create an accurate representation of African safari accommodation, as this varies so much throughout the continent.

Perhaps the most important single aspect of a guidebook about access is how it defines 'accessible'. I have tried not to, and the reasoning is simple. Within the field of 'limited mobility' there is an enormous range of abilities. It varies from people who can walk, but maybe struggle with more than one step or need to sit down regularly, to those who use an electric wheelchair and require full-time assistance. Consequently, what is accessible for one person may be completely inappropriate for the next.

What I have done is collected as much relevant information as possible and presented it in a manner that allows the reader to make an informed choice about whether the property will be accessible for them.

THE LISTINGS

The information describing accommodation (in *Part Two* of the book) may appear a little complicated at first glance, but it follows a standard sequence that quickly becomes easy to understand.

Firstly, each property has been assigned with access icons, which allow the reader to quickly locate places that are most likely to fit their needs. Secondly, the accommodation is described in more detail. This information usually starts in the public areas, and then follows on to give specifics about the most inclusive rooms or tents in that property. These are described in a standard order, beginning on entering the room, going through the sleeping area, entering the bathroom then dealing with the bathroom furniture from the washing to toilet facilities. Some specific terminology is used and the most important measurements are given; an explanation of these follows. The number of dollar (**$**) signs following the description denotes the price range of the property (see price codes, on the inside-front cover).

ACCESS ICONS

There is an access route with no steps from **inside** the entrance of the main building to at least **one** dining area and at least **one** accommodation unit. It may not be perfectly smooth or very direct and might have ramps steeper than 8%. There may also be steps to the entrance and to other public areas (including swimming pools, game-viewing areas, shops and bars). More details about these issues can usually be read in the description of the accommodation.

Denotes the number of unavoidable steps (1, 2 or '3 or more') between the main entrance, any dining area and any accommodation unit.

There is a bath having at least one of the following access features: support rail, lever taps, bath board, and seating.

There is a shower having at least one of the following access features: support rail and seating.

There is a level-entry ('roll-in' or 'wheel-in') shower. This may not have any further access features, but there will be no step, wall or lip more than 2cm high between the shower floor and the bathroom floor. If the entrance to this shower is less than 65cm wide, this is noted.

There is a shower that meets the requirements of both and above.

There is a toilet with at least one support rail.

TERMINOLOGY

Gradient/ramp (20%): The approximate slope of the ramp is 20% (or 1:5). A slope of 100% (or 1:1) is equal to 45° (degrees).

Round taps: Where the tap head has no protrusions, and therefore must be squeezed in order to grip and turn it. For this the user must have strong hand function. Also sometimes called 'derby' or 'crystal' taps.

Star taps: The head of the tap is shaped like a cross, meaning it can sometimes be opened or closed (with difficulty) by a user who has little or no grip function. Also sometimes called 'X' taps or 'capstan' taps.

Lever taps: The head of the tap is extended, becoming a lever (normally at least 10cm long). This allows easy use with the back of the hand, wrist or elbow for anyone with no hand function. Also sometimes called 'elbow' taps.

Support rail: Any rail fitted in the room that is designed to be held for support or balance. A towel rail is not a support rail. Also sometimes called a 'grab rail' or 'handrail'.

Showerhead: The final part of the shower from where the water comes. Also sometimes called a shower 'rose'.

Hand-held showerhead: The showerhead is connected to the taps by a flexible hose and can therefore be removed from its wall mounting, as opposed to a **'fixed' showerhead**, which is permanently attached to the wall. A hand-held showerhead is especially useful for wheelchair users. Also sometimes called a 'telephone' shower.

Fitted handles in bath: The two handles (usually about 20cm long) that many bathtubs have fitted to them as standard. They are almost always about halfway down the inside edge of each long side of the tub. They are not designed for users with disabilities, but are useful for anyone who is less steady on their feet.

Transfer space: 80cm of unobstructed space next to the object in question (bed, bath, seat, etc) to allow a wheelchair user alongside.

MEASUREMENTS

The important measurements are either incorporated in the text or are put in brackets next to the feature to which they relate. Where no unit of measurement is stated, centimetres are implied.

Threshold/lip (3): The top of the threshold or lip is 3cm vertically above the floor.

Step/drop-off (12): The vertical distance from the top of the step to the next one down is 12cm.

Door/doorway/entrance (76): The usable width in the doorway or entrance (from the face of the open door to the opposite door frame) is 76cm.

Table/desk (69): There is space under the table or desk for a wheelchair user to advance forward to some degree and the height of the underside is 69cm from the floor.

Seat (51): The top surface of the seat (the sitting area) is 51cm from the floor.

Highest switch/control/handle (165): The highest switch, control or handle in the room is 165cm from the floor.

Bed (55): The top of the mattress is 55cm from the floor.

Bath (49): The top of the bath rim is 49cm from the floor.

Step-in shower (10): The top of the barrier around the shower is 10cm vertically above the floor.

Roll-in shower (64): The entrance to the roll-in shower (see access icons on page xiii for definition) is 64cm wide.

Washbasin (71): There is space under the washbasin for a wheelchair user to advance forward to some degree and the height of the underside of the basin from the floor is 71cm. Sometimes the washbasin is curved underneath; in these cases the approximate midpoint is used.

Mirror (95): The lower edge of the mirror is 95cm from the floor.

Taps (88): The taps are 88cm from the floor.

Toilet (40): The top of the toilet seat is 40cm from the floor.

Support rail (85): When referring to **rails next to toilets or in showers**, the figure is the height of the lowest horizontal part of the support rail from the floor. When referring to **rails above baths**, the figure is the height of the lowest horizontal part of the support rail from the top of the bath. When referring to **diagonal or vertical support rails**, the point of measurement (usually midpoint) is stated and the figure is the height of this point from the floor.

NOTES
The symbols < (less than) or > (more than) are also used:

Highest switch/control/handle (<140): The highest switch, control or handle in the room is no higher than 140cm from the floor.

Table (>65): The height of the underside of the table from the floor is more than 65cm.

MISCELLANEOUS POINTS ABOUT LISTINGS
Parking: Where possible and relevant I have described the ground surface in the parking area and leading up to the property. However, except for inner-city hotels, finding parking spaces with enough room for wheelchair transfers is rarely an issue in the areas covered in this book, so this information is not included.

Telephone and light switch: Where there is a telephone and/or a light switch within reach of someone lying in bed, this is stated. In camps with no telephone there is very often a hooter or whistle present, and the grounds are usually patrolled by security staff.

Telephone dialling codes: In *Part One*, telephone numbers are given with their international dialling codes. In *Part Two*, they are given as you would dial them from within the country, and the international dialling code for each country is given at the beginning of that chapter.

Circulation space: Unless stated otherwise, it is safe to assume that bedrooms and bathrooms have access and turning space of at least 100cm x 70cm.

FEEDBACK REQUEST
Every effort has been made to ensure that the information in this book is as accurate and up to date as possible. However, things do change, especially in this field where proprietors are rapidly becoming aware of access needs. Any feedback – regarding general experiences on safari as well as access issues – would be greatly appreciated and will help when compiling future editions. Visitors are encouraged to take photographs of the important areas (access routes, bathrooms, etc) and these may be included in the online visual resource – ⌂ www.access-africa.co.uk – which supports this book.

Please write to Gordon Rattray at Bradt Travel Guides, 23 High St, Chalfont St Peter, Bucks SL9 9QE, England; **e** info@bradtguides.com.

PART ONE
GENERAL INFORMATION

1 **Planning and Preparation**

An African safari is often thought of as an adventure and sometimes even a challenge, but don't forget that it's also a holiday. Plan as much as you can before you leave to ensure you thoroughly enjoy the trip itself.

The first steps are planning where and when to go, followed by thinking about the general style of travel. You then need to decide how to book: by organising and booking everything independently, by using a travel agent or by dealing directly with an operator in Africa. Once that's done and bookings are at least partially in place, then the practicalities like passports, visas, travel documents and insurance must be arranged. Anybody requiring personal assistance will need to address this issue. Clothes and equipment must be sought, sorted and packed. As explained in *How to Use this Book*, pages xii–xvi, it will be useful to refer regularly to the information given in *Chapter 3*.

WHERE TO GO

All the countries featured in this book offer the full range of safaris, from exclusive trips with luxury accommodation to simpler lodgings where the emphasis is more on budget than banquet. Similarly, each area has its own unique climate, topography, flora and fauna; there is no ideal destination.

Having said that, there are generalisations that can be made. I do not want to list sweeping statements that may do more harm than good, but there is truth in all of the following and, if not taken too literally, these guidelines might help anyone who wants to go on safari and has no experience of Africa.

AUTHENTICITY

Kenya and Tanzania (and to a lesser extent, Botswana) are the destinations of choice if you really want 'African sensory overload' – in these countries it is easy to see, hear and smell the vitality of the continent without dilution. Namibia and South Africa also have areas where you can experience traditional Africa with little Western influence but it may require a greater diversion from the usual tourist trails. Whichever area is chosen, anyone who wants to escape from 'Westernisation' should aim to stay clear of the multi-star lodges and to stop in at lesser-visited villages.

INFRASTRUCTURE

One common observation is that the southern countries (especially Namibia and South Africa) are more 'developed' than east Africa. For less able travellers the main consequences of this are a greater choice of itineraries that use good-quality roads and a more predictable safari in general. In support of east Africa, routes that stick to smooth roads are quite possible and if this is a real issue then all the main game areas can be reached using light aircraft.

ACCESS

Namibia, and especially South Africa, have the greatest level of inclusion. The public in these countries expects access and there is a useful selection of adapted accommodation throughout. All the Kenyan and Tanzanian game reserves featured in this book have at least one adapted lodge and it is worth remembering that staff in all properties will gladly help people over and around small obstacles. Read about access in the countries themselves (at the beginning of each country chapter in *Part Two*) to get a deeper insight into the standards that are offered at each.

COST

Botswanan safaris are, in general, pricier than those in other countries. Apart from the fact that a large proportion of its camps are 'fly-in' rather than 'drive-in', this is because Botswana has the deliberate policy of low-impact tourism. This means it aims to limit the number of visitors, but keeps income from tourism high by encouraging those who can afford to pay more. Namibia and South Africa have the greatest range of accessible cheaper accommodation but Kenya and Tanzania have the edge on most international flight costs.

DISABILITY ADVENTURE TRAVEL: THOUGHTS FROM THE EXPERTS

Of all the tips and advice I received from disabled adventure travellers while compiling this book, the following themes kept reappearing:

- Research and be prepared, but be flexible and ready for change
- If you're not used to travel, prepare for a big trip by going away for a weekend or two first, maybe taking a short flight and getting used to living without home comforts
- There are always people prepared to help; accepting this not only makes your trip easier, but is a simple way to begin an interaction with the local people
- Think laterally – it may be as easy to remove a door as to search for another hotel with wider entrances
- A positive outlook, humility, a smile and a thank you are a traveller's most essential items

WHEN TO GO

Unless there is something seasonal that you particularly wish to see (the Great Migration in the Maasai Mara–Serengeti ecosystem, for example – see box on page 8) then I recommend taking your trip when it suits you and your home timetable best. Most areas are worth seeing all year round and as would be expected with such a huge range of habitats, there is always somewhere that is especially ripe to visit. However, if you are completely flexible, then weather conditions and the number of other tourists present are the most important considerations. The following gives some guide to these factors.

IS DRY-SEASON GAME VIEWING THE ONLY OPTION?

It is often said that the only time worth going on safari is the late dry season. While game is generally easier to spot at this time – lush vegetation is less abundant, forcing animals to come to waterholes to drink, and even when they are in the bush the lack of foliage means they have less cover – it's certainly not the only important issue. Do take into account that African landscapes are stunning at any time of year and that the game in most of the regions covered in this book is abundant enough to make a 'green season' safari quite rewarding. Indeed, the experienced Africaphile may consider travelling at this time specifically to see another face of the continent. Of course, due to poor-quality roads, some areas are inaccessible during the rains.

TRAVEL OUT OF SEASON

If all other factors are not important then travelling even slightly out of peak season will mean lower prices, relatively empty lodges and wonderfully serene game viewing. Being alone in the wilds of an African reserve – even if none of the famed 'big five' are within camera shot – is often more thrilling than watching a pride of lions surrounded by a horde of other tourists in minibuses. And when a big cat or another of the most coveted animal species does decide to share a quiet moment with you, the privilege you feel is indescribable.

SPECIFICS – KENYA AND TANZANIA

Although the weather patterns here are less defined than they used to be, the two main rainy seasons are expected from March until the end of May and from October to December. Temperature differences are minimal throughout the year because east Africa is spread around the Equator, but May through to September is slightly warmer than between October and April. If the midday and afternoon sun is avoided then unbearable heat is not a major factor. The Indian Ocean coast is typically humid, making it feel warmer than it is, but even here visitors will rarely have to cope with temperatures in excess of 30°C.

The game parks of east Africa are at their busiest from June until September, corresponding with drier weather and the summer holidays of many western countries. A major draw in Kenya at this time is the migration, the congregation of which usually peaks in the Maasai Mara in August. Visitors aiming for the January to April drier period are well advised to consider the southern plains of the Serengeti, where the wildebeest, having just calved, are preparing to trek north and westwards.

SPECIFICS – THE SOUTHERN COUNTRIES

Because these countries are further from the Equator, seasonal extremes of temperatures are more distinct. There are also regional topographical differences (rivers, mountains and deserts), making it difficult to generalise, but as with east Africa the basic rule is that June to October is most popular. Apart from being the Western holiday peak time, low rainfall and comfortable temperatures are the main reasons for visiting at this time.

The more northerly areas of these countries (including Etosha, Chobe, the Okavango Delta and Kruger) can feel uncomfortably warm in the wet 'summer' season from November to March. As a result, heat-sensitive travellers are advised to aim for the dry 'wintertime', when days are pleasantly warm, evenings can be refreshingly chilly and even localised frost is not uncommon in the mornings. Road networks in South Africa and Namibia and main routes in Botswana are extremely good, making it easy to get around at any time.

HIGHLIGHTS

This book explores the traditional safari regions, covering the most popular game parks and reserves as well as the towns and coastal resorts that both support and depend on the tourist trade.

Starting in east Africa, this means famous names like Kenya's **Maasai Mara** and Tanzania's **Serengeti**, two neighbouring reserves that together make up one of the world's greatest ecosystems. Colossal herds of herbivores chomp their way annually around these plains following timeworn routes and being harassed at every step by big cats, gargantuan crocodiles and a squabbling entourage of scavengers. Itineraries in Kenya are usually based on the Maasai Mara, then fattened either by detours north to the arid and remote **Samburu** region, or south, taking in the dusty plains of **Amboseli** (under the towering hulk of Kilimanjaro) and the wilds of the two **Tsavo national parks**. **Lake Nakuru and Naivasha** are unique highlights easily slotted into most tours that involve Nairobi. Visitors to northern Tanzania nearly always start in **Arusha**, aiming for the Serengeti and the wildlife-packed **Ngorongoro Crater**, and visiting one or both of **Lake Manyara** or the beautiful **Tarangire national parks** on the way. East African safaris are often rounded off by a beach break, with **Mombasa** and **Zanzibar** being the two countries' respective Indian Ocean treasures.

In southern Africa, highlights in Namibia include the shimmering saltpan reserve of **Etosha**, the towering sand dunes of **Sossusvlei**, and **Swakopmund**, a jovial holiday town flanked by the choppy, chilly Atlantic

Ocean. Trips to this region often work their way inland, snaking through the verdant **Caprivi Strip** to **Chobe National Park** (elephant country) in northern Botswana, and culminating at one of the world's most breathtaking sights, **Victoria Falls** in Zambia. The pristine wilderness of the **Okavango Delta** has fewer low-budget options, but is included partly because it can be explored on an accessible camping safari with a specialised local operator. For desert lovers, a trip to the desolate, yet surprisingly fascinating great salt pans of the **Kalahari** is a possible extension from Maun. South Africa is touched upon, with **Kruger National Park** in particular being dealt with in more detail. This flagship reserve is an example to any, not only because of its excellent habitat management, but also because its level of disability access is without equal. **Addo Elephant Park** and **the Cape area** are also highly accessible regions to visit, while Johannesburg is included more as a place of arrival and departure than a highlight in itself.

ITINERARY PLANNING TIPS

Complaints are not commonplace among people returning from their first trip to Africa, but if one can be picked out as being most regular, it is of fatigue. A standard safari can be a full-on experience, and operators, due to competition, are often forced to squeeze as many highlights as possible into their itineraries. Ideally, more time should be given to thoroughly appreciate the beautiful places. Although this applies to everyone, it is particularly relevant for people with mobility issues, as they will invariably take longer for ablutions, vehicle transfers and general getting around. Trying to follow a 'normal' programme when you need more time for the basics will just mean reducing rest times and eventually missing the important highlights.

Experienced agents and operators should take all of this into consideration, but it would do no harm to check when booking. If you are planning your own itinerary then base it on a mainstream trip (choosing the most accessible accommodation *en route*) and ventilate it slightly by following these guidelines:

• Miss out a highlight or add some extra days, making room for rest time

• Put in an extra rest day on arrival after a long flight and at various points through the trip. This is good for general recharging but might be essential for people who need to relieve skin pressure regularly.

• Plan in more time for toilet stops and rest stops on journeys

• Plan shorter drives, allowing later morning departures without forcing later arrivals, and where there are long drives, spread these over two days

• Fly instead of driving to avoid long journeys and/or rough roads

• Miss the occasional game drive. This may not mean missing the game, as many lodges and camps are set within game reserves and are regularly visited by birds and animals. Many have waterholes with viewpoints and these are often accessible.

- Include a relaxing beach (or similar) break at the end of the safari

If you do stay longer than normal in one game park, it's not difficult to find something new of interest; you might begin to recognise distinct bird calls or territorial animal movements, and if you come across a fresh lion kill one morning, it can be fascinating to watch the depletion of the carcass over the next day or two by a procession of different scavengers. More simply, many people say they only begin to relax after a few days in one place. Extra time like this is not time wasted; it's time to be treasured.

STYLE OF TRAVEL

I have split the most common styles of travel into two categories (see *Using an operator*, see opposite and *Going alone*, also opposite), although the majority of safaris are at least partly run using an operator. Giving actual prices is impossible because of the size of the region covered; therefore those mentioned below are only rough benchmarks (see *Where to go*, page 3 for a comparison in cost between countries). These are 'land-only' (including all costs apart from those involved in getting to Africa).

THE GREAT MIGRATION

East Africa's Great Migration is the annual traipse of up to two million wildebeest, gazelle and zebra around the Maasai Mara–Serengeti ecosystem. Huge herds instinctively follow the rain, thriving on the vast prairies of sweet, young grass it leaves behind. Resident prides of lion and other large carnivores gorge on this glut, and the various scavengers follow the pecking order, quickly removing all traces of the fallen animals. It is an unforgiving cycle, utterly fascinating and unforgettable.

August and September are usually the top months to see it in Kenya's Maasai Mara, when the herds are on the move, fording rivers *en masse* and providing a feast for waiting crocodiles. If you are lucky, then this is best witnessed at the crossing points on the Mara and Talek rivers in the north of the reserve. An altogether more languid sight is on the plains of the southern Serengeti from January until May, when the newborn calves are building strength before the northbound trek begins again.

It is worth remembering that even if the main herds are not passing through, a visit to these areas is always rewarding. Most species, including the predators, elephants and giraffes, do not migrate and a large population of plains game also remains fairly static, providing superb game viewing at all times of the year.

USING AN OPERATOR

Overlanding

Joining an overland truck trip means travelling in a large vehicle – usually a truck that has been adapted to carry passengers and equipment – with other people of mixed nationality and age. The most obvious gain from being on such a tour is that responsibility for the day-to-day running of the safari is not on your shoulders. It also allows you to see places that would be impossible to reach by public transport. Truck trips vary in style but usually involve a degree of participation in camp chores, and the biggest downside is that you must compromise your aims and goals with those of the group, which can be up to 20 in size. Accommodation is usually basic camping although one operator in Africa (Epic Enabled – see page 21) offers truck trips in South Africa using an adapted vehicle and accessible lodgings. Expect costs to start at around US$150 per person per day.

Joining a small group

Joining a small group safari following a set itinerary means meeting (and getting along with) strangers is still a prerequisite, but groups are typically fewer than ten people. Transport is usually in 4x4 safari vehicles or minibuses and these trips are normally fully serviced (the crew will perform all cooking and washing-up duties) or restaurants are used. Accommodation can be campsites, permanent tented camps or lodges and hotels, while true bush camping (in the wilds) is possible with Endeavour Safaris in Botswana. Several local operators (see pages 19–23) have wheelchair-accessible vehicles and staff trained to cater to this market. These trips can cost anything upwards of US$200 per person per day, depending on standard of service and accommodation required.

Small group – friends and family only

If money is less of a restriction then this method (travelling only as a couple or with people you know) gives the most freedom to absorb Africa without the need to take the whims of strangers into account. The same styles of transport and lodgings as in the previous option apply, and the same local operators run the safaris. Itineraries can also be 'off the shelf' but there is the added luxury of being able to plan your own trip. This means discussing your transport needs, your ideal type of accommodation and your preferred number of days in each area with a knowledgeable agent or local operator. Per-person costs vary according to number of guests and level of luxury, but will always be more than 'off-the-shelf' safaris.

GOING ALONE

Backpacking

The least expensive method of getting at least a taste of Africa's wild places is to organise everything independently and to use public transport and

MOBILITY IMPAIRED AS PART OF A MAINSTREAM GROUP

Joining a group safari undoubtedly brings many advantages. Not only does the individual cost come down, but fun moments are often more memorable if shared with other people, there are opportunities to form lasting friendships and there is greater security. For someone with a disability, being part of a mainstream group is even more appealing – after all, full inclusion into society is the ultimate goal – but anyone with mobility problems should think carefully before booking this way.

It is quite possible, even probable, that everyone's trip will be enriched by the presence of a wheelchair user, and it would be an excellent way to dispel myths about disability. But travel in Africa is littered with potential problems including vehicle breakdown and maddening bureaucracy. If a trip is not going to plan, and is also regularly hindered by one slower member, then tensions can erupt and that person can end up taking the brunt of the group's frustrations. These scenarios make for riveting reality television, but are absolutely no fun if you are the bad guy.

Before joining a group tour, think seriously about the potential of such a situation arising. The style and length of the trip will have a bearing on this, but your limitations, particularly if more time and assistance will be required, are the most important factors. Speak to your booking agent; maybe a note for other group members (letting them know that someone with limited mobility is joining the group) would be wise. It might be a perfect solution for you to bring or hire a personal assistant or just to choose an itinerary that is not too demanding. If you still have real doubts then consider using a specialised operator. Full inclusion is definitely worth fighting for, but maybe not at the expense of your or others' holiday time.

budget/backpackers' accommodation or campsites. Private transport of some kind will be required to get to and around the game parks and this is normally arranged by joining a small group tour with a local operator. This style of trip will take a lot more work to organise and will be the least accessible way to see Africa, as few budget hotels and no public transport cater to disability. It is, however, the cheapest option and should be possible for little more than US$100 per person per day for two people travelling together.

Self-drive

Using an operator and having a driver/guide means experienced professionals deal with all the logistical landmines. For complete autonomy, however, it is possible to hire vehicles on a self-drive basis in all the countries covered (see *Self-drive vehicle rental*, page 24). These can be sturdy 4x4s fully kitted out with camping and cooking equipment – although a prerequisite of taking equipment for self-sufficiency is that you know how to use it. The type of accommodation used is entirely the choice of the traveller.

This is a relatively new option in Kenya and Tanzania, where road conditions as well as general planning require a good degree of knowledge and skill. First-timers to this style of travel will find Botswana, Namibia, and South Africa offer challenges and rewards for all levels of experience. Road networks in the latter two countries especially are streets ahead of those in the rest of the continent, and consequently 2wd cars are readily available. In South Africa, cars with hand controls and self-drive vans with hydraulic wheelchair lifts can also be found. All that said, even here no independent trip should be taken lightly. (For further information see box in *Chapter 3, Driving in Africa*, page 89.)

Your own vehicle

This is the approach taken by people doing an extended overland trip through the continent and requires a serious depth of knowledge about vehicle maintenance, off-road driving and the documentation required. If you can afford it, using your own vehicle gives the greatest independence and such a trip is certainly not outwith the boundaries of people with restricted mobility. If more information is required about this style of travel, an inspiring starting point may be Colin Javens's website ✆ www.drivinghome.co.uk. Colin is quadriplegic and drove an adapted Land Rover from the UK to Cape Town in 2006, raising funds for research and grass-roots African charities. See also *Africa Overland: The Bradt Travel Guide*, by Siân Pritchard-Jones and Bob Gibbons.

BOOKING A SAFARI

In the not-too-distant past, the vast majority of safaris were booked through travel agents, most of whom had experience of the region visited and direct contact with the ground handlers they used. However, with the advent of the internet and email, obtaining information has become remarkably simple, giving travellers much more autonomy. It is now possible to be completely self-sufficient, planning your itinerary and arranging transport and accommodation via email, or to book a package directly with a local operator. For details of specific operators, see page 19–23.

BOOKING EVERYTHING INDEPENDENTLY

Only trips to South Africa and Namibia could be described as being easy to arrange without help. In these countries roads to and through the regions that this book covers are good quality, meaning 2wd cars suffice and no off-road driving experience is necessary. There are more self-drive options here than in east Africa, including vehicles with hand controls (see page 24), and communications are reliable enough to book everything – including accommodation – by email. Despite this, the independent approach will not suit everybody. Most African safaris, if not the whole trip then certainly the excursions into game parks, are still booked using an agent or local operator.

USING AN AGENT OR A LOCAL OPERATOR

If making and booking an itinerary yourself is not feasible, for whatever reason, then the choice narrows to using an agent in your home country or contacting an operator in Africa directly. The latter approach is increasing in popularity. Having no 'middleman' in this way reduces the chance of vital details being forgotten and you can glean a much more accurate 'feel' for the operator if you are speaking to them yourself. That said, some people still want the peace of mind of booking through an agent. They might have one they know and trust, or maybe they've found one with a real interest in and depth of knowledge about the subject. Don't forget also that there is no guarantee that your safari will be cheaper by booking direct, as many agents receive a commission for selling local operators' trips so do not need to sell above the direct prices. Both methods have financial safety nets: depending on where you live, agents may be bonded to a large organisation (AITO or ABTA in the UK) which automatically safeguards your money if the company goes into liquidation, while some credit-card companies offer similar guarantees on payments made directly to operators in Africa.

Whichever approach is preferred, there are precautions worth taking. Catering to disabilities is a niche market that tempts agents and tour operators alike. The idea of being expert in a field (therefore escaping the rat race of mainstream safaris) is obviously attractive, but the next stage (learning about the myriad mobility problems, and how to overcome them) is less so. This means that there are plenty of unscrupulous companies stating that they 'are different', because they sell or run tours 'for the disabled', but from these it's difficult to discern which are genuine and which aren't. Never book with an agent or operator unless you are sure of their credentials.

For agents, ask them if they have actually seen the places and used the accommodation and operators they're selling. Just because they have twenty years experience sending people with disabilities to the Mediterranean doesn't mean they know about African safaris. For both agents and operators, you can request photographs of the equipment and accommodation they use and references from satisfied past disabled clients. Gauge also how they respond once you start giving your limitations and requirements. Contact details of specialised agents and operators are given on pages 17–18 and 19–23 respectively and the following list may give some inspiration about the sort of queries to make.

ACCESS ISSUES

Whether you book independently, through an agent, or directly with an operator, take your time to go into enough detail about your particular needs. Do not feel embarrassed about drilling down to the fine points like exactly how wide doorways are; these details may be essential to know. The following checklist might help to clarify these thoughts.

That word 'accessible'
Most accommodation will welcome anyone. They usually state their limitations and give assurances that they'll do their best to improvise and try to overcome any problems. Nevertheless, be wary of any that consider their property 'accessible'. Some think this just means having a spacious bedroom. Surprisingly, the reverse is also true; it's not uncommon for places to play down their inclusive features. This may sound perplexing, but they refuse to put in writing that they are to any degree accessible because they worry that being unable to fulfil promises could lead to court action from dissatisfied clients. Asking the right questions will sift out the unsuitable places more quickly; for instance, do not pose questions like 'Are you wheelchair accessible?', as these are all too easily answered with 'yes' or 'no'. It is much more revealing to ask for a description of the facilities in the room.

The correct room
It is often the case that there are only one or two rooms that have been made more accessible. It is therefore all too easy for the reservations agent to mistakenly book a standard room. Be sure the correct room is booked, and double-checking nearer your departure date – or asking your agent to – is always a sensible precaution.

Pathways, lighting and room location
The distances between vehicle parking, public areas and rooms, as well as number of steps, presence of handrails, lighting and ground surface are all useful to know. If temporary wooden ramps are available to bypass steps, would this be acceptable for you? Such a solution is common – and easily constructed from available local materials in Africa – but is rarely fully compliant with health and safety regulations. An unfortunate side effect of choosing the accessible room is that because of their proximity to the main buildings, they are often less secluded and more noisy. If you can cope with standard room features, this may be a reason to compromise. Also, people aiming for accommodation in the higher price brackets may find that client privacy has been given higher priority, with the result that distances to rooms are greater; of course, it is often possible to take your vehicle right to the door of your accommodation.

Doorways
When asking about doorway widths, don't forget that the width measured might be the total width of the doorframe and not that which is actually useable (the distance between the face of the opened door and the frame). Also, canvas tent flaps are usually wider than standard solid doors, but may have a wooden threshold (usually around 2cm high) or a zip to roll over.

BE PC

The words and phrases that represent disability are a potential minefield. Tread lightly: apparently, disabled people (can I call them that?) are easily offended.

While researching this book, one lodge manager told me 'cripples are welcome'. A shocking statement maybe, but he didn't know it was outdated. In these situations it's in our own best interests not to let it spoil our day. Being overly sensitive will only repel people, and personally, if it's well meant then I'd rather be referred to tactlessly than avoided or ignored. If appropriate, I attempt to re-educate the person, but if that's not possible then I try to laugh about it.

That said, there are some points worth making. I don't want to get bogged in the quagmire of political correctness, but there are a few definite rights and wrongs, and some outdated terminology that only strengthens negative perceptions.

One of the worst of these is the aforementioned 'crippled' and this is closely followed by 'handicapped'. Less offensive, but still wildly inaccurate,

Bedrooms and bathrooms

Important points when enquiring about rooms might include:

- Height and type of light switches, door handles, cupboards and beds
- Transfer space next to beds
- Telephone or other emergency communication device (bush camps often have a hooter or whistle)
- Legroom under dining tables, writing desks and washbasins
- Support rails
- Height of bath and size of the step into the shower if it's not roll-in
- Type of taps, availability of a suitable shower seat and access to the toilet
- Presence of a fridge for storage of medicines

Lifts

If a hotel has no ground-floor rooms, do they have accessible lifts?

Swimming pools

Gradual steps are the most common means of entering pools, and these are sometimes flanked by handrails – invaluable for unsteady walkers – or accompanied by a ramp suitable for wheelchairs. Very occasionally, there might be a lift to hoist non-ambulant people into the water. Ladders are only suitable for people with less physical impairment.

are phrases like 'confined to a wheelchair' and 'wheelchair bound'. My wheelchair is liberating! If I didn't have it then I would be floor bound. Now that would be something worth pitying; indeed, it is the harsh reality for too many disabled people in developing countries where wheelchairs are a luxury.

Another word worth body swerving is 'special' (sadly, there's nothing special about me, and I have no special needs either), and while I'm on a rant, the word 'the', in front of disabled also raises my hackles. This may sound too pedantic, but I feel it ring-fences this group and immediately sets them apart from the rest of society. In my opinion it's better to say 'disabled people' than 'the disabled'. However, even this is inaccurate; although the person has a disability, they are only disabled if the environment around them is not accessible.

So what can be used? I have tended to flit between 'with a disability', 'with limited or impaired mobility', and various derivatives of these. I've also used 'disabled people' quite regularly, more for ease of reading than anything else, and hope not to have caused too much offence.

Jetty access and boats

Many properties are situated next to rivers or lakes. Although these locations are usually teeming with bird and animal life, meaning staying on dry land will be safari enough for some, excursions onto the water are often an intrinsic part of the experience. Camp staff are usually happy to help with boat transfers (see page 93) but jetties can have ramped, stepped or laddered access; it might be important for you to know which. Boats may be dugout canoes or larger craft with deep keels or flat bottoms. The latter are more common and more suitable if you prefer to stay in your wheelchair. Larger vessels – taking up to 40 passengers for river cruises – usually have stepped entry then enough space on their lower deck to allow wheelchairs to move around unobstructed. There will rarely be safety harnesses or tie-downs, but speed is not a priority in Africa.

Cool storage and electricity

If regular medication must be kept cool, check that your room (and possibly your safari vehicle) has a fridge. This leads to the need for 24-hour electric power – some bush camps have none and others using generators have only an intermittent supply. Having electricity may also be essential to charge a power wheelchair or to run breathing equipment.

Mobility equipment

For people who can walk but find longer distances taxing, some lodges and camps will be able to provide a wheelchair, shower chair, commode, crutches or similar. Contact them in advance to confirm this. Specialised operators will also be able to supply such equipment.

Safety
Some unfenced camps are truly in the wilds; dangerous animals can wander through at any minute, which is one of the major reasons people choose these places. It is extremely important the owners and management are aware of any mobility problem their guests may have, and they may actually refuse a booking on these grounds. That said, many have vehicle access throughout, meaning clients less fleet of foot can be ferried between their room and the dining areas.

Vehicles
Public transport does not enter game reserves in any of the areas featured in this book. To do this, a suitable vehicle will need to be used, either from a local operator, independently owned, or hired. Anybody who has arranged to use a particularly accessible vehicle to get around is advised to check that it may be used on game drives. Some privately owned guest farms and lodges (especially in Namibia) only allow game driving in their own trucks, which may not fit your access needs.

BOOKING FLIGHTS
Even if an agent is used, most safaris are booked 'land-only', meaning flights must be organised separately. This isn't a disadvantage – in fact, it's quite the opposite. It gives you the freedom to choose the cheapest or most accessible airline and the best-suited airport, and it allows the flexibility to add a few days' acclimatisation in Africa before the safari begins or a similar 'wind-down' period somewhere relaxing at the end.

Flights can be booked directly with the airline, but this is rarely the cheapest method. It is usually better to use a booking or travel agent, giving them the desired destination and dates and allowing them to bring up a choice of options to compare. The most commonly used European carriers include British Airways, KLM, Lufthansa, Brussels Airlines and Air France. The latter, however, regularly receive bad reports for their handling of people with disabilities, especially in Paris's Charles de Gaulle airport. Delta Airlines from North America and Qantas from Australasia are the two main airlines from those regions. From within Africa, Kenyan Airways, Air Tanzania, Ethiopian Airlines, Egypt Air and Air Namibia can be included as big players ferrying tourists from overseas, while South African Airways (SAA) is the largest, serving most areas worldwide. SAA has had a patchy reputation regarding its disability policy, but has significantly tightened up its practices after some recent high profile cases. People who require assistance at the airports must inform the airline of this in advance; see *Chapter 3, Getting there (air travel)* page 77, for booking, boarding and in-flight procedures.

AGENTS AND OPERATORS

SPECIALISED TRAVEL AGENCIES WORLDWIDE

The following list is a selection of travel agencies who either have genuine knowledge of accessible safaris, who work directly with a specialist ground handler in Africa or who have some experience of disability.

Belgium

Decalage Rue du Temps des Cerises 2/272, 1150 Brussels; ☎ +32 (0)2 772 1952; **e** info@decalage.be; 🖰 www.decalage.be

Canada

Accessible Travel 572 Weber St North Unit 1, Waterloo, Ontario N2L 5C6; ☎ +1 519 745 1860; **e** worldonwheelz@aol.com; 🖰 www.worldonwheelz.com

France

Akitsi Safaris 105 Rue de l'abbé Groult, 75015 Paris; ☎ +33 (0)153 447 430; **e** info@akitsi.com; 🖰 www.akitsi.com

Germany

Grabo Rennweiler Strasse 5, 66903 Ohmbach; ☎ +49 (0)6386 7744; **f** +49 (0)6386 7717; **e** info@grabo-tours.de; 🖰 www.grabo-tours.de
Outback Africa Am Südhang 10, 08645 Bad Elster; ☎ +49 (0)374 375 3804; **f** +49 (0)374 375 3805; **e** info@outbackafrica.de; 🖰 www.outbackafrica.de
Madiba Pölitzstrasse 4, 04155 Leipzig; ☎ +49 (0)341 240 9464; **e** info@madiba.de; 🖰 www.madiba.de
Weitsprung Reisen Gutenbergstrasse 27, 35037 Marburg; ☎ +49 (0)642 168 6832; **f** +49 (0)642 169 0581; **e** mail@weitsprung-reisen.de; 🖰 www.weitsprung-reisen.de

Netherlands

Buitengewoon Reizen Diezerkade 3, 8021 CW Zwolle; ☎ +31 (0)384 557 030; **e** info@buitengewoonreizen.nl; 🖰 www.buitengewoonreizen.nl
Stichting Gehandicapten Reizen Noothoven Van Goorstraat 11e, Postbus 109, 2800 AC Gouda; ☎ +31 (0)182 587 056; **f** +31 (0)182 587 059; **e** info@gehandicaptenreizen.nl; 🖰 www.gehandicaptenreizen.nl
Toegankelijk/Accesswise Expeditieweg 1, 6657 KM Boven Leeuwen; ☎ +31 (0)900 040 1410; **e** info@toegankelijk.com; 🖰 www.toegankelijk.com

South Africa

Enabled-Travel (EOL) 25 Atholl Rd, Camps Bay, 8005; ☎ +27 (0)21 425 7675; **f** +27 (0)866 564 594; **e** info@enabled-travel.com; 🖰 www.enabled-travel.com

Switzerland

Rolli-Travel Stadtstrasse 48, 6204 Sempach; ☎ +41 (0)41 982 0536; **e** info@rolli-travel.ch; 🖰 www.rolli-travel.ch

UK

2by2 Holidays 5–7 John Princes St, London W1G 0JN; ☎ +44 1582 766 122;
e claire@2by2holidays.co.uk; ⊕ www.2by2holidays.co.uk

Acacia UK Head Office, (agents in several countries, see website for details) 23A
Craven Terrace, Lancaster Gate, London W2 3QH; ☎ +44 20 7706 4700;
f +44 20 7706 4686; e info@acacia-africa.com; ⊕ www.acacia-africa.com

AccessAfrica 47 Kimbolton Close, London SE12 0JH; ☎/f +44 20 8851 3065;
e info@accessafrica.co.uk; ⊕ www.accessafrica.co.uk

Accessible Travel Avionics Hse, Naas Lane, Quedgeley, Gloucester GL2 2SN;
☎ +44 1452 729739; f +44 1452 729853; e info@accessibletravel.co.uk;
⊕ www.accessibletravel.co.uk

Can Be Done 11 Woodcock Hill, Harrow HA3 0XP; ☎ +44 20 8907 2400;
e holidays@canbedone.co.uk; ⊕ www.canbedone.co.uk

Chalfont Line Ltd 4 Providence Rd, West Drayton UB7 8HJ; ☎ +44 1895 459 540;
f +44 1895 459 549; e holidays@chalfont-line.co.uk; ⊕ www.chalfont-line.co.uk

Expert Africa Upper Sq, Old Isleworth, Middlesex TW7 7BJ; ☎ +44 20 8232 9777;
f +44 20 8568 8330; ⊕ www.expertafrica.com

Holiday Access Direct (Richard Thompson) The Ferns, Framilode, Gloucester GL2
7LH; ☎ +44 1452 741585; e info@holidayaccessdirect.com;
⊕ www.holidayaccessdirect.com

Kumuka Worldwide UK Head Office, (agents in several countries – see website
for details) 40 Earls Court Rd, London W8 6EJ; ☎ +44 20 7937 8855; f +44 20 7937
6664; e adventuretours@kumuka.com; ⊕ www.kumuka.com

Outposts Lydeard Farm, Broomfield, Bridgwater, Somerset TA5 2EG;
☎ +44 1823 451959; f +44 1823 451809; e info@outposts.co.uk;
⊕ www.outposts.co.uk

Wings on Wheels 8 Cornfields, Church Lane, Tydd St Giles, Wisbech,
Cambridgeshire PE13 5LX; ☎ +44 1945 871111; f +44 1945 871325;
e info@wingsonwheels.co.uk; ⊕ www.wingsonwheels.co.uk

Virgin Holidays The Galleria, Station Rd, Crawley, West Sussex RH10 1WW;
☎ +44 870 990 8350; f +44 870 990 4209; e customer.care@virginholidays.co.uk;
⊕ www.virginholidays.co.uk

US

Accessible Journeys Inc 35 West Sellers Av, Ridley Park, PA 19078;
☎ +1 800 846 4537 (toll-free), +1 610 521 0339; f +1 610 521 6959;
e sales@accessiblejourneys.com; ⊕ www.accessiblejourneys.com

Connie George Travel Associates PO Box 312, Glenolden, PA 19036;
☎ +1 888 532 0989; e info@cgta.com; ⊕ www.cgta.com

Eco-Adventures W6022 Creamery Rd, Fort Atkinson, WI 53538; ☎ +1 888 710 9453;
f +1 920 563 9162; e info@eaiadventure.com; ⊕ www.eaiadventure.com

Iantosca Travel 3310 LBJ Freeway Suite 1200, Dallas, TX 75234; ☎ +1 877 301 1110;
e ralph@iantosca.travel; ⊕ www.iantosca.travel

SPECIALISED OPERATORS IN AFRICA

Since the mid 1990s, several operators have invested serious time and money into this market; their details follow. I have also included a few companies who, although they do not have specialist equipment, will treat enquiries seriously and attempt to provide a realistic and workable trip.

The following table allows you to find a suitable tour operator at a glance; more detailed information can be found in the listings below.

	KENYA	TANZANIA	ZANZIBAR	ZAMBIA	NAMIBIA	BOTSWANA	SOUTH AFRICA	MOZAMBIQUE
Able Africa							■	
Access 2 Africa							■	
Africa Insight						■	■	
Albatros Travel	■	■						
Endeavour					■	■	■	■
Epic Enabled							■	
Flamingo Tours								
Go Africa	■	■	■					
Grant and Cam							■	
Hemingways				■				
McFarlane							■	■
Sama Tours		■	■					
SandyAcre					■			
Southern Cross	■						■	
Wild at Heart							■	

East Africa

Albatros Travel Standard St, 7th Floor Bruce Hse, Nairobi, Kenya; ☏ +254 (0)20 211 947; **e** tours@albatros.co.ke; ⊕ www.albatros-africa.com
Region covered: Kenya, Tanzania & Zanzibar
Albatros is a Danish-based company, but they have offices in both Kenya & Tanzania. They do not run any vehicles with specific adaptations, but they have experience of this market & remove seats from their minibuses (in Kenya) & Land Cruisers (in Tanzania) to make more space for clients with disabilities.

Go Africa Safaris PO Box 5410, Diani Beach 80401, Kenya; ☏ +254 (0)40 330 0102; **m** +254 (0)722 599 194 or +254 (0)724 710 356; **e** info@go-africa-safaris.com or goafricasafaris@wananchi.com; ⊕ www.go-africa-safaris.com
Region covered: Kenya, Tanzania & Zanzibar

Dutch-born Yvonne Matiba & Kenyan Esther Nthemba run Go Africa, & as well as aiming to provide quality safaris for all, they cater seriously to disabled travellers. They have been two of east Africa's main advocates of promoting inclusive accommodation, & consequently, their knowledge of access in these countries is very comprehensive. Go Africa is the best-equipped specialised operator in the region, their main safari vehicle being a custom-built 4x4 Toyota Land Cruiser fitted with ramps, clamps & safety belts. Plans are in place to purchase an adapted minibus in 2009. Drivers are used to dealing with mobility issues & experienced personal assistance is available. Go Africa also actively supports local disabled people & community projects.

Grant and Cameron Safaris Gogar Farms Ltd, PO Box 60, Rongai 20108, Kenya; ℓ +254 (0)720 441 819; **e** info@classicafricansafaris.com; ⌐ www.classicafricansafaris.com
Region covered: Kenya
Catering to the 'top end' of the safari market, this exclusive style of guided luxury camping will ensure you want for nothing. Owner Hamish Grant started the Vanessa Grant Trust (see page 140) & although Grant & Cameron do not specialise in disability or run any adapted vehicles, they have a genuine interest in, & pragmatic approach to, the subject.

Sama Tours Behind the House of Wonder, Gizenga St, PO Box 2276, Zanzibar; ℓ/f +255 (0)24 223 3543; **m** +255 (0)777 430 385; **e** samatours@zitec.org; ⌐ www.samatours.com
Region covered: Zanzibar
Sama Tours is a friendly & flexible tour operator operating on Zanzibar. They offer all the usual highlights & services, including spice tours, cultural visits, boat trips & transfers, & they are happy to provide a personal assistant for anybody who needs it.

Southern Cross Safaris PO Box 90653, Mombasa, Kenya; ℓ +254 (0)20 243 4600/1/2/3; **m** (Safaricom): +254 (0)720 600 200/+254 (0)721 240 840, **m** (Zain): +254 (0)733 622 022/+254 (0)734 122 022; **f** +254 (0)20 243 4610; **e** sales@southerncrosssafaris.com; ⌐ www.southerncrosssafaris.com
Region covered: Kenya, Tanzania & Zanzibar
A company whose robust reputation has been built by providing a reliable service over time, Southern Cross also takes an interest in this niche market. They have 1 safari minibus, which has ramps & space for a wheelchair, & they own & manage several safari properties with accessible features (see Elerai & Satao camps in Amboseli & Tsavo national parks in Kenya in Chapter 4). On top of this they have made efforts to gather information about accessible accommodation in the region.

Southern Africa
Able Africa PO Box 734, NoordHoek 7979, Western Cape; ℓ +27 (0)21 789 1250; **f** +27 (0)86 6106 324; **m** +27 (0) 83 216 3342; **e** mandyrapson@africanencounter.org; ⌐ www.ableafrica.com

Region covered: South Africa, extending north
This is a newcomer to disability, but one with a firm base in mainstream safaris as it is an offshoot of African Encounter (⁁ *www.africanencounter.org*). As with its mother company, Able Africa intends to work with deep involvement of the local communities, in this case people with disabilities in Africa. Endeavour Safaris (see below) are used for running some of the trips, so you can be confident it will be suited to your physical needs.

Access 2 Africa Safaris PO Box 159, Hluhluwe 3960, Kwazulu-Natal, South Africa; ☎ +27 (0)35 562 0614; **f** +27 (0)86 524 3482; **e** info@access2africasafaris.co.za; ⁁ www.access2africasafaris.co.za
Region covered: KwaZulu-Natal, South Africa
This is, at the time of writing, the newest specialised operator in South Africa. It is headed by Jennae & JJ Bezuidenhout (who is quadriplegic) & has mapped out itineraries in KwaZulu Natal (inc Durban & the Hluhluwe/Umfolozi game reserves). Although Jennae is a trained caregiver & can help out, fulltime qualified assistance can also be supplied. Vehicles used inc minivans with portable ramps & a Quantum minibus with a hydraulic lift.

Africa Insight PO Box 402942, Gaborone, Botswana; ☎ +267 (0)72 654 323; **e** info@africainsight.com; ⁁ www.africainsight.com
Region covered: Botswana & across southern Africa
Based in southern Botswana, Tim Race makes a point of welcoming disabled visitors. Although, at the time of writing, Africa Insight has standard equipment only, a Land Rover with a hydraulic wheelchair lift is on order.

Endeavour Safaris 23 Lark Crescent; 7441 Table View, Flamingo Vlei, Cape Town, South Africa; ☎ +27 (0)21 556 6114; **e** info@endeavour-safaris.com; ⁁ www.endeavour-safaris.com
Region covered: South Africa, Namibia, Botswana & Mozambique
One of the most dynamic companies in this field, Endeavour is owned & run by Mike & Silvia Hill. They are based in Maun, Botswana but have an office in Cape Town & run trips throughout the southern region. Vehicles are a selection of Land Cruisers & minibuses, most of which have been adapted with lifts & restraints for wheelchairs. The safaris are mainly mobile camping trips, but Endeavour can also run lodge- & fixed-camp based tours. This company has done much to promote accessible tourism in southern Africa, & not just content with the usual goals of offering safaris to all, Mike wants to provide meaningful employment to disabled people locally & has even voiced dreams of employing disabled guides.

Epic Enabled 3 Bodrum Cl, PO Box 1991, Sun Valley/Noordhoek 7985; ☎/**f** +27 (0)21 785 3176; **m** +27 (0)73 22 82825; (after hours): +27 (0)21 785 3156; **e** info@epic-enabled.com; ⁁ www.epic-enabled.com
Region covered: South Africa
Alfie & Sabine Smith have a proven history in the overland industry, & now run a wheelchair-accessible truck based near Kruger National Park & a minibus fitted

with ramps in the Western Cape. They offer a variety of fixed itineraries using accessible tented camps, bungalows & cottages, as well as tailor-made trips. An innovative couple, they have recently taken over management of 'The Blue Tangerine' (see page 315), a soon-to-be fully inclusive guesthouse in Cape Town.

Flamingo Tours PO Box 60554, Flamingo Sq, Table View 7439, South Africa; ☎ +27 (0)21 557 4496; e info@flamingotours.co.za; ☝ www.flamingotours.co.za
Region covered: South Africa
Pam & Jeff Taylor have been operating since 1995 & have built a solid base of knowledge about access in the Eastern & Western Cape areas of South Africa. They have fully adapted vehicles & can also provide equipment, oxygen & a qualified nurse. They specialise in Cape Town & the Garden Route, taking in game areas like Shamwari Reserve & are constantly seeking new accessible highlights to include in their itineraries.

Hemingways PO Box 60810, Livingstone, Zambia; ☎ +260 (0)213 320 996; e info@hemingwayszambia.com; ☝ www.hemingwayszambia.com
Region covered: Zambia
Pete Hemingway himself is an above-knee amputee, so already has more of an understanding than most about issues concerning personal mobility. His company, based in Livingstone, has a fleet of vehicles for hire, one of which is a Volkswagen minibus with a UK-fitted wheelchair lift & floor clamps to tie down wheelchairs. Hemingways can organise local transfers, self-drive holidays or driver-guided vehicle hire throughout the region. There are plans to adapt a Land Rover for wheelchair entry providing a 4x4 safari option in Zambia for those who have difficulty transferring into a vehicle seat.

McFarlane Safaris PO Box 983, Hoedspruit 1380, South Africa; ☎ +27 (0)15 793 3000; e res@mcfarlanesafaris.co.za; ☝ www.mcfarlanesafaris.co.za
Region covered: South Africa & Mozambique
Garth McFarlane runs a reputable mainstream safari operation, but has recently developed a South African itinerary specifically for people with visual impairments. Called 'Touch Trails', this tour takes in highlights of South Africa concentrating on stimulating the other senses.

SandyAcre Safaris PO Box 9970, Windhoek, Namibia; ☎ +264 (0)61 248 137; e info@sandyacresafaris.com; ☝ www.sandyacresafaris.com
Region covered: Namibia
Although SandyAcre has no specialised equipment & does not target this market, Managing Director Martin Webb-Bowen takes a positive approach when dealing with disability. With a fleet of 4x4 & 2wd vehicles, plus uncommonly professional & well-motivated staff, SandyAcre do their best to cater to all.

Wild at Heart PO Box 802, Hilton, 3245 KwaZulu-Natal, South Africa; ☎ +27 (0)33 234 4466; e andrew@zulusafaris.co.za; ☝ www.wildatheart.co.za
Region covered: South Africa

Andrew Anderson of well-established company African Insight
(⌂ www.africaninsight.co.za) is slowly developing this offshoot to his standard
business & now regularly hosts clients with disabilities. All the main South African
highlights are covered & wheelchair-accessible vehicles are used.

SELECTED MAINSTREAM OPERATORS
There is, of course, a gaggle of mainstream operators in every tourist hub in
Africa, and some travellers may still prefer to use one even though they do
not have any interest in or experience of disability. I have selected a couple
for most of the regions covered by this book, but before I list them, readers
are reminded that all the companies listed as specialised operators (above)
also run safaris for fully 'able' people, and, in tune with modern-day
thinking about disability, do not label themselves or their clients as 'special'
in any derogatory way.

Kenya
Basecamp Travel Ole Odume Rd, end of Argwings Kodhek Rd, Nairobi; ☏ +254 (0)20 387
7490–2; **f** +254 (0)20 387 7489; **e** info@basecampexplorer.co.ke;
⌂ www.basecampexplorer.com
Hoopoe Safaris Inside Wilson Airport, Nairobi; ☏ +254 (0)20 604 303; ☏/**f** +254 (0)20 604
304; **e** hoopoekenya@hoopoe.com; ⌂ www.hoopoe.com

Tanzania
Hoopoe Safaris India St, Arusha; ☏ +255 (0)27 250 7011; **f** +255 (0)27 254 8226;
e information@hoopoe.com; ⌂ www.hoopoe.com

Roy Safaris 44 Serengeti Rd, Arusha; ☏ +255 (0)27 250 2115/8010/7057/7940;
f +255 (0)27 254 8892; **e** roysafaris@intafrica.com; ⌂ www.roysafaris.com

Zambia (Livingstone)
Safari Par Excellence Zambezi Waterfront & Activity Centre; ☏ +260 (0)21 332 0606;
e zaminfo@safpar.com; ⌂ www.safpar.com, ⌂ www.safpar.net or
⌂ www.zambezisafari.com

Namibia
Chameleon Safaris 5–7 Voigt St, Windhoek; ☏ +264 (0)61 247 668;
f +264 (0)61 220 885; **e** chamnam@mweb.com.na; ⌂ www.chameleonsafaris.com
SWA Safaris 4 Independence Av; ☏ +264 (0)61 221 193; **f** +264 (0)61 225 387;
e swasaf@swasafaris.com; ⌂ www.swasafaris.com

Botswana
The Booking Company Tsheko-Tsheko Rd, Maun; ☏ +267 (0)686 0022; **f** +267 (0)686 0037;
e enquiries@booking.co.bw; ⌂ www.thebookingcompany.net
Travel Wild Mathiba I Rd, Maun; ☏ +267 (0)686 0822; **f** +267 (0)686 0493;
e reservations@travelwild.co.bw; ⌂ www.botswanaholidays.com

South Africa

Bophelo Tours & Safaris Postnet Suite 546, Private Bag x 4, Menlo Park 0102; ☎ +27 (0)12 567 6981; f +27 (0)86 502 7949; e marius@bophelo.com; ⌂ www.bophelo.com
Siyabona Africa 10 Dean St, Gardens, Cape Town; ☎ +27 (21) 424 1037; f +27 (21) 424 1036; e from ⌂ www.siyabona.com

SELF-DRIVE VEHICLE RENTAL

Most of the operators listed on pages 19–23, will be able to organise safaris, airport transfers and city transport. These may be with accessible or standard vehicles, depending on whether it is a specialised or mainstream operator, but in the majority of cases they will be chauffeur-driven. If you want to drive yourself, there are various options.

CARS WITH HAND CONTROLS

In South Africa both Avis and Budget car-rental companies can provide a car with hand controls at most of their major centres throughout the country. For these, it is sensible to book at least a month in advance, although four or five days is often quoted. I have heard of one person who managed to coerce Avis into providing such a vehicle in Namibia but this was after protracted negotiations with their UK office.

Avis Car Rental (South Africa) ☎ +27 (0)11 923 3402/600; ⌂ www.avis.co.za
Budget Car Rental (South Africa) ☎ +27 (0)11 398 0123; f +27 (0)11 398 0124; e reservations@budget.co.za; ⌂ www.budget.co.za

Your own hand controls

A further option is to purchase and travel with your own set of hand controls, then hire a standard automatic car. These are not expensive and can usually be installed in a matter of minutes, but do be sure that this method won't render your insurance invalid. One company selling such equipment is **Lynx Hand Controls** (⌂ *www.lynxcontrols.com*).

SELF-DRIVE ACCESSIBLE MINIBUSES

Exclusiv Coach Tours can supply minibuses with a hydraulic lift and capacity for wheelchairs at various centres in South Africa. Depending on the qualifications and experience of the driver, these may be self-drive, but if not a driver trained in disability handling will be provided. Budget (see contact details above) and QASA (QuadPara Association of South Africa) have such vehicles in Johannesburg and QASA has plans to develop similar services in KwaZulu-Natal and Cape Town by 2009. Flamingo Tours (see page 22) also plans to have such a vehicle for hire around Cape Town by early 2009. An accessible van with hydraulic lift is also now available at Durban Airport. Ask Jennae from Access 2 Africa Safaris for details (see page 21).

Exclusiv Coach Tours PO Box 32400, Totiusdal 0134, South Africa; ☎ +27 (0)861 114 953;
f +27 (0)86 508 5078; **e** info@exclusivcoachtours.co.za; 🖰 www.exclusivcoachtours.co.za
QASA (QuadPara Association of South Africa) PO Box 2368, Pinetown, 3600; ☎ +27 (0)31 767
0348; **f** +27 (0)31 767 0584; **e** pcqasa@iafrica.com

SELF-DRIVE 4X4

The following companies are two of the better-known options providing fully
kitted self-drive 4x4 vehicles, although these have no disability adaptions.

Offroad Africa PO Box 53453, Kenilworth 7745, South Africa; ☎ +27 (0)21 794 0806;
f +27 (0)21 794 4583; 🖰 www.offroadafrica.com. Offroad Africa is based in South Africa &
runs vehicles in South Africa, Namibia, Botswana & Zambia, among other countries.
Safari Drive Ltd The Trainer's Office, Windy Hollow, Sheepdrove, Lambourn, Berkshire
RG17 7XA UK; ☎ +44 (0)1488 71140; **e** info@safaridrive.com; 🖰 www.safaridrive.com. Based
in the UK, Safari Drive operates in Kenya, Tanzania, Namibia, Botswana & Zambia, among
other countries.

RED TAPE

The paperwork required for a safari is neither complicated nor difficult to
obtain, but it is essential. If you have everything necessary, and it is
organised in an orderly fashion, then your trip will run more smoothly.

ESSENTIAL DOCUMENTS

- Passport, with relevant visas
- Flight tickets including proof of purchase
- Standard and international driving licences (the former – or a
  photocopy of it – is useful as proof of identification, while its original
  plus the latter are essential if you plan to drive in Africa)
- A health card showing your immunisation status (including a yellow
  fever certificate)
- Doctors' letters and medical certificates
- Insurance policy including emergency contact numbers
- A sheet of paper with useful information, eg: contact details of friends
  and immediate relatives, travellers' cheque numbers, emergency
  contact details, travel insurance numbers and passport numbers

All these documents should be photocopied three times (including the main
page and any relevant visa page of your passport); two copies should be kept
separately in your hand luggage and main luggage, and the third left at
home with a friend or relative. If travelling as a couple, both parties should
be carrying copies of each. The internet can be accessed in most towns and
many hotels and lodges, so a sensible backup is to have all these documents
scanned and emailed to your web-based address.

PASSPORT, VISAS AND ENTRY REQUIREMENTS

There are several prerequisites when entering a country. It is easy to make sure that these are in order and although some visa offices and immigration officials will ignore some stipulations, it would be infuriating to have entry refused because of something avoidable.

- Your passport must be valid for a specific period from the proposed date of departure from Africa (for Kenya this is three months; for Tanzania, Zambia, Namibia, Botswana and South Africa it is six)
- Your passport must have enough blank pages for entry and exit stamps (normally two are required)
- To acquire a visa, you may also need proof of an onward or homeward journey after your safari plus evidence that you can support yourself financially during your stay (a credit card usually suffices here)

Country-specific requirements

Visa requirements and costs vary depending on nationality and destination, and they can change with little or no warning. It is therefore essential to check with the nearest appropriate embassy or high commission for current stipulations. The following simple guide shows current requirements for citizens of the UK, US, Canada, Australia, New Zealand and all major European countries.

Kenya

A visa is required and can be obtained at most land borders and at Nairobi International Airport. Prices vary but are usually around US$50 for a single entry and twice that for multiple entry. At the time of going to press there is talk of Kenya reducing visa prices by 50% until the end of 2010.

Tanzania and Zambia

Everybody, except citizens of the Republic of Ireland, currently requires a visa, and it can be obtained on arrival at major land borders and international airports. Prices vary according to nationality and point of purchase but usually vary between US$30 and US$60 for Tanzania and US$50 and US$100 for Zambia.

Namibia, Botswana and South Africa

Visas are not required for visits of up to three months.

Acquiring a visa

If a visa is required, it can be purchased either before departure at the relevant consulate in your home country, or obtained at land borders or airports on entry. If the second option is possible then the usual advice is to do it this way. However, I personally feel that acquiring the visa at home in advance can be a time-saver in the long run. People with mobility restrictions have enough to consider every day on their travels, and arriving at the border with a visa may make skipping a queue possible. Even if this is not the case, it will mean you've had to carry less hard currency (usually US dollars cash).

Visas may be valid for one or several months and may be single or multiple entry. Be careful to choose the cheapest option that covers your needs and it's sensible to exaggerate the length of stay slightly to ensure that the visa will still be valid if the flight home is missed for any reason.

EMBASSIES AND CONSULATES WORLDWIDE

KENYA

Australia (High Commission) Qe Insurance Bldg, 33–35 Ainsley Av, Civic Sq, Canberra; ℡ 02 6247 4788; **f** 02 6257 6613; **e** khc-canberra@kenya.asn.au; ⌂ www.kenya.asn.au

Belgium (Embassy) Av Winston Churchill 208, 1180 Brussels; ℡ 02 340 1040; **f** 02 340 1050; **e** info@kenyabrussels.com; ⌂ www.kenyabrussels.com

Canada (Consulate) 415 Laurier Av East, Ottawa, Ontario KIN 6R4; ℡ 613 563 1773–6; **f** 613 233 6599; **e** jbahemuka@mfa.go.ke; ⌂ www.kenyahighcommission.ca

Germany (Embassy) Markgrafen Strasse 63, 10969 Berlin; ℡ 030 259 2660; **e** office@embassy-of-kenya.de; ⌂ www.embassy-of-kenya.de

Sweden (Embassy) Birger Jarlsgatan 37, 2nd Floor, PO Box 7694, 10395 Stockholm; ℡ 08 218300/4/9; **f** 08 209261; **e** kenya.embassy@elia.com; ⌂ www.kenyaembassystockholm.com

UK (Consulate) 45 Portland Pl, London, W1B 1AS; ℡ 020 7636 2371; **f** 020 7323 6717; **e** consular@kenyahighcommission.net; ⌂ www.kenyahighcommission.net

US (Embassy) 2249 R St, NW Washington, DC 20008; ℡ 0202 387 6101; **f** 0202 462 3829; **e** information@kenyaembassy.com; ⌂ www.kenyaembassy.com

TANZANIA

Australia (Consulate) c/o Denes Ebner Lawyers, 32A Oxford St, Sydney; ℡ 02 9332 4944; **f** 02 9332 3902

Belgium (Embassy) 363 Av Louise, 1050 Brussels; ℡ 02 640 6500/27; **f** 27 12 646 8026

Canada (Embassy) 50 Range Rd, Ottawa, Ontario KIN 8J4; ℡ 613 232 1500–9; **f** 613 232 5184; **e** tzottawa@synapse.net

Germany (Embassy) PO Eschenallee 11, 14050 Berlin; ℡ 030 303 0800; **f** 030 3030 8020; **e** info@tanzania-gov.de; ⌂ www.tanzania-gov.de

Netherlands (Consulate) HA Van Karnebeeklaan 46, Amsterdam; ℡ 020 641 6060; **f** 020 18031 9158

Sweden (Embassy) Nasby Alle 6, 18355 Taby, Stockholm; ℡ 08 732 2430/1; **f** 08 732 2432; **e** mailbox@tanemb.se; ⌂ www.tanemb.se

UK (High Commission) 3 Stratford Pl, London W1C 1AS; ℡ 020 7569 1470; **f** 020 7495 8817; **e** tanzarep@tanzania-online.gov.uk; ⌂ www.tanzania-online.gov.uk

US (Embassy) 2139 R St, NW Washington, DC 20008; ℡ 0202 939 6125; **f** 0202 797 7408; **e** ubalozi@tanzaniaembassy-us.org; ⌂ www.tanzaniaembassy-us.org

ZAMBIA

Australia and New Zealand (Embassy) 10-2 Ebara I-Chome, Shinagwa-Ku, Tokyo 142;
📞 03 3491 0121; **f** 03 3491 0123
Belgium 469 Av Molière, 1050 Brussels; 📞 02 343 5649; **f** 02 347 4333
Canada (High Commission) 151 Slater St, Suite 205, Ottawa, Ontario K1P 5H3; 📞 613 232
4400; **f** 613 232 4410; **e** info@zambiahighcommission.ca; 🖰 www.zambiahighcommission.ca
Germany (Embassy) Botschaft Sambia, Axel-Springer-Strasse 54a, 10117 Berlin; 📞 030 206
2940; **f** 030 206 29419
Sweden (Embassy) Gardsvagen 18, 3rd Floor, Solna, Stockholm, Box 3056, SE-16903;
📞 08 679 9040; **f** 08 679 6850; **e** info@zambiaembassy.se; 🖰 www.zambiaembassy.se
UK (High Commission) 2 Palace Gate, London W8 5NG; 📞 020 7589 6655; **f** 020 7581 0546;
e immzhcl@btconnect.com; 🖰 www.zhcl.org.uk
US (Embassy) 2419 Massachusetts Av, NW Washington, DC 20008; 📞 0202 265 9717–9;
f 0202 265 9718; **e** embzambia@aol.com; 🖰 www.zambiaembassy.org

NAMIBIA

Belgium (Embassy) Av De Tervuren 454, 1150 Brussels; 📞 02 771 1410; **f** 02 771 9689;
e nam.emb@brutele.be
Germany (Embassy) Wichmannstrasse 5, 2nd Floor, 10787 Berlin; 📞 030 254 0950;
f 030 254 09555; **e** namibiaberlin@aol.com
Sweden (Embassy) Luntmakargatan 86–88, PO Box 19151, SE 104 32 Stockholm;
📞 08 442 9800; **f** 08 612 6655; **e** info@embassyofnamibia.se; 🖰 www.embassyofnamibia.se
UK (High Commission) 6 Chandos St, London W1G 9LU; 📞 020 7636 6244; **f** 020 7637 5694;
e namibia-highcomm@btconnect.com
US (Embassy) 1605 New Hampshire Av, NW Washington, DC; 📞 0202 986 0540 (also
responsible for Canada)

BOTSWANA

Australia (High Commission) 5 Timbarra Crescent, O'Malley 2606 ACT Canberra;
📞 0612 6290 7500; **f** 0612 6286 2566
Belgium (Embassy) 169 Av De Tervuren, B1150 Brussels; 📞 02 735 2070/6110;
f 02 732 6110/725 6318
Canada (Consulate) 30 Chinook Crescent, Ottawa, Ontario H2H 7E1; 📞 0613 596 0166;
f 0613 596 2342; **e** mbelanger1003@rogers.com
Germany (Consulate) Berzeliusstrasse 45, 22113 Hamburg; 📞 040 732 6191; **f** 040 732 8506
Sweden (Embassy) Tyrgatan 11, PO Box 26024, 10041 Stockholm; 📞 08 545 25880;
f 08 723 0087
UK (High Commission) 6 Stratford Pl, London W1C 1AY; 📞 020 7499 0031; **f** 020 7495 8595
US (Embassy) 1531–1533 New Hampshire Av, NW Washington, DC 20036; 📞 0202 244 4990;
f 0202 244 4164; **e** pmajingo@gov.bw; 🖰 www.botswanaembassy.org

SOUTH AFRICA

Australia (High Commission) Corner State Circle & Rodes Pl, Yarralumla 2600, ACT,
Canberra; 📞/**f** 02 6272 7364; **e** info@sahc.org.au or **e** consular@sahc.org.au;
🖰 www.sahc.org.au

Belgium (Embassy) Rue dr la Loi/Wetstraat 26 (8th Floor), 1040 Brussels; ✆ 02 285 4400;
🖷 02 285 4402; ℯ embassy@southafrica.be; 🖱 www.southafrica.be/consular.htm
Canada (High Commission) 15 Sussex Drive, Ottawa, Ontario K1M 1M8; ✆ 0613 744 0330;
🖷 0613 741 1639; ℯ rsafrica@southafrica-canada
Germany (Embassy) Tiergartenstrasse 18, 10785 Berlin; ✆ 030 220 730; 🖷 030 2207 3208;
ℯ berlin.consular@foreign.gov.za; 🖱 www.suedafrika.org/de/konsulat.php
Netherlands (Embassy) 36 Wassenaarseweg, 2596 CJ, The Hague; ✆ 070 310 5920;
🖱 www.zuidafrika.nl
New Zealand (Consulate) 22 The Anchorage, Whitby, Wellington; ✆ 064 4234 8006;
🖷 064 4234 8075; ℯ gfortuin@paradise.net.nz
Sweden (Embassy) Flemingatan 20, 4th Floor, 112 26 Stockholm; ✆ 08 243950;
🖷 08 660 7136; ℯ info.saemb.swe@telia.com; 🖱 www.southafricanemb.se
UK (High Commission) South Africa Hse, Trafalgar Sq, London WC2N 5DP; ✆ 020 7451 7299;
🖷 020 7451 7283; ℯ webdesk@southafricahouse.com; 🖱 www.southafricahouse.com
US (Embassy) 3051 Massachusetts Av, NW Washington, DC 20008; ✆ 0202 232 4400;
🖷 0202 265 1607; ℯ info@saembassy.org; 🖱 www.saembassy.org

INSURANCE

Comprehensive travel and medical insurance from a dependable organisation is essential for anybody planning to go on safari. Some operators won't accept you without it. For older travellers and people with disabilities, this may appear, at first glance, to be one of the first stumbling blocks in preparing for such a trip, but it shouldn't be. What is crucial is to be sure you have the chief hazards covered and to confirm that your age and/or any pre-existing or current medical conditions will not annul any potential claim.

CHOOSING TRAVEL INSURANCE

Current policies
Before spending money, it is worth checking that you do not already have sufficient cover in another guise. Many home and contents policies insure some personal effects, even on holiday, and banks and credit-card companies often include basic travel insurance as a standard part of their package. Even if the current cover is not sufficient, an upgrade may be cheaper than a new policy elsewhere.

Standard and specialised insurers
In the UK, the Disability Discrimination Act states that insurance companies may not treat people with disabilities less favourably than other customers. What this means – theoretically at least – is that everybody, irrespective of physical ability, has the same range of choice when buying insurance. Unfortunately, insurers may charge a higher premium if they

can show that the risk is greater. While I'd applaud anybody who would push an unwilling provider to these lengths, I suspect few travellers have neither the time nor energy to do this. If you are struggling to find adequate cover at a reasonable price, it might be most straightforward to contact a specialist company. This could be beneficial, not only because the cover might be more comprehensive, but because there is a higher probability that the agent you deal with will know what is being talked about when lesser-known terms like 'quadriplegia' or 'multiple sclerosis' are mentioned. For some people, using a specialised insurer may be the only option as they do not exclude pre-existing medical conditions and have no (or higher) upper age limits. See the end of this section for a list of inclusive insurance providers.

Age limits
Many insurance companies enforce an upper age limit, but you can shop around here, as there are some who have none. This limit will normally be higher if you are insuring a single trip as opposed to buying long-term insurance. Of course, for regular travellers an annual policy may be more economical. Conversely, disabled people, irrespective of age, may find it easier to obtain insurance from a company specialising in older clients as they are more used to discussing medical conditions. The onus here is on finding one with no lower age limit!

Pre-existing medical conditions
It could be important that your policy does not exclude recurrence of a pre-existing medical condition, which can mean anything from an ongoing medical or dental situation to a recent operation or even any ailment for which you take prescribed medicine. Note that this clause, if included, can sometimes be so broad as to cover the traveller, a travelling companion or a non-travelling family member. Most insurers demand that any pre-existing medical conditions are deemed stable before travel. Often 'stable' is interpreted as not having been in hospital for the past year.

Medical screening
In many cases medical screening will be necessary; some companies do this in-house, while others use an independent screening service. Some ask for a letter from your GP or usual doctor. In independent screening, the insurance company will give you a telephone number to call, various questions regarding your current medical situation and history will be asked, and through this process you will receive a reference number that is subsequently used by the insurance company to provide a quote. The agents you speak to should understand the medical condition or disability you have; this whole procedure should be completely confidential, but it is worth checking nonetheless. If you have any doubts about any of this, ask to speak to another agent or use a different insurer.

IMPORTANT POLICY CONTENTS

Medical costs

Medical and dental bills can quickly become large, and with no reciprocal health agreements between African countries and those of most safari tourists, it is essential to have solid coverage. Check and compare policies for which medical costs will be refunded and the maximum value of each.

Repatriation

Full repatriation insurance, which will pay for evacuation to your home country in the case of serious accident or illness to yourself, is extremely important. It is also possible to have costs refunded if an unexpected return home is necessary because of sudden family illness or bereavement.

Personal effects and baggage

Personal effects insurance is always recommended, but becomes more of an issue for travellers who have expensive equipment such as wheelchairs, scooters and walkers. Such items are invariably extremely expensive and can be damaged, stolen or lost at any stage of the trip. If you wish to be able to redeem their complete value then they must be itemised and insured separately, and may be more cheaply covered under a separate policy or home and contents insurance. Such equipment is most at risk during flights (see page 84), when it is out of your sight, so it is worthwhile checking with the airline or your flight agent if it is insured when in their care (it almost certainly won't be), and then to purchase travel insurance accordingly. General baggage can also go astray during flights, especially when there are several connections *en route* to Africa. Buying replacement clothes and equipment and transport costs for collecting late luggage are just some of the expenses that may need to be recouped here.

Cancellation and delay costs

Check and compare policy refunds and notification required if the trip has to be cancelled for any reason, medical or otherwise. Cancellation may not just be necessary because of personal problems, but in the event of death or illness of family members or travelling companions. If you arrive late for a group tour because of missed or delayed flights, there will be expenses involved in catching up as well as extra hotel costs. These may be refunded by the airline, depending who is responsible for the delay, but it is wise to be covered.

Free telephone 24-hour emergency assistance

There are mobile telephone networks covering most of the safari regions in Africa, and if not, then reliable communications are never far away. If there is an incident of any kind – medical, theft or loss – then it is imperative that your insurance company is notified as soon as possible. This is made easier if they guarantee free 24-hour, 7-day operator availability, and if you have this contact number noted, with policy number, and easily found by somebody else in your party.

Region visited and holiday type
There are sometimes important exceptions within policy documents, excluding travel to particular regions or countries or not covering certain activities (safaris may be one of these). Be sure that your provider knows exactly where you plan to go and what to do, then double-check the policy yourself to be sure these are not excluded.

Procedure and small print
Understand the procedure for reporting a claim, and read the small print thoroughly, tedious though it may be, as there could be details that render an apparently good policy impractical – for example there may be an extremely short time limit after any accident or theft within which a claim must be made.

INCLUSIVE TRAVEL INSURANCE PROVIDERS
The following companies cover pre-existing medical conditions and specialise in offering insurance for disabled and/or older travellers.

UK
Age Concern Insurance Services Fortis Hse, Tollgate, Eastleigh, Hampshire SO53 3YA; ☎ 0800 169 2700; ⊕ www.ageconcern.org.uk. No upper or lower age limit.

All Clear Travel Insurance Services 6th Floor, Regent Hse, Hubert Rd, Brentwood, Essex CM14 4JE; ☎ 0871 208 8579; **e** info@allcleartravel.co.uk; ⊕ www.allcleartravel.co.uk. No upper or lower age limit.

Atlas Direct 37 King's Exchange, Tileyard Rd, London N7 9AH; ☎ 0870 811 1700; **f** 0870 811 1800; **e** callme@atlasdirect.net; ⊕ www.atlasdirect.net. Upper age limit is 80. There is no lower age limit.

Chartwell Insurance 292–294 Hale Lane, Edgware, Middlesex HA8 8NP; ☎ 020 8958 0900; **f** 020 8958 3220; **e** info@chartwellinsurance.co.uk; ⊕ www.chartwellinsurance.co.uk. Upper age limit is 79 (single trip). There is no lower age limit.

Direct Travel Insurance Shoreham Airport, Shoreham by Sea, West Sussex BN43 5FF; ☎ 0845 605 2700; **e** info@direct-travel.co.uk; ⊕ www.direct-travel.co.uk. Upper age limit is 75.

Enroute Insurance Grove Mills, Cranbrook Rd, Hawkhurst, Kent TN18 4AS; ☎ 0800 783 7245; **e** info@enrouteinsurance.co.uk; ⊕ www.enrouteinsurance.co.uk. No lower age limit. Upper age limit for annual policies is 79 & for single trip is 85.

Freedom Insurance Services Ltd Richmond Hse, 16–20 Regent St, Cambridge CB2 1DB; ☎ 0870 774 3760; **e** from website; ⊕ www.freedominsure.co.uk. Upper age limit for single trip is 85.

Free Spirit Travel Insurance (PJ Hayman and Company Ltd) Stansted Hse, Rowlands Castle, Hampshire PO9 6DX; ☎ 0845 230 5000; **f** 023 9241 9049; **e** freespirit@pjhayman.com; ⊕ www.free-spirit.com. Safaris must be organised in the UK prior to departure. There's no lower age limit; upper age limit is 85.

J & M Insurance Services 14–16 Guilford St, London WC1N 1DW; ☎ 020 7446 7600; **e** jmi@jmi.co.uk; ⏱ www.jmi.co.uk. Upper age limit is 79 & there's no lower age limit. Medical screening is done in-house.

MS Society National Centre, 372 Edgware Rd, London NW2 6ND; ☎ 020 8438 0700; **f** 020 8438 0701; ⏱ www.mssociety.org.uk. No upper age limit.

Orbis Travel Insurance Charter Hse, 43 St Leonards Rd, Bexhill-on-Sea, East Sussex TN40 1JA; ☎ 01424 220110; **f** 01424 217107; **e** cover@orbis-insure.co.uk; ⏱ www.orbis-insure.co.uk. Upper age limit is 99 & there's no lower age limit.

Towergate Risk Solutions 288 Chase Rd, Southgate, London N14 6HF; ☎ 0870 920 2222; **f** 0870 920 2211; **e** marrs@marrs.co.uk; ⏱ www.marrs.co.uk. Upper age limit is 79 & lower age limit is 1.

Travelbility Peregrine Hse, Falconry Court, Bakers Lane, Epping, Essex CM16 5BQ; ☎ 0845 338 1638; **e** enquiries@travelbility.co.uk; ⏱ www.travelbility.co.uk. Upper age limit is 79.

US

An interesting point is that most US travel insurance companies offer a 'pre-existing condition waiver' as an incentive if the traveller purchases trip insurance within a certain time period (typically between seven and 15 days) of paying the deposit on their trip.

Access America PO Box 71533, Richmond, VA 23286 4684; ☎ 1 800 284 8300; **e** salessupport@accessamerica.com; ⏱ www.accessamerica.com

Travel Guard 1145 Clark St, Stevens Point, WI 54481; ☎ 1 800 826 4919; ⏱ www.travelguard.com

Travel Insured International 52-S Oakland Av, PO Box 280568, East Hartford, CT 06128 0568; ☎ 800 243 3174; **e** info@travelinsured.com; ⏱ www.travelinsured.com

Travelex Insurance Services PO Box 641070, Omaha, NE 68164 7070; ☎ 1 800 228 9792; **e** customerservice@travelex-insurance.com; ⏱ www.travelex-insurance.com. No upper or lower age limits.

Australia

In Australia, if pre-existing medical conditions are covered then the usual procedure is for the client to complete a medical assessment with their doctor, which is then reviewed by the insurer's medical assessor to determine the potential risk and premium applicable.

Aon Personal Insurance GPO Box 390D, Melbourne VIC 3001; ☎ 1300 134 256, (international direct-dial number) ☎ +61 3 9918 5609; **f** 03 9916 3776; **e** cgu_aonpi@iag.com.au; ⏱ www.personalinsurance.aon.com.au/travel.htm. Various age-related restrictions.

CGU Travel Insurance ⏱ www.cgu.com.au. Medical assessment forms & contact details for different states in Australia can be found on the website.

Travel Insurance Cover 7 Wrench Pl, Kenthurst NSW 2156; ☎ 02 9423 6940; **f** 02 942 3 6968; **e** info@travelinsurancecover.com.au;

🖰 www.travelinsurancecover.com.au. Upper age limit is 80 for international journeys & some health conditions are automatically covered.
Travel Insurance Direct ☎ 1300 843 843; **e** infoAUS@travelinsurancedirect.com.au; 🖰 www.travelinsurancedirect.com.au. Upper age limit for single trip is 81.
Travellers Assistance Insurance Jetset Travelworld Insurance Pty Ltd, Level 5, 24 York St, Sydney, NSW 2000; ☎ 1300 787 311; 🖰 www.travellersassistance.com.au. Cover is available for pre-existing conditions by completing the 'Under 81 Medical form' or 'Over 81 Medical form' that can be downloaded from the website home page (under 'Documents').

New Zealand
Mike Henry Travel Insurance Ltd Shortland St, Auckland 1010; ☎ 09 377 5958 or ☎ 0800 657 744; **f** 09 309 5473; **e** info@mikehenry.co.nz; 🖰 www.mikehenry.co.nz. No upper or lower age limits.

PERSONAL ASSISTANCE

Needing help with aspects of daily living does not mean that an adventurous holiday is off limits. Quite simply, if a personal assistant* cannot be taken with you then one can be organised in Africa. This subject may also apply to people who manage to cope alone at home, but who may need a bit of help when out of their comfort zone. Being used to independence, they will find it more difficult to accept assistance; however, it's worth remembering that not only is a holiday much more relaxing this way, but effectively managing assistance is a skill one should be proud to have.

The first point to note is that labour is relatively inexpensive in Africa, and very often, especially in the more upmarket camps and lodges, a member of staff can be dedicated entirely to one client. The drawback here is that this person will only be available for the duration of your stay in that property; they will not travel with you on the safari. If you need a helper throughout the trip, then there are several options. The ideal scenario is to take one of your personal assistants from home (and few would refuse the opportunity), but because airlines rarely offer free or reduced-cost extra seats for companions, this might not be financially viable. The second option is to use your travelling partner (spouse, family member or friend), which is quite straightforward but may greatly affect your and their enjoyment of the trip. Thirdly, you can employ someone locally and I'll discuss this in more depth.

The starting point when hiring an assistant locally is to contact a reputable operator (your safari organiser will usually oblige here) and explain exactly what you need. A safari company specialising in disability will be able to supply someone experienced, but even standard operators can often provide an able helper. Most have a list of people who have worked for them as guides or drivers and are therefore known to them and can be trusted. If an assistant with medical training is required, then the operator will usually know a local hospital, clinic or medical centre. From there, it is possible to spread the word to nursing or physiotherapy staff – or students of such disciplines – and find a suitably qualified person. You can, of course, contact such institutions yourself.

For the assistant, whether they come from a tourism or medical background, such work is not only valuable employment but glowing references straight from Western clients are good CV fodder. For the traveller, apart from not having to pay flight costs, this is a unique chance to relate one-on-one with someone from the country they're visiting. Many tourists pay for village visits and the like, but they rarely cross the massive economic and ethnic gulf that exists between the two cultures. If you use a local assistant, you will spend a lot of time together and the relationship will lose a degree of its informality; it becomes significantly more than just a fleeting exchange of words and the purchase of an artefact. Yet another bonus is that a local assistant will be streetwise. Wandering through markets not only becomes safer – so a more relaxing experience – but a local will know the traders and which shops give the best bargains.

There are two main drawbacks of this approach. Firstly, no interview or 'trial period' is possible (you will meet the assistant face to face for the first time on day one of your safari), so you must be as thorough as possible during the preceding email negotiations. Secondly, your food and accommodation costs will be greater. Some accommodation will offer free or reduced-rate rooms for assistants, but this is nowhere near standard policy in Africa. Failing that, in parts of the continent bed and board for drivers and guides is cheaper, but is less luxurious – sometimes squalid. This would obviously need to be discussed in full and agreed with your assistant beforehand.

As an aside, on a recent trip to Zanzibar a UK agent had warned me that because the bulk of local labour is Muslim, people would not be comfortable undertaking tasks of a personal nature. Nevertheless, I easily arranged an assistant through a reputable local operator. My PA had no qualms about any of the duties I presented, including bathroom work, and discussions with him assured me that his faith in no way precluded him from such tasks. Personal hygiene is given high ranking in Islam and when someone needs help with such issues, men apparently care for men and women for women.

* **Personal assistant:** Someone whose function, either paid or voluntary, is to help another person who has mobility difficulties. A personal assistant is also known as a 'PA', a 'carer', an 'attendant', an 'aide' or a 'care giver'.

WHAT TO TAKE

This subject is hugely personal, depending not only on how and where the safari is done, but also on the needs of the individual. Independent backpackers in Africa can easily be just that, living quite comfortably out of a light rucksack for three months, while it is quite normal for a two-week safari visitor to pack to (and sometimes beyond) their airline weight restrictions. There will always be essential items and any disability usually brings more of these. The skill (and it is one worth honing) is to take everything that you need for your style of travel, but nothing more. For those who have difficulties carrying or pulling luggage, help is always available in airports (see page 79), drivers will load vehicles and camps and hotels have porters to assist with lugging everything to and from rooms.

CLOTHING

Although it is traditional that safari dress is natural colours – usually green, brown and khaki – this is only really necessary if you are visiting more exclusive camps or going on walking safaris. On game drives, other colours are perfectly acceptable as long as they are relatively dull. At other times, more variation is fine; indeed, Africans are famed for their vibrant attire. Two thoughts to bear in mind are never to take military clothing – at best this will lead to mistrust and probing questions – and mosquitoes are attracted to darker colours, so wearing light-coloured clothing between dusk and dawn lowers the risk of being bitten.

Loose and light clothing is more comfortable in hot weather and cotton is generally preferred over synthetic fibres. T-shirts and shorts are fine in towns and cities where tourists congregate, and swimming costumes and sunbathing attire (including bikinis) are perfectly acceptable around lodge and hotel swimming pools. However, outwith these areas more care should be taken. When walking around towns it is disrespectful to dress scruffily – Africans don't if they can afford not to – and in villages less frequented by visitors men should think twice about wearing shorts (long sleeves and trousers also provide more protection against the sun and insect bites). Women should not wear anything that could be perceived as flirtatious (for example, underwear-revealing tops that are fashionable at home) and this is especially true in Muslim areas where such clothing will cause offence. Here, shoulders and knees should be covered (loose trousers, culottes or knee-length skirts are ideal for the latter). A very useful item for women to carry is a sari (*kikoi* in east Africa), which can quickly be wrapped around the body as a makeshift skirt if wearing shorts or a swimming costume. Such garments are cheaply bought in local markets, and are also super impromptu towels. Men should also heed Muslim traditions; wearing a vest can be perceived as arrogant in Zanzibar's Stone Town and going topless is unacceptable. A warm jersey or fleece is essential for cold evenings and morning game drives and a light anorak is recommended if travelling when there is any risk of rain.

Laundry facilities are available at virtually all hotels and lodges. Although this can be quite pricey, it is, in my opinion, not something worth scrimping on. Safaris are sweaty, dusty affairs at the best of times, and clothes enough for even a two-week trip require a large proportion of luggage space. For people who need to pack catheters, urine bags and incontinence pads, such space is at a premium. Another option is to take washing powder with you. This is a matter of personal choice, and one that depends on the budget of your trip, but I feel there are more pleasant ways of spending a Serengeti afternoon than wringing dirt from T-shirts.

OTHER USEFUL ITEMS
Once again, this is subjective, and this list is more intended to give ideas than to be all-inclusive:

- Guidebooks (though don't forget that most reasonable safari operators or guides will have bird and animal guidebooks either in lodges or vehicles; see *Further Information* for some recommended reading, page 337)
- Enough light reading material to fill time during air travel or by the pool. Don't expect to be reading on game drives and most people are too tired in the evening to manage more than a page or two.
- Water bottle
- Swiss army knife or similar
- Earplugs – it is almost a crime to block out the sounds of an African night, but because canvas provides no insulation, anyone with an aversion to snoring may wish to carry earplugs on a camping safari. These can also make it easier to sleep during a flight.
- Sunglasses
- If you use glasses, packing a spare pair might prove invaluable. Contact-lens wearers should bring all the fluids they need and might want to consider using only glasses, as dust and strong sunlight can be irritating.
- Hat – preferably with a brim providing shade over your face and neck
- A bed net and your own mosquito net could be useful if you plan to use cheap accommodation
- Toilet bag – but note that most of the usual contents are easily bought on the African tourist circuit
- Suncream of varying strengths, lipsalve (with UV protection) and insect repellent
- A box of baby wipes (or similar) is really handy for a quick freshen up when you're not near an accessible bathroom
- Basic medical kit (see page 61)
- Small torch (a head torch is the most practical type)
- Electrical adaptor (see box *Electricity and charging equipment*, page 48)
- Binoculars – again, many operators will provide these, but it's worth having your own pair especially during exciting moments when

everybody in the minibus wants a closer view. (People with limited hand function, see 'focus-free binoculars' in *Miscellaneous specialised equipment*, page 47.)

- Camera (a long lens is essential if you wish to photograph wildlife) and plenty of spare film or digital memory, spare batteries and recharger (some camps may not have recharging facilities, though most do – including everywhere in *Part Two* of this guide)

- Serious photographers may consider a laptop/notebook computer as important luggage. Modern models are slim and light and more and more hotels/lodges have Wi-Fi, allowing quick and easy communication with home. If you carry a separate backup drive, then don't forget to store it in a separate bag at all times.

SPECIALISED EQUIPMENT AND MODIFICATIONS

On top of the standard kit list, anyone with a disability will have an extra inventory of essential luggage. There is a huge range of such accessories, ranging from bathroom paraphernalia to mobility aids, and the trick is to know what would be more useful than burdensome.

As well as looking online, a visit to your local medical shop, rehabilitation unit or disability fair will also give great ideas. It may be simpler to locate heavier articles in Africa and hire them for the duration of the safari and in this case it's highly recommended that you book through a specialist operator (see pages 19–23); given enough warning, they can normally provide any equipment that might be needed. The following may be useful starting points when looking for ideas:

Disabled Accessories ☎ +44 1458 449028; f +44 1458 445988; e info@disabledaccessories.com; ⁰ www.disabledaccessories.com. A UK-based store with a huge range of equipment.

Gimpgear ⁰ www.broadenedhorizons.com. Gimpgear designs, builds & markets a range of products, but most notable for safari travel may be their 'comfort carrier' (see page 43, under *Slings, hoists and lifts*).

Spinalist Tips ⁰ www.spinalistips.se. This Swedish website is written in English & has a large selection of tips & equipment. The information has been sent in by disabled people & there is a category dedicated to travel.

Travel John ⁰ www.traveljohn.com. Has outlets in more than 20 countries & deals only in bathroom equipment.

Youreable ⁰ www.youreableshop.co.uk. Online only, but again, a UK-based resource with something for every situation.

Equal Adventure A'chaoruinn, Dulnain Bridge, Morayshire PH26 3NU; ☎ +44 1479 861 200; f +44 1479 780 538; e equal@equaladventure.co.uk; ⁰ www.equaladventure.org. This innovative company – based in the Scottish highlands – invents, researches & develops equipment designed to allow people with disability to take part in outdoor activities. This includes outdoor bathrooms & hoists.

The following items are by no means all-encompassing, but are a selection that may be handy. Basic everyday equipment that is used at home, including wheelchairs and incontinence material, is not included here.

Mobility aids

Punctures – avoidance and repair

There is undoubtedly a greater risk of having punctures on safari than at home. The usual culprits – sharp stones – are always around but Africa's greatest defence against wheelchair invasion is the ubiquitous acacia tree. Species of this genus are found throughout the continent, populating hotel, lodge and campsite compounds, and although their spreading canopy provides tempting shade from the sun, it has often laid a carpet of piercing thorns. Therefore, carrying a small hand pump and puncture-repair kit and having the know-how to use them is a wise precaution. That said, bicycles are a chief means of transport in Africa and most vehicle tyres still use inner tubes meaning roadside repairs are quick, cheap and efficiently done. I've had several punctures in various countries and although I do carry a repair kit, I've never had to use it.

What I would definitely recommend is that you take three or four new inner tubes with you. These can quickly replace the punctured tube, allowing you to get to a repair shop without damaging the tyre wall by running on a flat. It might be worthwhile carrying a spare tyre as well, but space and weight considerations have always dissuaded me from going to this extreme.

A different approach – one guaranteeing no risk of punctures – is to fit your wheelchair with solid tyres. The main drawbacks of this approach are extra weight and that they are generally softer than pneumatic tyres, making the chair heavier to push.

Wheels and tyres

Lightweight, everyday wheelchairs are usually fitted with narrow, high-pressure tyres. These make for effortless pushing on hard, smooth surfaces, but provide little grip on loose ground and sink into soft surfaces like grass or sand. As a result, if you plan to venture off the beaten track, it might be worth considering shoeing your wheelchair with something more practical. Off-road tyres with a more pronounced 'knobbly' tread can be bought for most wheel sizes, and this is definitely a worthwhile and relatively inexpensive first step if you want improved grip.

A greater investment is to buy wider wheels, which you can then use specifically for adventurous holidays. Rims of various sizes can be purchased for most types of chair and these can then be dressed with more gripping tyres. Obviously, the more contact with the ground that there is, the more strenuous pushing will be (even on hard surfaces), but the extra traction and flotation more than compensate for this. There is of course the

PHOTOGRAPHIC TIPS *Ariadne Van Zandbergen*

Equipment

Although you can take reasonable photos with a 'point and shoot' camera, you need an SLR camera with one or more lenses for more serious photography. The most important component in a digital SLR is the sensor. There are two types of sensor: DX and FX. The FX is a full size sensor identical to the old film size (36mm). The DX sensor is half size and produces less quality. The type of sensor will determine your choice of lenses as the DX sensor introduces a 0.5x multiplication to the focal length. So a 300mm lens becomes in effect a 450mm lens. FX ('full frame') sensors are the future, so I will further refer to focal lengths appropriate to the FX sensor.

Always buy the best lens you can afford. Fixed fast lenses are ideal, but very costly. Zoom lenses are easier to change composition without changing lenses the whole time. If you carry only one lens a 24–70mm or similar zoom should be ideal. For a second lens, a lightweight 80–200mm or 70–300mm or similar will be excellent for candid shots and varying your composition. Wildlife photography will be very frustrating if you don't have at least a 300mm lens. For a small loss of quality, teleconverters are a cheap and compact way to increase magnification: a 300 lens with a 1.4x converter becomes 420mm, and with a 2x it becomes 600mm. NB 1.4x and 2x teleconverters reduce the speed of your lens by 1.4 and 2 stops respectively.

The resolution of digital cameras is improving the whole time. For ordinary prints a 6-megapixel camera is fine. For better results, the possibility to enlarge images and for professional reproduction, higher resolution is available up to 21 megapixels.

It is important to have enough memory space when photographing on your holiday. The number of pictures you can fit on a card depends on the quality you choose. You should calculate how many pictures you can fit on a card and either take enough cards or take a storage drive onto which you can download the cards' content. You can obviously take a laptop which gives the advantage that you can see your pictures properly at the end of each day and edit and delete rejects. If you don't want the extra bulk and weight you can buy a storage device which can read memory cards.

Keep in mind that digital camera batteries, computers and other storage devices need charging. Make sure you have all the chargers, cables and converters with you. Most hotels/lodges have charging points, but it will be best to enquire about this in advance. When camping you might have to rely on charging from the car battery.

Dust and heat

Dust and heat are often a problem. Keep your equipment in a sealed bag, and avoid exposing equipment to the sun when possible. Digital cameras are prone to collecting dust particles on the sensor which results in spots on the image. The dirt mostly enters the camera when changing lenses, so you should be careful when doing this. To some extent photos can be 'cleaned' up afterwards in Photoshop, but this is time-consuming. You can have your camera sensor professionally cleaned, or you can do this yourself with special brushes and swabs made for this purpose, but note that touching the sensor might cause damage and should only be done with the greatest care.

Light

The most striking outdoor photographs are often taken during the hour or two of 'golden light' after dawn and before sunset. Shooting in low light may enforce the use of very low shutter speeds, in which case a tripod/beanbag will be required to avoid camera shake. The most advanced digital SLRs have very little loss of quality on higher ISO settings, which allows you to shoot at lower light conditions. It is still recommended not to increase the ISO unless necessary.

Generally, it is best to shoot with the sun behind you. When photographing animals or people in the harsh midday sun, images taken in light but even shade are likely to look nicer than those taken in direct sunlight or patchy shade, since the latter conditions create too much contrast.

Protocol

In some countries, it is unacceptable to photograph local people without permission, and many people will refuse to pose or will ask for a donation. In such circumstances, don't try to sneak photographs as you might get yourself into trouble. Even the most willing subject will often pose stiffly when a camera is pointed at them; relax them by making a joke, and take a few shots in quick succession to improve the odds of capturing a natural pose.

Ariadne Van Zandbergen is a professional travel and wildlife photographer specialised in Africa. She runs 'The Africa Image Library'. For photo requests, visit the website ⌁ www.africaimagelibrary.co.za or contact her direct e ariadne@hixnet.co.za

added drawback that more muck is carried in the tread, meaning you'll leave tracks indoors but again, this is usually an acceptable price to pay.

If buying new wheels is out of your budget, a common solution is to have a pair custom made. You'll need a pair of wheelchair hubs fitting your model of chair (you can pick these up secondhand from various sources, including your local wheelchair dealer, rehab centre or wheelchair sports clubs) and a pair of children's mountain-bike wheels, as these are normally 24in models and therefore fit standard wheelchairs. Most good bike shops will be able to spoke these rims to your wheelchair hubs and the whole process should not cost more than about £75, including work and materials.

Tools and mechanical repairs

When dealing with mechanical or electrical breakdowns, Africans excel at improvisation. This skill is common where there is not enough wealth to guarantee availability of correct tools and official spare parts, but is not something to be relied upon without caution. If you have a small, portable toolkit that was supplied with your chair, do bring it. If not, then assemble one, making sure you have a tool for most bolts and screws.

Similarly, skilled welders are not difficult to find in Africa, but sourcing somebody with the experience and equipment to deal with aluminium or titanium alloys will be less easy. The chances of such drastic repairs being necessary are extremely slight, but if you have a choice of wheelchairs that you're comfortable with then I'd recommend travelling with the cheaper option.

A sensible suggestion, if you are prone to worry about such occurrences, is to leave your second chair available with a friend at home. In the unlikely event of your chair being lost, stolen or damaged beyond repair, you have the peace of mind that your reserve could be sent urgently as a replacement. This would certainly be expensive, but if the circumstances are properly recorded – with police report or photographic evidence if possible – then insurance should pay the costs.

Luggage struts

A useful adaptation to wheelchairs of both independent users and those who need help pushing is luggage-carrying struts. These are strong lengths of durable plastic that clamp to the front of the wheelchair – one on each side – and provide a strong, level platform to carry luggage in front. They are hinged so fold up to sit flush with the frame when not in use. Apart from leaving the user's hands free to push the wheels or hold other items of luggage, the other obvious advantage is that your bags are always in sight. They can be purchased to fit specific wheelchairs or generic versions can be ordered that will suit various models.

Collapsible wheelchairs

Travellers who are not completely steady on their feet, but get by in their home life without any mechanical aids, may consider taking a lightweight, collapsible travel wheelchair. Other walking aids like sticks and frames can also be easily carried. Resorting to such aids may seem like a step backwards but once the idea is accepted, people generally appreciate the freedom such apparatus gives and forget about their initial reservations.

Slings, hoists and lifts

To reduce manual handling, various options exist that make transfers between chair, vehicle, bed, bath and toilet more comfortable for the user and assistants alike. Gimpgear's 'Comfort Carrier' is a sling with handles, which can be slid under the person and requires two helpers (see page 38). Portable, wheeled hoists exist that can be operated by one person, although one traveller does recommend carrying an extra battery – not because of a lack of charging possibilities, but because theirs simply stopped working on day one of their trip. For outdoor use, Equal Adventure have recently launched a frame designed to safely lift people in and out of boats, but which can also be used for high vehicle transfers (see page 88).

Bathroom aids

For the majority of travellers who have mobility restrictions, knowing that they will be able to answer nature's call in a dignified manner is the top priority when planning a trip away from home. With a bit of research, it should be possible to organise a safari with bathroom facilities to suit everyone's needs, but there is always the risk of having to improvise *en route*. As well as situations where toilets in accommodation are not ideal, distances are often great and toilet stops in the bush are a common occurrence. Depending on your ability to stand, sit or squat, various devices exist that will help to allow comfortable and private ablutions.

Privacy tent

If the journey from the vehicle to the bushes during a toilet stop is too daunting, then a privacy tent might be the answer. This construction is easily erected, ensuring you'll quickly be hidden from view. They have enough space inside to accommodate a wheelchair and have sufficient height to allow someone to stand up. Although they are only a few kilos, this extra weight might mean it is something that you expect your safari operator to provide, and it should be no problem for most specialised companies.

The long call

Emptying the bowels (or the 'long call' as it is known in Africa) is perhaps the topic that worries travellers the most, but the one they're least likely to want to discuss with strangers. Everyone handles this task in their own way, but the majority of people who are unable to transfer onto a toilet or a portable commode tend to use incontinence material. This is bulky and heavy, so it is worthwhile contacting the operator in Africa and arranging for it to be sent to or bought in Africa.

There are various 'field toilets' available in camping stores both in Africa and at home. These usually have a light, metal frame and canvas upholstery with a simple hole in the appropriate place. While they're designed for able-bodied campers in bush camps where the toilet is a hole in the ground, they can be a good solution for less-able people where the toilet is simply out of reach.

The short call

For the 'short call' (passing urine), there are funnels that can be easily washed and re-used, giving women (wheelchair users or those who find squatting uncomfortable) much more freedom. These can also be very useful during the flight. Popular brand names to look out for are 'Whiz', 'She-Pee', 'She-Wee' or a host of products from the manufacturer Travel John (see page 38 for contact details).

If you're not behind a bush or in a toilet, disposing of the urine is the next challenge. For this, 'portable urinals' (urine storage bags) are available and these are useful for both sexes. They contain dry crystals that turn to a semi-solid gel when mixed with urine. However, they're usually full after two or three uses so you'll need to bring several, meaning more luggage. Also, depending on whether they're made from biodegradable plastic or not, they may not be environmentally friendly.

Bedroom ablutions

For those who need an extremely accessible bathroom, but can't find one in their budget where they want to go, the solution most commonly used is the old-fashioned bed bath. These are never as pleasant as the real thing, or a shower, but may be a solution for a few days. The equipment required – two bowls and a sheet of plastic – is hardly technical and can be cheaply purchased in virtually any town in the continent.

Commodes and shower chairs

Portable, collapsible commode chairs are available in various styles, with legs or wheels, and hard plastic or soft padded seat cushions. Depending on what they're made of, some can be used as a shower chair. Those with legs are generally lighter to carry and more compact when folded, whilst wheeled versions allow the user to move between toilet, shower and bed. They often come with a 'catching pot', which fits underneath the chair, but this is bulky. Instead of this, I'd suggest you buy a cheap bowl on arrival in Africa, or use plastic bags. Taking the environment into consideration, it is possible to purchase biodegradable bags that are designed to securely enclose solid human waste.

Bath board

There is a huge variety of styles available. Choose one that's light, yet sturdy and adjustable.

Bath/shower cushions
A waterproof inflatable cushion with suction fixation points makes a bath safe and comfortable. These can also be used for shower seating, which is often stone, tile or stainless steel, but a towel, folded double, is the simplest solution here.

Toilet cushions
Although good-quality pressure-relieving toilet seat cushions are pricey and can be heavy, sensible advice is to remember that skin health is the most important priority. They usually have straps to allow them to be securely fastened to any toilet seat (so fixed toilets in bathrooms as well as portable commodes can be made comfortable) and if you shop around then differing thicknesses can be found, depending on whether you need the toilet height as high or as low as possible. U-shaped versions as opposed to those closed at the front allow easier hand access under the body for washing and digital stimulation.

Suction support rails
Bathrooms with level access and wide doorways are fairly common in Africa. Roll-in showers are also surprisingly prevalent. These features often exist in rooms which have no other adaptive features simply because there is enough space to allow such luxury. The next level of access – fitting support rails – is a conscious step towards inclusion and therefore is less commonly seen. Until the day when every property has bathrooms fitted with such features, one option is to carry suction grab rails with you. These come in various lengths and clamp to tiled walls using suction pads. They have the huge advantage that you can place them exactly where suits you best but they're only as strong as the tiles they're clamped on.

Tap turners
Despite the fact that many older people as well as some disabled people have limited grip, easy-to-use lever or push taps are some of the last features to be considered when adapting bathrooms. To counter this problem, simple plastic extension handles are available with fittings to suit 'star' or 'round' taps (see page xiv for definitions of these types).

These are small and light so pack easily, and although to many this may appear to be too fine a detail, having them with you could make your trip that little bit more relaxing.

Shower mat
Anti-slip tiles or floors with a traction material (like sand) embedded in the paint are not yet common features in bathrooms. This may not be relevant to many visitors, but those who are unsteady on their feet may wish to make standard bathroom floors that bit safer by laying down a shower mat. These have water drainage holes for use directly in the shower and suction cups to make sure they stay fixed to the shower floor.

EXTRA MOBILITY EQUIPMENT

Most airlines carry at least one piece of mobility equipment free of charge, though some may impose weight restrictions. Be sure to confirm with your carrier during booking that they can carry the extra equipment you need. If you are taking more than a standard wheelchair then it is prudent to check this at least once again before flying and even then to be prepared for a discussion at check-in. I have heard of people being given permission by airlines to greatly exceed their weight limits by calling incontinence items 'disability equipment'. While true, I don't recommend this approach; it would be wise to have this agreed in writing by the airline before arriving at check-in with armfuls of catheters.

If something like this is too heavy to pack, I'm reliably informed that a towel laid out on the ground is also an improvement on bare tiles, though I personally see this presenting more of a tripping hazard than slipping solution.

Portable mirror

It is astounding how few 'wheelchair accessible' bathrooms have mirrors at a height that is useful to someone in a wheelchair – and that's not just in Africa.

If you need to use a mirror, it's wise to pack your own.

Padding

Depending on your itinerary, journeys can be long and roads can be rough. Also, beds and seating away from home may not protect your skin to the degree you are used to. Anyone prone to pressure wounds, as well as those with joint pain and other conditions where comfort is a priority, might consider taking extra padding. Clinically proven inflatable pressure-relieving mattresses, cushions, pillows, footrests and knee supports are available, and offer the best protection, but can be expensive. If you want to improvise then there are no rules; ingenuity and common sense are what's important. I've heard of various types of material and apparatus being used and here is a selection of suggestions:

- Inflatable camping mattresses are cheap and easily packed, especially the half- or three-quarter length versions. However, they are not designed to alleviate pressure to a clinical level.

- Foam cushions from sun loungers make beds firmer

- Flight head pillows might make a huge difference to anyone with poor balance and don't have to be limited to either the flight or your head

- Sheepskin padding comes in various sizes and shapes can be wrapped around seatbelts and various fittings (like armrests) to reduce chafing

Miscellaneous specialised equipment

The list of extra equipment that could be of use is potentially infinite. Mobility and bathroom problems are without question the priorities, but the following may also be of interest:

- 'Focus-free' binoculars have no focus adjustment and are therefore useful for anyone with limited hand function. Quality of image is compromised slightly and they cannot focus on objects closer than approximately 20m, but these shortcomings are barely noticeable to the amateur eye; they will be a useful tool for some.

- Four pieces of wood (each about the size of a matchbox) can be invaluable for raising tables that are just too low for wheelchair users' knees

- A roll of masking or duct tape is perfect for temporary equipment tears and repairs, and any *en-route* improvisations

- Straws are the simple solution if you have trouble grasping mugs, cups and glasses of different sizes. It's surprising how few restaurants have them available.

- A light collapsible 'fishing stool' is an ideal footrest during flights (if you have been lucky enough to secure a seat with legroom) and has a multitude of uses during transfers into vehicles and in bedrooms and bathrooms

- For people whose body thermostat does not function properly, ice packs designed for pain relief or a sporting 'cooling vest' could help control core body temperature in hot climates (but take medical advice first before using these). A bandana and wristbands continuously soaked in cool water will do a similar function at a lesser cost

- A spray bottle designed to water indoor plants is the simplest skin coolant, working on the same principle as sweat

CARRYING YOUR LUGGAGE

Clothing and equipment will need to be distributed between your main baggage and hand luggage (daypack), and there are various options for each of these depending on your abilities and safari plans.

Type of bags

As main baggage, I use a large canvas holdall (duffel bag), which has a capacity similar to that of a reasonably sized suitcase but is lighter and can easily be carried across my knees when wheeling through airports. A suitcase is the most common alternative, is more securely lockable and offers more protection to breakable objects or neatly folded clothes. The wheeled versions have extendable handles and can easily be pulled, assuming the ground surface is smooth. A rucksack (backpack) is advised if your trip is going to require more extended periods of walking than from

ELECTRICITY AND CHARGING EQUIPMENT

All of the accommodation covered in this guide has some kind of electrical power available, ranging from 24-hour, reliable mains distribution to an intermittent supply driven by diesel generator or solar power. The latter will normally be switched on for several hours through the evening then switched off during the night, meaning a degree of planning may be necessary to ensure you have enough charge at the essential times.

Hotel rooms and substantial tented camps (where the 'tents' are semi-permanent structures) will almost always have electrical sockets within the rooms. Simple camps and authentic, wilder bush camps often use paraffin 'Tilley' lamps, torches or candles, but clients can usually charge items at the main reception or staff areas. This may sound like a security risk, but their remoteness means the only people around are employees or guests, making theft much less likely. Staff will be happy to take your scooter or power chair to charge overnight and return it in the morning. Specialised operators offering mobile camping safaris have equipment to allow charging of most appliances – including power chairs – in the bush.

Upmarket lodges and tented camps often give the opportunity to spend a night or two truly in the wilds in a 'fly camp', with or without substantial crew and equipment. In these cases, lighting will usually be battery or kerosene powered so you do need to be sure all your appliances are charged before setting out.

Electricity supplies are 220–240V/50Hz throughout. The UK three square-pin plug type is standard in Kenya, Tanzania and Zambia and is the most prevalent type in Botswana. Namibia and South Africa use the three round-pin South African type, which is essentially a derivative of the old UK type.

Important note: Anyone using medical or mobility equipment where guaranteed electrical power is essential should contact the lodges and operators in advance and check thoroughly that their particular requirements will be met.

baggage reclaim to safari vehicle (obviously few people with mobility problems will be able to use one, but their travelling companion might). If your itinerary includes a flight in light aircraft within Africa, then soft, manageable bags are recommended; hard 'Samsonite' style cases are not suitable for this.

Your 'daypack' should contain all the items you use regularly (sunglasses, sunblock, hat, guidebooks, maps, binoculars, camera) and doubles as hand luggage during the flight. Either handheld or with shoulder straps, it must be large enough to hold everything you need (the maximum size of carry-on baggage is dictated by the airline), yet easily carried as it will be with you almost every minute of your safari. A small rucksack (like those often slung from the backrest of a wheelchair) is ideal and it makes life simpler if it has a couple of compartments or outside pockets. If you travel with bulky yet valuable electronic equipment, be sure to consider this when choosing your daypacks. There are models that are designed to store a camera and accessories in a removable compartment and a slim, light notebook computer tucked against the back support.

Useful tips when packing

- If you take regular medication, it might be a good idea to take along a tablet dispenser with compartments for different days of the week. Being away from home can make usual routines easier to forget.

- Pack all medication in the daypack for the flight, especially that which will be difficult to replace in Africa. It is also highly recommended that you carry as much incontinence material as possible (at least enough to last several days on safari) ensuring that even if the main luggage is delayed or goes missing then you will have the absolute essentials with you.

- If you feel you are approaching the baggage weight limit, a useful tip is to pack heavy but less bulky items in your hand luggage, as this is not usually weighed at check-in

- As well as the obvious sharp objects, don't include wheelchair tools in hand luggage, as airport security will almost certainly confiscate them

- Put durable labels on all your luggage items. For the outward journey use the most practical address at your destination and for the return journey use your home address. It's worthwhile including email and mobile phone details as this allows a finder to contact you more quickly.

- Most theft from tourists' luggage is casual, so it might give extra piece of mind to padlock zips while bags are in transit or stored in rooms

- On bumpy roads ensure that items prone to damage (electronic equipment, binoculars and cameras) are well protected, either carried on your knee or wrapped in clothing in your bags. For the same reason, it is wise to store essential mobility equipment securely in vehicles (wheelchairs being the most obvious example). There is a greater risk of them being damaged if they are allowed to rattle around.

MONEY AND BUDGETING

For people who book a fully inclusive safari, the only 'in Africa' costs to consider are those for the everyday expenses like drinks, tips and souvenirs.

More independent travellers may need to budget for food, fuel, accommodation and transport in their travel money. For everybody, decisions must be made about which form to bring their hard currency in, and this depends largely on the region visited.

In all of the countries covered it is always prudent to carry a small amount of hard currency in cash for emergencies. Beyond that, most of Namibia, Botswana and South Africa can be treated like Europe and North America; credit cards are all that is necessary. Hotels and restaurants generally accept these and ATMs are easily found for when cash is required. In Kenya and Tanzania ATMs are becoming more prevalent in most large towns and more establishments now accept credit cards, but travellers' cheques and larger amounts of hard currency are still considered essential.

The next question is in which proportions? I always follow the rule of thirds, where I take two-thirds of the total amount in travellers' cheques and one in cash, with a credit card as emergency backup. Cash is the most instantaneous and trouble-free form to exchange, and has the best exchange rates, but using travellers' cheques is the most secure method because they are more easily refunded if stolen.

When choosing hard currency (for travellers' cheques and cash), US dollars, British pounds and euros are all useful, with dollars being the most widely accepted, while Visa, MasterCard and American Express are the most readily welcomed credit cards. The denominations of cash and cheques should vary from 100s down, and it is good planning to take some five- and single-dollar notes, keeping these in easily accessible pockets for tipping porters and any other opportune helpers. As instructed when buying travellers' cheques, always keep their proof of purchase separate from the cheques themselves.

When on safari, most itineraries will give the possibility to acquire cash at least every few days, so planning how much each time should be fairly predictable. Broadly speaking, lodges and hotels will often be able to change money but their rates will be very poor, while forex bureaux give better rates of exchange than banks and are open longer on weekdays and often on Saturdays. (See *Chapter 3*, *Security*, page 105, for guidance on carrying cash and documents.)

2 Health Issues

Personal health is high on the agenda of most visitors to Africa and is often a serious concern of first-timers. Of course these issues are important, and must be addressed, but it is worthwhile keeping things in perspective. Good preparation beforehand and taking care during your trip should make homesickness your greatest worry.

People with disabilities, through necessity, often know more than most about how their bodies work and how to take care of them; as a result they are usually quick to spot problems and are well prepared to deal with them. The same applies to seniors, who have years of experience looking after their wellbeing and are often better at reading the first signs of ill health. That said, the truth is that many in these groups do need to be extra careful, particularly in a situation where routines and external factors such as temperature, potential infections and disease are not what they're used to.

Planning travel health care, because it is so important, is a daunting task. I've simplified the process by dividing this section into three parts: *Before Leaving Home, On Safari* and *Returning Home*.

BEFORE LEAVING HOME

If you are not sure if you are physically capable of going on safari, it is wise to arrange to have a preliminary chat with your GP or usual physician before booking anything. Another visit, several weeks before you plan to leave is definitely recommended to go through the specific points detailed below.

CHECK-UP
Outline where you are planning to go, how long for and ask for a complete medical check-up. This is particularly important if you have recently had surgery (within a few months) or have a chronic medical condition that may be affected by such a trip.

CONSENT FORM
Depending on your physical condition, your travel agent and/or insurance company may require written consent from your doctor stating that you are fit to travel. There is usually a small charge for this but it can be a good

investment – such a letter has also proved useful for me on internal flights in Africa where officials struggled to believe that a wheelchair user was not necessarily a medical risk to others on the flight.

MEDICATION

- If you take regular medication, ask advice about how best to reorganise this to cope with differing time zones

- If possible, check if all the medication you use is available in the countries you are planning to visit. Your travel agent or local operator may be able to provide contacts for this. If there is any doubt about this, then it is wise to ask your GP to prescribe enough for the duration of your trip, including journey times, plus extra to cover for potential delays and possible losses *en route*. In the UK, NHS rules may mean you are charged for such extra prescriptions even if you don't pay prescription charges.

- Ensure you know the generic name and dose of any medicines you take

- If you will be carrying a lot of medication, or syringes, ask for a covering letter explaining that this is necessary. This may help smooth passage through customs where officers may suspect that you are planning to sell it once in the country.

- As with bulk medicines, a covering letter may be wise if you carry less common prescription medicines, as not all countries have the same legislation regarding which of these may be imported. Customs at the countries covered in this book are encouraged to be friendly to tourists, and will be especially lenient if you have a visible disability, but such a note could help.

EQUIPMENT AND SUPPLIES

As with medication, equipment like syringes, catheters, incontinence pads or urine bags will be more difficult to obtain in Africa, so anyone using these should take enough to cover their trip, with extra to allow for lost or delayed luggage. Even if such things can be found on safari, nobody will want to spend time searching for well-stocked pharmacies when there are game parks to be explored. Taking too much, apart from finding space in your bags, should not be an issue as local hospitals in Africa are always in need of such materials. If donating in this way, it is best to spend time finding the most responsible person in charge, as this reduces the risk that the goods will be sold on before reaching the needy end user.

WRITTEN INSTRUCTIONS FOR EMERGENCY USE

In case you need urgent help and are unable to communicate, a medical card, bracelet or pendant with your potential medical problems and their treatments could be a lifesaver. This should include standard information such as your blood type and allergies. The MedicAlert Foundation (⚕ *www.medicalert.org*) can advise about where to acquire this. There is a school of thought that believes that all people with limited mobility should carry a MedicAlert Bracelet, because it may be just as useful to say, '...This person has no medical illnesses or complications and is on no regular medication'.

METAL IMPLANTS
Airport security scanners, especially if they are at their most sensitive level, will pick up metal implants (including spinal fixators, fracture plates and hip/knee artificial joints). In most cases, a quick explanation will do the trick, but more zealous officers may need extra convincing. Offer to show them your scars. If the visual shock factor isn't enough then allow them to feel the metal under the skin. I have even heard of people taking photographs of their x-rays with them (even simply on their mobile phone) as proof of the presence of subcutaneous metal.

RISK OF DVT
If you are considered to have an even higher than normal risk of a blood clot or DVT then there are precautions to consider before flying: preventative measures include wearing flight socks or even pressure stockings (TEDs) and possibly blood-thinning injections or tablets. Be sure to carry enough for your return trip also. (See box *Clots and DVT*, pages 68–9.)

OXYGEN
There are several specialist safari operators in Africa who can cater for people who require oxygen (see *Chapter 1, Specialised operators in Africa*, page 19–23). It is also worth noting that since the cabin air is only pressurised to the equivalent of 6,000–8,000ft (1,800–2,500m), this may exacerbate any respiratory or heart problems and even those who have no oxygen requirement at sea level may need it when flying. Anybody who may need to use oxygen should inform the airline of this. It can be supplied, but a doctor's note will be required and there may be a charge. With all oxygen suppliers, ask if you should bring your own mask and cannula and whether taking empty tanks with you to fill and use on safari is worthwhile. Some good sources of information are ⚕ www.vitalair.co.uk and ⚕ www.breathineasy.com.

DENTISTS AND OTHER CONSULTANTS
A visit to your dentist (and any other medical consultant you have reason to see on a regular basis) may prove worthwhile, and if you have a lot of fillings and crowns, dental emergency kits are available from dentists and at some pharmacies. Treatment can be costly in Africa and suffering with toothache until you get home is not going to make for a relaxing holiday.

CONTACT DETAILS

Depending on where you live, this era of email and instant digital photography means specialist medical consultancy might not be more than a few mouse clicks away. Any unusual rash, wound or injury can be photographed and instantaneously sent to an expert for an opinion, which is particularly significant for people with reduced sensation who are at risk of pressure wounds. Make sure you ask permission from your doctor or specialist before leaving, and add their email address to your list of contacts.

TRAVEL CLINIC CONSULTATION

A consultation with your local travel clinic several months before departing for Africa is essential. Although the vast majority of medical and health problems among visitors to Africa are minor, it is important to protect yourself as much as possible against the serious disease threats. Tell the consultant where you are going and make sure your vaccinations and boosters are up to date, checking that there are no adverse reactions possible between these and the medicines you take on a regular basis. (See table *Vaccinations – country recommendations/requirements*, on page 58, page 59 for a full list of travel clinics, and pages 72–6 for more information on the diseases themselves.)

Prophylaxis and vaccinations

Malaria

Since most of Africa is very high risk for malaria, travellers must plan their protection properly. Seek current advice from a travel clinic on the best antimalarials to take: usually mefloquine, Malarone or doxycycline. These drugs work by inhibiting the life cycle of the plasmodium parasite that causes the disease. It is essential for them to be in your bloodstream when you arrive in a malaria area, and the course must be continued after you leave – for a week if taking Malarone and for four weeks if taking any of the other prophylactics.

If mefloquine (Lariam) is suggested, start this two-and-a-half weeks (three doses) before departure to check that it suits you; stop it immediately if it seems to cause depression or anxiety, visual or hearing disturbances, severe headaches, fits or changes in heart rhythm. Side effects such as nightmares or dizziness are not medical reasons for stopping unless they are sufficiently debilitating or annoying. Anyone who has been treated for depression or psychiatric problems, has diabetes controlled by oral therapy or who is epileptic (or who has suffered fits in the past) or has a close blood relative who is epileptic, should probably avoid mefloquine. In the past doctors were nervous about prescribing mefloquine to pregnant women, however, experience has shown that it is relatively safe and certainly safer than the risk of malaria. It is now an option at some stages, however there are other issues, and if you are travelling to Africa whilst pregnant, seek expert advice before departure.

Malarone (proguanil and atovaquone) is as effective as mefloquine. It has the advantage of having few side effects and need only be continued for one week after returning. However, it is expensive and because of this tends to be reserved for shorter trips. Malarone may not be suitable for everybody, so advice should be taken from a doctor. The licence in the UK has been extended for up to three months' use and a paediatric form of tablet is also available, prescribed on a weight basis. Another alternative is the antibiotic doxycycline (100mg daily). Like Malarone it can be started one day before arrival. Unlike mefloquine, it may also be used in travellers with epilepsy, although certain anti-epileptic medication may make it less effective. In perhaps 1–3% of people there is the possibility of allergic skin reactions developing in sunlight; the drug should be stopped if this happens. Women using the oral contraceptive should use an additional method of protection for the first four weeks when using doxycycline. It is also unsuitable in pregnancy or for children under 12 years.

Chloroquine and proguanil are no longer considered to be effective enough to protect travellers in Africa, but may be considered as a last resort if nothing else is deemed suitable. All tablets should be taken with or after a meal, and washed down with plenty of fluid.

Despite all these precautions, it is important to be aware that no antimalarial drug is 100% effective, although those on prophylactics who are unlucky enough to catch malaria are less likely to get rapidly into serious trouble.

There is unfortunately the occasional traveller who prefers to 'acquire resistance' to malaria rather than take preventive tablets, or who takes homeopathic prophylactics thinking these are effective against this killer disease. Homeopathy theory dictates treating like with like so there is no place for prophylaxis or immunisation in a well person; bona fide homoeopathists do not advocate it. Travellers to Africa cannot acquire any effective resistance to malaria, and those who don't make use of prophylactic drugs risk their life in a manner that is both foolish and unnecessary.

Yellow fever

Although not common in regions most visited by tourists, this potentially fatal mosquito-borne virus is endemic in Kenya and Tanzania, meaning vaccination may be recommended if travelling there. These days because of rare but potentially fatal risks from the vaccine, a risk assessment is carried out to see if the vaccine is appropriate for each individual. For all countries covered in this book, a certificate of vaccination is usually required if coming from areas where there is a risk of transmission. Ask your travel clinic where you can be vaccinated (UK-based travellers can locate their nearest yellow fever vaccination centre from ⌐ www.nathnac.org). The immunisation lasts ten years. If the vaccine is not recommended but a certificate is required to cross borders then an Exemption Certificate should be obtained from a travel clinic.

MALARIA – COUNTRY-SPECIFIC RISK AREAS

KENYA	Malaria precautions are essential all year throughout low-lying Kenya, including the coastal resorts. Although the risk is less in Nairobi and areas above 2,500m, passengers transiting the capital would also be well advised to consider precautions.
TANZANIA	As in Kenya, malaria is endemic throughout the country irrespective of the time of year, meaning precautions are essential. Infection is less likely above 1,800m, although even here there is no guarantee.
ZAMBIA	Precautions against malaria are essential all year in all areas of Zambia.
NAMIBIA	The areas around the Kavango and Kunene rivers present a year-round threat, while visitors to the northern third of the country (including Etosha National Park) should take precautions between November and June.
BOTSWANA	Precautions are essential in the north of the country, from the Okavango Delta through Chobe to the Zambezi River. These areas present a risk of malaria all year, but this is most serious between November and June.
SOUTH AFRICA	There is normally no risk in cities and resorts such as Cape Town, Johannesburg, Durban and Sun City, or the game parks surrounding them. However, malaria precautions are advised in lowlands of Mpungalanga (including Kruger National Park and neighbouring game reserves), northern Limpopo and the coastal areas of KwaZulu-Natal as far south as the Tugela River. The risk is present year round in these areas, although much less so between May and October. The malaria risk zone may increase after severe flooding.

Hepatitis A

This infection is acquired through contaminated food and water. The vaccine Havrix Monodose or Avaxim comprises two injections given about a year apart and costs about £100. The vaccine is excellent and a course of two injections lasts about 25 years. UK readers should be able to obtain it free on the NHS and it can even be administered close to the time of departure, although it takes ten days to become completely effective.

Tetanus, polio and diphtheria
Protection against these three is advised and can be acquired in one vaccine, Revaxis, which lasts for ten years.

Typhoid
The newer injectable typhoid vaccines (eg: Typhim Vi) last for three years and are about 85% effective. Oral capsules (Vivotif) are currently available in the US (and soon in the UK); if four capsules are taken over seven days it will last for five years. They should be encouraged unless the traveller is leaving within a few days for a trip of a week or less, when the vaccine would not be effective in time. It should be available free on the NHS in the UK, but do not be misled into thinking that the vaccines that are free are the 'best' or most important ones.

Hepatitis B
This serious blood-borne infection can be contracted if people undergo medical treatment with contaminated needles or equipment, if they receive unscreened blood, or through sexual intercourse. It is worth getting immunised if you plan long or repeated trips to regions that aren't well resourced, or if you are likely to be at social or occupational risk or if you're planning sexual adventures. The immunising course comprises three injections over a minimum of 21 days for those aged 16 or over (Engerix only). Other courses comprise three injections over two or six months with the latter regime preferred if time allows.

Tuberculosis
There is constant debate about whether the BCG vaccine should be given to travellers. It is generally the case that American physicians tend not to give it, whereas Europeans do. It is a one-in-a-lifetime injection that protects people from the rapidly fatal forms of tuberculosis. Discuss with your travel clinic.

Rabies
Pre-exposure vaccinations for rabies are ideally advised for everyone, but are particularly important for travellers going to risk areas that will be remote from a reliable source of vaccine. It is a wise precaution for those on safari holidays – in 2007, a woman was scratched on the face by a bat while she was camping in Kenya and died of rabies. Immunisation entails three injections over a minimum of 21 days. A reinforcing booster is given after three years.

Meningitis
The only vaccine for travel to Africa is the tetravalent Meningitis ACWY. This is a single injection that lasts for five years.

Cholera
There is no longer any international requirement for immunisation against cholera and ordinary travellers and tourists are at minute risk of catching

the disease. Dukoral fizzy drink vaccine is now available and gives slight additional protection to some forms of travellers' diarrhoea. Allow at least three weeks if you are planning to take this vaccine.

Influenza and pneumococcal vaccine for elderly people

Those travellers with health challenges that mean at home they are immunised each year against influenza should certainly be covered for travel. Pneumococcus is a once-in-a-lifetime vaccine, which is of considerable advantage to all travellers but is a must for those who have lost their spleen (but travellers must seek special advice about malaria risk) and also people with on-going health problems. Droplet-spread diseases such as flu and respiratory infections are commonly acquired on long-haul flights.

VACCINATIONS – COUNTRY RECOMMENDATIONS/ REQUIREMENTS

	Hep. A	Typhoid	Polio	Tetanus	Diphth.	Hep. B	Rabies	TB	Menin.	Yellow fever
KENYA										RP
TANZANIA										RP
ZAMBIA										
NAMIBIA										R
BOTSWANA										R
SOUTH AFRICA										R

Immunisation sometimes advised (depending on doctor/clinic)

Immunisation usually advised

R   Immunisation required for travellers over nine months of age coming *from* areas where yellow fever is endemic.

RP   Yellow fever is present so immunisation is recommended for travellers over nine months of age. Immunisation is also required for those coming from (or having passed through) areas with risk of yellow fever transmission.

Travel clinics in your area

A full list of current travel clinic websites worldwide is available on ⊕ www.istm.org/. For other journey preparation information, consult ⊕ www.nathnac.org/ds/map_world.aspx. Information about various medications may be found on ⊕ www.netdoctor.co.uk/travel.

UK

Adventure and Tourism Travel Health Clinic 2 Lindsay St, Edinburgh EH6 4EG; ☎ 0131 561 1945; ⊕ www.adventuretravelclinic.com

Edinburgh Travel Health Clinic 14 East Preston St, Newington, Edinburgh EH8 9QA; ☎/f 0131 667 1030; ⊕ www.edinburghhealthclinic.co.uk; ☺ Mon–Wed 09.00–19.00 Thu & Fri 9.00–18.00

Fleet Street Travel Clinic 29 Fleet St, London EC4Y 1AA; ☎ 020 7353 5678; e info@fleetstreetclinic.com; ⊕ www.fleetstreetclinic.com

Footprints Travel Clinic 32–34 Woodlands Rd, Glasgow G3 6UR; ☎ 0141 353 6738; e clinic@footprintsglasgow.com; ⊕ www.footprintsglasgow.com or ⊕ www.footprintstravelclinic.co.uk

Hospital for Tropical Diseases Travel Clinic Mortimer Market Bldg, Capper St (off Tottenham Ct Rd), London WC1E 6AU; ☎ 020 7388 9600; ⊕ www.thehtd.org. Runs a healthline (☎ *020 7950 7799*) for country-specific information & health hazards.

InterHealth Travel Clinic 157 Waterloo Rd, London SE1 8US; ☎ 020 7902 9000; e askus@interhealth.org.uk; ⊕ www.interhealth.org.uk; ☺ Mon–Fri 09.00–17.00

MASTA (Medical Advisory Service for Travellers Abroad) MASTA Ltd, Moorfield Rd, Yeadon, Leeds, W Yorks LS19 7BN; ☎ 0870 606 2782; ⊕ www.masta-travel-health.com. Provides travel health advice, antimalarials & vaccinations. There are over 25 MASTA pre-travel clinics in Britain; call or check online for the nearest.

NHS travel website ⊕ www.fitfortravel.nhs.uk. Provides country-by-country advice on immunisation & malaria, plus details of recent developments, & a list of relevant health organisations.

Nomad Travel Store/Clinic 3–4 Wellington Terrace, Turnpike Lane, London N8 0PX; ☎ 020 8889 7014; e turnpike@nomadtravel.co.uk; ⊕ www.nomadtravel.co.uk. Also at 40 Bernard St, London WC1N 1LJ; ☎ 020 7833 4114; e russellsquare@nomadtravel.co.uk; 52 Grosvenor Gdns, London SW1W 0AG; ☎ 020 7823 5823; e Victoria@nomadtravel.co.uk; 38 Park St, Bristol BS1 5JG; ☎ 0117 922 6567; e Bristol@nomadtravel.co.uk; 66–68 Bridge St, Manchester M3 2RJ; ☎ 0161 832 2134; e Manchester@nomadtravel.co.uk; 6 Civic Centre Rd, Southampton SO14 7FL; ☎ 02380 234920; e Southampton@nomadtravel.co.uk

The Travel Clinic at Berkeley Street 32 Berkeley St, London W1J 8EL (near Green Park tube station); ☎ 020 7629 6233; ☺ Mon–Fri 10.00–18.00, Sat 10.00–15.00

The Travel Clinic, Cambridge 41 Hills Rd, Cambridge CB2 1NT; ☎ 01223 367362; e enquiries@travelcliniccambridge.co.uk; ⊕ www.travelcliniccambridge.co.uk; ☺ Mon 10.00–16.00, closed Tue, Wed & Thu 12.00–19.00; Fri 11.00–18.00; Sat 10.00–16.00

Trailfinders Immunisation Centre 194 Kensington High St, London W8 7RG;

📞 020 7938 3999; 🖰 www.trailfinders.com/travelessentials/travelclinic.htm; ⊘ Mon, Tue, Wed & Fri 09.00–17.00, Thu 09.00–18.00, Sat 10.00–17.15
Travelpharm 🖰 www.travelpharm.com. The Travelpharm website offers up-to-date guidance on travel-related health & has a range of medications available through their online mini-pharmacy.

Irish Republic
Tropical Medical Bureau Grafton St Medical Centre, Grafton Bldgs, 34 Grafton St, Dublin 2; 📞 1 671 9200; 🖰 www.tmb.ie. A useful website specific to tropical destinations. Also check website for other bureaux locations throughout Ireland.

US
ASTMH (The American Society of Tropical Medicine and Hygiene) 111 Deer Lake Rd, Suite 100, Deerfield, IL 60015; 📞 847 480 9592; 🖰 www.astmh.org, 🖰 www.astmh.org/publications/clinics.cfm or 🖰 www.istm.org (International Society of Tropical Medicine)
Centers for Disease Control 1600 Clifton Rd, Atlanta, GA 30333; 📞 404 498 1515 or 📞 800 311 3435; e cdcinfo@cdc.gov; 🖰 www.cdc.gov/travel
IAMAT (International Association for Medical Assistance to Travelers) 1623 Military Rd, 279 Niagara Falls, NY 14304-1745; 📞 716 754 4883; e info@iamat.org; 🖰 www.iamat.org. A non-profit organisation that provides lists of English-speaking doctors abroad.
International Medicine Center 920 Frostwood Drive, Suite 670, Houston, TX 77024; 📞 713 550 2000; 🖰 www.traveldoc.com
Passport Health 📞 0888 499 7277; e customercare@passperthealthusa.com; 🖰 www.passporthealthusa.com/locations
TravelDoctor.com 617–619 South State St, Ukiah, CA 95482; 📞 707 462 9420; e contact@wwmedical.com; 🖰 www.wwmedical.com

Canada
IAMAT Suite 1, 1287 St Clair Av W, Toronto, Ontario M6E 1B8; 📞 416 652 0137; e info@iamat.org; 🖰 www.iamat.org
Public Health Agency of Canada 🖰 www.publichealth.gc.ca. Follow the links to travel health then travel health clinics.
TMVC Suite 314, 1030 W Georgia St, Vancouver, BC V6E 2Y3; 📞 1 888 288 8682; e info@tmvc.com; 🖰 www.tmvc.com

Australia, New Zealand and Singapore
IAMAT PO Box 5049, Christchurch 5, New Zealand; 🖰 www.iamat.org
TMVC 📞 1300 65 88 44; 🖰 www.traveldoctor.com.au. 31 clinics in Australia, New Zealand & Singapore, including:
Adelaide TVMC Hse, 27–29 Gilbert Pl, Adelaide, SA 5000; 📞 08 8212 7522; e Adelaide@traveldoctor.com.au
Brisbane 75a Astor Terrace, Spring Hill, QLD 4000; 📞 07 3815 6900; e Brisbane@traveldoctor.com.au
Melbourne Level 2, 393 Little Bourke St, Melbourne, VIC 3000; 📞 03 9602 5788;

e Melbourne@traveldoctor.com.au

Sydney Level 7, Dymocks Bldg, 428 George St, Sydney, NSW 2000; **☎** 02 9221 7133;
e Sydney@traveldoctor.com.au

Auckland Level 1, Canterbury Arcade, 170 Queen St, Auckland; **☎** 09 373 3531;
e Auckland@traveldoctor.co.nz; ⁀ www.traveldoctor.co.nz

Switzerland

IAMAT 57 Chemin des Voirets, 1212 Grand Lancy, Geneva; **e** info@iamat.org;
⁀ www.iamat.org

STI (Swiss Tropical Institute) Socinstrasse 57, PO Box CH-4002, Basle; **☎** 061 284 8111;
⁀ www.sti.ch

Germany

Institute of Tropical Medicine Spandauer damm 130, Haus 10, 14050 Berlin;
☎ 030 301166; **e** tropeninstitute@charite.de; ⁀ www.charite.de

Reisemedizineisches Zentrum am Bernhard-Nocht-Institut (Bernhard Nocht
Institute, Centre for Travel Medicine) Bernhard-Nocht-Strasse 74, 20359 Hamburg; **☎**
040 428180 (24h); **e** bni@bni-hamburg.de; ⁀ www.bni-hamburg.de

Belgium

Brussels Medical Centre of the Ministry of Foreign Affairs Rue de Namur 59,
1000 Brussels; **☎** 02 501 3511

Brussels Travel Clinic Hopital St Pierre, Rue Haute 290, 1000 Brussels; **☎** 02 535
3343

Universitair Ziekenhuis Gasthuisberg (Gasthuisberg University Hospital)
Herestraat 49, 3000 Leuven; **☎** 016 344 775

Netherlands

Tropical and Travel Medicine Clinic Academic Travel Center, University of
Amsterdam; Meibergdreef 9, PO Box 22700, 1100 DE Amsterdam; **☎** 020 566
4380/9111; **e** p.p.vanthiel@amc.uva.nl or trop.amc@amc.uva.nl;
⁀ www.tropencentrum.nl

Sweden

Kungsportslakarna Medical Centre Kungsportsavenyn 10, 400100 Gothenburg;
☎ 031 339 9970; **e** dn@kungsportslakarna.se; ⁀ www.kungsportslakarna.se

Norway

Volvat Medisisnke Senter (Volvat Medical Centre) Fanaveien 98, 5236 Radal,
Bergen; **e** vkoefoed@broadpark.no

MEDICAL KIT

The amount of medication people take on safari varies enormously. As a rule
of thumb, take the basics and add whatever you regularly use at home, but
remember that space in your bags is not boundless. If you are on an
organised tour there will be medical kits in hotels, lodges and vehicles, and

the majority of reasonably sized towns will have pharmacies stocking the everyday items at least.

Basic essentials

Medicines

- Antibiotic eye drops, for sore, 'gritty', stuck-together eyes (conjunctivitis)
- Antihistamine tablets
- Broad spectrum antibiotic for severe diarrhoea and one for urinary tract infections if applicable (ask your doctor or travel clinic for advice)
- Oral rehydration sachets and possibly Imodium (although Imodium should be used only when visiting a toilet is extremely difficult)
- Malaria prophylaxis
- Mild painkiller (ibuprofen or paracetamol) and a stronger version (with codeine)
- Tinidazole for giardia or amoebic dysentery (again, ask medical advice)

Skin care

- Antiseptic – cream is commonly used (simple burn cream is remarkably healing) but a dry version or spray is better if visiting humid, tropical areas
- Dressings – it may be preferable to take a selection of various sizes of absorbent, breathable compresses and at least two rolls of Micropore tape rather than sticking plasters (Band-Aids), as this gives more flexibility to deal with different sizes of wounds. Opsite (or similar) dressings or spray give a quick-to-apply, water-resistant defence against wound infection.
- If you are prone to frequent cuts and grazes then larger self-adhesive wound dressings provide padding as well as barrier protection
- Insect repellent
- Moisturising cream – skin can dry out in arid climates, and areas where chafing occurs can easily become open sores. Sudocrem is recommended for this.
- Calamine or other soothing lotion

Equipment

- Condoms or femidoms
- Equipment for injections – swabs, needles and syringes
- Eyebath and dropper

- Thermometer
- Small scissors
- Tweezers

ON SAFARI

FOOD AND DRINKING WATER

Food

If preparing food yourself, always wash fruit and vegetables with treated or bottled water. Meals on a fully inclusive safari are generally of a high standard and illness is rarely the result of poor hygiene. Where more care is needed is when eating in cheaper restaurants or from street vendors. If eating hot food, it should be freshly cooked and not just kept warm (deep-fried mandazis and similar doughnut-type foods found in east Africa are scrumptious and safe if eaten immediately, but potentially tummy upsetting if they've been sitting for some time). It is not the case that African kitchens are less clean, but that bacteria found on these foods readily grow in numbers because of the climate and they are also new to tourists' bodies and take time (and sometimes a bout of illness) to get used to. (See the following box *Avoiding and treating travellers' diarrhoea*.)

Drinking water

Dehydration is one of the most common problems among visitors to Africa. This is usually due to a lack of appreciation that the climate demands a greater throughput of liquid, although bizarrely cases have arisen because people have not drunk enough water fearing it was unclean and would make them ill. Always make sure you have water available and drink small amounts frequently. The simple rule for a healthy, well-irrigated safari is that your urine should always be copious and clear; however, don't overdo it, there's no need to be visiting the toilet every hour!

Although bottled water is widely available and most visitors on recognised safari circuits won't need to consider anything else, do remember the environmental impact of plastic litter. If buying bottles, care should always be taken to obtain recognised brands and check before purchase that the plastic seal on the top has not been broken.

If you are going off the beaten track, you may need to drink tap water and this should always be treated. Boiling is best but not always practical, so there are bacteriological filters and a large range of purification tablets available – the most effective are iodine-based – and these are reliable if the manufacturers' instructions are carefully followed. Always check with local people where is best to fill water and ensure you always take your water from the cold tap. If the water is very cloudy or has particles in suspension, then filter it through some fine-woven material before treating.

Avoid ice cubes if having cool drinks in cheaper establishments; they can be a vehicle for bugs if handled by another person on the way into your drink.

COMMON HEALTH PROBLEMS

Travellers' diarrhoea
See box *Avoiding and treating travellers' diarrhoea*, below.

Sunburn
Sunburn is at best uncomfortable, but can be painful and render you inactive for several days. More seriously, prolonged exposure causes premature skin wrinkling and increases the risk of melanoma: the incidence of skin cancer is increasing as Caucasians are travelling more. The equatorial sun can burn remarkably quickly and the following are useful tips:

- Build up exposure times gradually and keep out of the sun during the middle of the day
- Take extra care swimming or snorkelling – water reflects the sun's rays and its cooling effect can mask the fact that the skin is burning
- Wear long, loose clothing (shirts with collars), a hat and sunglasses
- Use sunscreen of 15–25SPF (sun protection factor)

Eye problems
Bacterial conjunctivitis (pink eye) is a common infection in Africa; people

AVOIDING AND TREATING TRAVELLERS' DIARRHOEA
Dr Jane Wilson-Howarth

By taking precautions against travellers' diarrhoea you will also avoid typhoid, paratyphoid, cholera, hepatitis, dysentery, worms, etc. Travellers' diarrhoea and the other faecal-oral diseases come from getting other people's faeces in your mouth. Apart from taking care with what you eat, the most important prevention strategy is to wash your hands more often, and always before eating. You can pick up salmonella and shigella from toilet door handles and possibly bank notes.

It is dehydration that makes you feel awful during a bout of diarrhoea and the most important part of treatment is drinking lots of clear fluids. Sachets of oral rehydration salts give the perfect biochemical mix to replace all that is pouring out of your bottom, but other recipes taste nicer. Any dilute mixture of sugar and salt in water will do you good: try Coke or orange squash with a three-finger pinch of salt added to each glass (if you are salt-depleted you won't taste the salt). Otherwise make a solution of a

who wear contact lenses are most open to this irritating problem. The eyes feel sore and gritty and they will often be stuck together in the mornings. They will need treatment with antibiotic drops or ointment. Lesser eye irritation should settle with bathing in salt water and keeping the eyes shaded. If an insect flies into your eye, extract it with great care, ensuring you do not crush or damage it otherwise you may get a nastily inflamed eye from toxins secreted by the creature. Small, elongated red-and-black blister beetles carry warning colouration to tell you not to crush them anywhere against your skin.

Prickly heat
A fine pimply rash on the trunk is likely to be heat rash; cool showers, dabbing dry, and talc will help. Treat the problem by slowing down to a relaxed schedule, wearing only loose, baggy, 100%-cotton clothes and sleeping naked under a fan; if it's severe you may need to check into an air-conditioned hotel room for a while.

Skin infections
Any mosquito bite or small nick in the skin gives an opportunity for bacteria to foil the body's usually excellent defences; it will surprise many travellers how quickly skin infections start in warm humid climates. It is essential to clean and cover even the slightest wound. Creams are not as effective as a good drying antiseptic such as dilute iodine, potassium permanganate (a few crystals in half a cup of water), or crystal (or gentian) violet. One of these should be available in most towns. If the wound starts

four-finger scoop of sugar with a three-finger pinch of salt in a 500ml glass. Or add eight level teaspoons of sugar (18g) and one level teaspoon of salt (3g) to one litre (five cups) of safe water. A squeeze of lemon or orange juice improves the taste and adds potassium, which is also lost in diarrhoea. Drink two large glasses after every bowel action, and more if you are thirsty. These solutions are still absorbed well if you are vomiting, but you will need to take sips at a time. If you are not eating you need to drink three litres a day plus, the equivalent of whatever is pouring into the toilet. If you feel like eating, take a bland, high carbohydrate diet. Heavy, greasy foods will probably give you cramps.

If the diarrhoea is bad, or you are passing blood or slime, or you have a fever, you will probably need antibiotics in addition to fluid replacement. A dose of norfloxacin repeated twice a day for three days (if you are planning to take an antibiotic with you, note that both norfloxacin and ciprofloxacin are available only on prescription in the UK). If the diarrhoea is greasy and bulky and is accompanied by sulphurous (eggy) burps, one likely cause is giardia. This is best treated with tinidazole (four x 500mg in one dose, repeated seven days later if symptoms persist).

to throb, or becomes red and the redness starts to spread, or the wound oozes, and especially if you develop a fever, antibiotics will probably be needed: flucloxacillin (250mg four times a day) or cloxacillin (500mg four times a day). For those allergic to penicillin, erythromycin (500mg twice a day) for five days should help. See a doctor if the symptoms do not start to improve within 48 hours.

Fungal infections also get a hold easily in hot, moist climates so wear 100%-cotton socks and underwear and shower frequently. An itchy rash in the groin or flaking between the toes is likely to be a fungal infection. This needs treatment with an antifungal cream such as Canesten (clotrimazole); if this is not available try Whitfield's ointment (compound benzoic acid ointment) or crystal violet (although this will turn you purple!).

Sexually transmitted diseases
Sexual encounters are much more likely on holiday; strangers meet, are more relaxed than at home, and (pertaining more to safaris) everybody looks better in the half-light of an evening campfire. Whether you sleep with fellow travellers or locals in Africa, the risks of sexually transmitted infection are extremely high – about 80% of HIV infections in British heterosexuals are acquired abroad. If you must indulge, use condoms or femidoms, which help reduce the risk of transmission and if you notice any genital ulcers or discharge, get treatment promptly since these increase the risk of acquiring HIV.

SPECIFIC CONSIDERATIONS FOR LESS-MOBILE TRAVELLERS
The following is a list of important points and tips, but nobody is better placed to predict problems than the traveller themselves. A good first step is to note the major issues you have learned to cope with at home and imagine if and how these will affect you on a safari.

Importance of communication
Your travel agent and safari guide may have been very accommodating in listening to your needs during booking, and may even be experienced and specialised in disability, but it is a huge subject with a wide range of prerequisites and the best expert on yours is yourself. Inform your guide and driver, and anybody else involved in your safari, of exactly what your needs are; they will be happy to oblige and your trip will be the better for it.

If, through your medical condition, there are potential emergency situations where you would have difficulty communicating (for example, autonomic dysreflexia), then ensure people around you know either what to do or where to find information about appropriate action. Consider wearing a MedicAlert Bracelet or necklace.

Clots and DVT
People with limited mobility are more susceptible to deep-vein thromboses. (See box *Clots and DVT*, pages 68–9.)

Taking blood thinners

Anyone taking warfarin risks potentially disastrous bleeding if a change in food or drinking habits puts clotting control awry, or if they are injured, for example in a road accident. Alert the travel clinic that you are taking blood thinners so that they can avoid potential reactions with vaccinations and antimalarials. People on warfarin should have their immunisations subcutaneously rather than intramuscularly if possible. They also need to try out their malaria tablets to see whether they affect the INR (clotting level). This should be done well in advance of the trip.

Personal hygiene

Despite the rapid increase of suitably accessible bathrooms on the safari circuit, a degree of compromise in washing and toileting may be necessary. If so, it is essential that the important areas – genitalia, stoma sites (suprapubic catheters, urostomies, etc) – are not neglected. With wheelchair users, these regions will always have less ventilation, and everybody is more vulnerable to infection in humid climates.

Temperature sensitivity

Some disabilities can lead to the body being unable to regulate its own temperature, resulting in a narrowing of the tolerance levels of hot and cold extremes. In a temperate climate, this is rarely a concern – usually meaning that more layers need to be added to stay warm. In Africa, however, it is more likely that high temperatures will be difficult to cope with. Despite the fact that the most active times on safari are early morning and late afternoon, and this is when temperatures are normally pleasantly cool, there may be occasions when travel requirements mean you have to be on the go in the heat of the day.

If your body is prone to overheating, then the old adage of avoidance being better than cure is very apt. Some tips are:

- Dress in light clothing – thin cotton is ideal; avoid polycotton or mixed fabrics
- Wear a light hat with a wide brim. This can be frequently soaked in water allowing your head to stay cool.
- Wristbands soaked in water also help cool the blood
- Use a plant spray-bottle to regularly drench your face, neck and arms in water
- Try using ice packs designed for pain relief. Obviously these will have to be cooled first so you need access to a freezer, but when worn on wrists and ankles they can subtly keep you comfortable.
- If you are in a vehicle with air conditioning, use it. Yes, it means you may need to close the windows and temporarily 'shut Africa out', but this is much better than the consequences of overheating.
- Don't forget to take regular drinks of water

If it all gets too much then the only solution is to pour cool water over your head and neck. This provides instant – albeit temporary – relief but does mean that carrying extra water at all times is a must.

Skin care
An African safari is not an especially physical activity with a heightened risk of bodily injury. In fact, for most trips, quite the opposite is true – it is a sedentary holiday with the bulk of the time being spent seated in vehicles, restaurants, game-viewing areas and other relaxing situations.

However, even though there is rarely anything arduous involved, people with less sensation will need to be more careful than most. You will know

CLOTS AND DVT *Dr Jane Wilson-Howarth*

A deep-vein thrombosis (DVT) is a blood clot that forms in the deep leg veins, causing swelling and redness of one leg and heat and pain, usually in the calf and sometimes the thigh. Although recent research has suggested that many of us develop clots when immobilised, most resolve without us ever having been aware of them. Occasionally, though, large clots form and these can break away and lodge in the lungs. This is dangerous but happens in a tiny minority of cases.

DVTs are most likely to occur during or following lengthy (more than five hours) periods of inactivity, making long-haul flights ideal conditions and putting people with mobility problems at more peril than most. The lower level of oxygen in aircraft, the mild dehydration that occurs and cramped seating only increase the likelihood of this happening.

Potential travellers in the following categories need to discuss travel plans with their doctor:

- Those who have had a clot before – unless they are now taking warfarin
- People over 80 years of age
- Anyone who has recently undergone a major operation (in the last few weeks) or surgery for varicose veins
- Someone who has had a hip or knee replacement in the last three months
- Cancer sufferers
- Those who have ever had a stroke
- People with heart disease
- Those with a close blood relative who has had a clot

Those with a slightly increased risk are:

- People over 40 years of age

the areas of your body that are normally prone to damage, but any changes in normal routines, sitting positions and transfers mean that other parts become subject to pressures they are not used to. With no pain warning available, pressure wounds can quickly form and these need to be recognised immediately. Examine your skin daily (you can also check for ticks if you've been brushing through scrub), and no matter how thoroughly you do this at home, go back to basics and make a point of checking everything.

Any red mark or change in appearance must be taken seriously and the appropriate course of action followed. This may mean an afternoon spent in bed, therefore missing a game drive, or its healing may require a longer

- Women who are pregnant or have had a baby in the last couple of weeks
- People taking female hormones or other oestrogen therapy
- Heavy smokers
- Those who have very severe varicose veins
- The very obese
- People who are very tall (over 6ft/1.8m) or short (under 5ft/1.5m)

Anyone who thinks that they might have a DVT needs to see a doctor immediately who will arrange a scan. Warfarin tablets (to thin the blood) are then taken for at least six months.

Prevention of DVT
To reduce the risk of thrombosis on a long journey:
- Exercise before and after the flight
- Keep mobile before and during the flight; move around every couple of hours
- During the flight drink plenty of water or juices
- Avoid taking sleeping pills and excessive tea, coffee and alcohol
- Perform exercises that mimic walking and tense the calf muscles if possible
- Consider wearing flight socks or support stockings (see ⌂ www.legshealth.com)
- Taking a meal of oily fish (mackerel, trout, salmon, sardines, etc) in the 24 hours before departure reduces blood clotability and thus DVT risk

The jury is still out on whether it is worthwhile to take an aspirin before flying, but this can be discussed with your GP.

period of inactivity. Either way, it is vital that pressure is immediately removed from the affected area. Try to work out what caused it and have this resolved before continuing, for example, extra padding in the vehicle. If you have to wait a while in one place, you will usually be surprised at how amenable and flexible your guide and the hotelier will be about this; Africans are used to – and often relish – dealing with the unexpected. Do make sure you see a doctor and obtain a signed report, and inform your insurance company immediately. It may be possible to reclaim extra accommodation, transport or medical costs that have arisen.

Similarly, because of lack of sensation of pain, there is an increased risk of open abrasions. Depending on how long the safari is, it is possible to be travelling through two or three different climactic zones; the aridity of the northern parks of Kenya or Namibia can cause dry, cracked skin, particularly around the knees and elbows, while lush tropical areas like the Indian Ocean coast make wound drying a slower process. Any open injury should be treated with greater care than at home as they can quickly become infected in tropical areas. (See *Skin infections*, page 65.)

Again, prevention is better than cure and adhering to the following rules is a good first step:

- Always use your prescribed pressure-relieving cushion. It is usually possible to replace aeroplane seat cushions with your own (see *Chapter 3, Getting there (air travel)*, page 82) and safari operators, if you explain the reasons why, will be happy to try to adapt vehicle seating.

- Safari vehicles are often more basic and less plush than standard cars, and roads will be rougher than you are used to. It is wise (and more comfortable) to pad elbows, knees and ankles, or the parts of the vehicle that will come into contact with them (seatbelts also chafe and are easily softened with foam or smaller cushions). If you tell your travel agent about this in advance, then the safari operator will normally be only too happy to provide extra padding. If you prefer to take your own, then custom-made protection can be bought in most medical stores and homemade equipment can be fashioned from items like scarves, inflatable neck pillows and swimming aids.

- When transferring, be even more careful than you would at home. Make sure your own comfort and safety are the priorities, as opposed to the schedule of the safari.

- Look out for protruding bits of vehicles – locks, door handles, etc – that can catch the skin

- Check beds for softness, and depending on your susceptibility to pressure wounds, either increase the frequency of nightly turns or travel with an inflatable anti-decubitus mattress

- If you need it, take your own inflatable waterproof cushion for showering. There may be facilities to transfer into baths and showers but they won't always be satisfactorily padded.

- Do not take risks. Go without a shower for a day if you are not completely sure there is enough skin protection.

Spasticity

Although involuntary muscle spasm can be adversely affected by temperature extremes, my personal experience and reports from others only suggest that such symptoms are reduced on safari. I suspect that this is either through being physically more active than at home or having no time to dwell on such thoughts. If you notice more muscle spasm than normal, do not just assume it's because you're not at home – check all possible causes.

Incontinence

Those with mobility problems, and especially those with bladder or bowel incontinence, need to know exactly how accessible bathrooms are. Apart from the lists of accommodation covered in this book, there are very few reliable and objective sources of such information in Africa.

Proprietors will be able to describe their facilities but rarely know what is really necessary, so their opinions – no matter how well meant – are always to be taken with some reserve. It is not wise to ask if a property is 'accessible', as the answer will invariably be yes. Better to ask them to describe their most accessible bathroom, with emphasis on features such as shower threshold height, presence of support rails or whatever is important for you. Similarly, local operators, unless experienced in this market, may be prone to inaccuracies.

Depending on your ability to stand, sit or squat, there are various aids (that can be either taken from home or acquired in Africa), which allow comfortable and private ablutions. (See *Chapter 1, What to take*, page 43–4.)

One tip worth noting is that if you use suppositories, remember that these are designed to melt at 37°C (body temperature). As the ambient temperature approaches this, your suppositories will soften and become impossible to insert. If you use them in the afternoons or evenings, wrap them in some kind of insulating material in the morning, when they're still hard, and keep them as cool as possible through the day.

Fatigue

Anyone, able-bodied or not, could find a safari tiring at times. Itineraries are often packed, with opportunities for game driving twice daily, plus other activities and full days of travel between highlights. People with mobility problems and especially those with more severe disabilities may need more time to get ready in the mornings, use the bathroom and transfer in and out of vehicles. To enjoy a safari to the full it is vital that these limitations are considered and a suitable, less hectic, schedule created. It is imperative that this is done at the planning stage during discussions with your travel agent.

MAJOR HAZARDS

Before diving into the murky waters of tropical diseases and what they can do to you, it is worth remembering that compared to the risk of accident, the likelihood of your safari being ruined by contracting one of these is very small. Of course, there is a real danger (malaria was only recently overtaken by AIDS as Africa's number-one killer), but if the proper precautions are taken, then the following descriptions should not be more than interesting reading.

Malaria

The symptoms of malaria can mimic many illnesses and it can kill within 24 hours of the first shiver. These are frightening facts, and must not be understated, but with prophylactic protection and precautions on safari, the risk is considerably reduced. The parasite causing the disease is carried by the *Anopheles* mosquito, which thrives throughout tropical Africa, especially lower-lying regions near fresh water (where it breeds). This genus of mosquito feeds between dusk and dawn, and being bitten by a single infected insect can be enough to contract malaria.

Prevention

There is no vaccine against malaria that gives enough protection to be useful for travellers, and although there are malaria pills, which are considered essential (see *Prophylaxis and vaccinations*, page 54), it is wise to avoid being bitten in the first place (see *Avoiding insect bites*, pages 74–5).

Recognition

Even those who take their malaria tablets meticulously and do everything possible to avoid mosquito bites could contract a strain of malaria that is resistant to prophylactic drugs. Untreated malaria can be fatal, but even strains resistant to prophylaxis respond well to prompt treatment. Because of this, your immediate priority upon displaying possible malaria symptoms – including a rapid rise in temperature (over 38˚C), and any combination of a headache, flu-like aches and pains, a general sense of disorientation, and possibly even nausea and diarrhoea – is to establish whether you have malaria, ideally by visiting a clinic.

No-one can diagnose malaria except through a blood test so it is sensible to consult a doctor if you get a temperature: there are other dangerous causes of fever in Africa, which require different treatments. Even if you test negative, it would be wise to stay within reach of a laboratory until the symptoms clear up, and to test again after a day or two if they don't. It's worth noting that if you have a fever and the malaria test is negative, you may have typhoid or paratyphoid, which should also receive immediate treatment.

Cure

Some travellers (especially those travelling independently to remote areas) like to carry tablets for the emergency treatment of malaria; if you choose to do this make sure you understand when and how to take them and carry a digital thermometer.

Most people on safari will either have an experienced guide with them or will not be far from qualified medical help. The priority, if malaria is suspected, is to seek medical advice, have a test done and allow the clinician to prescribe a course of medicine. Any course of treatment must be completed, even if symptoms disappear, and do not go too far from further medical help – if oral medicine won't stay down, intravenous treatment may be necessary.

Other insect-borne diseases

Malaria is not the only insect-borne disease to which the traveller may succumb. Others include sleeping sickness and river blindness. Dengue fever and similar arboviruses are rare in places safari-goers frequent, but these may mimic malaria and there is no prophylactic medication against them. The mosquitoes that carry dengue bite during the daytime, so it is worth applying repellent if you see any around. Symptoms include strong headaches, rashes, excruciating joint and muscle pains, and high fever. Viral fevers commonly last about a week or so and are not usually fatal. Complete rest and paracetamol is the treatment, with plenty of fluids; some patients are given an intravenous drip to keep them from dehydrating. It is especially important to protect yourself if you have had dengue fever before, since a second infection with a different strain can result in the potentially fatal dengue haemorrhagic fever. (See box *Avoiding insect bites*, pages 74–5.)

Hepatitis

The many potential causes of turning yellow (you notice the white of the eyes first) need to be properly diagnosed in a clinic or hospital.

Meningitis

Coughing, sneezing or kissing can transmit this disease, which affects the central nervous system, and bacterial strains (the most dangerous) occur most commonly in the dry season 'winter months' from November/December through to May/June. This rapidly life-threatening bacterial infection causes severe headaches (looking at light is unbearable) and fever. It needs urgent, immediate treatment; minutes can matter.

Rabies

Rabies is spread through bites, scratches or licks on broken skin from an infected animal and is always fatal once the symptoms start. Although the likelihood of this happening is minuscule, the resultant worry of being bitten when not immunised would be enough to ruin a holiday. Immunisation is wise, and good wound care after a bite or scratch from any animal is essential. This includes scrubbing the wound with soap and running water and applying an antiseptic. Even if pre-exposure vaccines have been received, urgent medical advice should be sought after any

AVOIDING INSECT BITES *Dr Jane Wilson-Howarth*

Ideally, shower at the end of the day and as the sun is going down, don long clothes and apply repellent on any exposed flesh. Pack a DEET-based insect repellent (roll-ons or sticks are the least messy preparations for travelling). You also need a permethrin spray so that you can 'treat' bed nets in hotels. Permethrin treatment makes even very tatty nets protective and prevents mosquitoes from biting through the impregnated net when you roll against it; it also deters other biters. Duct tape or sticking plasters are a useful temporary repair for large gashes but if the net is a fixture in the room then the proprietor has a responsibility to make sure it is bug-proof. Upmarket lodges and hotels will usually have robust nets, but it may be worthwhile to purchase and treat your own, especially if you are travelling independently or going on a cheaper safari. Permethrin treatment remains effective for six months.

Otherwise retire to an air-conditioned room, burn mosquito coils (which are widely available and cheap in Africa) or sleep under a fan. Coils and fans reduce rather than eliminate bites. Travel clinics usually sell a good range of nets, treatment kits and repellents.

Aside from avoiding mosquito bites between dusk and dawn, which will protect you from elephantiasis and a range of nasty insect-borne viruses, as well as malaria (see page 72), it is important to take precautions against other insect bites. During the day it is wise to wear long, loose (preferably 100%-cotton) clothes if you are moving through scrubby country; this will keep off ticks and also tsetse and day-biting *Aedes* mosquitoes which may spread viral fevers, including yellow fever and dengue.

Tsetse flies hurt when they bite and it is said that they are attracted

potential exposure. All mammals can carry rabies but be especially wary of stray dogs in villages, bats and the small monkeys you find around lodges and camps. Never attempt to feed them, and if repeatedly pestered by a persistent monkey (they can, despite their size, be frighteningly aggressive), the only responsible course of action is to report it to the lodge staff.

Snakebites

Getting bitten by a snake while on safari, apart from being unfortunate, is exceedingly unusual. Even seeing a snake is an occurrence worth noting, and in my experience is more likely to happen when you are in a vehicle than when on foot around camps and lodges. However, when walking in the bush there is a real risk, so always wear stout shoes and long trousers. If bitten, forget the 'cut the wound open and suck out the poison' technique of Wild-West movies; the priority is to limit the spread of any venom in the bloodstream until medical help can be found. To this end:

to the colour blue; locals will advise on where they are a problem and where they transmit sleeping sickness.

Minute pestilential biting **blackflies** spread river blindness in some parts of Africa between 190°N and 170°S; the disease is caught close to fast-flowing rivers since flies breed there and the larvae live in rapids. The flies bite during the day but long trousers tucked into socks will help keep them off. Citronella-based natural repellents (eg: Mosi-guard) do not work against them.

Mosquitoes and many other insects are attracted to light. If you are camping, never put a lamp near the opening of your tent, or you will have a swarm of biters waiting to join you when you retire. In hotel rooms, be aware that the longer your light is on, the greater the number of insects will be sharing your accommodation.

Tumbu flies or *putsi* are a problem where the climate is hot and humid. The adult fly lays her eggs on the soil or on drying laundry and when the eggs come into contact with human flesh (when you put on clothes or lie on a bed) they hatch and bury themselves under the skin. Here they form a crop of 'boils' each with a maggot inside. Smear a little Vaseline over the hole, and they will push their noses out to breathe. It may be possibly to squeeze them out but it depends if they are ready to do so as the larvae have spines that help them to hold on. In *putsi* areas either dry your clothes and sheets within a screened house, or dry them in direct sunshine until they are crisp, or iron them.

Jiggers or **sandfleas** are another flesh-feaster, which can be best avoided by wearing shoes. They latch on if you walk barefoot in contaminated places, and set up home under the skin of the foot, usually at the side of a toenail where they cause a painful, boil-like swelling. They need picking out by a local expert.

- Keep the patient calm (this helps reduce heartbeat, slowing blood flow)
- Immobilise all of the bitten limb (with a splint and crepe bandage if possible) and keep it below heart level
- Try to identify the snake, or even note its size and markings, as this will help when sourcing antivenom
- Seek medical advice

Tickbite fever

Ticks are avoided by wearing appropriate clothing and discouraging them with permethrin and insect repellents. Dangerous tick-borne infections are uncommon in Africa but if you find a tick on you it should be removed with special tick tweezers that can be bought in good travel shops.

Failing that, you can use your fingernails by grasping the tick as close to your body as possible and pull steadily and firmly away at right angles to your skin. The tick will then come away complete as long as you do not jerk or twist. If possible, douse the wound with alcohol (any spirit will do) or iodine. Irritants (eg: Olbas oil) or lit cigarettes are to be discouraged since they can cause the ticks to regurgitate and therefore increase the risk of disease. It is best to get a travelling companion to check you for ticks; if you are travelling with small children, remember to check their heads, and particularly behind the ears.

Spreading redness around the bite and/or fever and/or aching joints after a tick bite imply that you have an infection that requires antibiotic treatment, so seek advice.

Bilharzia or schistosomiasis
This parasitic infection is acquired from paddling or bathing in infected lake water. It is most prevalent among local people who spend a lot of time in or close to still or slow-moving waters; it is fairly unusual in travellers, but people who have paddled or swum in Lake Malawi often get infected. It tends to cause fever some days or weeks after immersion and is treatable. Take care where you bathe in Africa.

RETURNING HOME

Generally, if you feel well and have no symptoms after a trip then it is most likely that you are well. If, however, you become ill after returning home, even if it is up to a year later, be sure to tell your GP where you have been and what diseases you may have been exposed to. It is all too easy to mistake early signs of malaria – headache and fever – for flu symptoms, and a few illnesses can take months to surface. If you are at all unsure, make an appointment with your nearest tropical diseases clinic (UK readers will need to do this through their GP) and have a full examination, including blood and stool tests.

3 The Trip

GETTING THERE (AIR TRAVEL)

The flight is one of the greatest concerns of many travellers with mobility restrictions, yet in reality this fear is usually groundless. Airports in the home countries of the majority of safari tourists are some of the most accessible of all public places, and those in Africa often equal these standards. Yes, there are horror stories of wheelchairs being lost and damaged, and if you are unable to transfer yourself then you may lose a little dignity being helped aboard, but in general services are efficient and professional. With a bit of planning beforehand and a positive attitude (it's only a means to an end after all), the flight can be hassle-free and even become an enjoyable part of the trip.

A basic problem with air travel is that because of its international nature, worldwide access is difficult to standardise. This chapter is based on information about UK policy, but travellers from other Western countries can fly assured that the situation will be similar where they are based. Indeed, the USA's ACAA (Air Carrier Access Act) reaches further than the UK's DDA (Disability Discrimination Act), as the latter only presides over flight booking and airport facilities; it has no power in the aircraft hence uniformity takes a nosedive the minute you step on board. UK airlines must only follow a voluntary code of practice published by the Department for Transport and, predictably, this leads to differences in inclusive practice. I champion anyone who wants to raise public awareness of this, but in general, high-altitude services are predictable and of a high standard.

As well as UK airports having to conform to DDA norms of accessibility, new EC legislation dictates that if a passenger is unable to board independently then the airport is duty bound to organise assistance, with the costs being passed on to the airline. In short, this means that throughout Europe there should be free help available in whatever form needed, from arrival at the terminal to being seated in the aircraft.

Although such legislation is generally less effective in Africa, arrival in the continent – to the surprise of many – is often equally trouble-free. The major hubs can be relied upon to provide professional help and all the usual access features, and what provincial ports lack in infrastructure they usually make up for in enthusiasm and improvisation.

For a list of airlines, see page 16.

FLYING POSITIVELY

I'm being deliberately upbeat in my description of flying with a disability. This is because in the ten years that I've been a chair user (and having taken probably more than 75 flights through five continents in that time), the biggest problem I've had has been worrying that things will go wrong. Maybe I've just been lucky, but I do think air services and facilities are generally very good – better than in most areas of public services – and that if a flexible approach is taken then few problems should be encountered. Of course, serious incidents out of your control can and do occur, including lost or damaged wheelchairs, lack of trained assistance and absence of specialised equipment. For these, and indeed, for the minor imperfections, it will only help the industry to improve if complaints are made. But do remember that is your holiday. Having a positive outlook will not only mean things are easier for everybody around you but will make the journey less stressful for yourself.

BEFORE LEAVING HOME

The amount of preparation done before a flight depends on the individual, their needs and their experience of flying. Some people book the cheapest-possible option that suits their timescale, then begin to work on the logistics like organising assistance. For others it is essential to know details like what happens to their mobility equipment, how accessible the toilet will be and exactly where they'll sit in relation to it.

Contact the airline

If any kind of assistance is required then it is very advisable to inform the airline of this yourself at least 48 hours before flying. If you are at all unsure, are using a route or airline for the first time, or will require a lot of help, then it's sensible to inform them while booking and double-check nearer the date of departure. All international airlines have a department dealing with this (often called 'barrier-free travel' or 'special assistance') and contact numbers for these can be found on their websites (a useful resource is www.allgohere.com which carries general information about access policies on many airlines as well as their telephone numbers). Give as much information as possible. Although well-trained staff will usually ask the right questions, it is wise to stay a step ahead and be sure they understand what is required. Once the airline knows the needs of the traveller, the appropriate code is attached to the booking. If the journey consists of several connecting flights, then in theory this code should be on all the tickets to alert assistance staff automatically in each airport.

Airlines carry at least one piece of mobility equipment free of charge – usually a wheelchair – and most will not refuse anyone who has to travel with something extra – most commonly a hoist or a bathroom chair. Sometimes weight restrictions are enforced, apparently to stay within ground staff health and safety regulations. It is sensible to inform them in advance of anything that may be considered extra luggage.

It may be that the airline requests completion of a form (called MEDIF or INCAD) before granting travel. If this is so, and you travel regularly, it is worthwhile asking for a FREMEC card instead, which details the specific requirements of someone with a stable and permanent condition. It is valid for multiple journeys, eliminating the need to fill in forms every time, though it might not be accepted by different airlines.

CHECK-IN

It is worthwhile arriving at the airport with plenty of time to spare, even if seating is reserved, as there is no guarantee the seat position will be held. In some airports, people who require assistance have the right to bypass check-in queues or check-in through business class. This can be worthwhile, but it does take someone fairly brazen to go straight to the front of a queue. A more subtle approach is to go to the assistance counter or find a 'floating' airport employee, who'll usually be able to prioritise your check-in. Often, the person checking the flight in is the one who organises proceedings at the departure gate, so a diplomatic, friendly approach from the beginning can do wonders once the scramble for boarding begins. But do not allow your needs to be overlooked.

The two most important issues to organise at check-in are assistance and seating position on the plane. Check also that your assistance requirements are noted in the system for your onward flights. If they're not, ask the check-in clerk to do this. If possible, check luggage in all the way through to your destination. If you have to rush between connecting flights, collecting bags is just going to waste time.

It occasionally is the case that wheelchair users are asked to transfer to an airport chair at check-in instead of staying in their own to the gate. The reasoning usually is that your wheelchair can be boarded with the rest of the luggage. For most chair users, this is unacceptable. Don't be shy about explaining why you cannot do it; apart from being uncomfortable, unsightly and difficult to push, sitting in a different chair for even a short period of time can lead to skin breakdown from poor pressure relief. If the answer is that it's only going to be for a very short time, then ask what happens if the flight is delayed. Although I've never seen how a luggage hold is packed, I also think that keeping your own chair until you get to the cabin makes it more likely that it will be one of the last items loaded, meaning it is less likely to be stored under luggage and broken.

Assistance

Large airports can be cavernous, with a long traipse from check-in to the departure lounge through seemingly never-ending corridors. To make these journeys easier for slow walkers, wheelchairs, electric chauffeur-driven 'buggies', escalators and travelators (moving floors) are normally present. Assistants are also available to help push wheelchairs, to lift and transfer non-ambulant travellers and to handle baggage. Although sometimes drawn from security or ground staff, they should always be trained and experienced. However, it is good advice to be assertive; explain thoroughly how best you like to be lifted and stay in control of the procedure. This service is free for the user (paid for by the airlines). In some airports it is available from arrival in the car park while in others it begins at check-in. Even if you don't need assistants and are faster pushing yourself, it is shrewd to use them, as they'll skip queues at security and immigrations checks.

En route through the airport, assistants are usually prepared to take passengers via the toilet but they rarely have time for a browse round the shops. If they cannot take the client all the way to the departure lounge immediately, they will invariably leave him or her at a designated holding point and arrange for a colleague to take over. Although this process is meant to be 'seamless', the stitching is sometimes a little loose; it is wise, therefore, to make sure they have definitely passed the message on and to ask how long their colleague will be. Another option is to bring a non-flying friend or relative to the airport to help you; this way, everything (at least up to passport control) is done according to your timescale rather than that of the airport staff.

Seating

In general, seats are allocated on a first-come, first-served basis; therefore, the airline isn't obliged to prioritise requests from disabled passengers. The chance to choose the most suitable location comes at check-in. If transferring – either independently or with help – then seats with movable armrests make the process less troublesome while those closer to the entry door are easier to reach for everybody with mobility problems.

Window versus aisle

People who have difficulties walking are usually placed either next to the aisle or a window. Those who need to access the toilet during the flight generally prefer the former, and although it may be a more cumbersome process to get there, window seating is ideal for anyone else. Apart from the view, the rewards of window seating are that the wall/window makes a handy headrest for an in-flight snooze and nobody has to clamber over you to reach the toilet. It is disconcerting, but true, that a few airlines prefer not to give aisle seats to disabled people in case they hinder an emergency evacuation.

Exit row and last row

Exit-row seating is rarely afforded to passengers with disabilities, as people sitting here must be deemed fully capable of opening the doors in an emergency. The last row in any block might be impractical as this seating is often directly in front of a partitioning wall meaning there is no space allowing an assistant to get behind to help with transfers.

Business class and upgrades

If more space and comfort is necessary, paying the extra for business class might be worthwhile. I have also heard of people attempting to get an upgrade on the grounds of having mobility problems, but I have my doubts about the success rate here. I suspect that a valid medical reason backed up with a doctor's letter would normally be needed.

Bulkhead

These are the seats in the first row of a block of seating. They normally have no seats directly in front of them, suiting those who need more legroom. This space also makes it easier for transferring in and out of the seat from the aisle chair if two people are required to help, as the assistant carrying your legs has more room to manoeuvre. However, for those who transfer more independently, or have poor upper body balance, having a seat upright directly in front can be a useful support. This can be used as a prop during transfers, throughout the flight when changing position to relieve pressure and while landing to prevent the upper body falling forward. The occupant of the seat in front may find this occasional bumping irritating, but an explanation of why usually quells tempers, or at least results in a surprised silence.

BOARDING

After check-in, people able to do so can make their own way through the airport. For others, help is normally available. At security checks, wheelchair users are ushered around the metal detectors then checked with a handheld device or lightly frisked. This can be done in private and rarely takes much longer than for able-bodied travellers.

Once at the departure lounge, try to sit fairly close to the gate and make yourself known to staff when they arrive, as people needing assistance should be boarded first. Unfortunately, this doesn't always happen, but when it does it is easier for everybody, is much more dignified for the traveller and means they have first choice of empty overhead lockers.

Boarding is usually done via a loading bridge (also called a jetway) which is an extendable tunnel reaching the door of the aircraft from the departure lounge. If no loading bridge is present, there may be a hydraulic platform called an ambilift that elevates users from ground level to the door of the plane. Failing this, steps will have to be negotiated. Anyone who cannot manage any of these options unaided can use an aisle chair*, which is an extra-narrow wheelchair, usually with four small wheels. It is designed to fit snugly down the aisle between the rows of seats on board and has safety straps to securely fasten anyone who has poor balance. Two transfers occur: one from the user's wheelchair to this chair (usually at the aircraft door or the bottom of the steps) and one from the aisle chair to the aircraft seat. If unable to transfer independently, the assistants will help (see *Assistance* above). Note, if two people are required to lift you then do state this at check in. Aircrew may help with this task but are not obliged. To ease the process flip the armrests up out of the way, and to prevent bruising, take care to remove all metal safety belt buckles from the row of seats before being lifted across.

If you use a pressure-relieving wheelchair cushion, this can be used on the plane too, giving your skin the protection it needs for long periods. The aircraft seat cushions are just fixed with velcro and are easily ripped out, allowing your own model to be put in their place. It always helps to ask permission before doing this and aircrew may be a little surprised, but it is rarely a problem. It is quite possible to simply place the wheelchair cushion on top of the standard aircraft seat, but doing this results in an uncomfortably high sitting position. Even if you don't want to use your cushion during the flight, these items are invariably valuable and easily damaged, so take it on board with you.

A useful tip when using an aisle chair is to ensure that your trouser pockets are not hanging open. These can catch on seat armrests as you're being whisked backwards down the aisle of the plane, and unless your trousers have a tight waistband or belt, they can be inadvertantly pulled to your knees.

*Aisle chair: Also known as a boarding chair, transfer chair, small chair, narrow chair, sleep chair, wellington chair and slipper chair in different countries.

DURING THE FLIGHT

Help from cabin crew
Cabin crew should all be aware of the presence of someone with extra needs, and will usually assist with tasks like retrieving items from luggage and cutting food.

Toilet issues
It is rarely a problem for crew to help someone to get to the bathroom using an on-board wheelchair (this should be booked and double-checked in advance), but passengers should be capable of using the toilet unaided or travel with a personal assistant.

If getting to the toilet is going to be impossible (see above), then other measures may need to be taken. Anybody who does or can use an indwelling Foley catheter has a distinct advantage in the urinary department. An overnight bag can be connected to the leg bag then a travelling companion can surreptitiously take it to the lavatory to be emptied. Several people have reported that they are happy to discreetly pee naturally into containers (see *Chapter 2, The short call*, page 44) and either have these emptied by a friend or carry them off after the flight. This is best done during the hours of darkness or under a blanket and is easier to keep private if you are sitting next to the window. For bowel movements, colostomy bags pose few problems though wearers would be well advised to use a larger pouch than normal because intestinal gas can expand during flight, resulting in increased output. Unfortunately, there are fewer options when dealing with natural bowel movements and none are guaranteed. Short of wearing incontinence pads (not an option for everyone due to potential skin damage), the best that can be done is to plan the routine around the flight or vice versa.

Pressure relief

A flight to east or southern Africa is at least six hours from most Western countries. Because of this, it will be essential for people with sensory deprivation to relieve pressure on their sitting areas. This should be done more regularly than when at home because the sitting position in an aircraft seat will be different from that in the everyday wheelchair, meaning new areas will be subject to pressure. Consider whether having a window, aisle or bulkhead seat will make a difference, depending on your methods of doing this.

Temperature

The cabin is air-conditioned and can feel chilly, especially if you are unusually sensitive to temperature. Thin blankets are provided but pack a fleece (maybe even hat and scarf) in your hand luggage; they can always double as pillows if you're warm enough. If you are still cold, the captain may raise the temperature, if asked politely.

DISEMBARKING

People requiring assistance exit the aircraft last and the process is the reverse of boarding – if available, an aisle chair is brought to the passenger and their own wheelchair should be waiting at the aircraft door. Although it should not be essential, it is often beneficial to remind cabin crew that your wheelchair needs to be brought directly to the aircraft on landing instead of going to baggage reclaim. This is best done about an hour before arrival, giving the flight crew time to relay the message on to the destination airport where baggage handlers will be alerted.

Assistance to push the wheelchair and help with baggage reclaim can be expected from this point to the point of connection with onward flights or to the exit of the airport.

It might not all work as smoothly as this in practice and there could be a long wait, but patience and being aware of the correct procedure will be useful when help does come. It is worth considering this potential delay when booking; in other words, do not leave too short a time between connecting flights.

Facilities in African airports are discussed on page 92 and specifics about each are given in their respective listings in *Part Two* of this book.

OTHER POINTS TO CONSIDER

Advance booking
Although many carriers will allow people with disabilities to pre-book seats free of charge, this is no guarantee and written confirmation is difficult to obtain. A relaxed roll up to check-in, slightly late, believing that all is securely booked, can be met with the news that the reservation has been 'lost in the system' or that somebody else's need was deemed greater. However, there is one last chance; people who need assistance should normally be first to board, so even if it was not possible to get the ideal seat during booking or check-in, cabin crew will often listen to a polite request. They are sometimes aware which seats are free or will be prepared to swap two bookings around to help.

Assistants' seats
Many people need to travel with a personal assistant who may be a friend, colleague, partner or spouse. Turning this on its head, an airline may also dictate that a disabled person is 'not self-reliant', and therefore must travel with an escort. Even though this appears to open a door to claiming reduced-price seating for a companion, and the UK code of practice does recommend this policy, it almost never happens. Likewise, those who need two seats because of their disability are rarely given reductions for this, but that does not mean it is not worth asking for. Anybody travelling together with their assistant will normally be given adjacent seats.

A potentially useful resource for Australian readers is Air Travel Companion (☎ *02 8281 8222;* **e** *rosaleen@airtravelcompanion.com.au;* *www.airtravelcompanion.com.au*). This service provides experienced professionals who travel with anyone requiring assistance.

Storage of equipment
Wheelchairs can occasionally be stored in the cabin, but only if there is space foreseen or if they can fold small enough to fit into the overhead lockers. The more common scenario is for these to be taken to the hold, where they are usually kept separate from the main luggage. Smaller aids like crutches, braces and walking sticks may be taken on board but will need to be stored away for the duration of the flight.

Notes for wheelchair users
Before your wheelchair is taken to the hold, it is wise to remove all loose or breakable parts like side guards, footplates and cushion. These can be taken with you into the cabin. Alternatively, fix them firmly in position with packing tape or similar. All pieces going into the hold will have been tagged at check-in but it is also sensible to attach an address label.

A good strategy if travelling with a manual chair is to tell the porters that it cannot be folded or dismantled. This works on the principle that if the chair and wheels stay as one, there's less chance of anything going missing. Also, if they leave it alone, they're less likely to damage it.

People who use an electrically powered chair or scooter may need to have it reduced to its component parts. In this case it is worth attaching instructions for dismantling and assembly. Check this with your airline long before you plan to fly, especially because wet-cell batteries must be removed and dry-cell versions might need to be isolated. Knowing how to do this yourself can be useful and it is important to arrive even earlier (possibly three hours) at check-in. This will also lead to a delay disembarking. It is sometimes necessary to have a manufacturer's or supplier's certificate of the type of batteries present and it is worth noting that heavy equipment is more likely not to be allowed on smaller aircraft (potentially important for internal flights). Some airports have large plastic bags available, which can be taped over your chair giving it another layer of protection.

Finally, travelling with mobility gear will always be risky. It might be worthwhile taking an old wheelchair or walking aid (if you have one) instead of your 'everyday' model. Alternatively, if you can cope with something that's not made to fit then it is often possible to hire such equipment on a short-term basis, either from home or in the destination country. (See *What to take*, page 35.)

Aircraft

Depending on the type of aircraft, there are variations in location and accessibility of toilets, location and type of seating (extra legroom, movable armrests) and restrictions on allowed wheelchair weight and storage of mobility aids. Some or all of these issues may be crucial, and the airline should be able to describe what can be expected on any particular flight. A few minutes' browsing the websites of the major companies will find the types of aircraft used on each route, and a mouse click deeper can often locate the seating plans. These do not necessarily show which of the toilets are accessible, but such details can be hammered out during email or telephone discussions with the airline.

Medical issues

There are various reasons why medical consent may be required (see page 51), and although having a stable disability is not one of them, the following may be relevant:

- If oxygen may be needed (this might be provided but it will be at the cost of the user)
- If medical assistance or equipment is likely to be needed
- If the passenger has recently been injured, hospitalised, had an illness or undergone an operation
- If there is a history of heart problems

Ventilator users do not normally need a medical certificate, but it could be handy. If powered by dry-cell batteries, ventilators may be used on board but be sure you have enough battery power for the duration of the flight or check if power is available. Cabin crew will not be responsible for operation of ventilators so if help is necessary then a personal assistant must be present.

Anyone unsure of whether or not they need a certificate would be well advised to get one. Even if one is not required for the international flights, this extra piece of paper has been known to help persuade over-zealous officials governing airports within Africa.

Insurance
It is strongly advised that all mobility equipment, from walking aids to electric wheelchairs, is independently insured by the traveller. Some airlines will compensate for damage or loss incurred, but the amounts they are liable for under international regulations rarely come to the true value of the item. Always file any insurance claim as soon as possible. (See *Chapter 1, Insurance*, page 29.)

GETTING AROUND

Nowhere in Africa has seamless, fully inclusive public transport systems. Similarly, legislation is not yet sturdy enough to outlaw steps, sand and other hindrances to individual mobility. The result is that addressing these issues is mainly up to private vehicle and accommodation owners. Africa is at an early stage in this process, but options are already in place that should suit everyone and the more disabled people who visit the continent, the more the industry will take note and cater to them.

ON FOOT
Tourist accommodation, especially in the more upmarket lodges, tends to concentrate on natural materials to construct buildings and access routes. Indoor surfaces are commonly smooth, polished slate, cement, tiles or wooden decking, while pathways outside vary from natural foot-worn earth in the most bush of bush camps, through sand and gravel to stone 'crazy paving' and wooden boardwalks.

Unmade earthen tracks are usually ideal for wheelers in dry seasons but may be better avoided during wetter times. Of the hard surfaces, the stone crazy paving is the least predictable. Some lodges have made the effort to finish this so well that it is virtually ridge-free, whereas others appear to have left it deliberately uneven, to the point where it would be easy to catch a castor or stub a toe. I have tried to give a rough idea of how friendly these surfaces are in my write-ups. (See examples of typical safari paths in the colour section.)

Architects are under less pressure to incorporate inclusive design in Africa; consequently, the traditional use of steps instead of gently sloping inclines is still in force in many places. The icons within the listings in

Part Two of this book give an idea of the number of steps that exist around the properties described. However, as stated in *How to Use this Book*, pages xii–xvi, the symbol for 'level access' refers only to access routes linking at least one room, one eating place and the main entrance. These routes are step-free but might not be perfectly smooth and slopes may be steeper than 8%.

As with anywhere in the world, there are always people to help and alternative routes around barriers can often be found. Experienced disabled travellers will be used to using rear doors, service lifts and staff areas to avoid inaccessible public entrances, and Africa is no different. The key to not letting this spoil your holiday is to consider it a privilege to catch a glimpse of the parts of buildings nobody else sees!

BY ROAD

A chief concern when disability and safari are mentioned together is the scarcity of accessible vehicles in Africa. There are certainly fewer options than in western Europe or in North America, but specialised operators with adapted vehicles exist in all areas covered in this book (see pages 19–23). They run 4x4s and minibuses with hydraulic lifts, wheelchair clamps and extra padding and restraints and can organise fully inclusive safaris several weeks long or simply arrange a transfer between airport and hotel.

For those who can cope with standard transport there follows a description of the types of vehicles commonly used by tourists, both in private and public transport, and their suitability to people with mobility limitations. For anyone planning to do the driving themselves, I've included some basic guidelines about driving in Africa.

Private vehicles

For information on self-drive rental vehicles, see page 24.

Cars

Normal saloon and estate cars are available for hire in most major towns, but in general are only to be considered for use within city limits. Exceptions are many South African parks and Namibia's Etosha, where the roads are so good that virtually any type of vehicle can be used. If you are going to be doing great distances on unsealed roads, then a small 2wd car should be discounted. Similarly, rutted, sandy tracks are often the means of access to lodges and camps, and low-slung cars flounder quickly on these. Cars generally suit wheelchair users well, as the seating is at a similar height to that of their wheelchair cushion and it is what they are used to at home.

Minibuses

Nissan and Toyota vans and Volkswagen kombis are wonderfully versatile vehicles. They have more passenger space than a typical Land Rover, are more economical and are generally cheaper to hire. They are commonly used for airport transfers, but being higher off the ground means they are more agile off-road and give better game viewing. Many have a 'pop-up' roof, especially in Kenyan parks and when driven skilfully, minibuses – even 2wd versions – cope admirably with mud and sand. Also, because they are built as commercial vehicles, they are remarkably durable. The passenger seat height is usually between 90cm and 100cm from the ground and open doorways are generally roomier than those on Land Rovers and Land Cruisers, making assisted transfers easier. Most have a sliding side door, which can provide an even wider entrance.

4x4s

The majority of safaris in Africa are done in 4x4 vehicles (mainly Land Rovers and Toyota Land Cruisers). Apart from adding a little more of a daring, adventurous flavour to a safari, these machines give good game viewing (some have had their bodies adapted making them higher with greater visibility and some have pop-up roofs). They are designed and built to be driven off-road, so – with an experienced driver – provide a much greater range of travel. Potentially crucial if your body has no sensation is that older models, or those built specifically for off-road use, may be harder sprung and have less luxurious upholstery than modern versions. Anyone for whom comfort of ride is a priority is strongly advised to use the front passenger seat. Those further back, above the rear axle, take the brunt of the bumps. The passenger seat is generally between 85cm and 95cm from the ground and although doorways (in older models especially) are relatively narrow, many of these vehicles based at lodges have had their doors removed, so are more easily entered.

Higher vehicles: further access issues

Higher vehicles (minibuses and 4x4s) can actually be easier to enter for anyone who struggles to get up out of a car seat, and may even suit 'wobbly walkers'. They usually have one or two strong handles in strategic places near the doorway, and some operators and lodges provide a small, portable step to assist. I've even heard of a cheap African drum being carried around by one group as a step, though this seems a little wasteful.

For people who cannot stand at all, MalaMala Game Reserve in South Africa (see page 330 and the photo in the colour section) has built a raised wheelchair platform that may allow some people to do an independent transfer into 4x4 vehicles. A further possibility is the hoist recently developed by Equal Adventure in the UK (see *Chapter 1*, page 38). However, it is not an economical option for most single-visit travellers, so manpower (possibly using something similar to Gimpgear's 'Comfort Carrier', also listed on page 38) may be the only realistic method. The trick is to make sure you thoroughly explain to helpers how it must be done and stay in control throughout the process. Finding people in Africa who are good at lifting is much easier than in 'the west' and most are far too pragmatic to consider health and safety issues.

DRIVING IN AFRICA

Driving safely anywhere is about risk limitation, but this is even truer in Africa where the external dangers are greater. Driving standards are often lower than you'll be used to, vehicles are less well maintained and, most importantly, roads can be little more than tracks in the sand. This paints a bleak image, and South Africa and Namibia are exempt to a large degree from such sweeping generalisations, but the message is that your safety when driving in Africa is very much in your own hands. These are useful basic rules:

- Don't drive at night. Roads (even in urban areas) are badly lit; people walk on them, animals sleep on them (especially tar-sealed roads, which have soaked up the heat of the sun through the day) and pot-holes and speed bumps are less easily seen.

- Drive defensively when approaching other vehicles. A good rule anywhere, this is more relevant where people sharing the highway may be less predictable than you're used to.

- Distances will usually be greater (hence driving times will be longer) than those you're used to at home. Plan your days well, leave early in the morning and take regular breaks.

- If you are planning to venture seriously off-road then you should always travel in a group of at least two vehicles and be fully equipped for such a trip. All drivers should be capable and experienced and at least one should possess knowledge of basic 'bush' mechanics.

- Take extra care if driving a vehicle that you're not used to. 4x4s may give the impression of safety but are slower to accelerate and less stable when cornering than a car. Their greatest danger, however, is that they instil confidence. If you're not experienced with off-road driving then it is possible to venture further than the vehicle's capabilities. This, of course, applies to any type of vehicle, but a heavy 4x4 is significantly more difficult to pull or push than a lighter 2wd if it flounders in mud or sand.

Once inside the vehicle, as with flying, it may be possible to replace the vehicle cushion with your own pressure-relieving variety. (See *Chapter 1, What to take*, page 46 for suggestions about padding potential pressure areas.)

Public transport

Taxis

The most common method of transport used by most visitors in urban areas is the local taxi. In most cities, the bulk of these are standard saloon cars, so if a more spacious 'estate' version is required for storage of wheelchairs or other equipment, then an effort should be made to order this in advance. Although drivers are always willing to help, they will not have any specialist equipment and will have had no training in how best to assist people with mobility problems. That said, haste is not an issue in Africa so you will feel no vibes that you're wasting their time.

Vehicles may often be older and more worn than you're used to. If so, seating and suspension could have lost the best of its bounce, and although this just means a less comfortable ride for most people, those with reduced sensation ought to be extra careful; it might be prudent to place a cushion on top of the car seat. Interestingly, Nairobi and Johannesburg have wheelchair-accessible cabs. These cars have enough space inside for people using lightweight wheelchairs to enter and stay seated in their wheelchairs for the journey. Those in the Kenyan capital are ex-London black taxis and unfortunately I see fewer on the streets every time I return. The South African models are newer and more information can be found on ⏚ www.sacab.co.za.

Matatus, dala dalas and kombis

The most ubiquitous people carrier in and between African towns and cities is the minibus. These are usually Japanese (Toyota Hiace models or similar) and have a variety of local names from *matatus* in Kenya (the standard fare used to be three – *tatu* in Swahili – shillings) to *dala dalas* in Tanzania, and *kombis* in the southern lands. They are often lovingly spray-painted in psychedelic styles, proclaiming allegiance to anyone from Allah to David Beckham, and jostle for space in crowded streets packed with passengers.

Travelling in one is an in-your-face exposure to local culture, where you're as likely to be squeezed thigh to thigh with a suited businessman as be planted under the spreading elbows of a plump mother nursing her baby. *Matatus* follow set routes, starting and finishing in stations, but times are less reliable; they tend not to leave until full. The driver is supported by a 'tout', who mans the door, charging fees and instructing the driver when to go and stop. Anyone who needs it will always receive help to board, but you do need to be reasonably able; if you require a lot of legroom to stretch out, or two seats to sprawl a little, then forget it. The frantic style of this transport is thrilling but unforgiving. It is probably also the least safe way to take a road trip, as these are the vehicles most regularly involved in (if not the cause of) road traffic accidents.

Buses and coaches

The next stage up from the urban *matatu* is the inner and inter-city bus. Kenya has (thankfully) stamped an 80km/h limit on public vehicles recently, because these buses – decorated in vibrant colours like *matatus* – used to hurtle through the country at irresponsible and often frightening speeds. The shuttle from Nairobi down to Arusha is probably the service that will most commonly be used by tourists and runs modern, well-maintained vehicles. Southern African coaches have traditionally been more regulated

BORDER POSTS

All the border crossings relevant to this guide are on well-used tourist routes. Therefore, assuming the vehicle and passenger paperwork is in order, there should be no major delays on these; as a result, most are easily cleared within an hour or two. Few borders have accessible toilets. If you need such conveniences then private roadside stops should be planned accordingly. If a less mobile member of the group cannot enter the immigration and customs buildings then this will pose no problem. One person is often left with the vehicle for security anyway and potential thieves are not going to know that that person is unable to give chase. Also, officials rarely need to see everybody in their office; I've even had some who relish the excuse to stretch their legs coming out to check identities!

between the main cities in Botswana, Namibia and South Africa, and are usually of a high standard, sometimes with luxuries like air conditioning and on-board loos. However, apart from sightseeing tours in Cape Town (see page 320) and proposals for a 'kneeling' bus in Johannesburg, none of these public services provide officially 'accessible' vehicles.

Anybody who cannot make their own way up the steps into a coach will need to ask the driver and/or passengers to help. Bear in mind also that the on-board toilet will not have any access features and that unlike air travel, public transport services by road do not provide assistance with luggage. There will always be hands willing to help with your bags, but similarly there will be those less honest.

BY RAIL

Railways are not a significant means of tourist transport in Africa. Consequently, very few have made any provision for mobility-impaired passengers. Three of those that have are detailed below. For anybody unable to walk, any other train journey will mean a lot of help is required as there are steps, narrow doorways, narrow corridors and small toilet areas.

Kenya

Nairobi–Mombasa Overnight Sleeper ℰ +254 (0)20 224 8453;
e info@eastafricashuttles.com; 🖰 www.eastafricashuttles.com/train.htm. This journey is not as luxurious as the following two southern African services, but does offer a potentially more convenient overnight journey between Nairobi & the coast. There are no facilities for disabled passengers & passages are narrow, but help is available with stairs & first-class cabins are self-contained with beds at seat level. Meals can also be brought to the cabin.

Namibia

TransNamib Luxury Trains ℰ +264 (0)61 298 2175/2032/2083;

e pubrelation@transnamib.com.na; www.transnamib.com.na. The *Omugulu Gwombashe Star*, is the only train that has spacious bathrooms & toilets with support rails, & usually runs between Windhoek & Oshivelo in northern Namibia.

South Africa
Gautrain (providing rail services in Gauteng) +2711 891 7108; www.gautrain.co.za. This not yet fully inclusive, but made a commitment in 2008 to ensure that all passengers with disabilities will be catered to.
The Blue Train +27 (0)12 334 8459; **e** info@bluetrain.co.za; www.bluetrain.co.za. This luxury train runs between Cape Town, Pretoria & Durban & can cater to some wheelchair users. There is a suite designed for this purpose, which has a roll-in shower with 1 support rail. A wheelchair made specially to fit the aisles is available & lounge areas at both Pretoria & Cape Town stations can be reached without steps from the car parks. Non-ambulant passengers will need to be lifted onto the trains from the platform, as there are no ramps on hand for this purpose.

BY AIR
For a detailed description of the procedures involved when flying with a disability, see *Getting There (air travel)* on page 77.

International airports
Although airports in Africa are not as tightly bound by legislation as those in Western countries, most of the arrival points on the continent carry all the essential equipment, have adapted toilets and assistance staff are trained and experienced. See the respective country and city sections in *Part Two* of this book for more detailed information about particular airports.

Provincial airports
The smaller provincial hubs are sometimes less well appointed. They may not have an accessible toilet or an aisle chair, meaning non-ambulant passengers will have to be manhandled between two assistants, carried 'bride style' by one or lifted in their own wheelchair from the plane. As stated elsewhere in this book, Africans are generally very adept in using these techniques and I have even heard of the last method being used perfectly well when the traveller was seated in her heavy, electric wheelchair.

Small airstrips in and near game parks
Most small private airstrips in Africa will be little more than a strip of grass or gravel and a windsock. They rarely have an aisle chair – the aircraft are often too small to allow easy use of one anyway – and the toilet will usually just be standard, with normal door widths. The upside is that everything is usually at ground level or only up a solitary step and, as in provincial airports, helpers are to be trusted with transfers. One important point is that the camp or lodge you are travelling to may be more than 30 minutes'

drive away, and often, only a driver will be sent to collect you. Anyone who will need help from two people to exit the plane must state this in advance as there is no guarantee that the pilot will get involved.

BY BOAT

Waterways are depended upon by many land animals and are home to some of the most striking birdlife in Africa. They provide another dimension to game viewing and often the best photography is done looking onto land scenes from a canoe or small boat. For people with physical limitations, the tranquillity of this style of transport may be more suitable than game driving; there are no bumps, there's no dust and it is often cooler on the water than on dry land. The difficulties are entering and sitting in the boat.

Jetties

Of the countless camps and lodges with riverside settings, few have step-free approaches to their jetties. That said, getting to the boat in a wheelchair is rarely impossible. Of course it depends on personal levels of aversion to being manhandled, but it is only really where many steep steps or vertical ladders are present that this is dangerous. Capable and willing helpers are always available, and because no boats are adapted to allow roll-on entry, help will be needed to enter the craft anyway. A hoist has recently been developed in the UK for this task (see *Slings, hoists and lifts*, page 43), but as with vehicle transfers, the most useful method will still be manpower.

Transfers into canoes and boats

Mekoro (singular *mokoro*) are the dugout canoes used mainly in Botswana's Okavango Delta. Nowadays these are made from fibreglass to try to preserve the native sausage trees and ebony that were traditionally used, but they are still the same basic design. Passengers sit on cushions – with or without backrests – in the floor of the vessel. A pressure-relieving wheelchair cushion can be used here and the best method of transfer for non-ambulant people is in two stages as follows:

- Park the wheelchair on the jetty, alongside the boat but with about 1m between them
- Place a cushion on the jetty in the 1m between the wheelchair and the boat
- Lift the person from the wheelchair onto the cushion
- With the *mokoro* being securely held in position, bow and stern by two people, lift the wheelchair user into it (onto their wheelchair cushion if this is preferred). The lifters will find it easiest to have one foot on the jetty and one in the *mokoro*.

When lifting wheelchair users into small, flat-bottomed boats, the process is very similar. However, because there is usually room for the wheelchair, it is easier to lift the wheelchair with the user still in it. Again, the boat must be securely held at both the bow and stern and for this lift four people are required, two in the boat and two on the jetty. Any variation of these techniques can be used, depending on the style of boat or jetty and the wishes of the passenger, but with a bit of compromise, there are few situations where entering a boat is not possible. If it is, it is rarely a tragedy; it usually results in having to spend an afternoon sitting by an African riverside with a cool drink, a bird or animal guidebook and a pair of binoculars.

ACCOMMODATION

In surveying the accommodation that is described in *Part Two* of this guide, I concentrated on those places where the rooms have connecting (ensuite) bathrooms. I appreciate that a lot of travellers with mobility impairments can cope very well with the shared ablutions typical of hostels and campsites – and I've included descriptions of these styles below – but I feel that the level of access they offer does not vary enough to justify more coverage. Anyone considering a mobile camping safari is wholly encouraged, especially as some operators cater specifically to this market.

A fairly safe generalisation is that the majority of Africa's adapted rooms are found in properties in the mid-range bracket. Above and below this, inclusive accommodation exists, but establishments in these price categories are investing more time, effort and expense catering to fully able travellers in their specific markets rather than opening their arms to visitors of all abilities.

The following are descriptions of the most common types of accommodation, with the emphasis on their suitability to guests with mobility problems.

CAMPING

As in the days of the explorers, the traditional African safari is done carrying your own canvas. This means of shelter gives the greatest freedom and flexibility and undoubtedly brings you closer to 'real' Africa than any other. A tent does little to stifle the night sounds of Africa, and if your campsite is near or within a game park, the aural entertainment after dark can be every bit as mesmerising as the visual feast on the morning game drive.

The vast majority of campers use official sites, which are found in or near most game parks with security, ablutions and sometimes a restaurant. However, those in South Africa's Kruger National Park are the only ones I have seen with adapted bathrooms. People considering camping should also remember that sites are invariably set on grass, sand or packed dirt; electricity may be available at camping stands but this is by no means a standard facility; and, at basic venues, toilets can still be the long-drop hole-in-the-ground type (see *Chapter 1, What to take*, pages 43–4, for possible solutions for people who have difficulties squatting). If you are used to leaning against walls to get around, floppy tent sides may pose a concern, although I have been told that the proximity of beds and furniture usually makes up for this. Also, unless you use large walk-in varieties, space in tents will be severely limited and sleeping is often at ground level on thermarests or similar. Standing up from this height may be difficult if you are stiff of limb, and only the most independent wheelchair users can master a floor-to-chair transfer. Even if you use fold-up camp beds, these are usually significantly lower than a wheelchair.

Entering and exiting a sleeping bag may not be as simple as one might imagine. If you have mobility difficulties, or you are helping someone in this situation, it can save a lot of effort to open the bag completely, roll into it then zip it up again. If you need to be lifted into your chair, a useful tip is to allow yourself to be pulled out of your tent on your thermarest or sleeping bag for the transfer. This gives the lifters more headroom and your fellow campers something to talk about over breakfast, but is only practical in dry weather and always remember to check for thorns on the ground.

Mobility impairments – even serious ones – do not mean camping is excluded as a potential way of travel, but a lot of support may be required from travelling companions. If you choose a specialised operator – see pages 19–23 – then mobile camping safaris through some of the most unspoiled parts of the continent are possible. Going this way would overcome many of the obstacles, yet still expose you to the adventure and thrill of camping. These companies know where the ground most suits wheelchairs, they use custom-made tents with high camp beds and roll-in showers and they run 4x4 vehicles with wheelchair lifts. Staff are experienced in catering to mobility problems but the real bonus of this style of travel is that you'll often be alone in the bush with no other tourists for miles around.

BACKPACKERS' HOSTELS

Backpackers' hostels following the worldwide norm (clean lodgings aimed at independent budget travellers) have been present in the southern African countries for many years. They are also now appearing in east Africa, but unfortunately I have yet to find any with fittings that are designed with limited mobility in mind. Most sleeping and bathroom arrangements are communal, with rooms for four or more (sometimes using bunk beds to save space); however, singles, doubles and twins with ensuite bathroom facilities are also found. Cooking and dining may be on a self-catering basis (facilities will be provided if so) or there might be a restaurant.

TENTED CAMPS

As with 'camping', you will have only a sheet of canvas separating you from the wilds. Inside, however, there can be any level of opulence, from basic furnishings to mahogany beds and marbled bathrooms. The tents are usually pitched on a solid wood or concrete base and often sheltered by a thatched-roof structure. This prolongs the life of the canvas and gives the whole camp a more robust, rustic and natural look, yet doesn't compromise the fresh-air feel or shut out the night sounds. Tented camps, especially the most exclusive examples, blend perfectly with their surroundings. Natural vegetation spreads uninhibited between and around tents and, if in a game area, animals wander through, apparently oblivious to the human presence.

All but the most basic tented camps are sufficiently large to house a double or two single standard-height beds, with enough space to roll next to them in a wheelchair. Entrances are either tent flaps or fixed doorways and they usually have ensuite bathrooms, sometimes sporting roll-in showers and support rails. Electric power may be available, either intermittent or full time, and telephones may be present. If there is no telephone, then most camps will provide hooters or whistles to attract attention in the case of emergency. If all else fails, security guards (usually local tribesmen) patrol the grounds and will come running at the first call of alarm.

The separate dining area may also be under canvas or thatch, and food can be as basic or as elegant as your budget allows. Pathway construction varies: the most natural of wilderness camps try to interfere with their surroundings as little as possible – sleeping tents may only be linked with eating and reception areas by a network of tracks through the trees; more structured set-ups may have distinct paths marked out by stones or low fences; solid, permanent settings often use stone 'crazy paving', either set in sand or sealed with cement.

LODGES

Lodges are more solid structures, with walls of stone or wood and solid doors. The rooms may be within the main building, in semi-detached clusters or apart and freestanding, but will always have the integral strength and security of a permanent construction. Although it is easy to assume that the feeling of proximity to the wilderness will be entirely lost when using a lodge, many are designed with such care that the buildings are constructed to mimic traditional designs and are nestled unobtrusively within the natural ecosystem.

Throughout a lodge complex, access routes connecting the sleeping, eating, swimming, game-viewing and reception areas are usually made from some kind of hard-wearing material, normally either wood, stone, tile or cement; 24-hour electricity and lighting is standard, and telephones are often present.

Some lodges have tented camps and self-catering campsites linked to them (and the guests staying in these areas will have access to lodge facilities) but this is the exception rather than the rule. For anybody who needs a high standard of access – smooth, hard floors, wide doors, electricity and generous amounts of space – the 'lodge' option is the most likely to give the widest choice of suitable accommodation.

WORKING FARMS, GUESTHOUSES AND B&Bs

Homely and welcoming, this style of lodging is often an adapted or extended house, with the owner living on the premises. All standards and styles exist.

Even if there are no custom-made access features, the big advantage here for disabled guests is the personal nature of service – with the owner actually managing the property, the likelihood of your needs being catered to in a sympathetic fashion is greater. It is also much easier to obtain a feeling for the human culture of the region you are in, as these lodgings are small scale and owned and run by local people.

HOTELS

Hotels catering to all budgets are found throughout the countries covered. They can be broadly divided into two categories: those aiming to attract tourists, and those catering to local business travellers; which suits you depends on your own tastes. Local hotels are usually more basic and consequently cheaper but rarely have any access for disabilities. Tourist-grade establishments will generally have more attentive staff and more upbeat décor, but correspondingly, more Western prices will need to be paid. The larger chains and independent hotels catering to mid-range budgets are the most likely to have rooms designed for people with disabilities.

EATING AND DRINKING

Meals on a fully inclusive safari are usually of a high culinary as well as sanitary standard; in fact, if your budget stretches to it then it is quite possible to have exquisitely prepared delicacies in the middle of the bush. Even on cheaper trips, African chefs are famous for producing sublime dishes – refined cakes from the coals of a campfire always astound guests. Most establishments within game parks offer a mix of Western and more traditional African dishes and the availability of market-fresh fruits and vegetables means the menu can be as healthy as it is indulgent. As a result, although many travellers see going on safari as an opportunity to lose weight, few succeed!

Towns and cities in Africa have a wide range of independent restaurants catering to most tastes and wallets. However, during all my research trips for this book, I saw none with a designated disabled toilet. Even in South Africa, the most advanced of the countries covered, there is not enough effective disability legislation to mean many street restaurants have a significant degree of access. That said, the great majority are ground floor with no more than two steps from street level to enter them and staff, clients and passers-by will always happily help if help is needed. In any case, most safari tourists – disabled or not – tend to do the bulk of their eating in the place they are staying overnight and I have provided basic restaurant access information within the accommodation listings in *Part Two*. For the independent restaurants that are mentioned in *Part Two*, an explanation of the price codes used can be found on the inside-front cover of the book.

INTERACTING WITH AFRICANS

Requiring more help from the local people, as discussed in *Chapter 1, Personal assistance*, page 34, turns the usual tourist/local relationship completely on its head. Instead of the obvious issue being the economic gulf between the two (a tedious reflection of Africa's financial dependence on the West), the new point of focus is suddenly the tourist's dependence on the African. This reversal is healthy for both parties, but does make this topic especially pertinent to people with mobility problems.

ACCEPTING HELP

As a disabled tourist, you will probably be one of the first to be noticed as soon as you exit the airport or hotel. There's a fair chance that help with luggage and finding taxis will be spontaneously offered at this point, and there may be several people vying for your attentions. Depending on how urban and Westernised the area is, payment of some kind will normally be expected, and for the uninitiated this can be a stressful moment.

Remember that you are under no obligation to use anyone. Calmly choosing one person from the throng usually makes the others melt magically away. Don't leave the security of the airport or hotel forecourt until you've discussed and agreed terms and make sure there are no potential misunderstandings about tips. In general, if you ever feel unduly heckled by someone then be polite but assertive and tell him or her immediately that you're very grateful for the offer but that you don't need anyone. If help is not spontaneously offered but you need it, then a uniformed worker (policeman, airport worker or hotel employee) is a good first stop. If they have no time to assist, they will usually endeavour to find someone else trustworthy.

Africans generally have no qualms about hands-on contact with strangers and are readily prepared to lift and carry people without fear of injuring themselves or their pride. However, the gusto with which they approach the task can be risky. If you need assistance for transfers, be sure to emphasise that you are in charge and it should be done under your instruction and at your pace. Likewise, pushing wheelchairs is a learned skill; I've ended up in flowerbeds and against walls several times due to overenthusiastic but inexperienced first-timers.

Incidentally, this readiness to help – sometimes without asking – may be uncomfortable for some people, especially if your personal space is important. It might be useful to remember that it is meant with no disrespect; it is simply African nature to want to assist.

PAYING FOR HELP AND TIPPING

As a disabled person, I find it refreshing how often people in Africa offer help then refuse payment. However, this makes knowing exactly when and how much to give even more difficult. It is a skill that that can only be obtained through experience, and even then everyone will have moments of

AFRICAN REACTION TO DISABILITY

Life is harsh across much of Africa. In low-income countries there is little or no social support, with the consequence that the weaker members of society – including people with disabilities – are often ignored. They may not be seen as valued family members and therefore have less right to education and vocational training. The net result is that people with disabilities are often homeless and survive by begging, only enforcing the perception of their worthlessness. In some cultures, having a disabled child is even seen as being a curse, and horror stories of babies that are born with a disability being left in the bush for the hyenas do have some truth. These beliefs are frightening, but they do not affect the way Africans see a disabled tourist.

Unlike the reaction in wealthy Western countries, where passers-by look away rather than meet the eye of a disabled person, Africans tend to be unashamedly honest. Maybe this is because disability is more prevalent in this continent than any other. I have never heard of a situation where a disabled tourist was made to feel unwelcome, unworthy or uncomfortable. On the contrary; the reaction is sometimes pity, but mostly support and sometimes even surprise. It is a commonly held belief that Western medicine can treat almost anything, so one question you may need to prepare a stock answer for is 'Why has your disease not been cured?'

indecision. Good advice, if you are in doubt, is always to offer something.

It is prudent to always carry enough cash for this purpose (in local currency and/or small-denomination US dollars), but do not dish it out too readily without thinking of the repercussions. Although the gulf in wealth between tourists and the local people makes it easy to feel a responsibility to pay more (and more often) than you would do at home, being too generous will only lower the standard of service for future visitors. They will then be less likely to want to return and consequently local businesses will be affected with the workforce being the final losers.

In accommodation and eating places, if you feel the service you received merits a token of appreciation, then it is acceptable and polite to give a gratuity. I'd normally add between 5% and 10% of the bill. To make it simpler, some establishments will have a staff tipping policy (written in menus, on brochures or visible at reception), which may mean donating to a communal staff tip box. If hesitant about tipping hotel/restaurant employees, locate and ask management or owners for guidance.

It is customary to give drivers and guides a tip. To avoid making daily obligations for yourself, make a one-off payment at the last moment (the end of the safari, not after every game drive) with the amount depending on the budget of your trip and the standard of the guide. If these people have been helping with tasks beyond their normal duties (with wheelchair pushing or transfers) then it would not be overgenerous to offer a fatter tip than normal. See Bradt's *Tipping* guide for more advice on this.

REWARDING EXCHANGES

The single most effective way to flatten barriers is to greet people with an open smile. Beyond this, although sweeping generalisations are often inaccurate, there are several things to remember that may make interactions more productive.

Indulge in small talk

When Africans greet and converse with each other they have a genuine interest in the human issues in each other's lives. It is customary throughout the continent for the first few minutes – sometimes longer – of each conversation to be devoted to repartee about family health, wealth and local news. Only once these details have been dealt with will the issues of the moment be discussed. Taking time for small talk will not only be appreciated by your hosts, but it is worthwhile; these are the moments when you really learn about the culture.

Learn some basic language

When meeting strangers, if you can learn two or three words of the local language then this is an immediate respect-earner. In east Africa, saying *Jambo*! is standard banter, but this is 'tourist Swahili' and is not what Swahili speakers would say to each other. Instead of this, try *Hujambo* for a solitary person and *Hamjambo* for a group. If an African greets you with *Jambo*, try *Sijambo* in reply. Even better, especially if speaking to younger people, is to use some *sheng* (Swahili slang). Examples are *Mambo* or *Vipi*, meaning 'How are you?', which can then be answered by saying *Poa*, *Fresh* or *Safi*, meaning 'Okay' or 'Cool'. Similarly, southern Africa is peppered with different local languages. Delving a little deeper into your phrasebook than the majority of visitors is not difficult and the rewards are encouragement enough. If that's too much like self-study, then just ask the locals to teach you; they'll be delighted by your efforts and even if you come away with only a head full of soon-to-be-forgotten phrases the interaction will have been fun, and that was the point of the whole exercise anyway!

Respect customs

As well as what you say, what you wear and what you do can have a real bearing in how you are perceived. Regarding clothing, take note of the dress code mentioned in *Chapter 1, What to Take*, page 36. Showing physical affection to members of the opposite sex in public is generally frowned upon, but in a surprising contrast, in many areas it's common practice for people of the same sex to hold hands while talking or walking; this can just as easily be between two locals or between a local and a tourist. If this happens to you, don't be shocked, feel flattered; if you reach this stage of informality it is a sure sign you have been accepted and are someone worth spending time with.

Photography

Apart from the safety issues surrounding photography (see *Security*, page

108) it is worth remembering that a camera can be offensive if used disrespectfully. It is only human courtesy to ask before taking someone's photograph, even if he or she is not the main subject of the shot. Money might be expected and the final image may be more staged than natural – which is frustrating – but anyone would find it invasive to have strangers from an infinitely wealthier culture constantly taking pictures of their life. Having said all that, modern technology can be used as a tool for interaction with locals. Most digital cameras now allow instant viewing of images, and letting your subjects see these can be fun for all involved. A good next step is to record their names and addresses (email if possible) and fulfil your promises to send some pictures once you return home. For advice on photography, see the box on pages 40–1.

TRAVELLING POSITIVELY

Although international tourism per se cannot be described as environmentally friendly, we have learned that there are ways to limit our impact on the places we visit. Beyond this, most responsible travellers hope that their trip will in some way help preserve these ecosystems and habitats, and improve the lives of their inhabitants.

Of course, the idea of helping Africa is not new. Ever since colonial rule was abolished, a mixture of guilt and social awareness has driven

HAGGLING

One of the highlights of a trip to Africa is the verbal sparring that is often necessary before a price agreeable to both parties is reached. This may be for a taxi fare, a bunch of bananas or a guide's fee, but the majority of a tourist's haggling will be done at a souvenir stall.

The lack of fixed prices is something we are not used to, and there are two ways of looking at it. Firstly, it makes many people paranoid that they are being ripped off. Yes, it's possible that you'll pay more for some items than the bottom price, but instead of letting this irk, consider the seller's respective wealth. Secondly, being too generous will only make the process more difficult for the next buyer, and the haggling process is fun – get stuck in and enjoy it!

When bargaining hard, it does become obvious when the seller's bottom price is near. If you still think it's too much then wander further. You usually find many traders in the same market selling similar items, so it doesn't take long to work out the real value.

These interactions often have more worth, and are more memorable, than the item itself. On balance, I suspect that once the piece has pride of place at home, it's more likely to make you feel good if you know it cost you a couple of dollars more than if you forced the seller to their lowest profit margin.

Westerners to fund and advise struggling African economies. These well-meaning efforts do often provide the basic essentials of life, but pure charity can be humiliating and rarely leads to a self-sufficient and sustainable future for local communities.

So how can we help in a meaningful way? If you wish to donate money from home then I have added a list of very worthwhile international organisations below, and when you are in Africa there is no shortage of ways to spread your wealth.

Positive travel on the road

As stated earlier, there is little social support in Africa, with the result that less able members of society – for whatever reason – often have to resort to begging. Giving spare cash to (or buying food for) these people is seen as a duty of those who can, so it is perfectly acceptable to do so as a tourist. However, do be careful not to be too generous, as this will only cause resentment among onlookers whose week's work might not bring the same reward. Take care also that your beggar is genuine; every profession has its fraudsters. Similarly, it is common to be followed by a procession of children, all demanding anything from sweets to money. Obviously this is a learned behaviour, and while the only items worth considering are useful gifts (like pens) it is more sensible to locate a teacher and give to their school. More than anything here, I'm wary of strengthening the stereotype that wealthy white foreigners are to be milked for money; a continuation of this will only further impede future generations of Africans. Children are often easily satisfied with a quick game or just a fun chat.

To do something even more substantial, keep an eye open for worthy grass-roots projects, and donate, or use or buy their services or products. These can be anything from craft shops and training centres to schools or orphanages – basically any enterprise that is well organised and run, mainly by local people, and directly benefits members of the local community.

An excellent example of such a venture, and one pertaining specifically to people with disabilities, is **Paul's Coffee Shop** in Windhoek (see *Where to Eat*, page 231). This brasserie is named after Paul Hester, an early activist for rights for people with disabilities in Namibia. It aims to train and employ people with disabilities, not only to give them an earned income, but to spread the message into the community that these people are valuable members of society. It is as efficiently run and as competitive as any similar outlet in the capital, and will undoubtedly exist – under its own steam – for as long as its current management and policies remain in place.

Other projects following similar lines are **Wonder Welders** (see box, page 180) and **Sibusiso** (see Kigongoni Lodge, page 177), both in Tanzania, and the **Vanessa Grant Trust** (see box, page 140) in Kenya. If you want to find more, specifically in the region you're visiting, the local operators you use will usually be able to give suggestions. Alternatively, you can see if a project local to the area you are visiting has been posted on Stuff Your Rucksack (see opposite).

Selected international charities and NGOs

ADD (Action on Disability & Development) Vallis Hse, 57 Vallis Rd, Frome, Somerset BA11 3EG, UK; ℓ +44 1373 473064; **f** +44 1373 452075; ⌂ www.add.org.uk. ADD supports organisations of disabled people in Africa & Asia to influence policy & practice to end social exclusion & poverty.

Survival International 6 Charterhouse Bldgs, London EC1M 7ET, UK; ℓ +44 207 687 8700; **f** +44 207 687 8701; **e** info@survival-international.org; ⌂ www.survival-international.org. Survival supports tribal peoples worldwide. In the areas covered by this book these include the Bushmen in Botswana & the Maasai & Ogiek in Kenya.

VSO (Voluntary Services Overseas) 317 Putney Bridge Rd, London, SW15 2PN, UK; ⌂ www.vso.org.uk. VSO is an international development charity that tackles poverty by placing skilled people from around the world in positions of work within the local communities.

WWF (formerly known as the World Wildlife Fund) Av du Mont-Blanc 27, 1196 Gland, Switzerland (International Office); Panda Hse, Weyside Park, Godalming, Surrey GU7 1XR (UK Office); ℓ +44 1483 426444; **f** +44 1483 426409; **e** supporterrelations@wwf.org.uk; ⌂ www.wwf.org. WWF campaigns to stop the accelerating degradation of Earth's natural environment, & to help its human inhabitants live in greater harmony with nature.

STUFF YOUR RUCKSACK – AND MAKE A DIFFERENCE

⌂ www.stuffyourrucksack.com is a website set up by TV's Kate Humble which enables travellers to give direct help to small charities, schools or other organisations in the country they are visiting. Maybe a local school needs books, a map or pencils, or an orphanage needs children's clothes or toys – all things that can easily be 'stuffed in a rucksack' before departure. The charities get exactly what they need and travellers have the chance to meet local people and see how and where their gifts will be used.

The website describes organisations that need your help and lists the items they most need. Check what's needed, contact the organisation to say you're coming and bring not only the much-needed goods but an extra dimension to your travels and the knowledge that in a small way you have made a difference.

⌂ *www.stuffyourrucksack.com Responsible tourism in action*

STAYING IN TOUCH

As with researching the trip, modern technology makes staying in touch when travelling very easy. All major towns and cities have internet cafés and many have hotels with broadband Wi-Fi in place for travellers with their own laptops. Mobile phone networks are spreading rapidly and if your home provider does not allow enough roaming coverage, then local sim cards are cheaply purchased and loaded, giving a temporary number that you can be reached at. It is certainly still possible to escape the waves and find a news-free environment – some camps even advertise themselves as such – but in general, communication is getting rapidly easier. For those of the old school, postcards can be bought practically anywhere so the traditional poolside 'wish you were here' half-truth can still be written.

DEALING WITH MEDICAL PROBLEMS

In the game parks, most large lodges and camps will have a basic medical room with a doctor or nurse on standby. Any issue that is too great to deal with here will result in the patient being transferred by road or air to the nearest well-equipped hospital. This is the main reason why comprehensive medical insurance is essential (see page 29).

In populated areas, the standard of hygiene and medical expertise in clinics varies enormously, as does the availability of medication in pharmacies. Generally speaking, rural services are basic whereas in the big cities it is possible to locate almost everything that is available at home; although you may need to know the generic name of any prescription medicines you take to be able to identify local varieties.

Hotel staff and taxi drivers usually know where the best facilities are, and if cost is not an issue (it shouldn't be, with good insurance), then asking for those frequented by expats should mean you find what you need. Consultation fees and laboratory tests are remarkably inexpensive when compared with most Western countries, so if you do fall sick it would be absurd to let financial considerations dissuade you from seeking medical help. That said, any medical clinics and hospitals that offer services comparable with those in Europe or the US may charge rates to match. Ensure your travel insurance covers this and be prepared to have to prove that you have the funds or insurance cover before you receive treatment.

As with travelling anywhere, anyone with a disability or less common physical condition will find that it helps considerably to know and understand its medical implications. Local doctors, although they are to be trusted about general human health and illnesses typical to their region, cannot be expected to be experts in all fields.

See *Chapter 1* (page 29) for further reading about insurance and *Chapter 2* page 51 for health issues.

SECURITY

Africans are rightly renowned for their hospitality, but as with anywhere there are those who welcome wealthy visitors for less honest reasons. Hence, the continent has its share of petty and serious crime. That said, very few safaris are affected by security issues and it is important to consider that even if you find yourself in a serious situation, the best policy is usually compliance. This is something done equally easily by people with mobility impairments as by those completely able. Indeed, a surprising observation is that because disabled tourists (especially wheelchair users) are generally more noticed by passers-by, they are less likely to be targeted by petty thieves.

On top of this, a common fear is that there is a real threat posed by animals. The whole point of going on safari is to get into wild Africa, and the closer we can get to the wildlife, the more impressed we are. Despite this, injuries from animal attacks are very rare. People visiting bush camps (especially anyone who cannot skip nimbly behind the nearest rock) may want to consider some safety issues a little more carefully than most, but even here, safe visits are quite possible.

THEFT

It is worth trying to understand why tourists are at risk of robbery. This might help allay some anxieties and therefore make for a more enjoyable trip with a deeper understanding of African culture, or may simply make it easier to avoid being a victim.

To Africans, the idea of theft is abhorrent, so much so that an opportunist street thief runs a real risk of being set upon and beaten by an angry mob. Hotel staff and other hospitality workers know that tourism is their livelihood, making them even less likely to risk pilfering. All that said, there is an immense gulf in affluence between the average Westerner and the majority of people they will meet in Africa; standard contents of a wallet in Europe equal monthly earnings of qualified workers in some countries and designer clothing can be worth several months' food for a family. Therefore, it is the visitors' responsibility, and it is in their interest, to be discreet. Apart from anything else, flaunting wealth can be seen as undignified.

The countries covered in this book vary considerably – in general terms Botswana and Namibia are as safe as most of western Europe – but common rules hold for all; bus stations, busy markets and public places where tourists congregate are pickpockets' paradises, big cities after dark are not to be explored on foot and there are always localised danger areas which should be avoided. Disabled people have another advantage: if working with a local personal assistant, he/she will know which taxis to use, which market traders are most dependable, where to go, and, most importantly, where not to go.

If you are unfortunate enough to be the victim of theft, report it immediately to local police – it may take time, be patient – and obtain a signed statement, as your insurance company will probably need this. Also check your insurance policy for the time period within which incidents must be reported as missing this deadline will render any claim invalid. Observing a few simple rules and following them habitually rather than obsessively will greatly reduce your chances of being in such predicaments.

Money and documents

There is always the thorny choice to be made about whether to leave the most valuable items that you don't need – passport, travellers' cheques and credit cards – hidden in the hotel, or to carry them with you on your daily wanderings. If there is a safe in the room, I use it. If not, it then depends on the security of the hotel and my plans for the day. I am very wary of leaving anything of value in my room, even if hidden, and this is especially true if I am going to be accompanied by a local personal assistant or guide. Also, when staying in a safari lodge or similar where the only people around are staff and guests, the chance of theft from your person is even less. Another option is to ask to use the safe at reception; however, because several people may have access to this, it is sensible to put everything in one sealed envelope.

In public places, spread paper valuables and credit cards around your person and if you are travelling with someone, divide them equally between you. For the most important items, I prefer to use a more 'figure-hugging' money belt (hidden next to the skin under a T-shirt or trouser waistband) and not the more practical but bulky (and therefore less covert) 'bum bag' or 'fanny pack'. A handy tip is to keep paper items inside a plastic bag in your money belt, preventing them from being damaged by sweat. As well as this, a good option for wheelchair users is to conceal valuable and less frequently required items within the upholstery of the chair. If the backrest is fixed with velcro, then tucked inside and tied to the frame is ideal, but obviously this should be done in the security and privacy of your room. Of course, this means your chair becomes much more valuable, but how often is it out of your sight? There is a plethora of small wallets and zipped bags on the market that are specifically designed to be attachable to wheelchairs and used as storage space for valuables. My opinion on these is that they are extremely good if they're relatively concealed, but anything like this swinging from your brake handle or joystick is simply temptation. If you use such a device, make sure it's securely fastened somewhere under your chair, preferably between your legs near the front. This makes it difficult to see and reach by strangers, yet still easily accessible to you. Of course, if you use your wheelchair for any manner of money storage, then do not forget to strip it of your cash when you're separated from it (for instance, during flights or bus journeys).

Keep ready cash (local currency and a few dollar bills for tips) in zipped or deep pockets, or in a wallet that is easily accessible to you but difficult to reach by anyone else, and expose only a small amount when paying for items. Before leaving the privacy of your room, it is prudent to think ahead and estimate how much cash you'll need to have available; the last thing you want is to have to search in your socks for small change in a crowded bar. Finally, some feel it's shrewd to stash an emergency fund (maybe a US$100 bill) somewhere very safe.

Banks
When collecting money from banks and forex bureaux, take a taxi or go with a companion and always carefully count then pocket your cash before leaving the teller. While using auto teller machines (ATMs), the same precautions apply in Africa as anywhere; do not allow yourself to be crowded or become engaged in conversation and if your card is swallowed, report it immediately.

Other valuables
It is possible to purchase daypacks that are custom made with a removable compartment to store a camera and accessories, and space for a slim notebook computer tucked against the back support. These backpacks are padded for protection and do provide a degree of disguise, but your camera is not as readily accessible as it would be in a belt-hung pouch. When travelling light – on game drives or town visits – either leave your computer in the room safe or ask if it can be left securely in a safe at reception; however, remember that final responsibility lies with you. A separate hard drive with backups of your photographs should be kept apart from your primary storage at all times, and don't forget that while their small size makes MP3 players and similar items great travelling companions, they are also easily swiped bounty. Buy and take a cheap, waterproof watch if your own is very valuable and leave expensive jewellery at home. As well as potentially saving time and money, this will hugely reduce any worries about theft.

Street wisdom and discretion
When in towns browsing markets and using local transport, blend in and try to look as little like a tourist as possible. This may be difficult if carrying a backpack and camera, but at least appearing confident can be enough to put off a would-be pickpocket. Pack small, valuable items – like glasses or sunglasses – deep in your daypack, as a zipper is easily opened and the topmost item taken without the wearer being aware they've been robbed. Always hold bags securely and get into the habit of moving with purpose, projecting a self-assured air even if you're slightly lost. If you feel threatened or followed then walk near the street as opposed to under shady shop awnings, strike up conversation with a policeman or other official or hail a taxi. Taking care over your stance or location in crowded areas can also lower the risk of theft. One useful tip for wheelchair users who have a daypack slung from their backrest is to park with your back to the wall, making it more difficult for wandering hands to reach pouches containing valuables.

Personal safety first

If you are mugged, do not fight back, give chase or be argumentative. It is better to be as quick, safe and inexpensive as possible and to this end some people carry a 'dummy' wallet to give to a mugger instead of the real one. This would have local cash and a little hard currency but wouldn't include passport, travellers' cheques or credit cards. A holiday can be given a sour taste for a few days and be slightly inconvenienced by theft, but completely ruined if there is personal injury.

After dark

If it can be avoided, do not drive at night and don't walk in African towns and cities after dark. Rural roads are not lit but are littered with dangers – they may have deep pot-holes, pedestrians use them, vehicles often don't have working headlamps and animals like to stand or sleep on them as they are still warm from the heat of the day. Urban streets are often similarly hazardous, although being mugged is the biggest danger here. If you must go out after dark in cities, ask your hotel to organise a taxi or if going somewhere within walking distance, tip one of the security guards to escort you there and back.

DEALING WITH OFFICIALS

There is very little chance of a package tourist having bureaucratic problems while on an organised safari, as the guide will always do any negotiations with police officers or at borders. When, as an independent traveller, you need to deal with officials, always be patient. Procedures might seem infuriatingly slow or the easy way of doing things may appear painfully obvious to you, but it is wise to stay quiet and calm. Getting angry in situations like these will not only mean the process takes longer, but can also increase the risk of being arrested.

It is prudent to be respectfully dressed and to keep cameras out of sight. It is essential not to use them when crossing borders or near government buildings, as these are areas that could be construed as being important for national security and there will usually be a greater police or military presence. Bridges, dams and provincial airports are also areas where it is wise to ask before taking photographs.

Try to obtain receipts for everything paid for and never give bribes. Police officers may hint that money could solve a problem or, for a small gratuity, unscrupulous national park officials can offer to falsify entry documents, allowing a longer stay than that paid for. This is illegal and is at best irresponsible (theft of potential national park income) and at worst dangerous (criminal charges if caught).

VEHICLES

Keep doors locked when in a vehicle in cities, and close windows or hide valuable items if driving slowly through crowded areas. It is too easy for someone to reach into a car and take something – sunglasses or camera – then slip unnoticed into a throng of people. As at home, leaving valuable items visible in parked vehicles is inviting theft.

If you take longer to enter or leave vehicles than most people, be sure to have bags and cameras in full view of yourself or safely stowed away. Depending on how far off the beaten track you venture, tourists using wheelchairs can be an attraction and such spectacles are entertaining, drawing a crowd, causing confusion and consequently creating opportunities for an opportunist thief.

TERRORISM
Despite the car bombs in east Africa in 1998, there is as little chance of being involved in any terrorist attack in the regions covered in this book as there is in most cosmopolitan Western cities.

WILDLIFE
If booking a trip that includes bush camps or camping in a game park without security fencing, then there is the likelihood of wild animals wandering around. This is a wonderful feeling – for many, the whole reason to go on safari – but it does mean that some issues become more pertinent, such as pathway surface and lighting as well as the distances and number of steps between sleeping, dining and reception areas. Because guest safety is their priority, operators and lodge owners are usually very amenable here, providing information as required. They feel a genuine responsibility towards their guests and you may even find that some will refuse a booking if they feel a client is not mobile enough.

Before these fears end all thoughts of adventure, it is worth remembering that not only is such an encounter an extremely rare occurrence, the worst thing to do when threatened by a wild animal is to flee. This will only kick off the 'pursuit' instinct, and nobody – fully able or not – can match a curious cat, a cantankerous buffalo or confused hippo for speed. The best plan of action in the majority of these situations is to stay still, hope the animal loses interest, then make your way to safety.

More seriously, if this is an issue for you then arranging a safari that uses only enclosed lodges or tented camps, or places with built pathways and ubiquitous lighting is not difficult (indeed, more common). If the true wilderness experience is something you really want (and it is worth it) then invest a little more time in research. There are many truly wild places that will accept most levels of physical ability; you can either use your vehicle to drive to your tent or room or be escorted by spear-carrying warriors or armed rangers. In bush camps where the tents don't have telephones and there is no mobile phone reception, there are often compressed-air horns or simple whistles present to attract attention in an emergency.

EXPERIENCING THE WILDERNESS

The climax of the trip is the time spent in the wilderness, and there are few feelings finer than the anticipation of leaving your camp to enter the bush. Most commonly, this will take the form of a game drive, but transport options are not limited to vehicles alone. In some areas boat trips are possible, and game viewing from the water can be more relaxing yet just as rewarding as from rough country tracks. Walking safaris are wonderfully liberating, but probably won't suit most readers of this book, while patiently sitting in a hide or next to a waterhole is often equally exciting and gives more time to notice the little nuances of animal behaviour. Whichever approach you use, it is a game of chance. There are no guarantees but anything is possible. Even if nothing remarkable happens, being in the bush is always invigorating.

At most lodges and camps the traditional scenario is for there to be two game-viewing trips per day. The first usually leaves at sunrise and returns mid morning, while the second (normally the shorter of the two) leaves mid to late afternoon, aiming to return just after sunset. Depending on the trip style and your personal energy levels, the lunch hours can be as relaxing or as active as you wish. For complete luxury, you can read by the pool then slope off for a siesta after lunch; the more conscientious may write postcards sitting by the camp waterhole; and those most energetic might organise their morning photographs, tick off the list of birds spotted and read guidebooks about where they are going next.

There are several reasons why early morning and late afternoon are the most ideal times to see the game. The cool temperatures mean animals are at their most active (for humans, similarly, avoiding the midday sun is also wise), the light is at its softest, so suits photographers best, and the chances of sighting some of the more elusive nocturnal creatures before they find a secluded spot to snooze are very much higher.

For people who baulk at the idea of early starts, guides are flexible and will rearrange schedules as much as possible to suit their clients. This may be particularly relevant to those with disabilities who need more time to get ready. Africa also has an uncanny ability to make 'morning people' of the most practised long-sleepers. Lungfuls of fresh air all day, a short, sharp dusk and soporific campfires mean few stay up late. The constant chirr of insects through the night – interspersed with the warlike roar of a lion or the bold whoop of a hyena – is more of a comfort than a commotion and most people wake early, refreshed and ready to go.

If early mornings are simply not going to be possible, then do try to make full use of the afternoons. If for some reason going out at any time is completely impractical – perhaps only inaccessible boat trips or walking safaris are available – then this is not as gloomy a prospect as it sounds. Some of your most memorable African moments can be had at these times. The lodge or camp takes on a quieter air without other guests and if its location is remote enough then game often wander around, oblivious to the human

HOT-AIR BALLOONING

Floating serenely above a game park presents Africa from a completely different perspective. The silence, apart from the occasional, reassuring, blast of the burners, allows a completely unobtrusive approach to the animals and it is especially worthwhile in some of the larger reserves where a true appreciation of their sheer size can only be gained from above. Balloon flights are usually done in the early morning when the air is still and cool and the game active and visible. They last around an hour and often, at the landing point, are met by crew from the balloon company who prepare a sumptuous bush breakfast complete with champagne. Companies offering this service operate from lodges and camps in the most popular game parks, and are reasonably comparable in style and price.

Some companies will stipulate that the person with limited mobility is accompanied by an assistant, and some will only accept those who are reasonably fit and mobile. Anyone unable to clamber into the basket would need to be lifted, and once inside, a reclined standing position at least is advantageous to be able to have a good view. Some balloons have seating and if you are able to kneel and hold onto the padded sides then it may be possible to see through the floor to the ground. For landing, passengers must be able to sit upright and hang on tightly – often there are rope handles at shoulder height. The pilot will have the last say on whether a person is 'fit to fly' or not.

Balloon flights are a wonderful experience but at several hundred US dollars per person it is worth being sure you will enjoy it. Anyone with mobility difficulties ought to discuss their needs in full with the balloon company before booking.

There are ballooning options in many areas, but the most positive response I've had regarding disability is from the following company, operating in Kenya's Amboseli:

Airborne African Antics Ltd PO Box 38646-00623, Nairobi; ☎ +254 (0)20 204 3939; **e** info@kilimanjaroballooning.co.ke; ⏶ www.kilimanjaroballooning.co.ke

presence or perhaps using it as a screen from predators. Unlike being in a vehicle, there is no pressure from other people to continuously keep moving on, and a patient observer can be rewarded with thrilling experiences. Similarly, birds venture closer without the constant clatter of human activity. Sit still and share your time with them; you won't regret being left behind.

For those on game drives, there are a few tactics that may help you get the most out of your time in the park. Firstly, try not to fall into the trap of chasing only the 'big three'. Lion, leopard and cheetah are without doubt the most coveted species, and when a guide hears that one of these has been sighted, he will want to take you straight to it. While this is understandable, and the majority of clients would only encourage him, there may be other vehicles there too. This makes for unpleasant viewing and might disturb the animals. I'd suggest not lingering too long in this situation. Similarly, zipping around, frantically chasing the fashionable species only will mean you miss a lot of what's really out there. Try to make a point of waiting a little longer at each stop, or each waterhole. Whisper instead of speaking out loud and don't make any sudden movements. It's remarkable what you see and hear once there are no engines running. After a few moments, birdsong begins again, and once the small mammals feel safe, they'll emerge from cover. These moments of perfect serenity are what you came for and there's no need for cats to saunter onto the scene.

above left   **Evening meal at Huab Lodge, Namibia** (J&SH) page 244

top right   **Luxury bungalow at Ongava Lodge, Namibia** (IV) page 249

above right   **Enjoying brunch with Endeavour Safaris in Botswana** (ES) page 21

below   **Lodge on the Zambezi River, Zambia** (IV)

above left   *Mokoro* trip in the Okavango Delta, Botswana (AD) page 273
above right   Feeding the residents, Nairobi Giraffe Centre, Kenya (IV) page 129
below   Surveying the plains, Maasai Mara, Kenya (RJ) pages 145–51

above left **Taking it all in** (J&SH)
above right **Etendeka Crystal Mount, Namibia** (J&SH)

below **Travel by light aircraft within Africa is quite possible** (J&SH) pages 92–3
bottom **Boating at the confluence of the Zambezi and Chobe rivers, Botswana** (J&SH) pages 281–9

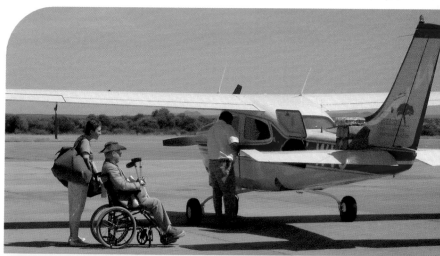

Opposite

top   **Diani Beach, Mombasa, Kenya**
(IV) page 161

middle   **Mt Kilimanjaro seen from Amboseli National Park, Kenya** (IV) pages 151–5

bottom   **Sossusvlei, Namibia** (J&SH) pages 240–3

This page

above left   **Sunset on the Zambezi River, Zambia** (IV) page 291

above right   **Coffee plantation, Tanzania** (IV)

below   **Baobab tree, Tarangire National Park, Tanzania** (IV) pages 181–4

PART TWO
THE GUIDE

KENYA AT A GLANCE

Location	East Africa, north of Tanzania, bordering five countries and with an Indian Ocean coastline
Size	582,650km²
Climate	Varies from tropical to arid, with more temperate highlands and two main rainy seasons (Apr/May and Nov/Dec)
Population	37.9 million (Jul 2008 estimate)
Capital (and largest city)	Nairobi (population almost 3 million in 2007)
Currency	Kenyan shilling (KSh)
Rate of exchange	£1=KSh117; US$1=KSh79; €1=KSh104; (May 2009)
Language	English (official), Kiswahili (official) plus multiple indigenous languages
Religion	Christianity, Islam and traditional beliefs
Time	GMT +3
Electricity	220V, delivered at 50Hz; British-style plugs with three square pins
Weights and measures	Metric
Public holidays	1 Jan, Good Friday, Easter Monday, Labour Day (1 May), Madaraka Day (1 Jun), Moi Day (10 Oct), Kenyatta Day (20 Oct), 25–26 Dec, Id-ul-Fitr
Tourist board	www.kenyatourism.org
International telephone code	+254

4 Kenya

The self-proclaimed 'home of the African safari', Kenya has long been the country most synonymous with this type of holiday. Accordingly, tourism is one of its main industries and those who work within it are experienced, self-assured and professional. There is a multitude of game parks and reserves (eight of which I have covered here) and they offer everything from the enchanting, arid landscapes of Samburu in the north to the world-famous Maasai Mara on the Tanzanian border. The southerly circuit includes the easy-to-visit Amboseli and the two enormous Tsavo national parks; from these, the palm-fringed beaches of Mombasa and the coast are only a short drive on smooth, tar-sealed highway. Nairobi, the capital city, is the hub of east African travel and is worth spending a day or two in for its own highlights.

GENERAL INFORMATION

ACCESS SUMMARY
There are active disability movements in Kenya but as yet there is little effective legislation to force hoteliers to provide access. That said, every Kenyan game park I've covered has at least one lodge or camp with adapted rooms. Although some of the main roads are pot-holed, they are improving and internal flights connect all the most-visited areas of the country.

LOCAL OPERATORS
For local operators catering to people with mobility issues, plus some mainstream operators that have shown a genuine interest in this market, see *Chapter 1, Specialised operators in Africa*, pages 19–20.

KENYAN NATIONAL PARKS AND RESERVES
The wildlife areas covered in this chapter are either national parks, managed by the Kenya Wildlife Service (⌂ *www.kws.org*) or are national reserves, which are run by local councils. The differences between the two are subtle, and most will not affect the majority of visitors. Broadly speaking, national reserves take the needs of the existing human populations more into account

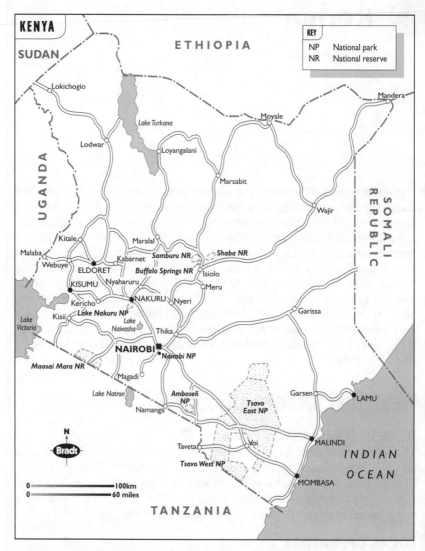

and because they are independent, their policies and styles of management are not as harmonised as those of the national parks.

Entry fees

Unless otherwise stated, non-resident entry fees per person in all parks and reserves covered are US$60/30 for adults/children. As a rule, an entry ticket is valid for 24 hours, though there is usually a bit of flexibility here.

Kenya Wildlife Service smartcards

One important issue is that of smartcards. If you are on an organised tour, this will not be relevant, as your operator and guide will deal with park

SMARTCARD – PARTICIPATING NATIONAL PARKS
The following national parks require Smartcards: Nairobi, Lake Nakuru, Amboseli, Tsavo East and Tsavo West.

Points of issue: Nairobi Park Main Gate, Lake Nakuru Park Main Gate, Tsavo East Park Main Gate (Voi) and Mombasa KWS Offices.
Points of sale: Nairobi Park Main Gate, Lake Nakuru Park Main Gate, Tsavo East Park Main Gate (Voi), Aberdare HQ, Mombasa KWS Offices, Malindi Marine Park, Amboseli Park Meshanani Gate, Tsavo West Park Mtito Andei Gate.

payment. However, if you are travelling independently, you need to take more care when planning your itinerary. Smartcards were brought in by the KWS to thwart corruption by unscrupulous officials at park gate level. They are required at some, but not all national parks and replace cash payments. The size of a credit card, they can be purchased at 'points of issue', 'loaded' by buying credit at 'points of sale' and are debited when you enter a participating park. It gets complicated because not all entry gates are 'points of sale' and fewer still are 'points of issue' (see above for details). If flying into these parks, your smartcard must be obtained and loaded in advance, as there are no points of issue or sale at park airfields. All other parks still require cash payments.

NAIROBI

This vibrant capital comes with an undeserved reputation for being significantly more dangerous than other African cities. There's no doubt that walking around after dark is not advisable, but I suspect Nairobi is better known in this respect because it has so many more foreign tourists than its contemporaries. Care must be taken in the city, but don't avoid it. Nairobi has many good faces and should be given more credit for these.

The modern-day city developed from a 19th-century railway supply camp. The site was chosen mainly because it had a high altitude (1,600m), which meant a relatively cool climate and consequently little or no risk of malaria. These factors hold true today, further enhancing Nairobi's appeal as a safe staging post for a safari. The population is currently just under three million people, and is very cosmopolitan in make-up. Unlike many cities in Africa, there's also a good spread of wealth between the various communities; when visiting a restaurant or attraction in Nairobi you are as likely to be sitting or standing next to a local Kenyan family (of any race) as next to an overseas tourist.

As the start or end point of the vast majority of east African safaris, most visitors will go through Nairobi, if not stay there. Don't panic if you discover

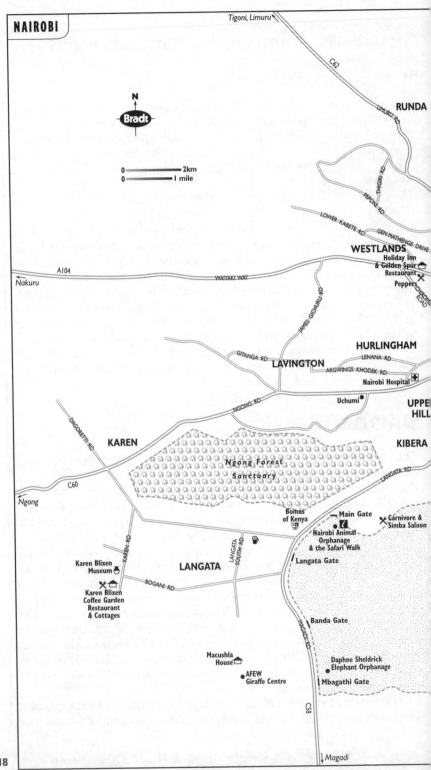

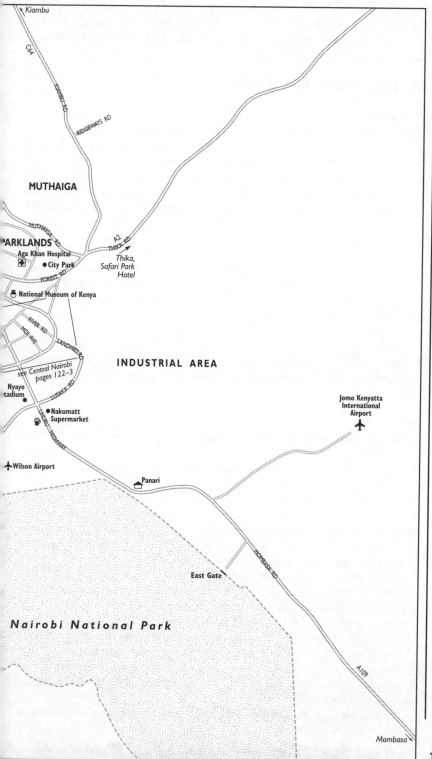

you have a day or two in the city – on the contrary, if possible, plan it in. It is a good place to recuperate after a long flight, and if you want to explore then there's plenty to see and do.

GETTING THERE AND AWAY

By road
Trunk routes from all directions are tar sealed and good quality as they approach Nairobi, but inner-city congestion can be horrendous. Although great efforts are being made to improve the situation, the current volume of traffic is too great for an infrastructure that was designed decades ago. The result is that a peak-hour arrival could mean hours of traffic jams. The Tanzanian border crossing at Namanga is approximately 170km south (2½ hours' drive) and Mombasa is just under 500km southeast (but can take anything up to nine hours, depending on traffic and roadworks).

Comfortable shuttle buses run daily from Nairobi to Arusha in Tanzania (leaving from the airport and major town centre hotels) and there is a good network of mainline coaches and minibuses to the other areas of Kenya. However, none of these services have facilities for disabilities; see page 89 for advice on using public transport.

By rail
As with public transport on the roads, none of Kenya's rail services have facilities for disabled travellers (see page 91 for the Nairobi–Mombasa journey).

By air
Jomo Kenyatta International Airport (20 minutes' drive from Nairobi) handles all heavy international traffic and consequently has aisle chairs and staff trained in their use. However, if you require your own wheelchair on arrival then it is essential to remind aircrew to inform the Kenyan ground staff of this about an hour before landing, otherwise you'll certainly be met at the aeroplane door by an airport chair. Any chair users who are not strong would be wise to ask for assistance too, because although there are no steps on the way, there is a steep ramp (about 15m long) down to immigration that most will require help with.

From immigration, a flight of stairs leads down to the arrivals hall, but this can be avoided by using a lift. If this is out of service then wheelchairs are diverted via a service lift, meaning they somewhat bizarrely exit the airport at a security gate and then must re-enter through the main door to reclaim their baggage. It's not something to worry about; airport workers and security staff have the system working perfectly, which suggests that the main lifts are quite often out of order. The pavement is level with the main doors (which are automatic) and there are kerb drop-offs at the parking area outside.

There are bathroom facilities with level entry for people of both sexes at

JKIA's departure lounges (low toilets) and arrivals hall (raised toilets).

Wilson Airport (a few kilometres from the centre of the city) caters only to light aircraft. This is the normal departure point if flying into the parks and reserves in Kenya. It is a basic airport, with no special facilities. Anybody needing help will receive it, but since the aircraft are all small, entering and exiting will mean more manhandling than with specialised equipment.

GETTING AROUND
A fleet of ex-London black cabs used to be dominant amongst Nairobi's throng of public transport vehicles. These were ideal for wheelchair users, but are less commonly seen nowadays. The current options (standard taxis, *matatus* and minibuses) are a cheap way of getting around but anyone who usually uses accessible vehicles should see *Public transport*, page 89. Go Africa Safaris (see page 19) does have accessible vehicles that may be available for daily hire in Nairobi.

WHERE TO STAY
Nairobi Serena (184 rooms) Kenyatta Av; ☎ 020 282 2000; **f** 020 272 5184; **e** from website; ⌂ www.serenahotels.com ③⁺ ♿
The Nairobi Serena's most inclusive feature is that there is a wheelchair available at the hotel. There are no rooms designed for disabled guests & although there is an accessible lift, the buffet in the main restaurant is up 12 steps & the Mandari Restaurant is itself only entered by using 12 steps. The swimming pool can be reached using ramps & pool entry is via 8 steps with no handrail.

Standard rooms have queen-sized beds (52); superior rooms have king-sized beds (61). Both have very small bathrooms with no support rails, no space to manoeuvre a wheelchair & bathroom doors are 60cm. Baths (49) have fixed showerheads. On a positive note, doorways into the rooms themselves are wide (80) & superior rooms have a large balcony with a small threshold (1).
Business suite: May suit someone who can walk, but is less steady on his/her feet. Doorway (60) is level; bath (49) has 2 fitted handles & 1 wall-mounted support rail (20); step-in shower (5) has 1 diagonal support rail (midpoint 105) & round taps. **$$$$$**

Sarova Stanley (217 rooms) Corner of Kimathi St & Kenyatta Av; ☎ 020 275 7000; **f** 020 222 9388; **e** thestanley@sarovahotels.com; ⌂ www.sarovahotels.com ⓪ ♿ ♿
A steep ramp from street level avoids several steps. The swimming pool is on the top floor – so reached using the lift & several custom-made ramps – & is entered via 6 steps or a ladder. Dining areas are level, with tables >65cm. The lift has automatic doors (90) & the highest control is 120cm. The Stanley has 4 rooms designed for ease of access, with baths but no showers.

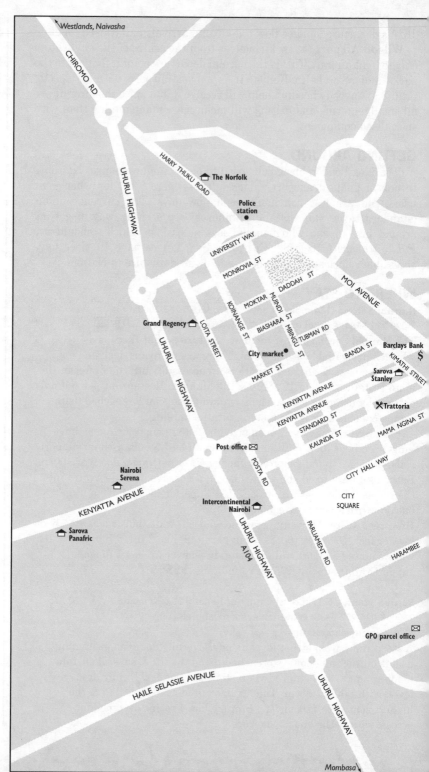

Westlands, Naivasha

CHIROMO RD

UHURU HIGHWAY

HARRY THUKU ROAD

The Norfolk

Police station

UNIVERSITY WAY

MONROVIA ST

MOKTAR MUNDI DADDAH ST

KOINANGE ST

BIASHARA ST

MBINGU ST

TUBMAN RD

MOI AVENUE

Grand Regency

LOITA STREET

City market

MARKET ST

BANDA ST

Barclays Bank $

KIMATHI STREET

Sarova Stanley

UHURU HIGHWAY

KENYATTA AVENUE

KENYATTA AVENUE

STANDARD ST

KAUNDA ST

Trattoria

MAMA NGINA ST

Post office

POSTA RD

CITY HALL WAY

Nairobi Serena

KENYATTA AVENUE

Intercontinental Nairobi

UHURU HIGHWAY

A104

CITY SQUARE

PARLIAMENT RD

HARAMBEE

Sarova Panafric

GPO parcel office

HAILE SELASSIE AVENUE

UHURU HIGHWAY

Mombasa

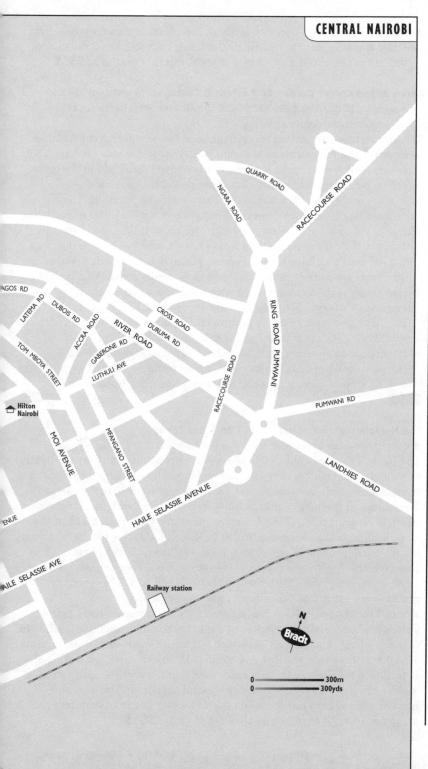

CENTRAL NAIROBI

QUARRY ROAD

NGARA ROAD

RACECOURSE ROAD

AGOS RD

LATEMA RD

DUBOIS RD

ACCRA ROAD

CROSS ROAD

DURUMA RD

RIVER ROAD

GABERONE RD

TOM MBOYA STREET

LUTHULI AVE

RING ROAD PUMWANI

RACECOURSE ROAD

Hilton
Nairobi

MOI AVENUE

MFANGANO STREET

PUMWANI RD

ENUE

HAILE SELASSIE AVENUE

LANDHIES ROAD

AILE SELASSIE AVE

Railway station

N

Bradt

0 ——————— 300m
0 ——————— 300yds

Adapted rooms: level doorway is 90cm; bed (45) has transfer space, light switches & phone; door to ensuite (90) is level; bath (50) has 2 rails (10); washbasin is 69cm; toilet (40) has 1 support rail (85) next to it. **$$$$**

Karen Blixen Coffee Garden Restaurant & Cottages (18 cottages) 336 Karen Rd, Karen; ✆ 020 882 138; f 020 882 508; e info@blixencoffeegarden.co.ke; ⌕ www.blixencoffeegarden.co.ke 🖳

The airy cottages are dotted around spacious lawns, offering comfortable seclusion & the Karen Blixen Museum (see *What to See and Do*, page 130) is a short walk away. Paths are irregularly shaped slabs laid in the grass, therefore not completely smooth but quite passable. Access to the swimming pool is level & entry is via 7 steps with no handrail. The restaurant has level entry from the front patio & a wheelchair is available. Entrance verandas of all accommodation are up at least 1 step from the path (usually 2) & the majority of rooms have a reasonably wide doorway (78). 2 sgl beds (66) have transfer space, phone & light switch & can be pushed together to make a dbl. Bathrooms generally consist of a bath (51), step-in shower (10) & a washbasin with no access underneath it.

Faraghani Cottage: Meaning 'private' in Swahili, Faraghani is the cottage with the most spacious bathroom. Dbl doors (139) are up 2 steps (6 & 5); dbl bed (74) has transfer space & light switch; highest switch is <140cm; door to ensuite (73) is level; bath (47) has transfer space & a slightly extended area at the foot end, which could be used as a seat to aid transfers; step-in shower is 10cm; toilet (41) has front transfer space. **$$$$**

The Norfolk (168 rooms) Harry Thuku Rd; ✆ 020 221 6940; e Kenya.reservations@fairmont.com; ⌕ www.fairmont.com 🖳 🛏 🖼 🖳

The Norfolk is spread out in 6 blocks with stairways in many areas. Rightly or wrongly, the policy is to try to 'confine physically challenged persons' to the 2 blocks which have the easiest access, & any steps here are ramped. The 6 steps at the main entrance have been bypassed with an extremely steep, brick-built ramp (50%) & similar measures have been taken at the steps leading to the swimming pool & health club. All this means that even the most independent of wheelers will need to accept help at times. However, there is 1 room (Room 715) that has been very well adapted & renovations are planned, after which there should be 4. The dining areas are accessed using low ramps & all tables are >65cm.

Room 715: Doorway (76) is ramped; bed (50) has transfer space, light switch & phone; highest switch is <140cm; bathroom door (82) is level; bath (54) has a long support rail (35), which follows its shape all the way around 1 long & 1 short side; the foot-end of the bath has an extended seating area to facilitate transfers & there is space next to it for a wheelchair; roll-in shower has seat, transfer space & horizontal support rail; washbasin (70) has low mirror, grab rail & round taps; toilet (40) has front transfer space & a support rail (77) that swings up out of the way. **$$$$**

Intercontinental Nairobi (376 rooms) City Hall Way; ☏ 020 320 0000;
e reservations@interconti.co.ke; ⌖ www.intercontinental.com 🄿 🄰🅁 🖳
This hotel has the most comprehensively accessible room in the city, if not
in Kenya. Public areas – including dining rooms – are all step-free, with
smooth floors, wide doors & regular seating. The pool has level access & 4
steps to enter the water. Lifts have automatic doors (105) plenty of turning
space & highest controls are <140cm.
Room 362: Adapted room, has features for sensory as well as motor
disabilities. Level doorway (83); bed (59) has transfer space, phone & light
switches; all switches & handles are <140cm; 2 phones (1 easily reached
from bed, 1 in bathroom) have extra-large buttons plus ring tone, flashing
light & pillow vibrator to alert about incoming calls; bathroom door (83) is
level; roll-in shower has seat, lever taps & 2 support rails (58 & 87);
washbasin (72) has lever taps & low mirror; toilet (40) has support rail
(85) within reach; both toilet & shower seat have front & side transfer
space; there is an emergency alarm cord above the bed & 1 in the
bathroom to alert staff; finally, Room 362 is connected to the neighbouring
room – 360 – via a connecting door, ideal if you travel with family or a
personal assistant. **$$$$**

The Panari Hotel (136 rooms) Mombasa Rd; ☏ 020 694 6000;
e info@panarihotels.com; ⌖ www.panarihotels.com 🄿 ▭
The Panari Hotel has mesmeric views out onto the distant Ngong Hills &
a spacious lift to reach this height. The swimming pool is up 7 steps & the
main Red Garnet Restaurant has level access, with tables of 61cm.
Deluxe rooms: Offer the most accessible accommodation, mainly on
account of space; there is 1 of these on each floor up to the 11th. Beds (59)
have transfer space, light switches & phone; highest control is thermostat
(160); door to ensuite (66) is level; inside the bathroom there is room to
turn around in a wheelchair, but no transfer space or rails next to the
toilet (40); the bath has a handheld showerhead, fitted handles, transfer
space & 1 support rail (which is near one end & designed to be used when
standing & showering in the bath); step-in shower (10) has doorway (55);
washbasin not accessible underneath & has star taps. Bathrooms in
standard & superior rooms are smaller – the former have only a bath &
the latter have a shower in the bath. **$$$$**

Sarova Panafric (153 rooms) Kenyatta Av; ☏ 020 272 0822; **f** 020 272 6356;
e panafric@sarovahotels.com; ⌖ www.sarovahotels.com 🄿 🄰🅁 🖳
This hotel has made admirable efforts in recent years to open its doors to
all. There are now 2 rooms dedicated to less-mobile guests & the Flame
Tree Restaurant near reception is on 1 level with dining tables >65cm.
Reception is up 1 step from the vehicle drop-off point, but this has been
ramped. Unfortunately, the adapted rooms are upstairs & even the
strongest of wheelchair users will need help with the next ramp, a short,
steep push from reception to the lift. Lift doors (86) are automatic &

highest control is 106cm. The swimming pool & poolside bar/restaurant are down 15 steps.

Rooms 407 & 408: Have accessible features – doorways (94) have slight ramps; beds (60) have transfer space & light switches, but no phones; all handles & switches are <140cm; level door into ensuite is 97cm; roll-in shower has curved threshold (3), handheld showerhead, lever tap (78) & 1 diagonal support rail (midpoint 110) within reach from the washing area; washbasin has 1 vertical support rail, lever taps & low mirror but no access underneath; toilet has side & front transfer space & 1 fixed horizontal support rail (80). **$$$$**

Holiday Inn (171 rooms) Parklands Rd; ☎ 020 374 0920; **f** 020 374 8823; **e** admin@holidayinn.co.ke; ☝ www.holidayinn.com 🅿️ 🖼️
This lush hotel has a pleasant earthy feel to it, with smooth brick & concrete pathways running through well-maintained lawns. Flowers, bushes & well-established trees make it unusually garden-like for a chain hotel & there's plenty of seating in public areas. It is also one of the more accessible hotels in the city, with (in 2008) 1 adapted room & plans for more inclusive developments. Although the main entrance is stepped, an accessible entrance is at the rear, with disabled parking & a ramp; a wheelchair is available at reception. The gift shop & reception are both up 1 small step but all other areas, including both restaurants, are level or ramped.

Room 103: Very close to reception. Doorway (85) is level; dbl bed (58) has transfer space, phone & light switch; doorway into ensuite (84) is level; roll-in shower has handheld showerhead & round taps (92), & although it is small (squeezed into a corner), it is possible to enter in a standard wheelchair; bath (45) has transfer space, handheld showerhead & fitted handles; toilet (40) is between the washbasin & the shower, meaning the sloped shower area must be entered if a side transfer is necessary; washbasin (72) has lever taps & low mirror. Other ground-floor rooms close by are similar, but do not have the roll-in shower. **$$$$**

Hilton Nairobi (287 rooms) Mama Ngina St; ☎ 020 279 0000; **e** hilton.nairobi@hilton.com; ☝ www.hilton.com 🅿️ 🛗
From street level, there is a ramp to reception. Once there, the dining area is entirely level & all tables are >65cm. The swimming pool is reached using the lift then wheelchairs must take a steep, temporary ramp. The pool itself is entered using a ladder. There are 2 identical rooms with accessible features & apparently portable ramps are available if wheelchair users prefer standard (stepped entry) rooms. The lift has automatic doors (85), turning space inside & highest control is 155cm.

2 accessible rooms: Level doorways (94); king-sized bed (60) has a light switch & phone; level bathroom door (85); bath (49) has fitted handles (but no support rail) & transfer space; the toilet & washbasin are surrounded by a plethora of rails, 2 vertical & 2 horizontal – 1 of the latter 2 swings up, allowing a side transfer; washbasin (93) has knee-space only. **$$$$**

Grand Regency Hotel (194 rooms) Uhuru Highway; **📞** 020 221 1199; **f** 020 221 7120; **e** reservations@grandregency.co.ke; 🕾 www.grandregency.co.ke 🔲 ▭
Entrances to the hotel & all public areas (apart from the swimming pool) are level. To reach the pool, 10 steps must be navigated then a ladder is the only means of entry. The main restaurant is on a mezzanine, which can be accessed using a lift. Many tables are >65cm. I was told there are 2 rooms (Rooms 411 & 416) with features for limited mobility, but these were occupied during my visit so have not been seen. The following is a description of the bathroom from a 'lounge room', which is apparently identical: doorway is 85cm; highest switch is 158cm; bath (58) has support rail (30) & 2 fitted handles; step-in shower (19) has no seat & or support rails; washbasin not accessible & toilet has front transfer space only. **$$$**

The Safari Park Hotel (205 rooms) Thika Rd; **📞** 020 363 3000; **f** 020 363 3919; **e** reservations@safariparkhotel.co.ke; 🕾 www.safaripark-hotel.com 🔲 ▭ ▭
A few kilometres northeast of the city centre on Thika Rd, the Safari Park is set in expansive grounds. Access throughout is reasonably smooth crazy paving that has been ramped next to all steps in public areas, & a wheelchair is available. The different restaurants vary in accessibility: African, Italian & international are all approached via ramps, albeit sometimes steep, while the Chinese/Japanese option is upstairs. Staff will help if Asian is the preferred option. Swimming pools can all be reached avoiding steps; 1 (decorative) pool has a roll-in ramped edge that could be used by wheelchairs while others have only ladders or steps to enter the water.
Room 620: The only officially 'wheelchair accessible' unit. Doorway (88) is ramped; bed (61) has transfer space & phone, but notably no light switch; highest switch is 151cm; bathroom doorway (94) is level; bath (49) has wall-mounted support rail (5), fixed showerhead, lever tap & transfer space; washbasin has lever tap but no access underneath; toilet (40) has transfer space next to it & a wall-mounted, fixed, horizontal support rail (87) within reach.
Block 100: Has rooms accessed with no step; other ground-floor rooms are up at least 1 step but temporary wooden ramps are available. Superior & deluxe versions have baths (52) with built-in handles & a fixed showerhead but bathrooms are tight for wheelchair space & some are up a step from the bedroom with standard doorways (75). Some standard rooms have step-in showers. **$$$**

Macushla House (6 rooms) Nguruwe Rd, Langata; **📞** 020 891 987; **f** 020 891 971; **e** macushla@africaonline.co.ke; 🕾 www.macushla.biz 🔲
The most strikingly accessible feature at Macushla House is the wheelchair-friendly wooden walkway. This leads to the owner's living quarters, but appears more like a tourist attraction, spanning over wild bush & cleverly incorporating a viewpoint looking out on to the Ngong Hills. The attractive pool is down 1 step from the house, has 7 steps to

enter & has a safety rope around the inside edge. The rest of the complex is not deliberately accessible, but 4 of the 6 rooms are inside the main building & therefore on the same level as the dining room, study & lounge. Dining tables are >65cm. Although bathroom doors can be narrow (68), there is enough space for wheelchairs inside & furniture consists of a bath, step-in shower & a toilet (40) with front-transfer space only. **$$**

WHERE TO EAT

There is no shortage of restaurants in and around the centre of Nairobi, and it should be possible to find something for every budget and taste. Most are ground floor and many have access without steps. However, apart from those connected with accessible hotels, I've yet to find one with a fully accessible toilet. Four that are worth mentioning are as follows:

The Carnivore & Simba Saloon Off Langata Rd; ☏ 020 605 935; **e** reservations@carnivore.co.ke; ⌂ www.carnivore.co.ke; ⊘ 12.00–14.30 for lunch & 19.00–22.30 for dinner daily. This popular restaurant is probably Nairobi's best-known eatery. The emphasis is on grilled meat, which waiters carry around the restaurant on huge skewers. There are no steps & just a slight downhill slope from the parking area into the building but toilets have no features for disability. Tables are >65cm. **$$$$$**

Peppers Restaurant Parklands Rd, Westlands (opposite the Holiday Inn); ☏ 020 375 5267/8; **e** peppersrestaurant@kenyaweb.com; ⊘ 12.00–15.00 for lunch & 18.00–23.00 for dinner Mon–Fri; 12.00–23.00 Sat–Sun. The extensive menu contains dishes from Europe, China & India. Situated only about 100m from the Holiday Inn, this is an ideal change of scenery if you have several days there. At night it is sensible to ask an *askari* (a guard or watchman in Swahili) from the hotel to escort you to the restaurant, as the street is unlit. The entrance is up 1 small step; otherwise, the building is level. Toilets are on ground level but are not adapted for accessibility. Tables are >65cm. **$$$$**

Golden Spur Restaurant (part of the Holiday Inn – see page 126) ☏ 0374 6769; ⌂ www.spur.co.za; ⊘ 07.00–23.00 daily. This wild-west themed eatery is more fun & family than class & culture, but the food's good & staff are friendly & efficient. It specialises in sizzling steaks, burgers & spare ribs, but chicken, fish & pizzas are available & the menu also covers b/fasts & lunches. Toilets are standard. **$$$**

Trattoria Restaurant On corner of Wabera & Kaunda St in the city centre; ☏ 020 340 855/240 205; **e** admin@trattoria.co.ke; ⊘ 07.00–24.00 daily. Good-quality Italian food but doesn't take credit cards. 1 step leads up into the building, but the terrace outside is at pavement level. There is no downstairs toilet. Tables are >65cm. **$$$**

OTHER PRACTICALITIES

Nairobi has several banks and bureaux de change in the city centre (main bank branches have ATMs). The main post office is on Kenyatta Avenue and pharmacies and internet cafés are in most street malls. For anyone who wants to stock up on food or buy equipment – anything from batteries to sleeping bags – the main Nakumatt superstore on Uhuru Avenue is the best one-stop shop.

Medical services

Nairobi's best hospitals are the **Aga Khan Hospital** (*3rd Parklands Av;* ✆ *020 374 2531;* ⊕ *www.agakhanhospitals.org*) and the **Nairobi Hospital** (*Argwings Kodhek Rd;* ✆ *020 284 5000/6000;* **e** *hosp@nairobihospital.org;* ⊕ *www.nairobihospital.org*).

WHAT TO SEE AND DO

With the exception of the National Museum (see below), few of the city's attractions have made access a priority. That said, most can be tackled, even if wheelchairs are involved. The following is a selection of some of the most popular:

Bomas of Kenya

(*Forest Rd, off Langata Rd;* ✆ *020 891 802;* **e** *info@bomasofkenya.co.ke;* ⊕ *www.bomasofkenya.co.ke;* ⊕ *14.30–16.00 Mon–Fri, 15.30–17.15 Sat/Sun;* 🎫 *adult KSh600, child KSh300*) The main amphitheatre at Bomas of Kenya – which hosts a wide range of cultural events performances – is approachable with no steps from the vehicle drop-off point several metres away. The public toilets have six steps and although there is (apparently) a ramp available, none are adapted for accessibility.

Daphne Sheldrick Elephant Orphanage

(*PO Box 15555, Mbagathi, 00503;* ✆ *020 891 996;* **e** *rc-h@africaonline.co.ke;* ⊕ *www.sheldrickwildlifetrust.org;* ⊕ *11.00–12.00;* 🎫 *viewing is a min of US$5 pp*) The David Sheldrick Wildlife Trust is involved in many conservation projects in Kenya. This centre, near Nairobi National Park, aims to rear and rehabilitate rescued baby elephants and rhinos. Daily feeding sessions are open to the public, but visitors must be there by 11.00. Although pathways are rough and there's no seating at the feeding area, the whole complex is at ground level or up a maximum of one step. A visit is well worth the discomfort.

AFEW Giraffe Centre

(*Langata;* ✆ *020 890 952;* ⊕ *www.giraffecenter.org;* ⊕ *10.00–17.30 daily;* 🎫 *adult KSh500, child KSh250*) Also known as the Giraffe Centre, the African Fund for Endangered Wildlife (AFEW) Kenya was set up to save the threatened Rothschild giraffe. Since its inception numbers in the wild have more than doubled. The education centre is set in more than 100 acres of indigenous forest and although the nature trail may be difficult, the feeding and viewing area is very worthwhile. Giraffes may be tall, but you'll not miss out just because you're not on top of the viewing gantry (which is up 13 steps). These graceful animals are also inquisitive, and if you have a handful of giraffe food (given out at the centre), then you can be sure they'll stoop to your level.

The bar and reception are on ground level and the shop is up two small steps (5). The ground is not uniformly flat (a mixture of concrete slabs, pebble stones and crazy paving) and the path to the toilets is particularly rough, though still wheelchair-pushable with help. The gents' and ladies' toilets are up one and two steps respectively. Everything is within a 50m radius.

Karen Blixen Museum
(*Karen Rd, Karen;* ℃ *020 882 779;* ⌂ *www.blixencoffeegarden.co.ke;* ⊘ *09.00–17.00 daily;* ℬ *KSh500*) Less than 1km from the Karen Blixen cottages, it's easy to feel part of Kenya's colonial history here. Blixen, of *Out of Africa* fame, lived here in the early 20th century while running a coffee farm. Her house is now a museum and still contains original furnishings. There is no more than 1 step to negotiate.

Nairobi National Park
(*Langata Rd;* ℃ *020 602 121;* e *nnp@kws.org;* ⌂ *www.kws.org;* ⊘ *06.30–18.00 daily; smartcard required; park entry fee US$40;* ℬ *vehicle entry fee KSh800*) This easy-to-reach park gives the chance to see much of Africa's wildlife without venturing far from the city centre. Game drives can be done in the park's vehicles – standard nine-seater minibuses – or in private cars. The aerial walkway (opened in 2000) runs 6m up in the trees and Kenya Wildlife Service assure me that it has ramped access but that wheelchair users will need assistance. I assume from this that it is steep. Pathways to the walkway are apparently mazeras (sandstone) and are therefore hard and smooth.

National Museum of Kenya
(*Museum Hill;* ℃ *020 374 2161–4;* e *nmk@museums.or.ke;* ⌂ *www.museums. or.ke;* ⊘ *09.30–18.00 daily – inc public holidays;* ℬ *adult KSh800, child KSh400*) This highly rated museum closed in 2005 for renovations and opened again in 2008. The plans included ramps throughout with slopes of not more than 5%, two lifts to the upper floor, wide doorways and accessible toilets. Having not yet visited or heard first-hand reports, I cannot be sure this is the case, but would be surprised if not.

Nairobi Animal Orphanage
(*Langata Rd;* ℃ *020 500 622;* ⊘ *08.30–17.30 daily;* ℬ *adult KSh500, child KSh250*) Just at the Langata Road entrance to Nairobi National Park, this

education centre is the easiest option here for wheelchair users. The enclosures are all on one level and pathways through the grounds are hard, smooth and weatherproof. Viewing the animals is generally as easy from a sitting as from a standing position. The negatives are that there is not a lot of seating (anyone who needs to rest regularly may find it tiring) and there is a peculiar trench in front of the toilet blocks, effectively barring wheelchairs.

NORTH TOWARDS SAMBURU

Mount Kenya has a lot of lodges and hotels dotted around its lower slopes, and although climbing the mountain is not going to suit most readers of this book, this area is an ideally located stopover to break the journey north to the Samburu reserves. With Sweetwaters and Lewa, there is also the opportunity to spend an extra day or two in a private and extremely well-run nature conservancy.

GETTING THERE AND AWAY

Main roads around this area are either good-quality tar or well-graded gravel. Either way, the accommodations listed here are all within about two hours' drive of each other and around three hours' drive north of Nairobi and south of Samburu. There are small airfields near Nyeri and Nanyuki and one on Lewa Downs estate, so those who prefer this method of transport can choose which best suits their destination. (For access issues in small airfields, see page 92.)

WHERE TO STAY

Lewa Wildlife Conservancy Safari Camp (12 tents) ☎ 020 600 457; **e** info@bush-and-beyond.com; ⏏ www.bush-and-beyond.com 🔲
Near Isiolo, Lewa Conservancy has a solid background in conservation in Kenya & now supports thriving populations of threatened species including the black rhino & Grevy's zebra. In early 2008, a tent at the Safari Camp was adapted to be 'user friendly'. It is close to the main house – hence a short walk from the bar & dining facilities – & the path to it is smooth. There is a level, stone walkway & entrance. The tent entry is zipped & beds (58), roll-in shower & toilet have transfer space. Game drives must be done in Lewa's vehicles, which are Land Cruisers with bench seats & a 'cut out' for easy entrance. **$$$$$**

Sweetwaters Tented Camp, Ol Pejeta Conservancy (39 tents) ☎ 020 284 2333; **f** 020 271 8100; **e** from website; ⏏ www.serenahotels.com 🔲 🔲
Close to Nanyuki, Sweetwaters is a highly rated camp. It has its own game conservancy, waterhole & – unique in Kenya – a chimpanzee sanctuary. There are level pathways through most of the complex though these are a little narrow in places, forcing wheelchairs onto the grass.

Restaurant access is also step-free. None of the bathroom facilities have support rails, but the newer tents near the front of the site apparently have roll-in showers & level entry to the toilet area. **$$$$**

Outspan Golf & Country Club (45 rooms) ☎ 020 445 2095–9;
e info@aberdaresafarihotels.com; ⌂ www.aberdaresafarihotels.com [🖱]
A colonial-style hotel situated in well-tended gardens in Nyeri, Outspan was in the midst of a much-needed renovation in 2008. The Kirinyaga conference room & tavern have level entry while the dining room & expansive veranda are down several steps, for which a solid wooden ramp is kept. The pool is reached via 4 steps or a grassy slope & there are many steps on the way to the river walk. The accommodation is mixed, & some is more accessible than others.
Room 25: Scheduled to be refurbished (& adapted) in late 2008 & will be the most suitable. It has a connecting door to the next room & will therefore be ideal if you are travelling with an assistant or family. Currently, Rooms 12a & 14 have spacious bathrooms (entrance doorway is 75cm) with standard baths, though toilets are in small separate rooms with narrow doorway (65). **$$$**

Naro Moru River Lodge (49 rooms) ☎ 062 62023; **f** 020 444 5309;
e mt.Kenya@africaonline.co.ke; ⌂ www.alliancehotels.com [3⁺] [🖼]
Between Nyeri & Nanyuki, this lodge is set on a slope, so inherently difficult to make completely accessible. As a result, there are several steps to negotiate around the grounds & paths are sloped in places. The attractive swimming pool is entered using shallow steps & the poolside café is up 1 step. The dining room is 5 steps up from the cement paving.
The most accessible chalet: Has a custom-built plyboard wooden ramp to mount the 2 steps at the doorway (72); beds (50) have transfer space, light switch & phone; bathroom door (75) is level; roll-in shower has round taps (125); toilet (40) has front & side transfer space but washbasin (65) has a high mirror & round taps. Other rooms (standard, superior & deluxe) have between 1 & 10 steps at doorways & have either step-in showers or baths. **$$**

Mountain Rock Lodge (28 rooms) ☎ 020 242 133;
e info@mountainrockkenya.com; ⌂ www.mountainrockkenya.com [🖱] [🖼]
Close to Naro Moru River Lodge & west of Mount Kenya, this is a traditional, basic & relaxed retreat. The majority of overseas guests are climbers tackling the mountain, but that doesn't exclude the lodge from the itineraries of those with less energetic plans. Reception is down a steep ramp from the car park then the cosy dining & bar areas are all on 1 level. Rooms are along hard, yet narrow, paved walkways & temporary, wooden ramps are available to cross the 1-step entry threshold. 'Superior' accommodation has log fires – a must during the colder months – & several rooms in this class have very small roll-in showers. **$$**

OTHER PRACTICALITIES

Road trips heading north from Nairobi to the Samburu region are invariably broken by food, fuel, toilet and supply stops in Nanyuki and/or Isiolo. Although Isiolo is the nearest town to Samburu with reliable services, Nanyuki is larger and the Barclays Bank here has a (steeply) ramped entrance.

SAMBURU, BUFFALO SPRINGS AND SHABA NATIONAL RESERVES

The Samburu ecosystem is the most northerly region covered in this guide and comprises three national reserves: Samburu, Buffalo Springs and Shaba. These reserves were initially established in 1948 within one boundary, called the Samburu Isiolo Game Reserve, but are now independently managed by Samburu and Isiolo local councils. Despite this, the communities co-operate well and entry fees for one reserve are now valid for all three, greatly simplifying a visit to the area.

Rugged and remote, the whole region is semi-arid and sparsely populated, with flat plains of scrubby acacia studded by volcanic outcrops. It is the traditional home of the Samburu people, a nomadic tribe similar in culture to the better-known Maasai and equally proud of their traditions.

The Ewaso Ng'iro is the one permanent river, and its meandering path through the Samburu and Buffalo Springs reserves is flanked by forest. Birdlife is prolific here and game viewing excellent as the animals are drawn to the water. The majority of tourist accommodation is located here too. The less-visited Shaba Reserve is similar, though generally drier and more mountainous, with sandy, seasonal river basins and dramatic natural rock sculptures. The unique geography and distinct location of these parks give the opportunity to see some less common – even threatened – animal species, including the graceful gerenuk, Beisa (east African) oryx, Grevy's zebra and reticulated giraffe.

Park fees are currently US$40/20 for adults/children, but will probably increase to US$60/30 during 2009. These are paid on entry at the entry gates.

GETTING THERE AND AWAY

At approximately 350km (six hours) from Nairobi, most journeys to Samburu are broken by either a lunch stop *en route* or an overnight stay near Mount Kenya. The road is good bitumen except the final 80km, which is corrugated gravel. This stretch was being worked on in 2008 and should be tar sealed by 2009. A scheduled flight from Nairobi's Wilson Airport takes just under an hour to Samburu airfields. (For access issues in small airfields, see page 92.)

WHERE TO STAY

Larsens Camp (20 tents) ↳ 020 532 329; **e** sales@wildernesslodges.co.ke; www.wildernesslodges.co.ke

2 tents in this luxurious tented camp have been designed with access in

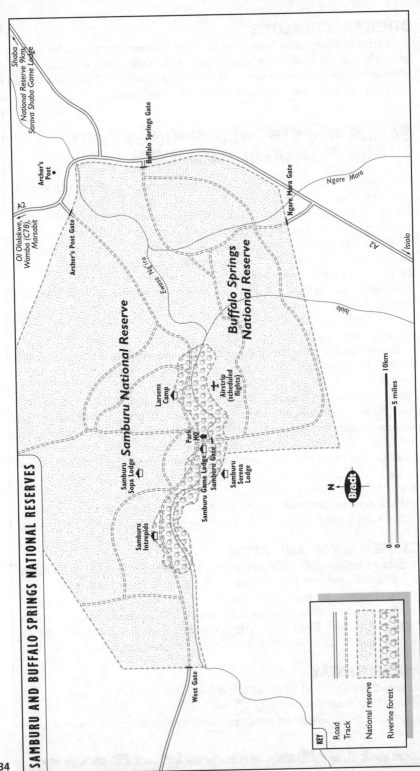

SAMBURU AND BUFFALO SPRINGS NATIONAL RESERVES

Samburu National Reserve

Buffalo Springs National Reserve

Shaba National Reserve 9km, Sarova Shaba Game Lodge

Archer's Post

Buffalo Springs Gate

Ngare Mara Gate

Ngare Mara

A2

Isiolo

Ol Ololokwe, Wamba (C78), Marsabit

Archer's Post Gate

Ewaso Ngiro

Isiolo

West Gate

Samburu Intrepids

Samburu Sopa Lodge

Larsens Camp

Park HQ

Samburu Game Lodge

Samburu Gate

Samburu Serena Lodge

Airstrip (scheduled flights)

N

Bradt

0   5 miles
0   10km

KEY	
	Road
	Track
	National reserve
	Riverine forest

mind. The camp is set on a level part of the riverbank, so is essentially slope-free, & although pathways are mostly just beaten earth, they are generally flat. The reception area is up 3 steps but other than this, all public areas (except jacuzzi & massage parlour, which are up 5 & 11 steps respectively) are ramped. The swimming pool has ladder entry.

Tents Heron & Shrike: Have ramped access: doors are wide tent flaps & rooms are spacious; beds (60) have light switches & all other handles are <140cm; doorway (110) is level to bathroom area; shower is large enough for a wheelchair, has a lip (6) to enter it, round taps (105), a fixed showerhead, horizontal rail (85) & no seat; the toilet (40) has transfer space & 1 fixed rail (83) within reach. **$$$$$**

Samburu Intrepids (27 tents) ☎ 020 444 6651; **f** 020 444 6600; **e** sales@heritagehotels.co.ke; ⌂ www.heritage-eastafrica.com

At the time of visiting, Intrepids had no adapted accommodation but a wheelchair is available & less mobile guests are currently assigned to tents close to reception. Access routes are generally hard & smooth. Pool & dining areas are level although the buffet is down 5 steps.

Tent 8: Has 2 steps at entry while others have at least 2. **$$$$$**

Samburu Game Lodge (61 rooms) ☎ 020 532 329; **e** sales@wildernesslodges.co.ke; ⌂ www.wildernesslodges.co.ke

This soundly built wood & thatch lodge is set in established woodland overlooking the Ewaso Ng'iro River. To get close-up views of the crocodile feeding or leopard baiting, you'll need to be able to navigate about 20 steps from the main lodge down to the riverside. Apart from this, there are no steps in public areas & 1 room has been adapted to be more inclusive. There are 4 steps & a ladder to enter the swimming pool, & even a roll-in shower – with narrow (65) doorway & no support rails – in the changing rooms. The dining room entrance is gently sloped & all tables are >65cm. Pathways are stone-built, lit & relatively smooth.

Room 36: The closest room to reception has been adapted. Entrance door is gradually ramped; beds (60) have light switch & transfer space; all switches are <140cm; level bathroom door (84); bath (40) has 2 fitted handles, a horizontal support rail (40) & transfer space; step-in shower (6) has built-in tiled seat in washing area, handheld showerhead, star taps & horizontal support rail (not within reach from seat); toilet (40) has 1 support rail (83) within reach & the washbasin (60) has star taps. There are more ground-floor dbl & trpl rooms, but the entry doorways (73) have 1 step, there's no bath & the shower is smaller with no seat. **$$$$**

Samburu Serena Lodge (62 rooms) ☎ 020 284 2333; **f** 064 30759; **e** from website; ⌂ www.serenahotels.com

On the other side of the river from Samburu Game Lodge, Serena's property is the less-accessible option of the two. Although there's a step at reception, a temporary ramp is available. Eating areas have level entry, tables are >65cm, & the swimming pool can be reached via a ramp & has ladder entry. Less positively, standard rooms' doors are narrow (doorways are 64cm) & bathrooms are small. Deluxe rooms are some 300m from reception & up 2 steps with, again, no adaptive features in their bathrooms. **$$$$**

Sarova Shaba Game Lodge (85 rooms) ✆ 020 276 7000; **f** 064 30481; **e** shaba@sarovahotels.com; ⌂ www.sarovahotels.com 🔲 ⬛
Sarova Shaba is located just inside the main entrance of Shaba National Reserve, which is about 9km from Samburu & Buffalo Springs. Of all the accommodations I've visited, this lodge has shown the most desire to become accessible, making some changes during my stay & more soon after. A wheelchair is available & all public areas are accessed via crazy paving & ramps (1 being steep). A drawback for slow walkers or wheelers here is that the main dining area is up a flight of stairs. However, the staff are very happy to set a table & serve food in the comfortable bar/lounge area at ground level. The swimming pool – unusually – has a roll-in entrance as well as steps.
Rooms have no accessible features but doorways (75) are level or ramped; beds (56) have light switches & transfer space; all other controls are <140cm; bathroom door (60) is level; bath (60) has 2 fitted handles, a fixed showerhead & 1 diagonal support rail (midpoint 40) designed for 'wobbly standers', not 'paraplegic sitters'; washbasin (66) has round taps, as does bath; toilet (42) has front transfer space & no rails. **$$$**

Samburu Sopa Lodge (60 rooms) ✆ 020 375 0235; **f** 020 375 1507; **e** info@sopalodges.com; ⌂ www.sopalodges.com 🔲 🔳
Being sited away from the river's edge, in gently rolling hills, makes Samburu Sopa unusual in this park. This open setting, however, allows for wonderful sunsets & is an environment more typical of the Samburu ecosystem, which is mostly arid. It is 700m from the new Oryx airstrip, lending itself nicely to air arrivals. A new lodge & impressively inclusive as a result, Sopa has 1 adapted room (Room 41). All public areas are on the same level or joined with smooth gradients & the 3 swimming pools are entered using steps. The pathway to the rooms is well lit & the cement is perfectly smooth.
Room 41: Ramped doorway (106) leads to a spacious room, & patio door (107) is level; bed (60) has light switch; all other controls are 140cm; bathroom doorway (106) is level; spacious roll-in shower with fixed showerhead & star taps; washbasin (66); toilet (40) has transfer space next to it; at the time of writing, there were no support rails in the bathroom & no shower seat, but these were 'on order'; Room 41 connects internally to the next room, allowing easy communication with family or personal assistant. All other rooms are up 1 or 2 steps & have standard doors & fittings. **$$$**

OTHER PRACTICALITIES
Drive-in visitors usually attend to their fuel and financial needs in either Nanyuki or Isiolo. Money can also be changed and payments made by credit card at the larger lodges.

Medical services
The bigger lodges usually have basic first-aid rooms, often with a nurse or doctor available. People with serious medical emergencies would be taken by air to Nairobi.

LAKE NAKURU NATIONAL PARK

Famous for its massive populations of pink flamingoes, Lake Nakuru National Park is also home to a superb variety of game making it an essential inclusion on any northern itinerary. Formed in 1968, the national park is centred on Lake Nakuru, one of the Great Rift Valley's soda lakes.

It has a wide range of habitats – all within reach of vehicles – including swampy lakeside marshlands, baboon-populated cliffs, acacia woodland and a euphorbia forest. There are no elephants but it is a sanctuary for Rothschild's giraffe and black rhino. As well as these rare species, lion are regularly seen and even leopard sightings are relatively common. Birding is superb: apart from the flamingoes (there can sometimes be millions of these) there are up to 450 species. Lake Nakuru's wildlife is also relatively habituated to humans, making game drives – and photography in particular – a pleasure.

Park fees are paid using the smartcard system (see page 116).

GETTING THERE AND AWAY
Only 160km from Nairobi, Nakuru is an easy drive on good roads through stunning Great Rift Valley landscapes. Scheduled flights from the capital take 25 minutes and are equally scenic, but local airfields have no facilities for disabilities (see page 92).

WHERE TO STAY
Nakuru Town has no accommodation catering specifically to disability. However, there are suitable options inside the park, plus nearby Mbweha Camp and Kembu (30 minutes' drive away).

Mbweha Camp (10 cottages) ✆ 020 445 0035/36; f 020 445 0037; e reservations@atua-enkop.com; www.atua-enkop.com
In the Congreve conservancy area flanking Nakuru National Park (20mins' drive from Nderit Gate), Mbweha (meaning 'jackal' in Swahili) offers a high standard of accommodation with some access. The bar & restaurant are reached using a ramp & public toilets are 'roll-in' but have no adaptations.

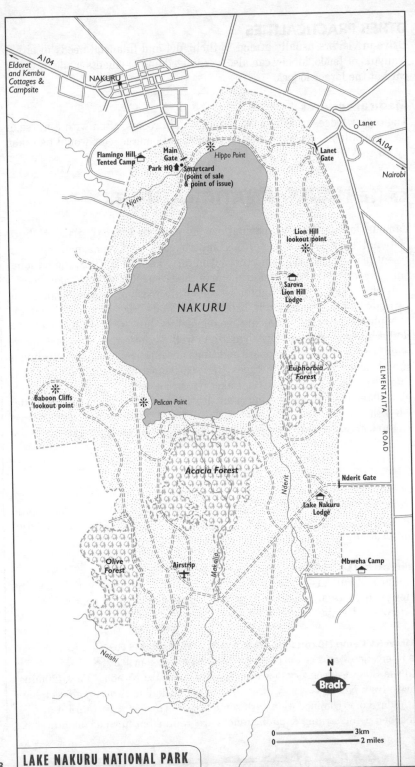

Eldoret
and Kembu
Cottages &
Campsite

NAKURU

A104

Lanet

Lanet
Gate

A104

Nairobi

Flamingo Hill
Tented Camp

Main
Gate

Hippo Point

Park HQ

Smartcard
(point of sale
& point of issue)

Njoro

Lion Hill
lookout point

Sarova
Lion Hill
Lodge

LAKE

NAKURU

Euphorbia
Forest

Baboon Cliffs
lookout point

Pelican Point

ELMENTAITA ROAD

Acacia Forest

Nderit

Nderit Gate

Lake Nakuru
Lodge

Olive
Forest

Airstrip

Makalia

Mbweha Camp

Naishi

N

Bradt

0   3km
0   2 miles

Dining tables are >65cm. Pathways are pebble stones meaning all but the strongest of independent wheelchair users will need help.

8 dbl cottages: These are similar regarding access. Doorways are mostly dbl doors; rooms are very spacious with light switches next to beds (53); entrances to ensuites (>80) are level; several have roll-in showers (with fixed showerheads, no seat & no rails) but toilets are surrounded by low walls, meaning none have side transfer space. The 2 family cottages have narrow bathroom doors (75) with a step (6). **$$$$$**

Sarova Lion Hill Lodge (67 chalets) ☎ 020 276 7000; **f** 051 221 0836; **e** lionhill@sarovahotels.com; ⌂ www.sarovahotels.com 🔲 🖼 ♿

Nestled into the steep escarpment above the lake, Lion Hill has done well to create a degree of access. Most public areas are stepped from reception (swimming pool down 12, gift shop up 14 & bar down 5) but the restaurant is ramped (tables are >65cm) & there is 1 twin room with adaptations.

Room 10: Door (75) ramped; beds (55) have light switches & space for transfers; all switches are <140cm; bathroom door (88) leads to a roll-in shower with fixed showerhead & no seat or rails; round taps (94); washbasin has no knee space; toilet (40) has support rail (57) within reach & transfer space. All other rooms have narrower bathroom door & a drop-off (5) into the shower. **$$$$**

Flamingo Hill Tented Camp (25 tents) ☎/**f** 020 884 485; **e** flamhillres@iconnect.co.ke; ⌂ www.flamingohillcamp.com 🔲 🖼

This luxurious, smoothly run & personable camp is also quite accessible. Attention to detail is everywhere & with French management, food quality is a priority. One slight drawback is that although it is geographically within the national park, its relative proximity to Nakuru Town can mean that howling hyenas compete with barking dogs for centre stage during the night. The setting is level & tents are <50m from other facilities. The dining area is ramped (tables are >65cm) & where there are steps (2 at reception & 1 into tents) temporary – though steep – wooden ramps have been made.

Tents have no specific disability aids but are cavernous: bed (56) has transfer space, light switch & all other switches are <140cm; entrance to ensuite (95) is level; spacious shower (enough for a wheelchair) has a lip (4), fixed showerhead & star taps (98) with a removable seat; washbasin (66); toilet (38) has transfer space but no rails. **$$$$**

Lake Nakuru Lodge (60 rooms) ☎ 020 273 3695; **f** 020 273 3698; **e** lakenakurulodge@wananchi.com; ⌂ www.lakenakurulodge.com 🔲 🖼

High above the lake, this functional lodge offers panoramic views over much of the park. The complex sprawls across a slight slope – from reception there are 4 steps (they are long & shallow, so can be taken 1 at a time in a wheelchair) down towards the rooms, then the swimming pool is down a further 8 & the bar is up 2. The large dining area – tables are

THE VANESSA GRANT TRUST

The Vanessa Grant Trust (VGT) supports a school for children with learning disabilities in Rongai, near Nakuru. It was started by Hamish Grant of Grant and Cameron Safaris, who also donated land for the school and dormitories, and initial funding was considerably helped by the UK's Department for International Development (DFID). The school is subject to Kenyan Ministry of Education regulations but is run by its own board of governors who make all the decisions regarding financing and day-to-day running.

The children are encouraged to learn life skills like tending animals and growing vegetables, and if possible, they proceed to a nearby vocational training centre where they can learn a trade. The ultimate aim is for them to be self-sufficient adults, or at least become less of a burden on their families. Although the school is live-in, close bonds with parents are maintained; a small part of the fee must be paid by the family, ensuring their commitment to the child.

There are always ongoing projects and plans for the future; current priorities, among others, are to develop a reliable water supply and disabled horse riders' courses. Long term, the VGT wants to expand the present school and also establish a quality secondary establishment for girls (there are none in the area). For these and the general upkeep of current projects, donations are always welcome. The Vanessa Grant School is not officially open to visitors, but anybody in the area is welcome to call by (*ring* **m** *0722 619117 to arrange to drop in*). More information can be obtained from Naomi Ndungu (**e** *naomi@vanessagranttrust.org*) or online (*www.vanessa granttrust.org*).

64cm – is up a ramp. Rooms are reached via a slightly sloped but continuous concrete pathway after the initial 4 steps.

Deluxe rooms: The most accessible, mainly because they're more spacious. Door (76) is level; bed (55) has transfer space & light switch; level door into ensuite (67) leads to a small but surprisingly accessible bathroom: roll-in shower has transfer space (though no seat), no support rail & fixed showerhead; taps (102) are round type; washbasin (65) has lever taps & toilet has side & front transfer space. Other rooms are smaller & have steps into their bathrooms. **$$$**

Kembu Cottages & Campsite (9 cottages) **m** 0722 361102 or **m** 0722 355705; **e** kembu@africaonline.co.ke; www.kembu.com
Situated on a working farm near Njoro (about 20km from Nakuru on the A104 then C56), Kembu's cottages have been tastefully designed by Andrew & Zoe Nightingale. Each unit is unique, & most are set apart in rambling grounds. The campsite bar & restaurant are not particularly

accessible but meals can be taken inside the house, which has 1 step at the main door. This is an ideal option if staying in the 'Yellow Room', which has level access with the rest of the house, though no en-suite bathroom.
Kinana Cottage: 2 identical rooms designed with access in mind & equipped for self-catering. Being a few hundred metres from the house, a vehicle is necessary to get there, but once inside, everything is on 1 level: narrowest doorway is 87cm; bed (65) has light switches & transfer space & all controls are <140cm; roll-in shower has tiled seat, transfer space, fixed showerhead & lever tap (110); washbasin (66) has lever taps & toilet (42) has front transfer space & horizontal support rail (85) within reach. The other rooms are all up at least 2 steps, with 'Acacia' having the fewest (2). **$$**

OTHER PRACTICALITIES
All banking, post, communication and shopping needs can easily be attended to in Nakuru Town, which is less than 1km from the main gate to the park. The majority of organised safaris stop for fuel and supplies here.

Medical services
The bigger lodges usually have basic first-aid rooms, often with a nurse or doctor available. People with serious medical emergencies would be taken either by road or from the nearest airfield to Nairobi.

LAKE NAIVASHA

A common stopover on the way to the Maasai Mara, but also a worthwhile place to visit in its own right, Lake Naivasha has long been a desirable destination for Kenyans looking for a break. It is shallow (averaging only about 5m deep) and, in an afternoon breeze, can be choppy. Because of this, the Maasai named it 'Nai'posha' which, loosely translated, means 'rough water'. Despite its proximity to the Equator, the lake's altitude – almost 1,900m above sea level – means the climate is comfortable.

As with all the Rift Valley lakes there is a myriad birdlife and a good range of game is attracted to its shores. Various other water- or land-based activities are on offer if reading a book and writing postcards proves to be too mundane.

GETTING THERE AND AWAY
Naivasha Town, at the head of the lake, is 85km from Nairobi on good sealed roads. Moi South Lake Road, which leads to all the accommodation described below, was resealed in 2006 and is now smooth tar. There are several small airstrips around the lake, but no scheduled flights. (For access issues in small airfields, see page 92.)

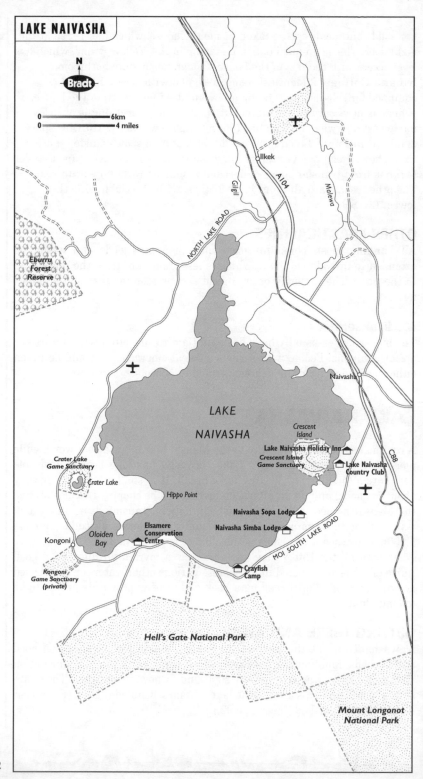

N

Bradt

| 0 | 6km |
| 0 | 4 miles |

Ilkek

Gilgil

A104

Malewa

NORTH LAKE ROAD

Eburru
Forest
Reserve

Naivasha

LAKE
NAIVASHA

Crescent
Island

Crater Lake
Game Sanctuary

Crater Lake

Lake Naivasha Holiday Inn

Crescent Island
Game Sanctuary

Lake Naivasha
Country Club

C88

Hippo Point

Naivasha Sopa Lodge

Naivasha Simba Lodge

Kongoni

Oloiden
Bay

Elsamere
Conservation
Centre

MOI SOUTH LAKE ROAD

Kongoni
Game Sanctuary
(private)

Crayfish
Camp

Hell's Gate National Park

Mount Longonot
National Park

WHERE TO STAY

There are extremely inclusive rooms in several lakeside lodges and Elsamere (the home of George and Joy Adamson of *Born Free* fame) offers reasonably accessible accommodation.

Naivasha Simba Lodge (70 rooms) ☎ 020 434 3960–2; f 020 434 3963; e sales@simbalodges.com; www.marasimba.com
Solidly built on a level site, Simba Lodge has the basics of good access & 1 adapted room. Paving to all public areas is hard & smooth with no steps. Dining tables are >65cm & the swimming pool is entered using steps (no handrail) or a ladder. Changing rooms & health club are up 1 step.
Room 43: The most accessible. Door (85) is level; bed (90) has transfer space, light switch & phone; bathroom door (86) is level; roll-in shower has 2 support rails (1 vertical, 1 horizontal), fixed showerhead & star taps (111) but no seat; washbasin (68) has star taps; toilet (39) has hinged horizontal support rail & both side & front transfer space. **$$$$**

Naivasha Sopa Lodge (84 rooms) ☎ 020 375 0235; f 020 375 1507; e info@sopalodges.com; www.sopalodges.com
With 2 adapted rooms a wheelchair available & tightly fitting laid brick pathways with ramps almost everywhere, this Sopa Lodge caters to most abilities. The bonus of colobus monkeys parading along the rooftops & hippos moseying through the expansive gardens makes this lodge more alluring. There are 2 steps to reach the swimming pool & it has stepped entry with rails. The dining tables are >65cm & the adjoining public toilet has wheelchair space & rails.
Accessible rooms: 10mins' walk from reception but can be reached using a vehicle. Doorway (111) is level; bed (56) has light switch, phone & transfer space; all controls are <140cm; door to ensuite (111) is level; spacious roll-in shower has seat & transfer space, no support rail, fixed showerhead & star taps (96); washbasin (67) has star taps; toilet (40) has transfer space but again, no rails. **$$$**

Elsamere Conservation Centre (8 rooms); ☎ 050 202 1055; f 050 202 1074; e elsa@africaonline.co.ke; www.elsatrust.org
As one of the main attractions in the Naivasha area, George & Joy Adamson's home – of *Born Free* fame – is worth including, despite not having any custom-designed access features.
Joy's room (in the main house): The easiest to access & is on the same level as the museum & dining area: doorway is 75cm; beds are 58cm; bath (56) & toilet (41) are each in own small rooms with doors (70) opening inwards, therefore limiting wheelchair space.
Room 5: Down a narrow concrete path (60) then doorway (80) is up 2 steps; bathroom has door (65) & contains step-in shower (6).
Room 6: next door, is similar, but has a standard bath as well. **$$$**

Lake Naivasha Country Club (52 rooms) South Lake Rd; ☎ 020 236 7300/237 0368; **e** reservations@kenyahotelsltd.com; ⤵ www.kenyahotelsltd.com 🔢
It is charming, in a colonial way, but the Country Club is in need of a spruce-up. Access is similarly dated with no rooms having a step-free approach (the rooms in 'C' block have only 1 step). Bathrooms have baths (52) with a shower hose & narrowest doorway is 70cm. The dining area & the swimming pool have ramped & level access respectively. **$$$**

Lake Naivasha Holiday Inn (25 rooms) ☎ 020 235 0149; **f** 020 354 5319; **e** info@lakenaivashaholidayinn.com; ⤵ www.lakenaivashaholidayinn.com 🔢
The new kid on the lakeside, this hotel is clean & furnished in a minimalist & rustic fashion. However, pathways are a mix of styles, including round cement 'stepping stones', which are a tripping hazard & will flummox wheelers. No rooms have completely level access. Baths have fitted handles & step-in showers have a low entry lip, so it may be fine for some slow walkers, but one for full-time chair users to avoid. **$$**

Crayfish Camp (75 rooms) ☎ 050 202 0239; **e** info@crayfishcamp.com; ⤵ www.crayfishcamp.com 🔢 🔢
Basic yet very well run with good food & lively bar, Crayfish offers wheelchair users a cheaper option. Access routes (including swimming pool & dining) are level or lightly ramped throughout, but narrow (60) in parts, meaning 1 wheel must take to the grass alongside. Rooms vary in accessibility.
Room 2: The easiest to explore. Doorway (74) is ramped; bed (50) has light switch & transfer space; bathroom door (75) is up 1 step (11); roll-in shower access is a squeeze (79) between the toilet & the wall & the shower has round taps & fixed showerhead; toilet (40) has side transfer space.
Rooms 1 & 4: The next-best options, but have more steps. There are no support rails installed in any rooms. **$**

OTHER PRACTICALITIES
The larger lodges will have email access but banking and shopping needs will have to be attended to in Naivasha Town, just northeast of the lake. All road arrivals come through Naivasha.

Medical services
The bigger lodges usually have basic first-aid rooms, often with a nurse or doctor available. People with serious medical emergencies would be taken either by road or from the nearest airfield to Nairobi.

WHAT TO SEE AND DO
The lodges and camps around the lakeside usually offer lake activities like boating, water skiing and fishing trips at little extra cost (usually less than US$10 per person) or these may be included in the price of your trip.

Hell's Gate National Park

(*Main entrance 2km south of Naivasha; contact Kenya Wildlife Service, www.kws.org; adult US$20, child US$10*) This small and scenic park usually has no dangerous predators, so walking and cycling safaris are often done. It is not designed to be wheelchair accessible but the main tracks are mainly hard and smooth and it might be a chance for everyone to explore a bit of wild Africa without a vehicle.

MAASAI MARA NATIONAL RESERVE

Possibly the most famous park in Africa, the Maasai Mara's reputation is wholly justified. Game viewing here is especially suited to first-time visitors because of the dense concentrations of the 'big five' – the most coveted species – but there is a huge variety of fauna present. Being the northern part of the Maasai Mara–Serengeti ecosystem, at certain times of the year it plays host to the Great Migration, the scale of which is inconceivable until witnessed.

The Maasai Mara is a reserve, as opposed to a national park, and is therefore run by local councils. First declared a game reserve in 1948, it was increased in size in 1968 by adding the land east of the Mara River, creating the current Maasai Mara National Reserve. The Mara Conservancy has been managing the Mara Triangle (www.maratriangle.org) since 2001, while the Musiara and Sekenani regions are under the control of Narok County Council. Maasai people still live in the Greater Mara Area Group Ranches around the actual reserve, and land for tourist accommodation in these parts is often leased from the villages with an agreement where a 'per visitor' rate is also added to a basic rent.

The 1,500km^2 reserve consists mainly of rolling grasslands broken by the Mara, Talek and Sand rivers. These are flanked by dense forests – the favourite haunt of leopard – and support large pods of hippo as well as providing permanent water for plains game. Birdlife is profuse in all the reserve's environments and black rhino are among some of the endangered species supported here. For visitors seeking the most dramatic wildebeest crossing points – where literally thousands of animals run a gauntlet of hungry crocodiles in their search for fresh pastures – the best are on the Mara and Talek rivers in the north of the reserve. This area can be reached from most lodges and camps but may require a day trip including packed lunch, depending on where you are based. If this is your primary goal in the Maasai Mara, then be sure your operator knows it in advance to be able to plan it in. The climate is generally mild and moist – hence the lush growth – but rarely uncomfortably hot. Main roads through the park are well maintained but smaller tracks can be muddy and less predictable during rainy seasons.

Park fees are currently US$40/20 for adults/children, but will probably

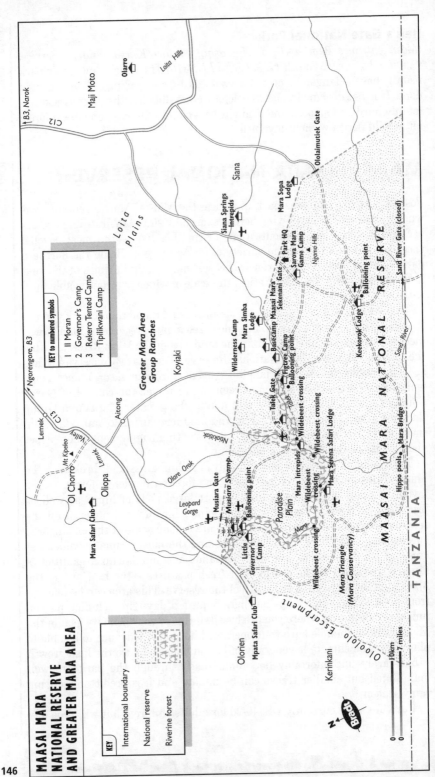

MAASAI MARA NATIONAL RESERVE AND GREATER MARA AREA

KEY

International boundary	— · — · —
National reserve	
Riverine forest	

KEY to numbered symbols

1 Il Moran
2 Governor's Camp
3 Rekero Tented Camp
4 Tipilikwani Camp

Greater Mara Area Group Ranches

Loita Hills

Olarro

Maji Moto

↑ B3, Narok

C12

Siana

Loita Plains

Siana Springs Intrepids

Mara Sopa Lodge

Park HQ

Sarova Mara Game Camp

Ngama Hills

Sekenani Gate

Basecamp Maasai Mara

Mara Simba Lodge

Wilderness Camp

Koyiaki

Keekorok Lodge

Ballooning point

Sand River Gate (closed)

MAASAI MARA NATIONAL RESERVE

Sand River

Ngorengore, B3

C13

Lemek

Ol Chorro

Mt Kipeleo

Oliopa

Lemek Valley

Aitong

Olare Orok

Ndtaktrack

Tatek Gate

Tipilikwa

Ol Kiombo

Mara Intrepids

Ballooning point

Wildebeest crossing

Mara Serena Safari Lodge

Mara Safari Club

Musiara Gate

Musiara Swamp

Leopard Gorge

Ballooning point

Little Governor's Camp

Paradise Plain

Mara

Wildebeest crossing

Wildebeest crossing

Mara Triangle (Mara Conservancy)

Hippo pools

Mara Bridge

TANZANIA

MAASAI MARA NATIONAL

Oloololo Escarpment

Olorien

Mpata Safari Club

Kerinkani

Ololaimutiek Gate

N

Bradt

0   10km
0   7 miles

146

increase to US$60/30 during 2009. These are paid on entry at the entry gates.

GETTING THERE AND AWAY

By road

Driving from Nairobi can take up to six hours (between 300km and 400km) depending on which area of the park you are visiting, and none of these roads are in excellent condition (although I have observed great improvements in the Narok to Sekenani section in recent years). Expect the last two hours approaching the park to be bumpy where there is pot-holed tar and sometimes dusty when on rough, corrugated gravel.

By air

A quicker and more comfortable method is to fly. Several airstrips serve the various regions of the reserve and there are daily scheduled flights from Nairobi, Nanyuki, Samburu and Mombasa. These are small airfields with no disability facilities. (For access issues see page 92.)

WHERE TO STAY

Governor's Camps (3 camps) ↆ 020 273 4000; **e** info@governorscamp.com or **e** responsibletourism@governorscamp.com
Of these famously lavish camps, Governor's itself & Governor's IL Moran apparently have ramped entrance at tents & dining areas. Reaching the third of the camps, Little Governor's, entails a river crossing with 20 steps on each bank. **$$$$$**

Mpata Safari Club ↆ 020 221 7015/244 987; **f** 020 310 859/222 9420; **e** mpata4@africaonline.co.ke; ◌ www.mpata.com
This exclusive lodge is regularly promoted as accessible, but although suite 6 apparently has a widened doorway, there are no particularly inclusive rooms. There is a special 'detachable chair' for one of their safari vehicles, & I've not seen it but Mpata tell me that clients who are unable to walk still need to be manually lifted into the car. **$$$$$**

Wilderness Camp (5 rooms) Near Talek Gate; ↆ 020 387 7490–2; **e** info@basecampexplorer.co.ke; ◌ www.basecampexplorer.com
Helping to provide funding for nearby Maasai Koiyaki Guiding School (◌ www.koiyaki.com), Wilderness Camp is managed by Basecamp Explorer (see below). It's off the usual Mara tourist circuit, yet provides good game viewing & has 1 room that is especially accessible. The reception/dining area is level, with tables >65cm, but pathways around the camp are rough meaning vehicle transfers are essential to & from the room.
The accessible room: Doorway (111) is level; bed (42) has light switch & transfer space & door to ensuite (111) is also level; spacious roll-in shower has fixed showerhead & star taps, but no seat or rails; the 2 washbasins

are at different heights (40 & 70) & the toilet has front transfer space; as with Basecamp, improvements were planned. **$$$$$**

Basecamp Maasai Mara (16 tents) Near Talek Gate; **℡ /f** 020 387 7490–2; **e** info@basecampexplorer.co.ke; ⏁ www.basecampexplorer.com 🄋 🖼
Basecamp is already renowned for being one of Kenya's most forward-thinking camps. Their eco-friendly policies are stringent & the local Maasai community is involved & supported at many levels. It all leads to a soothing feeling of being welcomed 'on their territory' in a standard of luxury you want, without having to worry about your environmental footprint. On top of this, the camp has attempted to include travellers with mobility difficulties. Crazy-paving pathways are level, but not smooth enough to make for easy wheeling, the dining area has level access & all tables are >65cm.
2 tents: These are more accessible. Tent entry is ramped; beds have transfer space & light switches (solar-powered lights); roll-in showers have fixed showerheads, but there are steep ramps into the bathroom; 'throne' style toilets are high & beyond the reach of wheelchair users, but I suspect changes will have been made by the time this book is published. **$$$$$**

Mara Intrepids (30 tents) ℡ 020 444 6651; **f** 020 444 6600; **e** sales@heritagehotels.co.ke; ⏁ www.heritage-eastafrica.com 🄋 🖼
Intrepids is built in dense woodland, giving a cool, shady feel to the camp. Access routes are hard, but sometimes uneven, the restaurant is ramped (though the buffet is up 1 step), the bar is up 1 step & the swimming pool has level access & stepped entry. A wheelchair is available at reception.
Tents 7 & 12: These are apparently 'going to be further adapted for disabled visitors' but currently have level access; beds (54) with transfer space & light switches; roll-in showers with fixed showerheads, star taps (107) but no seat or handrails. **$$$$$**

Rekero Tented Camp (8 tents) **m** 0721 486272; **e** rekerocamp@africaonline.co.ke; ⏁ www.rekero.com 🄁 🖼
Tidily dotted around a quiet, grassy glade within the Maasai Mara, Rekero's en-suite tents have no disability adaptations but are at ground level. They are connected by trails that have been worn into the lawn-like surroundings over time, & the main dining area is under canvas (up 1 step).
Tent 2: Closest to the mess tent; beds (54) have a light switch & a pressurised air horn is present to attract attention in an emergency; has a roll-in shower. **$$$$$**

Mara Safari Club (50 tents) ℡ 020 221 6940; **e** Kenya.reservations@fairmont.com; ⏁ www.fairmont.com 🄁 🖼 ♿

This chic lodge receives consistently good reports and, with 1 extremely accessible tent (number 28), is one of the Mara's most inclusive properties. Reception is down 1 small step from parking; dining areas & internet room are on the same level. Reasonably smooth, well-lit crazy paving links the various areas.

Tent 28: Ramped entry; beds have transfer space & light switches; ensuite is level; roll-in shower has handheld showerhead & star taps, but has a short, steep drop-off into it (only strong pushers will do this independently); washbasin has lever taps; toilet has front transfer space & 1 support rail. **$$$$$**

Tipilikwani Camp (20 tents) 📞 020 445 0035/6; **f** 020 445 0037; **e** reservations@atua-enkop.com; 🖰 www.atua-enkop.com 📱
On the banks of the Talek River, Tipilikwani is open, airy & relatively new. It followed (up to a point) the advice of a specialised local operator in trying to make the camp inclusive. Although not ideal, it will suit some. The site is level & crazy paving links the buildings. Stone ramps (some steeper than 8%) avoid steps around the restaurant.
4 tents: Have level access. Doors are tent flaps; beds (45) have lights & transfer space; other controls are <140cm; bathroom door (72) is level; shower has a handheld showerhead, but, although it has room for a wheelchair, there is a drop-off (6) to enter; toilet is approachable diagonally in a wheelchair. **$$$$$**

Siana Springs Intrepids (38 tents) 📞 020 444 6651; **f** 020 444 6600; **e** sales@heritagehotels.co.ke; 🖰 www.heritage-eastafrica.com 📱
There's an air of tranquillity about Siana Springs – maybe the natural setting in solid, mature woodland brings it on. It's also one to visit if you can't do steps because there are none to any of the public areas or to 5 of the rooms. Pathways are crazy paving but unfortunately, dining-table knee clearance is only 60cm.
Tent B20: The closest to reception. Door (tent flap) is level; bed (54) has light switch & transfer space; the entry gap to the ablutions area (60) could be widened by moving furniture; step-in shower (12) has no seat; toilet (38) has front transfer space only. **$$$$$**

Sarova Mara Game Camp (75 tents) 📞 020 276 7000; **f** 020 271 5566; **e** sarova.mara@sarovahotels.com; 🖰 www.sarovahotels.com 📱 🖼 📱
A comfortable tented camp, the Sarova Mara is more accessible than most & has a wheelchair available. There are several flights of 1–3 steps connecting public areas, all of which are flanked by short (sometimes steep) stone ramps. The swimming pool has ramped & stepped entry with handrails & dining tables are >65cm.
1 standard tent: Has adaptations including: level entry (door is tent flap); beds (50) have light switch & transfer space; door to ensuite (76) is level; narrow (85) roll-in shower has fixed showerhead, no seat & star taps

(107); toilet (39) has 1 shaped rail & front transfer space; washbasin (58) has low mirror & star taps. Club tents are more spacious but have several steps at their entrances. **$$$$**

Fig Tree Camp (79 tents & chalets) **☎** 050 22131/163; **f** 020 603 595;
e figtree@kenyaweb.com; ⏚ www.madahotels.com [0] [🖼]
Set on the Talek River, with a dramatic (& flat) boardwalk bridge at the entrance, Fig Tree has a wide range of accommodation types. Paths are crazy paving, which is fairly smooth but with the occasional step. The dining area is up a small ramp & the bougainvillea-shrouded swimming pool has level access & stepped entry. All chalets have level access & step-in showers.
Superior tents: Have steps at the tent flap & a narrow entrance (72) to a roll-in shower with star taps (96), fixed showerhead & no seat. Toilets & washbasins are not wheelchair accessible & there are no handrails. **$$$$**

Keekorok Lodge (101 rooms) **☎** 020 532 329; **e** sales@wildernesslodges.co.ke;
⏚ www.wildernesslodges.co.ke [0]
Meaning 'place of black trees' in Maa (Maasai language), this grand lodge has made an attempt to include everyone. Reception & eating areas are level, tables are >65cm & there's a 20% gradient leading down to the huge gardens, swimming pool & hippo-viewing area. The last is reached using a level, wooden boardwalk with guide rail, while there are several steps up to the swimming pool then hand-railed steps to enter it. There are currently no rooms with support rails.
1 of the newer chalets: The most accessible – main door (89) has a small threshold (2); beds (58) have light switches & transfer space; bathroom door (82) is level; step-in shower is 9cm; toilet (40) has front transfer space. **$$$$**

Mara Serena Safari Lodge (74 rooms) **☎** 020 282 2000; **f** 020 272 5184;
e from website; ⏚ www.serenahotels.com [3]
The Serena's stunning escarpment setting – close to one of the migration's favourite Mara River crossing points – immediately makes access a challenge. The lodge's ageing design doesn't help. There are 4 then 8 steps up to the 2 dining levels & 10 to the swimming pool. Rooms 1, 2, 50 & 51 have level access once reached from reception, but shower trays are sunken. **$$$$**

Mara Simba Lodge (84 rooms) **☎** 020 434 3960–2; **f** 020 434 3963;
e sales@simbalodges.com; ⏚ www.marasimba.com [1]
The Simba Lodges' Mara representative has a wheelchair on site, but is the only property I've viewed in Africa where management actively discourages disabled visitors. If you wish to visit, dining areas are level & swimming pool is up 5 steps. Room doorways (76) are up 1 step; bathroom doors (67) are level; showers are step-in (9) with no rails or seat; toilets (39) have front transfer space. **$$$$**

Other notable accommodation
Mara Sopa Lodge (☎ *020 375 0235;* f *020 375 1507;* e *info@sopalodges.com;* 🖰 *www.sopalodges.com*) and **Olarro** (☎ *020 375 2481;* f *020 375 2476;* e *archers@archersafrica.com;* 🖰 *www.archersafrica.com*) These properties are built on steep hillsides. Mara Sopa has more than 20 steps from the parking down through reception to the eating and accommodation areas.

These lodges are popular bases in the Maasai Mara, but are particularly unsuitable for guests with limited mobility.

OTHER PRACTICALITIES
The larger lodges have small shops and internet access but banking, post and shopping needs ought to be fulfilled *en route* to the Maasai Mara. The majority of trips stop in Narok on the way from Nairobi and here these services are available.

Medical services
The bigger lodges usually have basic first-aid rooms, often with a nurse or doctor available. People with serious medical emergencies would be taken from the nearest airfield to Nairobi.

AMBOSELI NATIONAL PARK

Ideally located in the centre of the Nairobi–Arusha–Mombasa triangle, Amboseli slots well into many itineraries. The park itself, at 392km², is relatively small but is part of the 3,000km² Amboseli ecosystem. This includes several Maasai-owned ranches where people, cattle and wild animals co-exist. Because of its proximity to the safari centres and excellent stocks of game, it attracts large numbers of tourists.

The climate is essentially hot and dry, but Amboseli is well watered by run-off from Kilimanjaro, giving rise to swamp marshes. In years of heavy rainfall a temporary lake forms in the lowest part of the pan. The name 'Amboseli' comes from the Maasai word *empusel*, which means 'salty dust'; it's apt, as the area has been blanketed by showers of ash from Mount Kilimanjaro since it first erupted between two and four million years ago, and this is whipped up by the dust devils (miniature whirlwinds) that regularly spin over the plains. Roads are good, though will be dusty in dry seasons and some may be impassable during the rains.

The five different habitats support numerous herbivore species and their usual predators – lion, leopard, cheetah and hyena. Birdlife is abundant and game drives are easy as distances are small. With arguably the most stunning views of Kilimanjaro in either Kenya or Tanzania, and plenty of impressively tusked elephants to fill the foreground, Amboseli is a photographer's dream.

Park fees are paid using the smartcard system (see page 116).

AMBOSELI NATIONAL PARK

N

Bradt

0   3km
0   2 miles

Namanga 80km

Meshanani Gate

C103

Lake Amboseli (seasonal)

Namanga 70km dry season only

Kitirua Gate

Tortilis Tented Camp

Lake Kioko

Observation Hill

Ol Tukai Swamps

Airstrip

Erimito Swamps

Erimito Gate

Makutano, Emali 260km

Ol Tukai Lodge

Amboseli Serena Lodge

Satao Elerai

views to Mt Kilimanjaro

Kibo Safari Camp

C103

Park HQ

Kimana Gate

Amboseli Sopa Lodge 19km, Loitokitok 50km

GETTING THERE AND AWAY

Most visitors reach Amboseli from Nairobi via Namanga. The road to the border town is good quality but the 80km from there to Meshanani Gate is unsealed and can be bumpy in places. The total journey of around 250km can take four–five hours. Many trips continue southeast from Amboseli to Tsavo West National Park, a journey of about 2½ hours (100km) on dirt roads. Safari minibuses currently travel in convoy with armed police on this stretch, as it was the scene of bandit attacks in the 1990s.

Daily scheduled flights of about 40 minutes connect Nairobi and Amboseli but the local airfield has no access facilities. (For access issues in small airfields, see page 92.)

WHERE TO STAY

Tortilis Tented Camp (17 tents & 1 house) ☎ 020 604 054; e safaris@chelipeacock.com; ☞ www.chelipeacock.com [3]
Hidden amongst low hillocks in southern Amboseli, this small camp deals with its inherent inaccessibility by ferrying less mobile guests around in a vehicle. Reception is up 3 steps from the gravel parking area. From there, the swimming pool & the majority of accommodation is down 4 steps then a steep trail. The **family tent** (which is more spacious & has a bath) & **tent 17** (near the bar/dining area at the top of the hill & with a shower) are those most suited to restricted mobility. **$$$$$**

Amboseli Serena Lodge (92 rooms) ☎ 020 282 2000; f 020 272 5184; e from website; ☞ www.serenahotels.com [i] [A]
Major renovations in recent years have given this lodge a facelift, but surprisingly – for part of a major chain – it still targets walking guests only. Public areas are all level, with hard, smooth stone access. Dining tables are >65cm & the pool has steps to enter, though without a handrail. There are no rooms without a step at the entrance & no temporary ramp. Of the renovated rooms, some have baths & some have showers. Baths (51) have fitted handles & transfer space. Shower cubicles are 1 step-down (10) & have a diagonal support rail (midpoint 112). Doors are generally 78cm & doors to ensuites are 68cm. Washbasins have no underneath access. **$$$$**

Satao Elerai ☎ 020 243 4600/1/2/3; m (Safaricom): 0720 600 200/0721 240 840, m (Zain): 0733 622 022/0734 122 022; f 020 243 4610; e sales@sataocamp.com; ☞ www.sataoelerai.com [0]
This attractive new camp is smoothly run & ideally situated; looking north gives sweeping views down onto the Amboseli Plains, whilst south confronts you with the towering face of Mount Kilimanjaro. A wheelchair is available & the only area accessed by steps is the viewing deck, which is up 4. The dining room & bar are reached using a low ramp & in 2007, rooms were along a level-paved pathway with 2 steps (which were apparently levelled in 2008).
Room 2: Level doorway (86); beds (66) with light switch & transfer space;

level bathroom door (87); bath (57) has a step next to it, so cannot be reached in a wheelchair; large step-in shower (17) with fixed showerhead & star taps (100); washbasin (79); toilet (41) has no transfer space – but does have a stunning view onto Amboseli; support rails were due to be added in 2009. 9 safari tents are also due to be completed in 2009, though access plans are unknown. **$$$$**

Ol Tukai Lodge (80 rooms) ☎ 020 444 5514; f 020 444 8493;
e oltukai@manrikgroup.com; ⌂ www.oltukailodge.com [0] [AR] [♿]
If access is your main concern, then friendly & relaxing Ol Tukai is the top choice in Amboseli. The whole complex can easily be reached on wheels (small ramped sections bypass steps where necessary), restaurant tables are >65cm & the pool has steps as well as a ladder. 2 rooms have level entry & adapted bathrooms; other rooms have stepped entry at doorways & step-in showers.
Rooms 49 & 50: Doorway (98) has threshold (2) on low-tiled ramp; beds (47) have light switch & transfer space & all switches are <140cm; ensuite door (88) is level; roll-in shower has 2 supports rails (1 horizontal & vertical), handheld showerhead, round taps (128) & a plastic removable seat; toilet (42) has front & side transfer space & 2 support rails (104) within reach. NB: the roll-in shower is sunken & narrow, so only suited to rolling shower chairs (there is no space for transfers from a manual wheelchair to the shower seat). **$$$$**

Amboseli Sopa Lodge (83 rooms) ☎ 020 375 0235; f 020 375 1507;
e info@sopalodges.com; ⌂ www.sopalodges.com [0] [R]
The Sopa Lodge is about 19km east of Kimana Gate but the road is hard, smooth gravel, so this will not hugely affect game-drive times. Access routes are a mixture of crazy paving, concrete & interlocking bricks – all fine for wheelers – & stone ramps bypass all steps except the 3 to the swimming pool. This attractive pool (with natural stone bottom) is itself entered using 2 steps & has seating all around its inside edge. The viewpoint onto the waterhole is reached using a long ramp. Dining areas are ramped & tables have knee clearance (68).
2 rooms (Rooms 20 & 21): Doorways (108) are level; bed (53) has light switch & transfer space; all switches are <140cm; bathroom door (109) is level; roll-in shower has fixed showerhead & round taps (80); washbasin (65) has round taps; toilet (40) has front transfer space. **$$$**

Kibo Safari Camp (61 tents) ☎ 020 445 0532/2918; f 020 445 0392;
e info@kibosafaricamp.com; ⌂ www.kibosafaricamp.com [1]
With a slightly ramshackle feel to it, Kibo Safari camp dissuades wheelchairs with its loose gravel pathways. However, slow walkers may be tempted by the completely level site with only 1 step into tents, dining or bar area & 4 up to the swimming pool. Trpl tents can be made more spacious by removing 1 bed & ablutions consist of step-in showers (14). **$$$**

OTHER PRACTICALITIES
The larger lodges take credit cards and have small gift shops, but any major banking, post and shopping needs ought to be fulfilled before arriving in Amboseli. This usually means in Nairobi, Mombasa or Arusha, depending on your itinerary.

Medical services
The bigger lodges usually have basic first-aid rooms, often with a nurse or doctor available. People with serious medical emergencies would be taken either by road or from the nearest airfield to Nairobi.

TSAVO EAST AND WEST NATIONAL PARKS

The two parks are geographically separated by the main Nairobi–Mombasa highway and together, at nearly 22,000km², they make up Kenya's largest area dedicated to wildlife preservation. For those who seek it, Tsavo does provide the opportunity to experience true wilderness.

Established in 1948, Tsavo National Park was almost immediately split into east and west to make administration simpler. Their landscapes differ: in broad terms, Tsavo West is more varied, with lava flows, rocky outcrops and ridges, woodlands and thorny scrub; Tsavo East is generally drier, flatter and more open. The Galana River flows through Tsavo East and large numbers of game are drawn to it. The northern part of this park recently reopened to the public after being closed for years to fight poaching, but the network of navigable roads there is still limited.

The name 'Tsavo' was made infamous by the man-eating lions that terrorised railway workers in 1898. Now, despite horrific losses due to poaching between 1970 and 1990, it is better known for its large herds of elephants. In Tsavo East, these often appear red-orange in colour, after bathing in the red dust that typifies parts of the park. The size of the parks (and the dense undergrowth in parts of Tsavo West) can make game spotting more tricky, but this can also be looked upon as a challenge.

The main roads throughout are 'all-weather', hard and fairly well maintained and its proximity to the coast makes Tsavo an ideal complement to a beach break.

Park fees are paid using the smartcard system (see page 116).

GETTING THERE AND AWAY
Voi Town, which lies between the two Tsavos, is only 160km (or two hours' drive) on shimmering asphalt from Mombasa. Nairobi is 330km north, but can currently take up to seven hours' driving, depending on roadworks and traffic near the city.

There are several airstrips in the park for light, chartered aircraft, but there are no scheduled flights. (For access issues see page 92.)

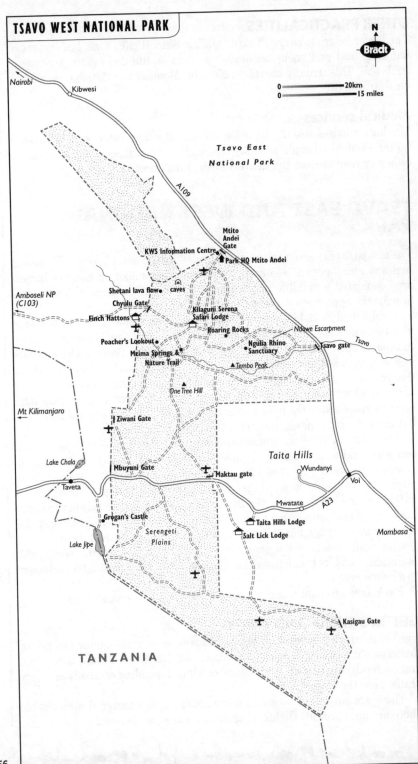

TSAVO WEST NATIONAL PARK

N

Bradt

0 ———— 20km
0 ———— 15 miles

Nairobi

Kibwesi

*Tsavo East
National Park*

A109

Mtito
Andei
Gate

KWS Information Centre

Park HQ Mtito Andei

*Amboseli NP
(C103)*

Shetani lava flow

caves

Chyulu Gate

Kilaguni Serena
Safari Lodge

Finch Hattons

Roaring Rocks

Ndawe Escarpment

Poacher's Lookout

Ngulia Rhino
Sanctuary

Tsavo

Tsavo gate

Mzima Springs &
Nature Trail

▲ *Tembo Peak*

Mt Kilimanjaro ←

▲ *One Tree Hill*

Ziwani Gate

Lake Chala

Mbuyuni Gate

Maktau gate

Taita Hills

Wundanyi

Voi

Taveta

Mwatate

A23

Mombasa

Grogan's Castle

Taita Hills Lodge

*Serengeti
Plains*

Salt Lick Lodge

Lake Jipe

Kasigau Gate

TANZANIA

WHERE TO STAY

Tsavo West

Finch Hattons (35 tents) ℡ 020 553 237/8; **f** 020 553 245;
e finchhattons@iconnect.co.ke; ⁀ www.finchhattons.com [3⁺]
As far as the setting, food, wine & service are concerned, Finch Hattons
has few equals. If, however, access means more to you, then you may need
to look further. The swimming pool is up 11 steps, restaurant 7 & tents
several. Access routes vary from open ground to rough paving, but none
are ideal on wheels. Some of the step-in showers do have a diagonal grab
rail. **$$$$$**

Kilaguni Serena Safari Lodge (56 rooms) ℡ 020 282 2000; **f** 020 272 5184; **e**
from website; ⁀ www.serenahotels.com [0⁻] [A⁻]
The waterhole – with magnificent viewing from the bar/dining room – is
the main attraction at Kilaguni; we missed a pack of wild dogs (including
pups) by a matter of hours. General access is reasonable; there are no
more than 3 steps anywhere & short (steep) ramps are present next to
these. There are no modified rooms, but **Room 1** (closest to reception) is
the best option: door (74) has a threshold (3); bed (53) has transfer space,
light switch & phone; bathroom door (68) is level; shower is down 1 step
(11), has round taps (107), fixed showerhead & vertical support rail
(midpoint 145); an authentic shower chair (on legs) is available; toilet (39)
has front transfer space only. The suites have rougher access routes, are
further from the main complex, have 2 steps to enter & their bathrooms
have fixed showerheads in baths. **$$$$**

Tsavo East

Galdessa ℡ 040 320 2630; **f** 040 320 3466; **e** reservation@galdessa.com;
⁀ www.galdessa.com [1⁻]
Furnished in timeless fashion, this picturesque camp won't suit everyone.
Tracks are soft river sand & there are 1 or 2 steps up into the tents. On
top of this, Galdessa isn't fenced, meaning you may need to be able to give
way quickly to wandering wildlife. If you can cope with this, then tents 5
& 6 have the most accessible ablutions, with step-in shower (4) & level
access to the toilet. **$$$$$**

Man Eaters (31 tents) ℡ 020 712 5741/2; **e** info@voiwildlifelodge.com;
⁀ www.voiwildlifelodge.com [0⁻]
About 5km north of Manyani Gate, & built on the site where Lieutenant-
Colonel Patterson shot the famous man-eating lions, this new camp has
cleverly inherited a unique history. The rushing torrent of the Tsavo River
& proliferation of wildlife coming to it ensure that a modern-day stay here
can be just as thrilling. This was the newest lodge in Tsavo East at the
time of research, & has tried to include everyone. From the vehicle drop-
off point (where there's shaded seating) the smooth stone access routes

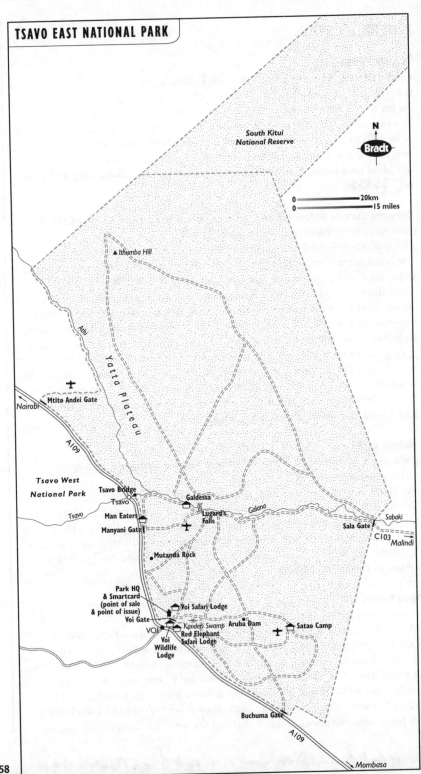

TSAVO EAST NATIONAL PARK

South Kitui
National Reserve

N

Bradt

0 ⟶ 20km
0 ⟶ 15 miles

▲ Ithumba Hill

Yatta Plateau

Athi

Nairobi

✝ Mtito Andei Gate

A109

Tsavo West
National Park

Tsavo Bridge

Tsavo

Tsavo

Man Eaters

Manyani Gate

● Mutanda Rock

Galdessa

Lugard's
Falls

Galana

Sabaki

Sala Gate

C103
Malindi

Park HQ
& Smartcard
(point of sale
& point of issue)

Voi Gate

VOI

Voi
Wildlife
Lodge

Voi Safari Lodge

Kanderi Swamp

Red Elephant
Safari Lodge

Aruba Dam

✝ Satao Camp

Buchuma Gate

A109

⟶ Mombasa

link the bar, restaurant, rooms & swimming pool. In parts they're steeper than 8%, but there are no steps. Dining tables are >65cm.

3 tents: including tent number 8 next to the restaurant: entry is level, though the tent flap does require a bit of effort to push over in a wheelchair; bed (58) has light switch, phone & transfer space; shower door (75) has drop-off (3) into shower itself, which is large enough for a wheelchair & has fixed showerhead & round taps (93); toilet door (78) allows frontal access to toilet (40) only; washbasin (74) has round taps & low mirror; the spacious patio at tent 8 has a small wooden threshold (2) from the tent & gives an unobstructed view on to one of the main approach tracks for animals coming to drink. **$$$$**

Voi Wildlife Lodge (72 rooms) ✆ 043 30762/691; **e** info@voiwildlifelodge.com; ᐃ www.voiwildlifelodge.com 🄌 🖼 🖥
Voi Wildlife Lodge is one of Kenya's best examples of accessible safari accommodation & is only a couple of hours' drive from Mombasa on tar-sealed roads. From the entrance through reception is all 1 level. This continues out past the dining areas & the smaller swimming pool (entered using steps) to the large, covered wildlife-viewing point. It's all comfortable pushing even for weaker chair users. Dining tables are >65cm & there's a public toilet with support rail in the main building.

2 adapted rooms: In the luxury category. Door (76) is level; bed (50) has light switch, phone & transfer space; highest switch is 142cm; doorway into ensuite (79) is level; roll-in shower has a wall-mounted flip-down plastic seat in the washing area, lever tap (85), handheld showerhead & horizontal support rail within reach opposite the seat; washbasin (84) has low mirror but round taps; toilet (41) has front transfer space & 1 horizontal support rail (71) beside it. There is 1 step up to some tents, which have just enough room to manoeuvre a wheelchair & have a small step-in shower. **$$$$**

Satao Camp (20 tents) ✆ 020 243 4600/1/2/3; **m** (Safaricom): 0720 600 200/0721 240 840, **m** (Zain): 0733 622 022/0734 122 022; **f** 020 243 4610; **e** sales@sataocamp.com; ᐃ www.sataocamp.com 🄌 🖼 🖥
Seriously accessible tents with views directly onto a busy waterhole make this long-established camp a worthwhile consideration for visitors to Tsavo. Staff are used to wheelchairs & are prepared to help in a useful manner if necessary. The camp is level & the large dining area is up permanent stone-built ramps (next to 2 or 3 steps) from the packed-sand paths.

Tent 7: Short ramp (around 30%) leads to cement-floored tent; doorway (tent flap) is level; bed (64) has light switch & transfer space; bathroom door is wide; roll-in bush shower (with gravity feed) has wooden stool, handheld showerhead & hot & cold taps (150 & 187); toilet (39) has 2 wooden horizontal support rails (70), 1 of which swings away, allowing front or side transfer; washbasin (71) has star tap.

Tent 6 also has a ramp & rails while **tent 8** has ramp but no rails. Of the 4 suites, 1 has ramps but no rails. **$$$**

Voi Safari Lodge (53 rooms) ☎ 041 471 861–5; **e** voilodge@kenya-safari.co.ke;
🖰 www.voilodge.kenya-safari.co.ke 🔲
This older lodge is perched on an escarpment, but is planning to make 5 rooms (those closest to reception) suitable for mobility-impaired guests. Parking to reception is down 10 steps or a very steep incline. The dining area is down another slope then up 2 steps (which are avoided using a temporary wooden ramp). The swimming pool is down 10 steps then a ramp & the scenic waterhole is several hundred metres further – not a walk to try in a hurry.
The most suitable rooms: Currently have a level doorway (75); the bed (55) has light switch & transfer space, but to reach the bedside a narrow gap (58) must be navigated; the bathroom is very small with a shower in a standard bathtub. **$$$**

Red Elephant Safari Lodge (12 rooms) ☎ 043 30749; **m** 0727 112175;
e redelephanteak@aol.com; 🖰 www.red-elephant-lodge.com 🔲
Reception & the bar are down 3 & 2 steps respectively, the small, round swimming pool is not sunken so has step-ladder entry. Standard rooms have 1 step at the doorway, 1 into the shower & a lip (10) at the entrance to the patio. Entry to the bush houses is up 2 steps & the shower has a drop-off (3). The bush houses are much more spacious & airy than standard rooms. **$$**

Other notable accommodation
Both **Taita Hills Lodge** and **Salt Lick Game Lodge** (*run by Sarova Hotels;* ☎ *020 271 4444/6688;* **f** *020 271 5566;* **e** *centralreservations @sarovahotels.com;* 🖰 *www.sarovahotels.com*) are in Taita Hills Game Sanctuary, a small reserve situated between Tsavo East and West. This area is sometimes used as an extra highlight in southern Kenya, but both lodges have flights of many stairs, no lift and no rooms with inclusive features.

OTHER PRACTICALITIES
Larger lodges in the Tsavos have basic shops, and Voi Town has a bank and limited provisions, but all important purchasing, post and finance tasks are better done in Mombasa, Nairobi or any other major conurbation *en route*.

Medical services
The bigger lodges usually have basic first-aid rooms, often with a nurse or doctor available. People with serious medical emergencies would be taken either by road to Mombasa or from the nearest airfield to Nairobi.

MOMBASA

A coastal break is the perfect complement to a safari, and for those who wish to lie back for a week, the beaches here have accommodation of all classes.

Palm trees lean into the breeze and turquoise waters lap endless kilometres of white sand, making it easy to forget the frenetic pace of life at home. But if culture and history are more appealing, then the region also has centuries of stories to discover. Mombasa has always been at the heart of African trade and discovery – having been ruled by the Portuguese, the Arabs and the British – and the Swahili civilisation that has developed is as intriguing as it is exciting.

With a population of 700,000, Mombasa is Kenya's second-largest city. It is a busy modern-day port – the country's only deepwater point of entry for sea freight – and is therefore still the main trade window for much of east and central Africa. Temperatures are rarely extreme, hovering around the high 20s most of the year, but being equatorial and at sea level it is usually humid and therefore gives the impression of being hotter. Energetic activities are best done early in the day before the sun reaches its zenith.

Accommodation from cosy guesthouses to hotels and resorts exists – mainly on the beaches – both north and south of Mombasa Island. Diani Beach on the south coast attracts the majority of overseas visitors, and correspondingly has the greatest choice of accessible hotels. I have described some properties on the north coast, but the bulk of the *Where to stay* and all of the *Where to eat* information given below refers to Diani.

GETTING THERE AND AWAY

By road
Mombasa is about 500km from Nairobi, but the journey can take up to nine hours depending on traffic and roadworks. Buses ply this route several times daily (leaving from Kenyatta Avenue in the centre of Mombasa Island) but none cater specifically to disabled passengers. Tsavo East and West national parks are just over two hours' drive away, on good, sealed roads.

By rail
As with public transport on the roads, none of Kenya's rail services has facilities for disabled travellers (see page 91 for the Nairobi–Mombasa journey).

By air
Moi International Airport receives some European flights and handles connections (45 minutes) from Nairobi. It is about 10km from the city and has level access and lifts between floors. There are also three toilets for people with disabilities, one downstairs in the departure lounge, one in the international departure lounge and one in the domestic departure lounge; all have wheelchair-accessible washbasins and support rails and transfer space next to the toilets. An aisle chair is also available to help non-ambulant passengers from the plane. However, if you need your wheelchair brought to the door of the plane, then it is recommended that you ask aircrew before arrival to inform ground staff of this.

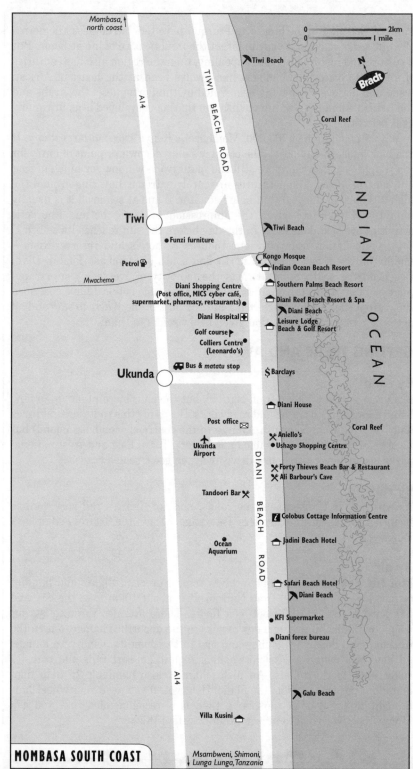

Mombasa,
north coast

TIWI BEACH ROAD

A14

0   2km
0   1 mile

Bradt

N

Tiwi Beach

Coral Reef

INDIAN

Tiwi

Funzi furniture

Petrol

Mwachema

Diani Shopping Centre
(Post office, MICS cyber café,
supermarket, pharmacy, restaurants)

Diani Hospital

Golf course

Colliers Centre
(Leonardo's)

Ukunda

Bus & matatu stop

Tiwi Beach

Kongo Mosque
Indian Ocean Beach Resort

Southern Palms Beach Resort

Diani Reef Beach Resort & Spa

Diani Beach

Leisure Lodge
Beach & Golf Resort

OCEAN

Barclays

Diani House

Post office

Ukunda
Airport

DIANI BEACH ROAD

Aniello's
Ushago Shopping Centre

Coral Reef

Forty Thieves Beach Bar & Restaurant
Ali Barbour's Cave

Tandoori Bar

Colobus Cottage Information Centre

Jadini Beach Hotel

Ocean
Aquarium

Safari Beach Hotel
Diani Beach

KFI Supermarket

Diani forex bureau

A14

Galu Beach

Villa Kusini

162   MOMBASA SOUTH COAST

Msambweni, Shimoni,
Lunga Lunga, Tanzania

Ukunda Airfield is a smaller airstrip near Diani with daily flights to the Maasai Mara. It has no specific disability facilities but is all level. (For access issues in small airfields, see page 92.)

GETTING AROUND

Standard taxis, *matatus* and minibuses are a cheap way of getting around the coast but anyone who usually uses accessible vehicles should see *Public transport*, page 89. Go Africa safaris (see page 19) does have accessible vehicles and is based in Diani.

WHERE TO STAY

Mombasa North Coast

Vipingo Beach Resort (7 cottages) Kuruwitu Rd 28, Vipingo, Mombasa; **m** 0724 831926; www.vipingo-resort.de
About 25km north of Mombasa, this small & exclusive resort is German owned & run. One of the owners uses a wheelchair, & although it is on a high bluff above the beach, it has been built to suit disabled guests. 4 cottages are designed to be accessible, a shallow ramp rises to the dining area & from there, a long, cemented track leads down to the pool & the idyllic private beach. The pool is surrounded by a low wall (36cm high), an accessible path runs to the beach-viewing platform & 2 public toilets near the beach bar have support rails. A shower/commode chair & a lightweight wheelchair are available.
Cottage 1: Doorway (84) has threshold (2); dbl bed (60) has light switch & transfer space; door to ensuite (87) is level; roll-in shower has handheld showerhead, round taps (99) but no support rail; washbasin (79) has short lever tap; toilet (41) has front & side transfer space & 1 horizontal support rail (53). **$$$$**

Sarova Whitesands (338 rooms) ℓ 020 276 7000; **f** 020 271 5566;
e centralreservations@sarovahotels.com; www.sarovahotels.com
10km north of Mombasa, Whitesands is a large hotel, but still feels warm & welcoming. It was being refurbished in 2008 & by the time of publication should have 3 extremely accessible rooms near reception with roll-in showers & support rails. Routes through the rest of the complex are generally flat & hard, with tiles, interlocking bricks & well-finished crazy-paved surfaces. The Lido Seafood Restaurant is up 5 steps but the Italian Minazi & Pavilion buffet are (steeply) ramped. A wheelchair is available from reception. **$$$$**

Voyager Beach Resort (233 rooms) ℓ 020 444 6651; **f** 020 444 6600;
e sales@heritagehotels.co.ke; www.heritage-eastafrica.com
A maritime theme prevails through this smart resort, which is fun, but it's not all plain sailing if access is your priority. It is only some 5km north of Mombasa but beach access is with steps. Although there are some

restaurants, pools & bars that are navigable without steps, not all are & ramps can be steep. A wheelchair is available but beach access is difficult. Less able guests are usually pointed to the ground-floor standard rooms, some of which have no step at doorways (76) & step-in shower cubicles. Ablutions in superior rooms & junior suites are similarly furnished, though the latter do have baths with fitted handles. There are portable ramps available for the sgl step at the doorway. No bathrooms have enough space for comfortable wheeling. **$$$**

Nyali Beach Resort (170 rooms) ✆ 041 471 551; **f** 041 471 987; **e** sales@nyalibeach.co.ke; ⌂ www.nyalibeach.co.ke 🔲 🖼 🔲

Nyali is about 3km north of Mombasa, & being constructed on a steep slope above the beach, it wouldn't appear to be ideal for wheelers & slow walkers. In fact, it's admirably well armed, with 2 adapted rooms & good thoroughfares around the hotel. The challenge is working out which suits you. Room 126 is on the top level, near reception & the main dining area whilst room 522 is at beach level, near the beach & several other eateries. They are similarly accessible, though Room 522's bathroom has grab rails in more useful positions. To get down to beach level from reception you must follow a long slope (around 150m), which is steep in places. There is a lift, but bizarrely it stops 7 steps from reception, so is only of use to able-bodied walkers.

Room 126: Doorway (86) is slightly ramped; dbl bed (57) has transfer space, light switch & phone; doorway into ensuite (70) is level; roll-in shower has handheld showerhead & star taps (88) plus 2 support rails, 1 vertical (high point 80) & 1 horizontal (83), but both are too far from washing area; washbasin (69) has lever taps; toilet has front transfer space with 1 horizontal support rail (70).

Room 522: Doorway (75) is level; dbl bed (57) has light switch, phone & transfer space; bathroom door (68) is level; roll-in shower has handheld showerhead, 2 vertical rails, a horizontal rail & 1 swing-up rail (80) shared with the toilet; washbasin (71) has low mirror & lever taps; toilet (42) has front & side transfer space. **$$$**

Mombasa South Coast

All the hotels listed below are approximately 20–25km south of Mombasa, around Diani Beach.

Diani Reef Beach Resort & Spa (143 rooms) ✆ 040 320 2723; **f** 040 320 2196; **e** info@dianireef.com; ⌂ www.dianireef.com 🔲 🖼 🔲

Diani Reef is sleek & chic, & has a wheelchair available. Polished wooden boardwalks connect smooth tiles & crazy paving & from the parking area all public areas – except the gym – can be reached without steps. The main restaurant is level – tables >65cm – while the Chinese, Japanese & Indian eateries are accessed by ramps via the tempting pastry area. The swimming pool has steps with no handrail to enter.

Rooms 36 & 37: Adapted & identical: door (90) has a slight ramp; beds (58) have light switch & phone; door to ensuite (88) is level; roll-in shower has plastic chair available, handheld showerhead, lever tap (80) & a vertical support rail (low point 81); washbasin has no knee space but has low mirror & lever tap; toilet (42) has 1 dbl support rail that swings up against the wall giving front & side transfer space.

The gargantuan presidential suite has a bathroom up 1 step with another roll-in shower & vertical handrail (120) on the wall. **$$$$**

Villa Kusini (2 rooms) ☏ 040 320 4015; **e** info@dmtours.net; ☝ www.dmtours.net

This smart 2-storey villa is not on the beach, but has access to the nearby Neptune Hotel & free use of its facilities. The owner's brother uses a wheelchair, so it has been adapted, & the most striking first impression is the innovative sitting-height 'slipway' ramp into the swimming pool. The pool also has steps & seating around its inside edge. There's the option of self-catering (fully equipped kitchen) but staff are included in the price to buy food, cook & clean. A wheelchair & shower/commode chair with 24in wheels are available.

The house entrance is ramped or up 3 steps, there are 2 ground-floor bedrooms with a dbl bed (69) with transfer space, light switches & phone; shower has a lip (3) so almost roll-in, handheld showerhead & round taps (103); toilet (39) has front transfer space only & there were no support rails (though apparently 1 was installed in 2009); upstairs, under makuti thatch, is a cool & airy lounge. I'm told the toilet seat now has a 'soft cover' & there is a shower stool available. **$$$$**

Indian Ocean Beach Resort (100 rooms) ☏ 040 320 3730; **f** 040 320 3557; **e** infoiobc@jacarandahotels.com; ☝ www.jacarandahotels.com

Not as accessible as Leisure Lodge (see following entry), though slightly more personable, this resort still caters to less mobile guests. Reception, swimming pool & rooms are interconnected with a mix of bricks, crazy paving & ramps, though some of these are too steep for independent pushing. The main restaurant is up 6 steps, however, the Ocean Terrace & Bahari ('sea' in Swahili) restaurants are within reach. The pool has entry steps but no handrails. When asked about disability aids, not only was a wheelchair wheeled out but elbow crutches were also proudly presented.

Room 113: Has adaptations including ramped door (87); bed (53) with light switch, phone & transfer space; level doorway into ensuite (89); roll-in shower with removable seat, 2 support rails (1 horizontal, 1 diagonal with midpoints 101 & 130), fixed showerhead & star taps (117); toilet has 2 diagonal support rails (102) & front transfer space only; flat, wide entry to patio. **$$$**

Leisure Lodge Beach & Golf Resort (249 rooms) ☏ 040 320 3624/2620; **f** 040 320 2046; **e** exec@leisurelodgeresort.com; ☝ www.leisurelodgeresort.com

With everything necessary for a comfortable beach break already in place,

the choice of 4 accessible rooms completes Leisure Lodge's picture. This is
the most accessible hotel I saw on the Mombasa coast. Only the
Fisherman's Cove Restaurant is down stairs, otherwise all the main public
areas – including beach access – are continuously level or ramped
(sometimes steeper than 8%). Access routes vary but all are smooth
enough to allow independent pushing. Dining tables are >65cm &
swimming pools are easily reached & entered using steps with handrails.
Adapted Bahari rooms (Rooms L1 & J1): Very close to reception. Level
door (85); beds (48 & 64) have light switches, phones & transfer space;
highest control (143) is the power key; level door to ensuite (87); roll-in
shower with plastic stool, 2 shaped support rails (horizontal part 80),
transfer space, handheld showerhead & lever tap (126); toilet (42) has front
& side transfer space & support rail (80); washbasin (69) has round taps.
Adapted Bustani Club rooms (numbers 1 & 28): Closer to dining &
swimming areas. Level door (76); bed (52) with light switch, transfer space
& phone; level door to ensuite (72); roll-in shower is as in Bahari rooms,
but with round taps (64) instead of lever taps; toilet (40) is as in Bahari
rooms; washbasin (64) has lever tap. No standard rooms have accessible
features. **$$$**

Southern Palms Beach Resort (294 rooms) ☎ 040 320 3721; **f** 040 320 3381;
e infodesk@southernpalmskenya.com; ⊕ www.southernpalmskenya.com 🔳 🚽
The step at the entrance of this large hotel is no warm welcome for guests
using wheels. Once inside, most restaurants, bars & pools are interlinked
with level paths, but room entrances (73) are all up a step. The Lebanese
restaurant is on an island in the pool (up 4 then down 4 steps). Showers
are all 'step-in' (15) & none have grab rails. The 2 positives I found are
that 1 swimming pool has a gently sloping roll-in entrance & the corner
ground-floor rooms have a support rail above the bath (the latter cannot
be verified as these rooms were occupied during my site inspection). **$$$**

Diani House (6 rooms) ☎ 040 330 0084; **e** info@dianihouse.com;
⊕ www.dianihouse.com 🔳 🚽 🪟
Relaxed, homely hospitality & superb cuisine epitomise Diani House. Set
amidst lush gardens on the beachfront, the old building has been kept up
to date without losing its charm. The house itself, including a dining area
on the veranda, is up no more than 1 small step. The path to the beach is
about 50m down a shallow slope through the garden. Of the 6 rooms,
Turtle (nearest to the main house) is most suited to limited mobility, as it
has both shower & bath & has the greatest circulation space.
Room Turtle: Doorway (86) has 1 low step; 2 'Zanzibar' beds (76) can be
replaced with lower Western-style beds if this is preferred; bathroom door
(70) is level; bath (49) has a tiled extended seating area at the foot-end
allowing for transfers; roll-in shower has fixed showerhead & round taps
(114); washbasin (82) has round taps & low mirror; toilet (41) has front &
side transfer space. **$$$**

Other notable accommodation
The following information may also be of interest.

Safari Beach Hotel and **Jadini Beach Hotel** are located near Diani and owned by Alliance Hotels (🖰 *www.alliancehotels.com*), and were undergoing extensive renovations at the time of writing. They will be open in early and late 2009 respectively and will each have at least three very accessible rooms.

WHERE TO EAT
The majority of resort visitors tend to eat in their hotels, but for the more adventurous, the Diani area offers several noteworthy eateries. None of these go as far as having deliberately accessible toilets, but several have few, or no, steps to enter and get around.

Ali Barbours Cave Restaurant & Forty Thieves Beach Bar ✆ 040 320 2033/3003; 🖰 www.dianibeachbar.com; ⊘ from 09.00 daily. Under the same management, these 2 well-known local haunts differ greatly in access. Ali Barbours has lots of steps, so people keen to taste its excellent seafood specialties may need help. The Forty Thieves Beach Bar, however, serves b/fasts, snacks & bar food, & although it has sand, the owners were planning ramped access in 2008. **$$$$**

Leonardo's m 0720 501707; **e** glt@leonardoskenya.com; ⊘ 08.00–22.30 daily. In the Colliers Centre, this eatery advertises wood-oven pizzas & homemade ice cream. It has 1 step to enter. **$$$**

Shan-E-Punjab ✆ 040 320 2116; ⊘ 13.00–23.00 daily. Again, in the Diani Shopping Centre, this Indian restaurant has good access from the parking area & is all level inside. **$$$**

Tandoori Bar Situated on the Beach Rd. This relaxed pub is all level, if not overly spacious. **$$$**

Aniello's m 0721 894045. In the Ushago Shopping Centre, this Italian restaurant was going to open in 2008. It looked relatively accessible at the time of writing, with level entry from the parking area. **$$**

Onjinko's ✆ 040 320 2303; ⊘ all day daily. In the Diani Shopping Centre, bread & pastries are freshly baked daily & an international menu includes pizzas. **$$**

Ushago Shopping Centre ⊘ during daytime. This new complex was opened in 2008 & has several restaurants & a small food court. Nyama choma (roasted meat) & other traditional Swahili dishes are available as well as pizzas. **$$**

OTHER PRACTICALITIES

Both north- and south-coast resort areas have banks, post offices and pharmacies, and the majority of the larger hotel complexes contain basic shops and gift stores.

Medical services

On the south coast is the **Diani Hospital** (*next to the Diani Shopping Centre;* \ *040 320 2435/6;* **m** *0722 569261;* **f** *040 320 3080/16;* ⏚ *www.dianibeachhospital.com*). In Mombasa itself, the **Aga Khan Hospital** (*Vanga Rd, Kizingo;* \ *041 222 7710–5;* ⏚ *www.agakhan hospitals.org*).

WHAT TO SEE AND DO

For water lovers, all the usual **aqua-activities** are available, including snorkelling, scuba diving, deep-sea fishing, sailing and jet skiing. Most hotels and resorts will be able to arrange these on request, and although there are no operators who have made any exceptional efforts to include clients with disabilities, all will attempt to organise something to suit your abilities.

A flavour of Mombasa's past still exists in the **old town**. It doesn't take much effort or imagination to transport yourself back a few centuries when wandering along the docks amongst the wooden fishing dhows, or through the narrow, winding streets leading to Fort Jesus. Smooth pavements are rare, but vehicles are also not common in the old part of town, meaning wheelchair users can feel safe wheeling the streets. Most shops and stalls are up a step, but traders are delighted to bring their goods out to you, or help you inside. *Matatus*, taxis and buses run up and down the coast roads all day, but none of these are designed to be accessible. (For further information on public transport in Africa, see *Chapter 3*, page 89.) For **souvenir shoppers**, the streets around most beach resorts are packed with curio stalls and these are almost all at street level.

TANZANIA AT A GLANCE

Location	East Africa, with an Indian Ocean coastline, bordering eight countries including Kenya to the north and Zambia to the southwest
Size	945,087km²
Climate	Varies from tropical to arid, with more temperate highlands and two rainy seasons (Apr/May and Nov/Dec)
Population	40.2 million (2008 estimate)
Capital	Dodoma (population 170,000 approx in 2002)
Largest city	Dar es Salaam (population 3 million in 2006)
Currency	Tanzanian shilling (TSh)
Rate of exchange	£1=TSh1,991; US$1=TSh1,336; €1=TSh1,773 (May 2009)
Language	English (official), Kiswahili (official) and numerous indigenous languages
Religion	Christianity, Islam, indigenous beliefs; Zanzibar is 99% Muslim
Time	GMT +3
Electricity	220V, delivered at 50Hz; three round pins and British-style plugs with three square pins
Weights and measures	Metric
Public holidays	1 Jan, Zanzibar Revolution Day (12 Jan), CCM Day (5 Feb), Good Friday, Easter Monday, Union Day (26 Apr), International Workers' Day (1 May), Saba Saba (Peasants') Day (7 Jul), Nane Nane (Farmers') Day (8 Aug), Nyere Memorial Day (14 Oct), Independence Day (9 Dec), 25–26 Dec, Id-ul-Fitr, Islamic New Year, Prophet's Birthday
Tourist board	ᐩ www.tanzaniatouristboard.com
International telephone code	+255
Further information:	For a more in-depth analysis, including background information and mainstream travel information, see Philip Briggs's Bradt safari guides to Tanzania and northern Tanzania and Chris and Susan McIntyre's Bradt travel guide to Zanzibar.

5 Tanzania

The purists would say that northern Tanzania's game viewing is unequalled anywhere in the continent, and, with the area boasting names like Serengeti and Ngorongoro, few can argue. The sense of space and abounding wilderness is sometimes breathtaking, and because the tourism industry here is still relatively young, it never feels overrun by visitors. Lake Manyara and Tarangire are lesser known but are beautiful national parks, and Zanzibar is Tanzania's Indian Ocean paradise. The Tanzanian people themselves are more reserved than their confident northerly neighbours, but give them time and they are just as warm and welcoming, and are genuinely delighted to have you visit their country.

GENERAL INFORMATION

ACCESS SUMMARY
'Inclusion for everyone' is far down Tanzania's list of priorities. Nevertheless, like Kenya, all the game areas I visited have at least one lodge or hotel with accessible features. The road network has been given a major boost in the last ten years with the previously atrocious route from Arusha to Karatu being tar sealed. The final leg of the journey into Ngorongoro and the Serengeti is still rough – be prepared for several hours' badly corrugated gravel – but these areas can always be reached by light aircraft.

LOCAL OPERATORS
For local operators catering to people with mobility issues, plus some mainstream operators that have shown a genuine interest in this market, see *Chapter 1, Specialised operators in Africa*, pages 19–20.

TANZANIAN NATIONAL PARKS: ENTRY PAYMENT
In November 2007, Tanzania National Parks (⏚ *www.tanzania parks.com*) introduced a system of electronic cards to pay for park entry. These are now the recognised method of payment and are carried by all safari companies. For Tarangire, Lake Manyara and Serengeti national parks independent travellers can buy one-off cards in various denominations (US$50, US$70,

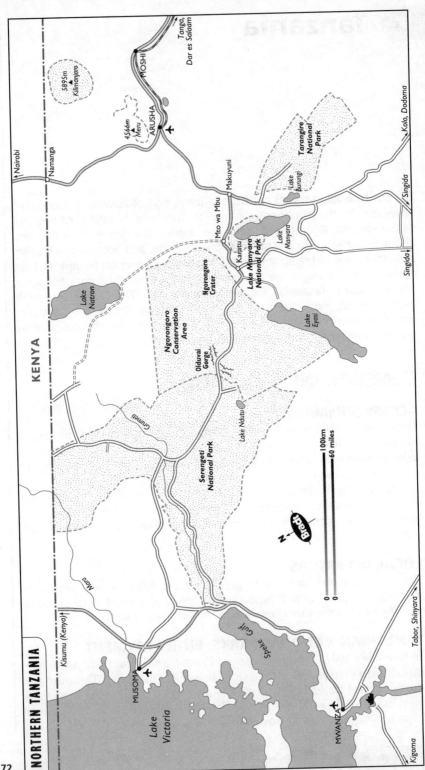

NORTHERN TANZANIA

US$100, US$250 and US$500) from EXIM banks in Arusha. MasterCards are also accepted at entry gates but not VISA cards. Travellers' cheques are no longer a valid method of payment and a penalty of 50% (of the total fee) is charged if cash is used.

ARUSHA

The hub of all safari activities in northern Tanzania, Arusha is a big, busy town with a thriving, commercial air to it. At first glance you could be forgiven for thinking everything depends on tourism. However, if you look beyond the swarms of safari vehicles and the hordes of affluent tourists followed by their predatory touts and curio sellers, it is not difficult to see a typical African metropolis. The fruit and vegetable markets are a throng of bodies, the public transport system bulges and sways with the weight of its passenger load, yet, despite the apparent chaos, a smile and personal eye contact are never far away.

Arusha has a picturesque setting, guarded over by the towering 4,566m bulk of Mount Meru, and as a result of its high altitude (1,500m) it is usually pleasantly cool, belying its tropical location. The town also has a strong history as an important centre of commerce – agriculture has long been the biggest employer (dominated by coffee, vegetable and flower growing) and several large factories make use of its good road links and proximity to Kenya. Politically, Arusha is also a known name on a world scale, having hosted the International Criminal Tribunal for Rwanda.

GETTING THERE AND AWAY

By road
Main routes into Arusha are good quality. Coaches from the main bus station run to the coast; Dar es Salaam is around ten hours' drive. Various companies operate shuttle buses across the border to Nairobi, starting in Moshi and taking in Nairobi's Jomo Kenyatta International Airport. From Arusha to Nairobi takes about five hours, including the efficient Namanga border post. There is not yet any means of public transport that has specific features for disabled passengers, so anybody who needs help with luggage and to board vehicles should see *Chapter 3, Public transport*, page 89.

By air
Kilimanjaro International Airport (⊕ *www.kilimanjaroairport.co.tz*) is less than an hour's drive from Arusha and receives daily European arrivals from the Dutch airline KLM, as well as within-Africa flights from Air Kenya, Kenya Airways, South African Airlines and Ethiopian Airlines. Air Tanzania connects Arusha with Dar es Salaam's international arrivals and flies to the other Tanzanian ports, including Zanzibar.

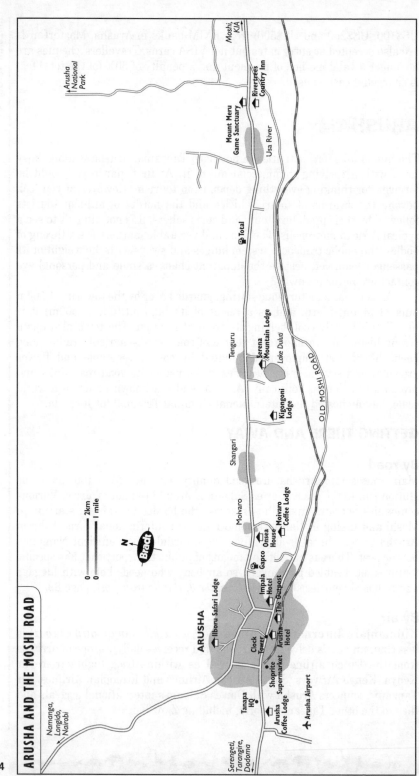

ARUSHA AND THE MOSHI ROAD

Namanga,
Longido,
Nairobi

Serengeti,
Tarangire,
Dodoma

ARUSHA

Clock
Tower

Shoprite
Supermarket

Tanapa
HQ

Arusha
Coffee Lodge

Arusha Airport

Ilboru Safari Lodge

Impala
Hotel

The Outpost

Arusha
Hotel

Gapco

Onsea
House

Moivaro
Coffee Lodge

Moivaro

Shangari

Kigongoni
Lodge

Serena
Mountain Lodge

Lake Duluti

Tengeru

OLD MOSHI ROAD

Total

Mount Meru
Game Sanctuary

Usa River

Rivertrees
Country Inn

Moshi,
KIA

Arusha National
Park

N

Bradt

2km
1 mile
0
0

174

There are no steps through the airport but also no disability toilet and no aisle chair. If you're unable to walk, you will be carried in your wheelchair or 'bride style' down the steps from the aircraft. Shuttle buses run from here to Arusha town centre but none have specific access features.

Arusha Airport is about 5km west of town on the Serengeti road and connects with Dar es Salaam, Zanzibar and the small airfields dotted around the northern circuit. It is serviced by domestic carriers using light aircraft. (For access issues and transfer procedures in small airfields, see page 92.)

GETTING AROUND
Arusha is swarming with taxis, *dala dalas* and minibuses. These are a cheap way of getting around but anyone who usually uses accessible vehicles should see *Chapter 3, Public transport,* page 89.

WHERE TO STAY
A huge amount of accommodation is available with several options for all wallets, but as yet, Rivertrees is the only lodge that stands out as being proactive towards disability access.

In Arusha
Arusha Hotel (65 rooms) opposite Clock Tower on Old Moshi Rd; ℓ 027 250 7777; **f** 027 250 8889; **e** info@thearushahotel.com; ⌂ www.thearushahotel.com
The Arusha Hotel has been renovated recently but has not lost its charm, earned from more than a century of being the main point of rest for travellers through northern Tanzania. As with most large hotels, hallways are smooth, wide & hard, but there are several steps – remnants of the era in which it was designed – & outdoor flagstone pathways are sometimes bumpy. Corridors are carpeted. The lift has space for a wheelchair & goes to all floors, including the basement with the business centre & casino, though the bar has a narrow, stepped access. There are many steps to the pool & fitness centre, but the dining room is level & tables are >65cm. There are no rooms adapted for disabled guests; however, all have level access & plenty of space.
Typical standard room: Main doors are 80cm; beds (54) have light switches, phone & transfer space; highest switch is 133cm; bath (57) has transfer space (but it's tight) & fixed showerhead; washbasin has no knee space whilst the toilet is approachable in a wheelchair only from the front. **$$$**

Impala Hotel (160 rooms) Old Moshi Rd; ℓ 027 250 8448/51; **f** 027 254 3088/9; **e** impala@kilinet.co.tz; ⌂ www.impalahotel.com
The Impala will suit some disabled visitors, but its claims of having 'fully accessible' rooms are, at best, a little hopeful. It's a busy hotel, catering to tourists as well as business clients & is good value & dependable if not stimulating. Entry from parking is level. 1 restaurant (Italian) is up stairs

only, but there are Chinese & Indian options on level floors. Public toilets are standard & are up 2 steps with narrow doorways (59). There are 5 steps on the way to the attractive pool & 7, or a ladder, to enter it. The lift has enough space for wheelchairs.

Room 116B: The most accessible, but has no view. Doorway (77) is level; beds (49) have transfer space, light switches & phone; bathroom door (74) is level; bath (53) has fitted handles, showerhead & transfer space; washbasin has no knee space & toilet (42) has side transfer space. **$$**

Ilboru Safari Lodge (30 rooms) **m** 0754 270 357; **e** reservations@ ilborusafarilodge.com; www.ilborusafarilodge.com [3]
High above the town centre, this lodge is a good escape from the bustle of Arusha, yet close enough to still be considered 'in town'. I'm told the owner manager is a 'Lieutenant-Colonel Mika Metili', but although Ilboru is obviously a well-run establishment – clean & organised – it still felt comfortable & friendly & not at all militaristic. Access routes are hard, flat flagstones but there are many steps around. Parking to reception is up 4 & down 3 steps, then the large swimming pool & rondavel cottages are up 3 from there. There are about 20 steps from reception up to the restaurant.
Rondavel 1: The closest to reception. Doorway (77) has a drop-off (2). Beds (50) have light switch & transfer space; bathroom door (66) & shower are both down 1 step (5); washbasin (67) has round taps & toilet (38) has front transfer space only. **$$**

The Outpost (23 rooms) 7A Serengeti Rd; **℡** 027 254 8405; **e** outpost@bol.co.tz; www.outposttanzania.com [0]
The Outpost is just off the centre of town, so is a cheaper base to explore Arusha on foot. It's tidy & unpretentious & the relaxed atmosphere might stem partly from its Australian ownership. Reception is up 2 (relatively steep) ramps from street level then the rooms are situated around a close-knit complex incorporating swimming pool (up 2 steps) & restaurant/bar (up a small ramp. Pathways are a mixture of smooth stone & 50x50cm flagstones set level in hard lawns. The latter may be tricky for wheelchairs in wet weather, but dry season should be fine for most strong pushers or those with help.
Room A6: This is the room we saw, which is apparently as accessible as any. Doorway (76) has a slight, sloped threshold (5); bed (52) has transfer space & light switch; other switches are <140cm; bathroom doorway (75) is level; step-in shower (19) has round taps & fixed showerhead; washbasin (65) has round taps & toilet (33) has transfer space, although it may need a slightly diagonal approach. **$**

Around Arusha
Arusha Coffee Lodge (23 chalets) 99 Serengeti Rd; **℡** 027 250 0630–9;
f 027 250 8245; **e** info@elewana.com; www.elewana.com [1] [R]
In many ways, Arusha Coffee Lodge is flawless. However, for disabled

travellers, the important points to note are that not only are the rooms up steps, but they are split level inside. Therefore, if you do need help negotiating a step then your room privacy will also be invaded. If this is not an issue then it delivers everything you would expect for a property in this price bracket. The public toilet is spacious with wide doorway (80). Pathways are gravel but some rooms can be reached by vehicle. There's 1 step *en route* to the swimming pool & the dining area is level. Some rooms have roll-in showers (with wide doorways but no rails or seat) but toilets (43) here have front transfer space only. **$$$$**

Onsea House (5 rooms) **m** 0784 833 207; **e** info@onseahouse.com; www.onseahouse.com [3+]
Onsea is extremely welcoming & the Belgian chef produces some of the most polished cuisine in Arusha. Sadly, its exquisite location amidst the low hills outside the town doesn't encourage limited mobility. There is a games room & a bar level with the parking area, but from there it's 22 steps up to reception, the restaurant & main rooms. Less able travellers might prefer to use it as a chance to eat out in style while in Arusha (accepting help up & down the steps) rather than a place to spend a few days.
The closest room to reception: Has doorways (84) up 2 steps, beds (48) with light switches & transfer space; bathroom doorway (67) is level & there is a bath (49) with round taps, a handheld showerhead & transfer space; the washbasin (87) has lever taps & toilet (40) has front transfer space only. There is a cottage near the swimming pool, down around 20 steps from the parking, which has 2 self-catering rooms; main doorways here are 84cm. **$$$$**

Kigongoni Lodge (18 cottages) **☎** 027 255 3087; **f** 027 255 3073/99 (lodge reception); **e** manager@kigongoni.net; www.kigongoni.net [3+]
Similar to the Onsea in setting – with buildings dotted around a hillside – this striking lodge may only suit more mobile visitors. However, it's worth including not only because the rooms themselves are level & spacious, but also because the lodge also heavily subsidises the nearby Sibusiso home for local children with learning disabilities. This organisation (www.sibusiso.nl) was started by the lodge owners (a Dutch GP & nurse/teacher) & is one of the most respected of such projects in the area. Reception is up a long, steep ramp & several steps from the parking area, the appealing swimming pool is 18 steps down from there (has 4 steps to enter) & the restaurant/bar is up 8. Rooms – with balconies giving sublime views of either Mount Kilimanjaro or Mount Meru – are various distances & elevations from reception.
Room 3: One of the closest to reception. The doorway (76) is 30 steps from reception; bed (55) has transfer space & light switch but the phone is out of reach; bathroom door (78) is level; bath (46) has extended, level seating area & a handheld showerhead; spacious step-in shower (11) has wide

entry (79), a fixed showerhead, a cute corner seat (41) which is not in the water flow & round taps (114); toilet (41) has front & side transfer space but narrow doorway (65). **$$$**

Mount Meru Game Sanctuary (17 rooms) ☎ 027 255 3643; **e** reservations@intimate-places.com; ⌒ www.intimate-places.com ⦿⊟
This cosy lodge has two distinct advantages over some local rivals: Firstly, there is wildlife on site – including a selection of antelopes & a myriad birdlife – & secondly, all the buildings are relatively close together on a fairly level site with decent pathways. The entrance has 3 steps & removable ramps available for other raised areas in the grounds. The restaurant is ramped with all tables 72cm. No adapted rooms, but most conform to: doorway (81) with 1 step but ramp available; bed (65) has transfer space & light switch; bathroom door is level (68); step-in shower (7) with plastic chair available; washbasin (67); toilet (41) has front transfer space only. **$$$**

Moivaro Coffee Lodge (16 cottages) ☎ 027 255 3243; **f** 027 255 3885; **e** reservations@moivaro.com; ⌒ www.moivaro.com ⦿⊞ ⦿
Set amidst lovely gardens on a coffee farm, this spacious, stylish lodge has a feeling of solidity. The food is fine, service good & its level setting will suit many visitors. Reaching reception from the parking area is the stiffest climb (5 steps). Beyond that, the eating areas are 1 step down & the swimming pool 1 down again, then a short walk over a neat lawn. There are 4 steps to enter the pool. Rooms are also 1 step down from the dining area, then less than 50m along a loose pebble path & a hard earth track.
The nearest room: Doorway (82) is up 1 step; beds (51) have light switch & transfer space; bathroom door (72) is level; bath (62) has transfer space & star taps; roll-in shower has fixed showerhead & star taps (103); washbasin has star taps but no knee clearance. **$$$**

Rivertrees Country Inn (14 rooms) ☎/f 027 255 3894; **e** info@rivertrees.com; ⌒ www.rivertrees.com ⦿⊟ ⊟ ⦿ ⊟
Regarding inclusion, owner/manager Martina Gehrken-Trappe is the most forward-thinking proprietor in Arusha, & Rivertrees, a tastefully renovated farmhouse & outbuildings in extensive leafy gardens, is testament to her enthusiasm. There are currently 2 river cottages with accessible features & plans are in place to adapt 1 room (Room 2) in the main house. The dining room is ramped & the path to the pool (which has stepped entry but no handrail) is level. Access routes are not yet ideal, being a mix of gravel, crazy paving & sand.
2 river cottages (numbers 1 & 2): These are very spacious & have ramped access. Bed (60) has transfer space & light switches (touch lights); doorway to ensuite (80) is level; bath (48) has fitted handles & extended sitting area that may help wheelchair transfers; roll-in outside shower (with step-free access via the main door of the room) has fixed showerhead

& seating (not in washing area); toilet (44) has shaped support rail (horizontal part 76) but front transfer space only. **$$$**

Serena Mountain Village (42 rooms) ℡ 028 262 1519/07; **f** 028 621 520; **e** from website; ⬡ www.serenahotels.com [3⁺] [⬚]
This attractive, colonial-style hotel is set in verdant gardens, but – living up to its name – has several steps to negotiate through the public areas. There are 6 up to reception & the gift shop, then a further 3 up to the bar & 3 down to the dining area. The closest rooms are down a crazy-paving slope & across a tricky little arched bridge. Public toilets are up several steps & not designed for disabled access.
Rondavel 6: Doorway is up 1 step (4); only 1 bed (57) has transfer space; entrance to ensuite has sharp turns (difficult for larger wheelchairs); shower is down 1 step (8) & has fixed showerhead & 1 support rail (high) but limited wheelchair space; washbasin not wheelchair accessible & toilet user would block bathroom door. **$$$**

WHERE TO EAT

While it is true that the majority of safari tourists tend to eat where they are staying, a special meal out is often done at least once on a trip. Arusha might be the place to choose for this; with such a steady flow of tourists it has eateries catering to every taste. For people with mobility problems, although there are no restaurants with custom-built accessible lavatories, the vast majority are ground floor with one or two steps.

Local recommendations are **Pizzarusha Restaurant** (next to Pizza Hut, north of the town centre), which serves all the usual popular dishes, the **Impala Hotel's Indian restaurant** and **Spices and Herbs Ethiopian Restaurant** (next to the Impala Hotel). The last is my pick; it may be an acquired taste but Ethiopian food is unique and the fare you'll receive here is just as good as the real thing. It is up a couple of steps but staff will gladly help.

OTHER PRACTICALITIES

As the launch pad of the majority of Tanzanian safaris, Arusha is well equipped to supply travellers. Apart from a bank in Karatu and small kiosk shops and expensive money changing in lodges elsewhere, most urban facilities can be forgotten once you leave town. Banks with ATMs and several bureaux de change are dotted around the centre of Arusha, the main post office is opposite the clock tower and internet cafés are easily found.

For independent travellers, the Shoprite Supermarket on the way out towards the Serengeti is a one-stop shop for all packaged food supplies and the fresh food markets can be plundered for perishables.

Medical services

The **AICC Hospital** (*Old Moshi Rd;* ℡ 027 250 2329) has a good reputation. It is clean and well run, and has a reliable X-ray machine among other facilities. Another (probably cheaper) option is **Ithnasheri Charitable**

WONDER WELDERS

When buying souvenirs it is always worthwhile noticing where and by whom the items were made. One producer worth supporting is Wonder Welders in Tanzania.

In 2004, a group of polio victims in Dar es Salaam – some of whom had previously been begging on the streets – got together and, with help from various sources, established a welding workshop. They started off making animal designs and after several months were visited by Scottish artist/welder Heather Cummin, who helped enhance their skills in the finer art of metal sculpture. A successful exhibition helped fund the launch of Wonder Workshop as a Tanzanian NGO, and the organisation is now self-sufficient, employing 40 full-time workers and constantly training more.

The range of products runs from masks to all different kinds of birds and animals; recent diversifications include training local disabled women in the art of making soap, using recycled glass to make jewellery and fashioning handmade wooden toys from renewable wood sources within Tanzania.

Various outlets throughout the mainland and on Zanzibar stock Wonder Welders' products, plus purchases can be made by mail order or donations can be given to help raise funds for a new premises.

You can also visit their workshop at Plot 44, Galu Street, Ada Estate, Dar es Salaam, Tanzania.

Wonder Welders PO Box 70045, Dar es Salaam, Tanzania ☎ + 255 (0)754 051 417; **e** info@wonderwelders.org or wonderwelders@bol.co.tz; 🖰 www.wonder welders.org

Hospital (*Sokoine Rd;* ☎ *027 250 2320*). People with serious medical emergencies would be evacuated from Kilimanjaro International Airport to Nairobi.

WHAT TO SEE AND DO

For most travellers, the main use of free time in Arusha will be buying souvenirs, and this will probably be one of the best places on your safari to do this. If you are going to be returning through the town then a worthwhile tip is to look around, note prices and if you don't see anything similar or better during your journey then buy in Arusha on your return visit. The majority of vendors are based near the clock tower roundabout, and although a step will occasionally need to be navigated, all are ground floor and most haggling is done at street level. Several of the more upmarket shops, including the superb Cultural Heritage Centre (which is on the outskirts of town in the direction of the Serengeti) will accept credit-card payment and can organise your purchases to be packed and shipped home.

TARANGIRE NATIONAL PARK

Of all the main highlights in northern Tanzania, Tarangire is usually the last to be considered when planning an itinerary. However, this says more about the standard of the competition than about Tarangire itself. This park is top quality on many counts. For avid game viewers, it can compete with the best, especially during the dry season when the perennial Tarangire River draws animals from afar. Huge herds of elephant are not uncommon and substantial populations of wildebeest, zebra, buffalo and smaller antelopes sustain the usual feline and canine carnivores. On one drive, we had the remarkable privilege of witnessing a lion kill, spying a treed leopard and watching a feeding cheetah (with cubs), all in the space of two hours. But that was exceptional.

For those who appreciate space, Tarangire may only be 2,850km², but it never feels crowded. For the purist, the timeless landscape, studded with ancient baobab trees, is quintessential Africa. More pragmatically, for people with mobility issues, the road network in the northern – most toured – part of the park is relatively well-graded gravel, meaning comfortable game drives, and there are two accommodation options inside the park that have access features. If you were pushed for time, then I would recommend Tarangire over Lake Manyara, mainly because of the access options inside the park, and if there is no time to include the Serengeti, then Tarangire is a reliable substitute. It is one of my favourite parks in Africa.

Park fees Tarangire is managed by Tanzania National Parks so uses the electronic payment scheme (see page 171). From July 2007 the entry fee is US$35 per adult and US$10 per child (<16 years) for 24 hours.

GETTING THERE AND AWAY

Tarangire is about 100km from Arusha, 8km off the main Arusha–Dodoma highway. This road is smooth tar until the Tarangire turn-off. Arrival by small aircraft is also possible, but local airstrips are small with no facilities designed for disability. (For access issues in small airfields, see page 92.)

WHERE TO STAY

Tarangire Treetops (20 luxury tents) ☎ 027 250 0630–9; **f** 027 250 8245; **e** info@elewana.com; ⏏ www.elewana.com [3+] [⛶]

Anyone who's not completely sure-footed will probably flinch at the name alone; surprisingly however, if it's in your budget then it could be in your plans. Thoughtfully designed & sumptuously furnished, the room types vary from those built around baobab trees, which have spiral stairways, to some with ramped access. The main entrance is up 2 steps, the bar 3 & dining room 3. There are 5 steps to the swimming pool & steps with a handrail to enter it. Pathways are relatively smooth gravel & polished wooden boardwalks take over leading into tents.

Ramped rooms: Door is 77cm; bed (52) has transfer space, light switch & a whistle for emergencies; highest switch is <140cm; doorway to ensuite

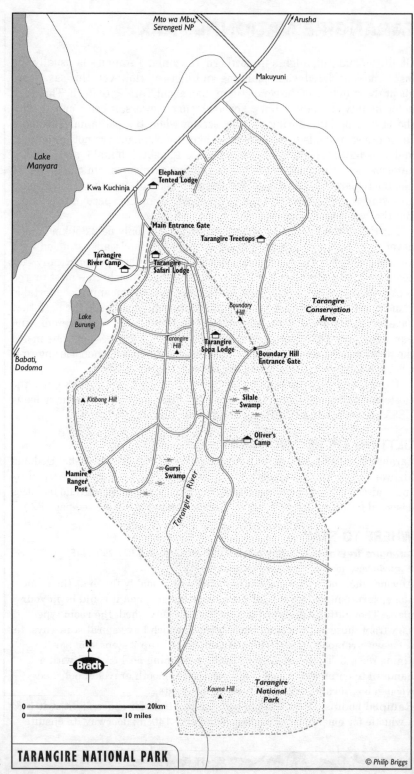

TARANGIRE NATIONAL PARK

© Philip Briggs

(110) is level; dbl roll-in shower has canvas seat & transfer space, lever taps (120) & fixed showerheads; washbasin has no knee space but toilet (43) has front & side transfer space. **$$$$$**

Oliver's Camp (8 tents) **e** info@asilialodges.com; ⊕ www.asilialodges.com [0⁻]
Rustic & secluded, Oliver's is right off Tarangire's beaten track & offers a true – yet very comfortable – bush experience for those who want it. It's on a level site (no steps into dining, lounge or accommodation tents) but soft, sandy tracks run throughout.
Nearest tent: Wide, tent-flap doorway; bed (62) has light switch, whistle (to attract attention if necessary) & transfer space; bathroom doorway is 92cm; bush shower is performed on a wooden duckboard, which is roughly level with the ground but not seamless enough for independent chair users; toilet (50) is boxed in by a square wooden frame with transfer space. **$$$$$**

Tarangire Sopa Lodge (76 rooms) ✆ 027 250 0630–9; **f** 027 250 8245;
e info@sopalodges.com; ⊕ www.sopalodges.com [0⁻] [🖼]
Sopa's Tarangire lodge is typical of the chain – clean, airy quality without being too swanky. It has a wheelchair available & 4 reasonably accessible rooms but the one drawback for mobility-impaired visitors here is its setting, which is on several levels. The access routes are all smooth & hard & the main dining area is ramped – with all tables >65cm – but the swimming pool is down a long (75m) steep slope. There is a temporary ramp available for the step leading to the public toilets & bar.
Rooms 46, 47, 50 & 51: These rooms are close to the reception & dining areas & are ground floor; doorway (80) is ramped; beds (50) have transfer space & light switch but no phone; highest switch is 140cm; bathroom door (107) is level; roll-in shower has threshold (3), narrow entrance (60), fixed showerhead & 2 vertical handrails at the shower doorway; washbasin (65) has round taps; toilet (39) has front transfer space only. **$$$$**

Tarangire River Camp (20 rooms) ✆ 022 213 0553; **e** info@mbalimbali.com;
⊕ www.mbalimbali.com [3⁺]
With an impressive setting – high above a sweeping bend of the Minjingu River – this camp is stairway heaven. The main building has been built to further enhance the river views & consequently all main public areas – including the lounge & dining room – are on the first floor with around 20 steps to reach them. Getting to the lodge in the first place is 10km of bumpy, dusty track from the park gate, & the least number of steps into a tent is 4. Ablutions are step-in showers (6) & (if you can handle the steps) some of these are large enough to accommodate a wheelchair. **$$$$**

Tarangire Safari Lodge (35 tents & 6 bungalows) ✆/**f** 027 254 4752; **e** bookings@ tarangiresafarilodge.com; ⊕ www.tarangiresafarilodge.com [0⁻] [🖼] [⏎]
This is the pick of the Tarangire bunch if scenery is your priority; the tents & chalets are lined up along a high cliff, giving stunning views down

onto the Tarangire River. It's also one of the cheaper options & another major bonus is that access is good. Pathways are packed earth & crazy paving, & although there are 2 steps to reach the swimming pool, level access is possible over short grass. The pool has laddered entry. The main entrance to the dining room is level (rear entrance ramped) & all tables are >65cm. Twin tents are more spacious than dbls.

Tent 1 (a twin): Hard-earth ramp up to tent-flap doorway (>100); beds (52) have transfer space but light switch is not within reach; bathroom doorway is >100cm; spacious (enough for a wheelchair) shower has step (4), fixed showerhead, round taps (83) & horizontal support rail (119); roll-in shower has support rail (119); washbasin (72) has round taps; toilet (40) has 1 horizontal support rail (80) within reach & front transfer space.

Chalets: Of these, numbers 1 & 2 have fewest steps (3) from the connecting pathway; beds are 46cm; door to ensuite is 76cm; shower door is 76cm & shower has threshold (3) & round taps (100); washbasin (69) has round taps; toilet (41) only has front transfer space & no rails. **$$$**

Elephant Tented Lodge (12 tents) ☎ 027 275 4949; **f** 027 275 4929; **e** sales@kilimanjarosafari.com; ⌂ www.kilimanjarosafari.com 3+
Situated just outside the park, this new camp has a good location. Pathways through it are concrete & level, but have been roughly finished so give a bumpy ride. The dining area has level access with all tables >65cm & the standard public toilet is likewise with doorway 74cm. The tents are set on stilts & all are up 4–6 wooden steps from ground level; tent door flaps are zipped but the horizontal part is not flush with the ground, leaving a threshold (up to 17); beds (64) have light switches; spacious showers have a step (18) to enter & toilets do have side & front transfer space; washbasins have no knee clearance. **$$**

OTHER PRACTICALITIES

Larger lodges in Tarangire have basic amenities and will be able to change money, but most practical issues are best dealt with in Arusha.

Medical services

The lodges usually have basic first-aid rooms, often with a nurse or doctor available, but the nearest reliable hospital by road is the AICC in Arusha. People with serious medical emergencies would be taken from the nearest airfield to Nairobi.

LAKE MANYARA NATIONAL PARK

Lake Manyara National Park is one of Tanzania's lesser-known highlights, but is still worth including in most itineraries. This is especially so for first-time Africa visitors or for people who are looking for shorter, easier journeys, as the park is less than two hours' drive from Arusha and has a well-organised and maintained game-drive circuit.

It is only 33km², but with dense forests, grassy plains and being based around a shallow soda lake, there is a large variety of bird and animal life. Elephants are especially numerous but perhaps Lake Manyara's most-talked-about feature is its tree-climbing lions. Why exactly they do this is still a topic of debate, but it's a commonly seen characteristic here and one that does add a new slant to game-drive priorities.

Mto wa Mbu is the village at the base of the escarpment, next to Lake Manyara's entrance gate. It is aptly named: in Swahili *mto wa mbu* means 'river of mosquitoes' and the lakeside location of this village is obviously a good breeding ground for these prolific pests. Otherwise, it is unremarkable, although it does have a reasonably good selection of curio stalls.

Park fees Lake Manyara is managed by Tanzania National Parks so uses the electronic payment scheme (see page 171). From July 2007 the entry fee is US$35 per adult and US$10 per child (<16 years) for 24 hours.

GETTING THERE AND AWAY

Karatu is just under an hour's drive up and onto the escarpment on smooth tar; Ngorongoro Conservation Area is about 20 minutes further on a hard gravel track. Arusha is about 120km (less than two hours' drive) east of Mto wa Mbu, again on gleaming tarmac. Arrival by small aircraft is also possible, but local airstrips are small with no facilities designed for disability. (For access issues, see page 92.)

WHERE TO STAY

Only Lake Manyara Tree Lodge is actually inside the park. The other properties covered are either on the outskirts of Mto wa Mbu or are on the escarpment above, looking down onto Lake Manyara.

Lake Manyara Tree Lodge (10 tents) Contact Conservation Corporation Africa (South Africa) ☎ +27 (0)11 809 4300; f +27 (0)11 809 4400; e safaris@ccafrica.com; ⌂ www.ccafrica.com

With an unsurprisingly arboreal feel to it (surrounded by woodland & most structures are timber built) this exclusive lodge is low key with excellent cuisine & faultless service. Access routes are a mix of soft sand, sawdust & wooden boardwalks, & there are 10 steps up to the main restaurant. Meals can be taken in the comfortable ground-floor lounge & – weather permitting – dinner is often served in the outside *boma* (a Swahili word meaning 'enclosure' or 'compound'). There are 4 steps up to the swimming pool.

Tent 7: Has ramped access (the others have 13–14 steps). Doorways (160) are level; bed (40) has light switch & phone; highest control <140cm; door to ensuite (77) is level; standalone bath (57) is on raised duckboard platform, hence not possible to roll alongside; roll-in shower has star taps (87), fixed showerhead & a wooden bench seat; toilet (39) has front transfer space & no support rail. **$$$$$**

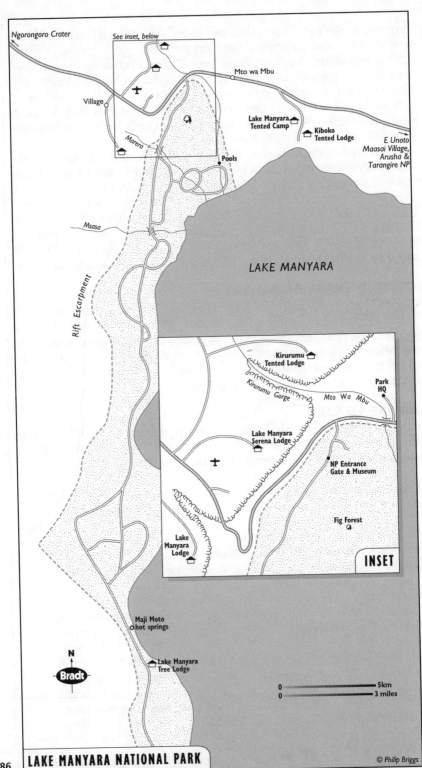

Ngorongoro Crater

See inset, below

Mto wa Mbu

Village

Marera

Lake Manyara
Tented Camp

Kiboko
Tented Lodge

E Unoto
Maasai Village,
Arusha &
Tarangire NP

Pools

Msasa

LAKE MANYARA

Rift Escarpment

Kirurumu
Tented Lodge

Park
HQ

Kirurumu Gorge

Mto Wa Mbu

Lake Manyara
Serena Lodge

NP Entrance
Gate & Museum

Fig Forest

Lake
Manyara
Lodge

INSET

Maji Moto
hot springs

N

Bradt

Lake Manyara
Tree Lodge

0   5km
0   3 miles

LAKE MANYARA NATIONAL PARK

© Philip Briggs

E Unoto Maasai Village (25 bungalows) **m** 0744 360 908; **e** eunoto@
maasaivillage.com; www.maasaivillage.com [0] [AR] [⌨]
A few kilometres outside Mto wa Mbu in the direction of Arusha, E Unoto
Maasai Village is signposted about 2km off the main road. It is a luxurious
lodge that has been designed to mirror a traditional Maasai *boma*. With
poured concrete paths, attempts have been made to make it suited to
wheelchairs, but the resulting ramps are simply too steep to allow much
independence. The dining & swimming areas are, however, reached
without steps & 1 room has inclusive features.
Adapted room: Doorway (80) has threshold (4); bed (75) has transfer
space & light switch; roll-in shower (entrance 76cm) has 1 diagonal
support rail (140) & star taps (110); washbasins are too high for chair
users; toilet (36) has 1 high, diagonal support rail but its entrance door is
70cm. **$$$$$**

Lake Manyara Serena Lodge (67 rooms) 📞 028 262 1519/07; **f** 028 621 520;
e from website; www.serenahotels.com [0] [AR]
This Serena lodge follows their policy of trying to echo local styles in
construction – Maasai *boma* is the theme here. Vibrant colours & natural
shapes are prevalent & as well as being well maintained & run, the lodge
is quite accessible. There's ramped access to the infinity pool & bar via the
car park, therefore avoiding 9 steps at reception. From here, the
restaurant is ramped, though the buffet is up 3 steps, & paths are
generally hard & smooth. As with all the escarpment accommodation,
views over the Great Rift Valley are magnificent.
Rooms 39 (with panoramic views) & 40: The most accessible. Doorway
(107) has shallow ramp; bed (46) has light switch, phone & transfer space;
bathroom doorway (109) is level; small roll-in shower has diagonal support
rail (midpoint 93), fixed showerhead & round taps (118) but no transfer
space; washbasin is 68cm & toilet (39) has front & side transfer space.
Standard rooms have steps at main doorways (77) & step-in shower (16)
with the same diagonal rail. Otherwise identical to Rooms 39 & 40.
$$$$$

Lake Manyara Lodge (100 rooms) 📞 027 254 4595/807/798/795; **f** 027 254 8633;
e res@hotelsandlodges-tanzania.com; www.hotelsandlodges-tanzania.com
[1] [⌨]
Whether by chance or design, this 1970s lodge is surprisingly comfortable
for wheelchair day visitors. Overnight accommodation may require more
mobility. Like the Serena & Kirurumu, it's built on the escarpment.
Although the design is dated & appearance a little worn, it still functions
well & commands panoramic views from its dining area, pool & gardens
over Lake Manyara & the Great Rift Valley. There is 1 step up from the
parking area & there are 2 distinct levels in the restaurant, which are
joined by steps; but apart from this, access round & between public areas
is smooth & level, or with shallow ramps. The swimming pool has

laddered entry. Family rooms are up >20 steps.

Twin/dbl rooms: Doorway (74) is level; bed (52) has transfer space, light switch & phone; doorway to ensuite (65) is level but there's no circulation space inside bathroom; bath (62) has 1 small vertical support rail (midpoint approx 50). **$$$**

Kirurumu Tented Lodge (22 rooms) ✆ 027 250 7011/7541; **f** 027 254 8226; **e** info@kirurumu.com; ✆ www.kirurumu.com [0]

Kirurumu is perched on the edge of the Great Rift Valley escarpment close to a deep gouge in the rock face from where a stream spews; hence the name, which relates to 'waterfall' in Swahili. As well as having stunning views onto the plains below, the camp gives a traditionally rustic bush experience. All the essentials (good food, efficient, jovial service, hot water & electricity) are provided with few frills, leaving the bush setting to take centre stage. The tents are dotted around a large area & 1 (Chui) has a perfectly smooth cement path connecting it with the reception & dining areas, where tables are 65cm. The bar is reached from here using at least 9 steps. Other tents have rocky pathways & some are progressively more difficult to reach, being further down the escarpment.

Chui (tent 1): Shallow ramped entry & wide, tent-flap doors; beds (48) have light switch; highest control in the room is 153cm; step-in shower is 16cm; washbasin is 88cm; toilet (41) has front transfer space only. **$$$**

Lake Manyara Tented Camp (19 tents) ✆ 027 255 3243; **e** reservations@moivaro.com; ✆ www.moivaro.com [3+]

In a copse of trees just off the main road, this camp is only 15mins' drive from Lake Manyara National Park. Paths through the flat, grassy enclosure are stone, but too bumpy & narrow to suit independent wheeling. The dining area is up 3 steps & all the tents are up 2 or 3 steps.

New units: Tent-flap entry & threshold (3); beds (66) have transfer space & light switches; door to en-suite is tent flap; step-in shower is 14cm; toilet has front transfer space only; washbasin (71) has round taps.

Older units: These have fixed wooden doors (72) hence no threshold to enter; beds (44) have transfer space but no light switch; highest switch is 160cm; en-suite door (75) is level; step-in shower is 17cm; toilet (39) has front & side transfer space; washbasin (70) has round taps. **$$$**

Kiboko Tented Lodge (12 tents) ✆/**f** 027 250 2617; **e** equatorial@habari.co.tz; ✆ www.equatorialsafaris.com [2]

Another new property, built on a level site just behind Lake Manyara Tented Camp, Kiboko may suit slow walkers but wheelchair users could struggle to reach the bathrooms. There are short, steep ramps up to reception from the parking area. The dining area is level with reception but – rather bizarrely – the main entrance is a door that is hinged in the middle (becoming a very narrow revolving door). The useful width is then only around 50cm, excluding almost all wheelchairs. Although the packed-earth pathways are wide, tents we saw were all up at least 2 steps & the gap (46) between the 2 sgl beds is narrow. Showers could be described as roll-in & toilet rooms are spacious but getting there from the sleeping area involves 1 step down then 1 up so are really not suited to wheelchairs. 4 new rooms were to be constructed in 2009, each with accommodation for 4 people. Access in these is unknown. **$$**

OTHER PRACTICALITIES
Larger lodges in the area have basic amenities but post, communication and money changing issues are most easily and economically dealt with in Arusha.

Medical services
The lodges often have basic first-aid rooms, but the nearest reliable hospital by road is the AICC in Arusha. People with serious medical emergencies would be taken from the nearest airfield to Nairobi.

KARATU AND SURROUNDING AREA

Karatu is the last staging post before the road disappears into the wooded slopes of Ngorongoro and further off into the Serengeti. As well as there being a couple of older accommodations, tourism in the area has flourished in the last decade and several new budget and moderately priced lodges have sprung up. Although none are particularly wheelchair accessible, reasonable options are available.

GETTING THERE AND AWAY
Karatu is less than four hours from Arusha on the newly surfaced tar road. The entrance to Ngorongoro is about 20 minutes' drive on hard gravel. Arrival by small aircraft is also possible, but local airstrips are small with no facilities designed for disability. (For access in small airfields, see page 92.)

WHERE TO STAY
Gibb's Farm (14 cottages – 6 more planned by 2009) ℡ 027 253 4040; **f** 027 253 4418; **e** reservations@gibbsfarm.net; www.gibbsfarm.net
Still a commercial coffee-growing enterprise, Gibb's Farm is also one of Tanzania's oldest guesthouses. It nestles into the slopes of Ngorongoro, high above Karatu, & has splendid views down to the village & beyond. The cuisine is superb & recent developments – luxurious new cottages – have not affected members of the resident bushbaby population, who are often heard serenading one another after dark. When we visited there was a long, steep ramp from the parking area up to the rooms, then several steps into the dining room – tables are >65cm – & bar area. From 2009, renovations are planned which will apparently remove these steps & make 1 'fully accessible' room.

New cottages: In these, room doorway is level but there is a small step (6) once inside; beds (69) have transfer space & light switch & all switches are 113cm; the highlight is an atmospheric – & romantic – roll-in shower next to the rustic stone hearth; if this is too risqué, then a substantially cooler (also roll-in) version can be found on the patio; both have fixed showerheads & star taps (140); washbasin (62) has lever taps & toilet (39) has front transfer space only. **$$$$**

Tloma Lodge (20 cottages) ☎ 027 250 4093; **e** twc-reservations@habari.co.tz; ⌂ www.africawilderness.com
This new lodge – a sibling of Ngorongoro Farm House (see following entry) – was built in 2007 & is refreshingly accessible as a result. It also has a wheelchair available. Very open plan, it sits prominently in the hills above Karatu, giving good views over a nearby waterfall & down the valley. Access round the grounds is hard, pebbled paths, which are doable in a wheelchair but don't allow freewheeling. Rooms are on concrete pads, but some have been ramped with cement. The swimming pool has short, steep, ramped access bypassing 6 steps, & has steps with no handrails to enter. Dining room is ramped & tables are >65cm. The standard public toilet has threshold (3) & doorway is 76cm.
Hondo Hondo: Doorway (82) is ramped; bed (65) has light switch & phone; highest switch is 142cm; bathroom door (80) is level; spacious step-in shower (12) has fixed showerhead; washbasin (67) has star taps & toilet (40) has front transfer space only. Other rooms are similar. **$$$$**

Ngorongoro Farm House (40 cottages) ☎ 027 250 4093; **e** twc-reservations@habari.co.tz; ⌂ www.africawilderness.com
The rooms are spread over extensive grounds in a coffee plantation, & the smooth, hard paths are pleasantly edged with peach trees & rambling gardens. Once wheelchairs are helped up the near 100% ramp from the car park, most routes are relatively level. The dining area is ramped, tables are 60cm & the public toilet here has level doorways (76) but no adaptive features. The business centre is up 1 step & the path to the pool is step-free but sloped. The pool itself is entered using steps with no handrail. Some rooms have support rails in showers & a wheelchair is available.
Duma: Down a steep slope from reception. Doorway (100) is up 1 step; bed (72) has transfer space, light switch & phone; ablution facilities are under the same roof as the bed; step-in shower (9) has doorway (86) & 1 support rail (midpoint 111); toilet (39) has doorway (76) & front transfer space.
Hondo Hondo: A virtually level 500m from reception. Doorway (76) has small threshold; beds are same as Duma; bathroom door (69) is level; doorway (73) to step-in shower (19) with same support rail as Duma; toilet has side & front transfer space. **$$$$**

Plantation Lodge (18 rooms) ☎ 027 253 4364; **f** 027 253 4405; **e** reservation@plantation-lodge.com; ⌂ www.plantation-lodge.com

Plantation's longstanding reputation as a classy lodge is well deserved; the service is refined – you get the feeling that it's effortlessly done – & rooms are stylish without being pretentious. The pathways through the grounds are hard & smooth, but there are many steps. There's 1 step up to the (standard) public toilet & 22 to the swimming pool (which is easily entered with steps & handrails). Of the 18 rooms, the following are the most accessible:

Forest Left & Forest Right: Main door is 84cm; beds are 70cm; bathroom doorway is 63cm; step-in shower with step of 21cm.

Zanzibar: Main door is 76cm; 3 beds are 85cm, 67cm & 60cm; bathroom door is 76cm; step-in shower (26) has a seat in the washing area.

Avocado: Has a dbl door; king-sized bed (57); bathroom door is 77cm; step-in shower (21) has cement seating; washbasin is 79cm. All have 3 steps up to main doors, the beds have light switches & transfer space & toilets have front transfer space only. **$$$$**

The Octagon Safari Lodge (14 rooms) ☎ 027 254 8311; **f** 027 253 4525; **e** reservation@octagonlodge.com; ⏀ www.octagonlodge.com 3️⃣
This comfortable & uncomplicated lodge has a compact layout on a level site. Paths are brick & bumpy in some places with cement & brick access. There is 1 step up to the restaurant & 4 up to the bar. Dining tables are all >65cm. The rooms all have several steps at their entrance doors.

Room 2: Doorway (88) is up 3 steps; bathroom doorway (60) is level, but furniture could be moved to make it larger; step-in shower (10).

Room 13: Doorway (88) is up 4 steps; more spacious bathroom; step-in shower (12); toilet has front transfer space. **$$$**

Kudu Lodge (20 rooms) ☎ 027 253 4055/4268/4412; **f** 027 253 4268; **e** kuducamp@iwayafrica.com; ⏀ www.kuducamp.com 3️⃣ 🖼️
This camp has expanded considerably since its modest beginnings in 1996. It's still clean & friendly, but now has a selection of room types as well as camping. The site is level, all the rooms are within a 50m walk from the dining area (up 6 steps) & bar (up 7 steps), & the access routes are hard (paved) but occasionally narrow.

All Kilimanjaro Cottages & the Ruaha Rondavel: Up at least 1 step from the pathways & most have a step up into the bathroom or into the shower.

Serengeti Suites: Up 3 steps but are more spacious; Suite 3 has a roll-in shower but the entrance is narrow (59).

Tembo family room: Has doorway (78) up 5 steps; bathroom is up 1 step but has roll-in shower with wider door (91). **$$**

OTHER PRACTICALITIES

Apart from the Bank of Commerce on the right side on the road as you drive north through town, Karatu is more of a rest point than a stocking-up place.

Medical services

The lodges usually have basic first-aid rooms, but the nearest reliable hospital by road is the AICC in Arusha. People with serious medical emergencies would be taken from the nearest airfield to Nairobi.

NGORONGORO CONSERVATION AREA

The Ngorongoro Conservation Area is part of the Serengeti ecosystem, and as such is one of Africa's greatest wild places. However, although it is more than 8,000km² in size, the focus of virtually all visits is Ngorongoro Crater, which stands out as a distinct highlight of Tanzania's northern circuit in its own right.

Descriptions of 'the crater', no matter how flowery, cannot prepare you for the scale of the setting or the wealth of wildlife that it contains. Yes, Ngorongoro is a collapsed volcano, but had it not fallen it would be comparable with Mount Kilimanjaro; and yes, there are animals, but there is simply nowhere else that gives such a guarantee of seeing so many of the coveted species (including the 'big five') in one small area. Furthermore, the wildlife is precisely that, wild and free to enter or leave the crater at will. Animals are very habituated to tourist vehicles, making Ngorongoro an ideal location to watch their natural behaviour and rendering it a photographer's paradise. The area's status as a conservation area means it also supports the Maasai people, herding cattle and living in as traditional a manner as can be seen anywhere on east Africa's tourist trails.

Although entry is not cheap, a visit to the crater is one of the first inclusions on virtually all northern Tanzanian itineraries. To pass it by without taking an extra day to drop in *en route* to the Serengeti would be utter madness.

Unfortunately, it is very important to note that the roads in and around Ngorongoro are some of the worst in the northern game areas. If possible, try to ensure you hire or use a reasonably new, well-sprung vehicle and do not scrimp on personal padding and cushions.

Park Fees Ngorongoro is managed by the Ngorongoro Conservation Area Authority (⊕ *www.ngorongorocrater.org*). Since 1 July 2007 an entry permit costs US$50 for adults and US$10 for children. On top of this the 'crater service fee' (to reduce congestion) is US$200 per vehicle. All permits are paid at entry gates and are valid for 24 hours.

GETTING THERE AND AWAY

The recent tar sealing of the road all the way to the conservation area gate has made Ngorongoro an easy and comfortable four-hour drive (about 185km) from Arusha. There is a small airfield on the crater rim and many fly-in safaris use Manyara airstrip, which is less than two hours' drive away. These facilities are not designed with disabled passengers in mind. (For access issues, see page 92.)

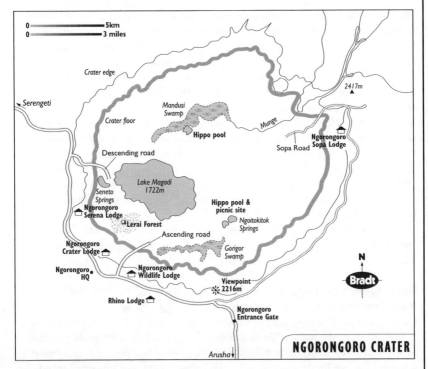

NGORONGORO CRATER

WHERE TO STAY

Ngorongoro Crater Lodge (30 rooms) Contact Conservation Corporation Africa
(South Africa) ✆ +27 (0)11 809 4300; f +27 (0)11 809 4400; e safaris@ccafrica.com;
⌂ www.ccafrica.com 3+

As well as the luxury of ringside seating on the crater edge, CC Africa's
Ngorongoro option is lavishly decorated with glittering chandeliers, gilt-
edged mirrors & raw-silk curtains. Pathways are generally good, being
wide, with decorative flagstones, but 18 steps lead to the shop & reception.
There are 3 clusters of rooms: North Camp, South Camp & Tree Camp. All
have similar bathroom facilities – large, standalone bathtubs & step-in
showers – but none cater specifically to mobility restrictions. Broad
guidelines are that the Tree Camp requires most step climbing while only
the South Camp has a room (number 20) with level boardwalk entry.
Rooms at North Camp all have at least 2 or 3 steps at their doorways. All
lounge/dining/bar areas have a long flight of stairs at the front, but at
North Camp there is a rear entrance, which uses only 4 steps. **$$$$$**

Ngorongoro Serena Lodge (74 rooms) ✆ 028 262 1519/07; f 028 621 520; e from
website; ⌂ www.serenahotels.com

This is one of those places where wheelchair users are treated to a free
tour of staff-only areas, only because it is essential to use a steep ramp at
the service entrance to avoid steps. Once this is done, the 2 adapted rooms

(Rooms 34 & 35) & the bar/lounge areas are all on the same level. The dining room is upstairs, but staff will happily serve people food in the lounge if the ramp is too much twice in one day. Clinging to the wall of the crater, the adapted rooms are enclosed on at least 2 sides so may feel slightly dark, but the breathtaking balcony vistas – each one looks directly into the caldera – more than make up for this. The public toilets are standard but have a level entrance.

Rooms 34 & 35: Once approached using the service entrance the doorway (99) is level; twin beds (45) have light switch, phone & transfer space; en-suite bathroom doorway (102) is level; roll-in shower has a short, diagonal support rail (midpoint 80) with fixed showerhead & round taps (120); washbasin has round taps, high mirror & no free space underneath for wheelchair knees; toilet (40) has diagonal support rail (midpoint 83) & both front & side transfer space.

Other (standard) rooms are similarly kitted out; they have the same rail in the shower, but it has a step (15) to enter & the toilet has no support rail. **$$$$$**

Ngorongoro Sopa Lodge (91 rooms) ✆ 027 250 0630–9; **f** 027 250 8245; **e** info@sopalodges.com; ⌂ www.sopalodges.com 🔲 🔲 🔲

Clean lines & simple design epitomise Sopa lodges & Ngorongoro's version is no different. As with other crater-rim lodges, it has a ringside position looking into the caldera, but unlike most, 1 room (number 37) has been adapted for use by disabled guests. All public areas are interconnected using fairly smooth crazy paving & are either on the same level or reached via short stone ramps, though these are not ideally graded. A bonus of staying here is that there is an access track leading into the crater that may be used for both descents & ascents; this is not only a great time saver, but means less bumping along rough roads.

Room 37: Entrance door (90) is ramped; beds have transfer space & light switches; doorway to ensuite (90) is level; roll-in shower has 1 (high) diagonal support rail & a fixed showerhead; the toilet has front transfer space & 1 support rail. NB: the rails are designed to help those who stand unsteadily, rather than to take the weight of a non-ambulant chair user. **$$$$**

Ngorongoro Wildlife Lodge (78 rooms) ✆ 027 254 4595/807/798/795; **f** 027 254 8633; **e** res@hotelsandlodges-tanzania.com; ⌂ www.hotelsandlodges-tanzania.com 🔲

This 1970s lodge has a dramatic outlook onto the crater, but is in need of renovation. The various levels are stepped (3 up to reception, 8 down to the viewing/dining area then another 10 down to the next viewing plateau).

Standard rooms: Doorways (74) are level; beds (48) have light switches & transfer space; narrow bathroom door (57) is level; bath (56) has handheld showerhead in tub; toilet (39) has front transfer space only. Junior suites are closer to the dining area, but have steps up to the bed area. **$$$**

Rhino Lodge (24 rooms) **m** 0762 359 055; **e** rhino@ngorongoro.cc;
🖥 www.ngorongoro.cc 🔲 🖼
Sited about half a mile from the rim – therefore without direct views down
into the crater – Rhino Lodge is the newest accommodation in the area. It
was being constructed when we visited, but paths were cement paving
(wide, smooth & fairly level) & eating areas were either going to be
ramped or up 5 steps. It looked simple, clean & a good option if low budget
is important.
The first completed room has: doorway (78) up 1 step (20); 2 sgl beds with
transfer space; level bathroom door (75) & shower door (64); roll-in shower
with slight drop-off (2), round taps (113) & fixed showerhead; washbasin
(67) with round taps; toilet (40) with no transfer space. **$$**

OTHER PRACTICALITIES
Larger lodges in the area have basic amenities but post, communication and
money changing issues are most easily and economically dealt with in
Arusha.

Medical services
The lodges usually have basic first-aid rooms, often with a nurse or doctor
available, but the nearest reliable hospital by road is the AICC in Arusha.
People with serious medical emergencies would be taken from the nearest
airfield to Nairobi.

SERENGETI NATIONAL PARK

Arriving from Ngorongoro by road – as most visitors do – few can fail to be
stunned by the sight that greets them. The track winds down the steep
shoulder of the crater, and as it descends, the folds of the landscape begin to
open, eventually revealing a flat land with distant, hazy horizons. This is
the Serengeti (which, aptly, means 'endless plain' in Maa) and it is well
worthy of its UNESCO listing as a World Heritage Site.

This huge park (almost 15,000km²) has several distinct areas, but the
majority of tourist activity is found around the Seronera River and the short
grassed plains running back towards Ngorongoro. Short, easy drives are
possible on well-organised – if slightly rough – circuits and longer trips can
be taken out to lonesome, eerie rock koppies where majestic prides of lions
are often found lolling lazily in the shade. Game is varied and plentiful on
the plains at all times – this is ideal cheetah country – but numbers of
ungulates (hoofed animals) swell greatly in the early part of the year, with
the arrival of the eternally mobile Great Migration. This area is the best
suited to mobility-impaired travellers who need accessible accommodation,
as both the Serena and Sopa lodges have adapted rooms.
The less-visited northern reaches of the Serengeti offer the tourist-phobic
traveller an escape from their peers. There are few permanent camps: Lobo

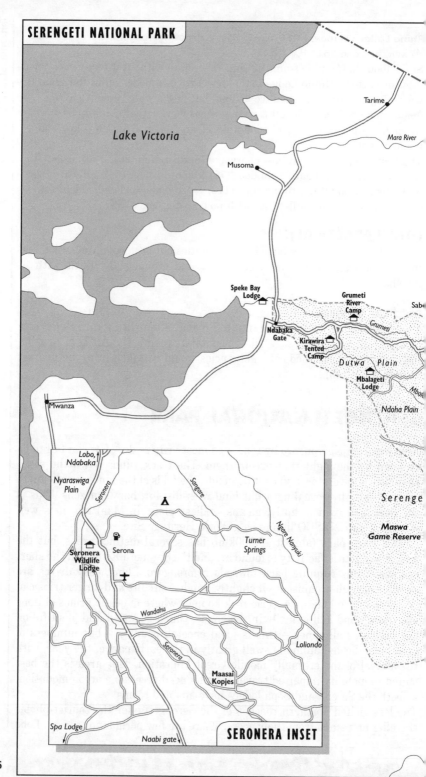

SERENGETI NATIONAL PARK

Lake Victoria

Tarime

Mara River

Musoma

Speke Bay Lodge

Grumeti River Camp

Sab

Grumeti

Ndabaka Gate

Kirawira Tented Camp

Dutwa *Plain*

Mbalageti Lodge

Mbal

Ndoha Plain

Mwanza

Serenge

Maswa Game Reserve

SERONERA INSET

Lobo, Ndabaka

Nyaraswiga Plain

Seronera

Sangare

Ngare Nanyuki

Serona

Turner Springs

Seronera Wildlife Lodge

Wandahu

Seronera

Loliondo

Maasai Kopjes

Spa Lodge

Naabi gate

196

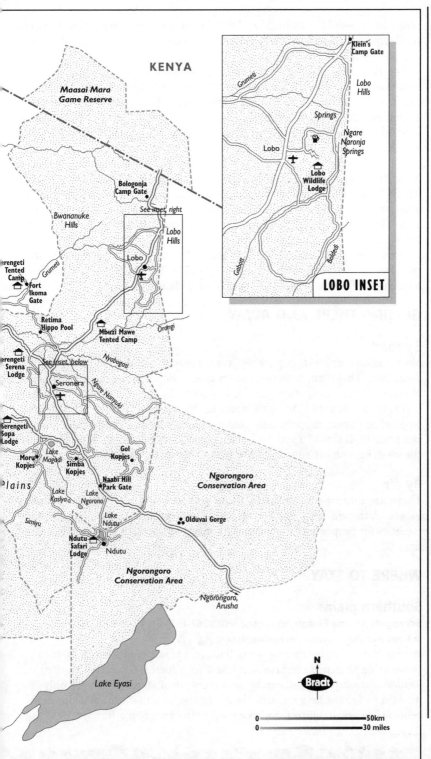

KENYA

Maasai Mara
Game Reserve

Bologonja
Camp Gate

See inset, right

Bwananuke
Hills

Lobo
Hills

Lobo

Serengeti
Tented
Camp

Fort
Ikoma
Gate

Grumeti

Retima
Hippo Pool

Mbuzi Mawe
Tented Camp

Orangi

Serengeti
Serena
Lodge

See inset, below

Nyabogati

Seronera

Ngare Nanyuki

Serengeti
Sopa
Lodge

Moru
Kopjes

Lake
Magadi

Simba
Kopjes

Gol
Kopjes

Naabi Hill
Park Gate

Ngorongoro
Conservation Area

Plains

Lake
Kasiya

Lake
Ngorono

Simiyu

Lake
Ndutu

Olduvai Gorge

Ndutu
Safari
Lodge

Ndutu

Ngorongoro
Conservation Area

Ngorongoro,
Arusha

Lake Eyasi

N

Brad

0 ———————— 50km
0 ———————— 30 miles

LOBO INSET

Klein's
Camp Gate

Grumeti

Lobo
Hills

Springs

Lobo

Ngare
Naronja
Springs

Lobo
Wildlife
Lodge

Gabati

Bologa

Lodge is the established building but is a maze of steps, Migration Camp is similarly protected from wheelchair attack while the most accessible option is probably Mbuzi Mawe.

The Western Corridor has for decades been the exclusive haunt of fly-in safaris only. The three main lodges in this area are upmarket and the black cotton-soil road was often a rainy mud bath. However, several cheaper accommodations are springing up outside Ndabaka Gate and the access road has been fortified and is now officially 'all-weather'. Treed plains dominate the landscape, which is split by the Grumeti and Mbalageti rivers, and the whole length of the corridor has the jagged Kianguge Mountains as its northern backdrop. Like the northern area, game driving here will be a lonely, lovely experience. Fewer tourist vehicles mean the wildlife is slightly more skittish, which for some is a drawback (there will be more photos of bums than of heads); for others this just enhances the feeling of being in the wilds.

Park fees The Serengeti is managed by Tanzania National Parks so uses the electronic payment scheme (see page 171). The entry fee is US$50 per adult and US$10 per child (<16 years) for 24 hours.

GETTING THERE AND AWAY

By road
Most visitors enter the park by road through Naabi Hill Gate in the Southeast. This road, however, is very rough. Be prepared for several hours of bone-jarring corrugations all the way from the end of the new, tar-sealed highway at Karatu. As with visiting Ngorongoro Crater, if you can, emphasise during preparations that a well-sprung and comfortable vehicle is a priority. If this is a serious issue, then consider flying in. If coming from the west, smooth tar runs from Mwanza to Musoma, passing Ndabaka Gate.

By air
There are airstrips at Seronera, Lobo and servicing most of the exclusive lodges. Although they are set on solid, level ground, none of these have facilities for people with disabilities. (For access issues in small airfields, see page 92.)

WHERE TO STAY

Southern plains
Serengeti Serena Lodge (66 rooms) ☎ 028 262 1519/07; f 028 621 520;
e from website; ⊕ www.serenahotels.com 🔲 🔳
In true Serena style the rooms are built in a traditional African fashion, these being thatched rondavels. It has 2 with increased access, but getting around the complex itself can be an adventure of steps, which are only avoided by taking long detours via the (attractive, thankfully) swimming pool. There are 10 steps from reception to the bar then a further 10 to the

dining area, which is split across 3 levels. The swimming pool has ramped access from the dining area, 6 steps to enter it & a useful bench seat around its inside edge. A wheelchair is available.

Rooms 29 & 30: These are adapted – doorway (107) has shallow stone ramp; beds (47) have transfer space, light switch & phone; bathroom door (107) is level; roll-in shower has 1 diagonal support rail (midpoint 90), no seat, a fixed showerhead & round taps (120); washbasin is 68cm & toilet (40) has front & side transfer space.

Other rooms have narrower doorways (67) with several steps & step-in showers. **$$$$$**

Serengeti Sopa Lodge (69 rooms) ✆ 027 250 0630–9; **f** 027 250 8245; **e** info@sopalodges.com; ⌂ www.sopalodges.com 🄍 🖼
This lodge has recently been renovated &, like most Tanzanian Sopa lodges, provides some of the most inclusive safari accommodation in the park. The dining area is reached using a removable ramp, the rooms are level from here & access to the swimming pool (currently with 4 steps) will be made level in the next phase of refurbishment.

Room 27: Close to reception, on the left wing, this is the most accessible. Main doorway (110) is level; 2 queen-sized beds have light switches & transfer space; bathroom door (110) is also level; spacious shower has threshold (13) on entry (75cm wide) and 1 high support rail; the washbasin, although the mirror is low, has no knee space for chair users; toilet has front transfer space. **$$$$**

Seronera Wildlife Lodge (75 rooms) ✆ 027 254 4595/807/798/795; **f** 027 254 8633; **e** res@hotelsandlodges-tanzania.com; ⌂ www.hotelsandlodges-tanzania.com 3⁺ 🖥
One of the first lodges to be built in the Serengeti, Seronera has an enviable location close to some of the park's most fruitful game-driving circuits & in the path of the annual wildebeest migration. It was built in the 1970s hugging a towering rock koppie, which gave stunning views but has rendered access a challenge – at that time, less mobile guests were not considered. The dining area is up 2 flights of stairs. Some rooms close to reception have level doorways (74) but bathroom doorways are generally narrow (53); baths (43) do have 2 support rails (24 & 67) & a handheld showerhead in the tub. **$$$**

Ndutu Safari Lodge (32 rooms) ✆ 027 250 2829/6702; **f** 027 250 8310; **e** bookings@ndutu.com; ⌂ www.ndutu.com 2⃣
Functional rather than elaborate, but very good value, Ndutu may suit those for whom stairs are a problem. It's on a flat site close to Lake Ndutu, & consequently public areas are at ground level or ramped. Paths are broad & are beaten earth, gravel & stone. The stone-built chalets are up 2 steps but we were assured a wooden ramp would be constructed if necessary; they have beds (63) with light switches & transfer space, level

bathroom door (80), step-in shower (5) & toilet (42) with front transfer space. **$$$**

Northern Serengeti

Mbuzi Mawe Tented Camp (16 tents) ☎ 028 262 1519/07; **f** 028 621 520; **e** from website; 🖰 www.serenahotels.com [0]

Mbuzi Mawe may be Swahili for 'klipspringer', but you don't need to be a mountain goat to get around this lavish new camp. The dining area & all the tents have ramped access using crazy paving, which is wide, has shallow slopes but is a little bumpy. There's no swimming pool yet & no outside seating for slow walkers but these were apparently coming in 2008.

Tent access is via zipped doorways; 4-poster beds (56) have transfer space & light switches; the spacious shower is 1 step (11) down & has a tiled seat, but this is not in the washing area; toilet (42) has front & side transfer space; dbl washbasins have no knee clearance. **$$$$$**

Lobo Wildlife Lodge (75 rooms) ☎ 027 254 4595/807/798/795; **f** 027 254 8633; **e** res@hotelsandlodges-tanzania.com; 🖰 www.hotelsandlodges-tanzania.com [3+] 🖵

From the same era & built in a similar style to that of the Seronera (see previous section), Lobo has a splendid rock-top setting but will prove equally uninviting to people with walking difficulties. It's also under the same management, but staff here are extremely welcoming & helpful. There are several flights of stairs between reception, dining & swimming areas. Standard rooms have doorways of 72cm, bathroom doorways (64) are down 1 step & baths (52) have a horizontal support rail (27). Suites have more space but ablutions are similar. **$$$**

Western Corridor

Kirawira Tented Camp (25 tents)
☎ 028 262 1519/07; **f** 028 621 520; **e** from website; 🖰 www.serenahotels.com [3+]

The ultimate classic safari camp, Kirawira is opulent to the extreme. Brass, leather & mahogany abound in Edwardian-era furnishings & there's even a working gramophone in the meeting tent. Unfortunately, the disabled rights of the day are also still in place & the steep, hilltop situation doesn't help. A wheelchair is available, but the pathway from parking to reception is long & built from broken stones. The stunning swimming pool is down 39 steps & all rooms have step-in showers or baths & several steps at their entrances. **$$$$$**

Grumeti River Camp (10 tents) Contact Conservation Corporation Africa (South Africa) ☎ +27 (0)11 809 4300; **f** +27 (0)11 809 4400; **e** safaris@ccafrica.com; 🖰 www.ccafrica.com [2]

This stylish camp lies in a gully next to deep pools of the Grumeti River;

expect, therefore, to be regularly heckled by grunting hippos. Of the 3 western Serengeti options, this is the most level & has the shortest walking distances around the site. The main camp is reached via all-weather grit pathways, which a strong wheelchair user could cope with. The swimming pool & sun-lounging areas are also step-free, but unfortunately, there are 3 steps into the dining area & then 4 down to the outside *boma* where meals are often taken – tables are 66cm.

The tents are cavernous & colourful. The most accessible (about 30m from the lounge area) has 2 steps to enter it: king-sized bed (65) has light switch & transfer space; access to ensuite is level but narrow (60); shower has wooden trellis floor, which could be removed to make a roll-in washing area but the showerhead is fixed. **$$$$$**

Mbalageti Lodge (35 rooms) **☎/f** 028 262 2387; **e** info@mbalageti.com; ⌂ www.mbalageti.com 3️⃣

Mbalageti has a stunning setting on Mwamveni Hill, with panoramic views onto the rolling plains of the Serengeti. Designed with an artist's eye & meticulously decorated, it is worth its luxury label, yet it also has accommodation catering to more frugal budgets. Mbalageti is spread out: tracks between rooms & restaurant are surfaced with small gravel of red & yellow sandstone, some slopes are steeper than 8% & there is the occasional step. There are 5 steps up to the restaurant, which has a ramped public toilet with support rail & side or front transfer space & dining tables are >65cm. A wheelchair is available & of the 3 classes of accommodation, the following are the most inclusive:

Chalet 14: Door (62) has no steps but is reached by a steep sandy slope; bed (70) has light switch & transfer space; highest control is 95cm; roll-in shower has cement seat, fixed showerhead & star taps; bath (47) has fitted handles; toilet only has front transfer space.

Exclusive suite: Door (77) up 7 steps; beds (68) have light switch & transfer space; phone is in the lounge; 1 bedroom has bathroom with step-in shower (3) & portable seat is available; another bedroom has bathroom with a huge, sunken bath; toilet has front & side transfer space.

Of the less expensive Lodge rooms **Sunrise Corridor** has the view out to the plain, but 6 steps to enter, while **Sunset Corridor** has no view but steeply ramped approach: door (78) is up 3 steps; bed (58) has light switch, transfer space & whistle; bathroom door (74) is level; step-in shower is 8cm; washbasin is 69cm; toilet has front transfer space only. **$$$$**

Serengeti Tented Camp (10 tents) **☎** 027 255 3243; **e** reservations@moivaro.com; ⌂ www.moivaro.com 1️⃣

This is a refreshingly simple camp compared with the exuberance of some Serengeti lodges, but is still clean, spacious & provides the essentials for a comfortable stay. Situated just outside the park at Fort Ikoma Gate, it's on hard, open, level ground. Gravel paths lead from reception (1 step up) & the dining tent (with level access) to the accommodation tents, none of which are designed to be fully accessible.

Closest tent to restaurant: Tent-flap doorway is up 1 step from path; bed (60) has light switch, transfer space & highest switch is <140cm; roll-in shower has star taps & fixed showerhead but no seat or rails; washbasin has no knee space; toilet (40) has front transfer space only.
$$$$

Speke Bay Lodge (9 tents & 8 bungalows) ☎ 028 262 1236; f 028 262 1237; e spekebay@africaonline.co.tz; ⏚ www.spekebay.com ▮
One of the more established options outside Ndabaka Gate west of the Serengeti, Speke Bay is currently the most accessible. Although it has no specifically adapted accommodation, Dutch owner Jan is a character, & will do everything he can to ensure your stay is comfortable. The food here is excellent, though you may need to fight with the local Speke's weaver bird population for sugar & butter at breakfast time. The fixed tents share basic ablutions but the rondavels have their own en-suite bathrooms.
Rondavels: Main door (74) is up 1 step, which they will 'ramp' with small stones if you wish; beds (45) have light switch & transfer space; highest switch is 150cm; bathroom door (74) is level; there is a seat available for the step-in shower, but it has no other accessible features; both shower & washbasin (72) have round taps; toilet (42) has front transfer space only.
$$

OTHER PRACTICALITIES

Main lodges will accept credit cards, be able to exchange money and may have small curio outlets, but main purchases should be done in Arusha (or possibly Mwanza, depending on your itinerary). Fuel can be obtained at Seronera.

Medical services

The lodges usually have basic first-aid rooms, often with a nurse or doctor available, but the nearest reliable hospital by road is the AICC in Arusha. People with serious medical emergencies would be taken from the nearest airfield to Nairobi.

WHAT TO SEE AND DO

As well as game viewing, a common side trip from the Serengeti is the **Olduvai Gorge**. The steep sides of this dry ravine expose layers of volcanic ash, in which fossilised homonid forms have been found. Some of these specimens are more than two million years old, and when discovered, were the first evidence that our human ancestors lived on the plains of east Africa. The gorge is about 3km from the main road that runs from Ngorongoro to the Serengeti, and if timings are right it can make a handy lunch stop. There is no food available but the small museum is interesting and easily accessed. The more able and adventurous visitor can take guided walks down into the gorge, but be warned – it is rocky and steep.

ZANZIBAR

The name smacks of exoticism and the place does not disappoint. Situated in the Indian Ocean about 30km from the Tanzanian coastline, this group of islands is renowned for being a tropical paradise. But it has more than just heavenly beaches; there is enough depth of history here to keep the most culture-hungry visitor plundering for days. Zanzibar's position – at east Africa's gateway to world trade routes – means the main island (Unguja) has always been a strategic stronghold for the ruling powers of the day. The Arabs, Portuguese, Omanis and British have all had their time as top dog here and as a result, the vibrant and unique Swahili civilisation – fundamentally African Bantu in origin – has been heavily influenced. Although the most valuable commodities on Zanzibar have been ivory, slaves and spices, the latter – mercifully – is the only one remaining, and tourism is now climbing the ladder of priority.

There are resorts, hotels and smaller guesthouses dotted all around the coastline, and each area has its own attractions and characteristics. Broadly speaking, the west coast is rockier but more sheltered from ocean winds than the east. Also, because the sun sets in the west, shadows fall inland in the afternoon giving more time on the beaches. The eastern shores are much more sandy (this is where you will find true visions of paradise) but afternoons can be breezy and tidal changes are more marked than on other parts of the island. Most areas can be reached in a couple of hours' drive from Stone Town and although roads around Zanzibar are tarred and generally in excellent condition, the last few kilometres to the hotel will often be dirt or gravel.

GETTING THERE AND AWAY

By boat
Being an island, the most obvious method of approach is by sea. However, people who cannot walk will find this tricky, as boarding on Zanzibar is via a gangplank, which is steep at low tide and can be difficult even for able-bodied people with luggage. On board there are various decks with stairways between them and there are no facilities to make mobility easier. Anybody arriving at the port might want to consider using a taxi to get to Stone Town itself; the journey is level and only about 1km, but this might be a struggle in the heat of the day.

By air
The simplest way of reaching Zanzibar is to fly. Several airlines do the short (30-minute) hop from Dar es Salaam and it is also possible to fly from Kilimanjaro International Airport near Arusha. Zanzibar Airport has no aisle chairs, but staff are careful to ask how a person should be lifted and there are standard wheelchairs available in the terminal. All main public areas are ground floor and the occasional single step is ramped, but there is no disability-adapted public toilet.

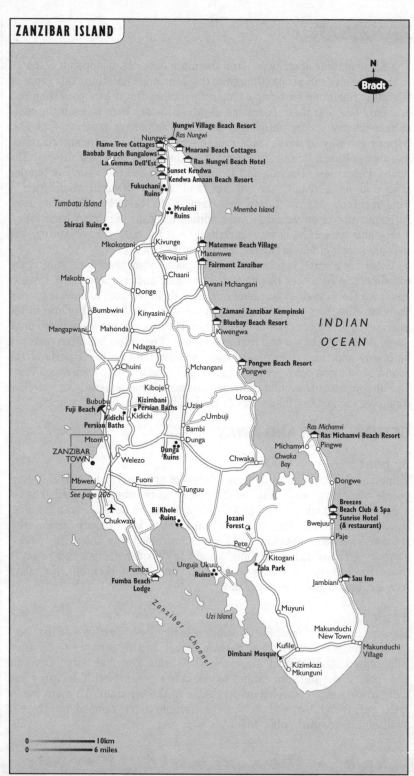

N

Bradt

Nungwi Village Beach Resort
Nungwi   *Ras Nungwi*
Flame Tree Cottages
Baobab Beach Bungalows   Mnarani Beach Cottages
La Gemma Dell'Est   Ras Nungwi Beach Hotel
Sunset Kendwa
Kendwa Amaan Beach Resort
Fukuchani
Ruins

Tumbatu Island

Mvuleni
Ruins   *Mnemba Island*

Shirazi Ruins

Mkokotoni   Kivunge
Mkwajuni   Matemwe Beach Village
Matemwe
Makoba   Chaani   Fairmont Zanzibar

Donge   Pwani Mchangani

Bumbwini   Kinyasini   Zamani Zanzibar Kempinski
Bluebay Beach Resort
Mangapwani   Mahonda   Kiwengwa

Ndagaa   INDIAN
OCEAN
Chuini   Mchangani
Pongwe Beach Resort
Kiboje   Pongwe

Bububu   Kizimbani   Uroa
Fuji Beach   Persian Baths   Uzini
Kidichi   Kidichi
Persian Baths   Umbuji   *Ras Michamvi*
Bambi   Ras Michamvi Beach Resort
Mtoni   Dunga   Michamvi   Pingwe
ZANZIBAR   Dunga
TOWN   Ruins   *Chwaka*
Welezo   Chwaka   *Bay*   Dongwe
Fuoni
Mbweni   Tunguu   Breezes
See page 206   Beach Club & Spa
Sunrise Hotel
Bi Khole   (& restaurant)
Chukwani   Ruins   Bwejuu
Jozani   Paje
Forest
Fumba   Pete
Fumba Beach   Unguja Ukuu   Kitogani
Lodge   Ruins   Zala Park   Sau Inn
Jambiani
Uzi Island   Muyuni

Zanzibar Channel   Makunduchi
New Town
Kufile   Makunduchi
Dimbani Mosque   Village
Kizimkazi
Mkunguni

0   10km
0   6 miles

GETTING AROUND

As well as the standard advice given in *Chapter 3*, page 89, about using public transport in Africa it is worth noting that when you take buses and *dala dalas* (small converted trucks) on Zanzibar, they may only run as far as the dirt track leading to some coastal resorts, leaving you to walk a short distance in potentially stifling heat.

WHERE TO STAY

Visitors who need good access will need to look hard on Zanzibar. The sultry climate here means it is easier to sleep upstairs, and I only know of seven properties in Stone Town with ground-floor rooms. There are many around the coastline, but wheelchair users and those prone to stumbling might find the sandy pathways and beaches problematic.

The sleek, new Fairmont Hotel had the only fully accessible bathroom on the island in 2008. Having – rather depressingly – stated all of that, it is well worth remembering that this is Africa. A solution will always be found for practical problems, usually using manpower and a little ingenuity.

In and around Stone Town

Zanzibar Serena Inn (51 rooms) ☎ 028 262 1519/07; f 028 621 520; e from website; ⌂ www.serenahotels.com 3+

With its ideal location – seafront & old town – Serena have chosen their Zanzibar flagship well. They've also restored the building responsibly, & although level access was obviously not a priority, it does have 14 ground-floor rooms. From the street, the main entrance has 6 steps. The restaurant is up several steps & the pool is down 6 then entered via steps with no handrail. The ground-floor rooms with baths have 2 sgl beds & are reached via a drop-off (12); those with showers have dbl beds & are level with reception. Bathrooms are small.
A wheelchair is available.
Room 12 (with bath): Doorway (71) is up 1 step (10); beds (55) have transfer space & light switches; highest switch in room is 140cm; bathroom door (69) is level; bath (53) has transfer space, diagonal rail (midpoint 69) & handheld showerhead; washbasin has no knee space; toilet (43) has front transfer space only.
Room 5 (with shower): Doorway (79) is level; bed (55) has transfer space & light switches; highest switch in room is 140cm; bathroom door (64) is level; step-in shower (5) has star taps (102), fixed showerhead & 1 diagonal support rail (midpoint 107); washbasin & toilet, like Room 12.
$$$$$

Africa House Hotel (15 rooms) m 0774 432 340; e info@theafricahousehotel.com; ⌂ www.theafricahouse-zanzibar.com 3+
As with most Stone Town hotels, there are no ground-floor rooms. However, watching the sunset with a cool drink (or eating there) is still a thriving tradition amongst visitors to Zanzibar. There are 4–5 steps into

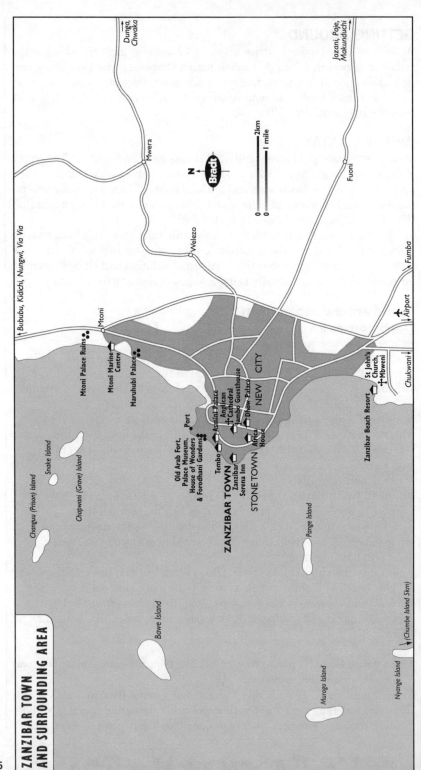

ZANZIBAR TOWN AND SURROUNDING AREA

206

ZANZIBAR TOWN

STONE TOWN

NEW CITY

Old Arab Fort,
Palace Museum,
House of Wonders
& Forodhani Gardens

Tembo

Zanzibar
Serena Inn

Africa
House

Anglean
Cathedral

Assnini Palace

Tambo Guesthouse

Dillow Palace

Port

Mtoni Palace Ruins

Mtoni Marine
Centre

Maruhubi Palace

Mtoni

Welezo

Mwera

Fuoni

Dunga,
Chwaka

Jozani, Paje,
Makunduchi

Fumba

Airport

Chukwani

St John's
Church,
Mbweni

Zanzibar Beach Resort

Changuu (Prison) Island

Snake Island

Chapwani (Grave) Island

Bawe Island

Pange Island

Murogo Island

Nyange Island

(Chumbe Island 5km)

Bububu, Kidichi, Nungwi, Via Via

N

Bradt

0   2km
0   1 mile

the building at the front & 1 at the rear. Of course, there's always a flight of stairs to be navigated to get to the balcony. **$$$$**

Zanzibar Beach Resort (70 rooms) ✆ 024 223 0208; **f** 024 223 0556; **e** bookings@zanzibarbeachresort.net; ⬦ www.zanzibarbeachresort.net [0]
This long-established complex is 10mins' drive from town & closer still to the airport. Big – but handsome – 2-storey chalets are set in pleasant gardens round a large swimming pool. Reception is up 1 then down 3 steps from the tar-sealed parking area. From reception, the Spice Restaurant (the main dining area) & the pool have step-free approach routes. The rooms are reached using a pathway – narrow (70) in places – with 2 ornamental bridges. A track runs between the rooms & the pool (which is entered using steps), but this is also narrow (60) at one point. There are several ground-floor rooms; some (Rooms 102, 103, 105 & 106) have level access & similar furnishings.
Room 106: Dbl-door entry is level; bed (78) has transfer space & light switch; door to ensuite (75) is level; shower is almost roll-in – it has a lip (3) – & has fixed showerhead; washbasin is 65cm; toilet (40) has front transfer space only.
Of the other ground-floor rooms, Rooms 101, 104, 118 & 119 have 1 step of varying heights at their entrances but their bathrooms are less accessible. **$$$**

Tembo Hotel (37 rooms) Forodhani St; ✆ 024 223 3005/2069; **f** 024 223 3777; **e** tembo@zitec.org; ⬦ www.tembohotel.com [0]
The splendid Tembo Hotel has 2 (long) entrance steps (7 & 10) & follows Stone Town style with a wooden threshold to cross at the doorway itself. The swimming pool has level access from reception (with laddered entry only) while the restaurant is ramped with low tables (61). There are 5 ground-floor rooms, all with similar ablution facilities.
Room 108: Doorway (79) has threshold (2); 2 sgl beds (79) have transfer space, phone & light controls; highest switch is 149cm; doorway to ensuite (61) is level; step-in shower is in a small Persian bath with tiled seating & fixed showerhead; toilet & washbasin not wheelchair accessible. **$$**

Dhow Palace Hotel (16 rooms) Kenyatta Rd; ✆ 024 223 3012/0304; **e** dhowpalace@zanlink.com [3+]
This sister of the Tembo Hotel is an old building & its relaxed, friendly atmosphere & antique furnishings give a genuine flavour of traditional Zanzibar. The swimming pool is down 5 steps from reception & is entered using ladder or steps. The main restaurant is on the top floor. Reception is up 3 steps from parking & there are several ground-floor rooms. These all have wide doorways (>80) up or down 1–3 steps. Beds are high (>75) with transfer space, phones & light controls & bathroom doorways (around 68) are up a step. Persian-style bath/showers also have 1 or 2 steps to enter them. **$$**

Asmini Palace Hotel (9 rooms) Kiponda St; ☎ 024 223 3369; **m** 0774 276464;
e info@asminipalace.com; ⌂ www.asminipalace.com [0▪]
With several floors & 4 steps plus the customary Zanzibar doorway
threshold at the entrance, the Asmini Palace looks foreboding from street
level. The Chinese-built lift is apparently Zanzibar's only modern lift but
when we visited, it was out of action, awaiting an instruction manual from
the Far East. However, there is 1 room & the dining room on the ground
floor.
Ground-floor room: Doorway (86) is level; dbl bed (77) has transfer
space, light switch & phone; bathroom door (71) is up 1 step; step-in
shower (12) has plastic seat available; toilet (43) has front transfer space
only, but there is no space to close the door once you've entered the
bathroom in a wheelchair. **$$**

Mtoni Marine Centre (46 rooms) ☎ 024 225 0140; **f** 024 225 0496;
e mtoni@zanzibar.cc; ⌂ www.mtoni.com [0▪] [▨]
Being just outside Stone Town can have its advantages; Mtoni is spread
out, lush & green & has a beach. An indication that it's good is its
popularity with the locals; the Mcheza Sports Bar & decent cuisine are
two of the main draws. The beach & the 2 restaurants can be reached
without steps from reception (removable wooden ramps are available for
main dining area) & the swimming pool is down 2 steps.
Ground-floor rooms: All this accommodation has at least 1 step, but a
sturdy wooden ramp has been made to fit Club room 18, which is close to
reception. Doorway (76) is up 2 steps (removable ramp); bed (58) has
transfer space & light switch; doorway into ensuite (75) is level; the
shower has entrance (73) with small drop-off (3) so is almost seamlessly
roll-in, has handheld showerhead & round taps (125); washbasin (71) has
round taps; toilet (41) has front transfer space only.
The older rooms are reached via a hard, level path. They are also up a
couple of steps but are less spacious in general, with the bathroom being
notably smaller. The shower is not possible in a wheelchair. **$$**

Via Via (5 bungalows) **m** 0744 286369; **e** viavia@zanlink.com;
⌂ www.viaviacafe.com [3+]
6km north of Stone Town, the Zanzibar representative of this relaxed
Belgian group of cafés/hotels has ground-floor rooms, but it is set on a
steep slope with about 13 steps from the accommodation up to the
restaurant. **$**

Jambo Guesthouse (8 rooms) Off Mkunazini St; ☎ 024 223 3779; **m** 0777 496571;
e info@jamboguest.com [3+]
This well-respected backpackers' guesthouse has ground-floor rooms,
though there are several steps at the entrance, ablutions are shared with
other guests & showers are step-in. **$**

Northern Zanzibar

Ras Nungwi Beach Hotel (32 rooms) ☎ 024 223 3767; **f** 024 223 3098;
e info@rasnungwi.com; ⌂ www.rasnungwi.com 3⁺

This upmarket hotel has smooth, hard access routes, but being sited on a
slope there are many steps. Reception down to the restaurant is about 15
then it's another 4 down to the swimming pool (entered using ladder &
steps). The beach is down 4 more.

Room 32: The most accessible, but is up 14 steps from reception: door is
94cm; bed is 77cm; door to ensuite (64); step-in shower (9). **$$$$**

La Gemma Dell'Est (138 rooms) ☎ 024 224 0087; **e** info.gemma@planhotel.com;
⌂ www.planhotel.com 0

This classy resort overcomes its inherent inaccessibility – being set on a
steep slope – by ferrying clients around in a golf car. Access routes
throughout are wide, hard & smooth & the only public areas that are not
ramped are the 2 sun-lounging pads – these are down several steps. A
wheelchair is available.

Room 421 (a villa): This is typical of the most accessible options.
Doorway (80) is up 1 step; bed (64) has transfer space, light switch &
phone; doorway into ensuite (70) is level; step-in shower (6) has handheld
showerhead, seat & lever tap (114); toilet has front transfer space only.
Deluxe rooms have similar bathrooms but are less spacious & there is no
seat in the shower. **$$$$**

Nungwi Village Beach Resort (36 rooms) ☎ 022 215 2187;
e relax@nungwivillage; ⌂ www.nungwivillage.com 3⁺

This large complex is under the management of a forward-thinking Swede,
& apparently there are plans to make between 3 & 6 'fully accessible'
rooms by 2009. When we visited, the public toilets were not adapted but
ramped & pathways were a mixture of packed sand & flagstones. All
public areas & all the rooms had several steps up to their entrances. **$$$**

Mnarani Beach Cottages (27 rooms) ☎ 024 224 0494; **f** 024 224 0496;
e mnarani@zanlink.com ⌂ www.lighthousezanzibar.com 1

Mnarani (meaning 'near the lighthouse' in Swahili) is located right on one
of the island's most beautiful beaches. Unfortunately for chair users,
access onto the beach is down about a dozen steps, but the complex itself
is reasonably level. A removable ramp avoids the 2 steps up to the dining
room, the swimming pool (entered using steps or a ladder) is virtually next
to the restaurant & the (most accessible) standard sea-view rooms are
lined up above the beach. Access routes are generally a mix of smooth
mosaic tiled paths & interlocking hexagonal paving.

Ground-floor rooms: All have ample space for wheelchairs but are up 1
or 2 steps; doorways vary from 68cm to 78cm. The sea-view standard
rooms have a threshold (6) entering the bathroom, but these in the family
cottages are level. All showers are step-in (approx 10). **$$$**

Flame Tree Cottages (14 rooms) ✆/f 024 224 0100;
🖰 www.flametreecottages.com 🔲
Owned & run by a friendly – & knowledgeable – Scottish/Zanzibari couple,
Flame Tree is new & therefore reasonably inclusive. The spacious rooms
are spotlessly clean & the whole place feels pleasantly alone near the
northern tip of the island. The pathways are sand, which become soft as
you near the dining area, & there are no steps onto either. There is no pool
& the beach here is not ideal for swimming – a more suitable shore is a
short walk away.
Most accessible rooms: Up 1 step (15) onto the patio (a wooden ramp is
available) then main door (80) is level; bed (62) has light switch & transfer
space; doorway into ensuite (69) is level; spacious shower has threshold
(4), handheld showerhead & a lever tap (104); washbasin (64) has low
mirror & lever tap; toilet (40) has front & side transfer space. **$$**

Baobab Beach Bungalows (50 rooms) ✆/f 024 223 0475; **e**
baobabnungwi@zanzinet.com; 🖰 www.baobabbeachbungalows.com. 🔲² 🖼
Baobab's buildings (including restaurant & rooms) are on 1 level & all are
up 1 or 2 steps from bumpy, sandy pathways. Of the 2 beach areas, 1 has
5 steps to reach it & the other has many more. There are various room
styles, with the most accessible being the standard & the lodge rooms. In
some of these, the shower is part of the room – without walls – making it
into a roll-in type. Several also have handheld showerheads. Main
doorways are generally 77cm but bathroom entrances can be as narrow as
65cm. **$$**

Kendwa Amaan Beach Resort (39 rooms) **m** 0777 492552;
🖰 www.kendwabeachresort.com 🔲
Kendwa Amaan is relatively compact & step-free. Reception is up 3 steps
from the car park, but beyond this, most small differences in height have
short (steep) cement ramps & a similarly sheer slope leads down to the
beach. From here, the Tutti Frutti Restaurant is a short walk over sand &
up 2 steps. The Indian eatery has level access & all tables are >65cm.
Garden-view rooms 31, 32 & 33: These have a drop-down (8) at the
doorway (80); beds (45) have transfer space & light switches; highest
switch is 154cm; bathroom door (65) has threshold (7); step-in shower is
12cm; toilet (39) is up 1 step (12). **$$**

Sunset Kendwa (31 rooms) **m** 0777 414647; **e** info@sunsetken dwa.com;
🖰 www.sunsetkendwa.com 🔲³⁺
The car park is level, there's ample seating at reception & the beautiful,
bougainvillea-clad archway is inviting, but that's where it may end for
full-time wheelers. There are steep pathways down, then several steps up
to rooms (which are extremely spacious), showers have step-in trays &
some toilets have transfer space. **$$**

Eastern Zanzibar

Zamani Zanzibar Kempinski (117 rooms) **m** 0774 444477; **f** 024 224 0066;
e sales.zanzibar@kempinski .com; www.kempinski-zanzibar.com 〇▪
The Kempinski aims to be the island's leading international resort. It's
certainly chic & unique & although it provides super-smooth wheelchair
terrain – polished stone floors abound – some finishings don't reflect its
glowing reputation. There is 1 step then a short ramp to reception. A
walkway of about 150m runs to the garden rooms & the main restaurant
& pool have step-free approaches from here. The pool bar is up 1 step (4) &
the jetty bar is down a long, steep ramp. All tables are >65cm. Golf cars
are available as transport around the complex.
Garden rooms: Most suited to limited mobility. Doorway (132) is level;
beds (43) have light switches, phone & transfer space; highest control is
117cm; bathroom consists of a standalone bath (62) with support rail (17),
but toilet & showers are behind narrow doorways (62 & 56). **$$$$$**

Fairmont Zanzibar (109 rooms) ✆ 024 224 0391; **e** zanzibar@fairmont.com;
www.fairmont.com 〇▪ 🖼 🖳
Recently taken over & renovated by the international chain Fairmont, this
large hotel is by far the most accessible on the island. It is designed &
furnished in contemporary style with a faint Swahili flavour. Smooth
bricked, tiled & cemented paths interconnect all main public areas
including reception, swimming pools, food outlets & the public toilets. The
pools can be entered using steps with handrails while the sun-lounging
area & the beach are down 3 & 5 steps respectively. Gradients are all
<8%. 1 room has disability adaptations with level access & there is a wide
range of other room & bathroom types, most with sgl-stepped entry.
Room 635: This is designed for disabled guests – doorway (76) is level;
bed (66) has transfer space, light switch & phone; bathroom doorway (77)
is level; roll-in shower has flip-down seat (49), handheld showerhead, lever
tap (113) & support rail (70); washbasin (62) has lever taps (though the
mirror is absurdly high) & the toilet (48) has front & side transfer space &
2 support rails (70), 1 beside & 1 behind it; broad sliding doors with
threshold (1) lead to a level patio & pathway to the pool. **$$$$**

Breezes Beach Club & Spa (74 rooms) ✆ 024 224 0102; **f** 024 224 0450;
e info@breezes-zanzibar.com; www.breezes-zanzibar.com 〇▪
A large, well-organised resort, Breezes is one of the older beach hotels on
Zanzibar. 1 step (12) takes you to reception, from where a (standard)
public toilet, TV room & business suite have level access. A wheelchair is
available. At least 1 swimming pool & 1 restaurant can be reached without
steps & several rooms have level doorways (81). There are no roll-in
showers or adapted baths but accommodation is spacious & for several
rooms, no more than 1 step must be negotiated either at the entrance or in
the bathroom. **$$$$**

Bluebay Beach Resort (112 rooms) ☏ 024 224 0240; **f** 024 224 0245;
e mail@bluebayzanzibar.com; ⊕ www.bluebayzanzibar.com 🔲 🖾

A slick resort with a wide range of accommodation types, Bluebay has also
been recognised for its strenuous recycling & energy-saving efforts. It does
not have rooms specifically designed for disability, but has features that
will make life easier for some. The beach is reached using several steps &
the Bahari lunch restaurant is up 4 steps; other than that, all public areas
including pool, main restaurant, bar & reception are level or ramped with
gradients (mostly <8%). Access routes are tiled or hard paths & the
swimming pool is entered using 4 steps.
Superior rooms 140 & 141: These are designated 'disabled', because
there are removable wooden ramps for the 3 steps at the entrance doorway
(87); bed (60) has light switch, phone & transfer space; door to ensuite (66)
is level; step-in shower (21) has seat (not in washing area), fixed
showerhead & lever tap; washbasin (72) has lever tap & toilet has front
transfer space only. **Most deluxe suites** are split-level – there are 2 steps
up to the bed area – & all garden rooms are up at least 2 steps with no
ramps. **$$$$**

Pongwe Beach Resort (16 rooms) **m** 0784 336181; **e** info@pongwe.com;
⊕ www.pongwe.com 🔼

Despite the worrying name, this is one of Zanzibar's treasures. It's well
run & simply decorated, & the generally unfussy atmosphere leaves you
with nothing else to do but enjoy the idyllic setting. As with most
Zanzibari hotels, however, there are steps & sandy paths. Reception is up
2 steps then there are 2 long drop-offs (10) down to the dining area, where
all tables are >65cm. Another half-dozen takes you to the sandy track,
which in turn leads to the gorgeous infinity pool & beach. The rooms have
traditional Zanzibari beds (higher than normal) & step-in showers. The
biggest distinction between rooms regarding access is the number of
doorway steps (varies from 1 to 6) & the distance from reception.
Room 1: The closest (<50m) from reception. Door (80) is up 3 steps; beds
(75) have transfer space & light control; doorway into en-suite (63) is level;
step-in shower (7) has fixed showerhead & entrance is 72cm; washbasin
(65) has lever tap; toilet (41) has side transfer space. **$$$**

Matemwe Beach Village (23 rooms) Contact Africa Travel Resource (UK) ☏ +44
(0)1306 880770; **e** nick@africatraveltesource.com; ⊕ www.matemwebeach.com
🔲 🖾

Locally owned & efficiently run, Matemwe caters to a range of budgets.
The standard rooms are basic but good value, the more popular suites are
more swish, & deserving of their higher price tag, & the extravagant Asali
suite ('meaning 'honey' in Swahili) is a honeymooner's paradise with
secluded location, personal chef & cool plunge pool. From the car park,
reception is down 4 steps & the swimming pool is up 5 then has 3 shallow
steps to enter it. The dining area is level with reception & all tables are

>65cm. Pathways throughout the rest of the lodge are a mix of sand & soft & hard surfaces, but there are occasional kerbs.

Standard rooms 1 & 2: The most accessible, & also have AC. A kerb must be crossed to reach the door (77); bed (58) has light switch & transfer space; door to ensuite (76) has small drop-off (2); step-in shower is 21cm; washbasin is inaccessible; toilet has front transfer space only.

Suite rooms: Doorways (narrowest 74) are up 3 steps; dbl beds are on concrete bases, which are wider than the bed hence blocking wheelchair access, though a free-standing sgl can be brought in; step-in shower is 7cm; 'throne' toilet is inaccessible to wheelchairs.

Asali suite: Pathway is a short plod through sand; doorway (98) is up 4 steps; a mobile phone is available for communication; kitchen area is up 1 step (5) & lounge is up 1 step (11); bed (67) sits on a wider cement base, which blocks wheelchair access; dbl step-in shower (9) indoors has fixed showerhead & sgl roll-in shower outdoors has fixed showerhead & round tap (85); toilet (39) has front & side transfer space. **$$** (Asali suite **$$$$$**)

Sunrise Hotel Restaurant (12 rooms) **m** 0777 415240; **e** sunrise@zanlink.com; ⌂ www.sunrise-zanzibar.com 🖫

This modest & colourful hotel has all the essentials to unwind – prime beach setting, clean rooms & genial staff. On top of this, it's owned & run by Georges, a Belgian chef, & the gourmet food is excellent. Pathways are generally cement. From the car park to reception & restaurant is up 1 step then it's down 2 to the pool, which has a ladder or 4 steps for entry. The beach is down 1 step.

Poolside rooms: The most accessible, all 8 have European dbl or twin beds. Doorway (73) is up 1 step; bed (52) has light switch; bathroom door (72) is level; step-in shower is 20cm; washbasin (64) has lever tap; toilet (40) has front transfer space only. **$$**

Ras Michamvi Beach Resort (15 rooms) ☎ 024 223 1081; **f** 024 223 8696; **e** info@rasmichamvi.com; ⌂ www.rasmichamvi.com 🖫 🖾

This new hotel (opened in 2007) has a stunning location perched high above the ocean. It does mean many (around 100) steps down to the serene shoreline, but there are plans to build an accessible route to another nearby bay, called 'Coconut Beach'. The hotel itself has been designed very much with access in mind. There is a ramp (albeit too steep), which avoids 6 steps at the parking area, & then the rest of the complex is linked via well-constructed, canopied wooden boardwalks. The restaurant is ramped & level; tables are 64cm but blocks are available to raise these. The infinity swimming pool sits proudly halfway down the cliff, with unobstructed views onto the ocean, but has >10 steps to reach it. 1 block of 3 rooms is 'accessible', but was not yet complete in late 2008 – confirm before booking.

Adapted rooms: Doorway (>80) is level; bed (78) has transfer space & light switch; door to ensuite (68) is level; roll-in shower has handheld showerhead & lever tap (103); washbasin (64) has round taps & toilet (40) has front & side transfer space.

The standard rooms have 1 step up to the main door, but level entry from the rear. Ablutions have step-in showers, but are otherwise similar to the 3 adapted rooms. **$$**

Sau Inn Hotel (39 rooms) **\/f** 024 224 0169/0205; **m** 0777 457782; **e** sauinn@zanlink.com 3⁺ ▨

This compact hotel is welcoming & homely. Pathways are cement & tiles though rooms are all up at least 1 step. The pool is virtually level with reception & to get to the beach is a climb then a descent of 6 steps. The b/fast restaurant is up 3 steps & the main dining room is on the first floor, but food can be brought down. The public toilet is up a vertiginous stairwell, not for those weak at the knees! Deluxe rooms are all upstairs. **Standard room 14:** Doorway (79) is up 1 step; beds (66) have transfer space & light switch; door to ensuite (63) is up 1 step (6); roll-in shower has fixed showerhead & lever tap (96); washbasin (63) has lever taps & toilet has front transfer space only. **$$**

Southwestern Zanzibar

Fumba Beach Lodge (26 rooms) **** 0774 878701; **e** reservations@fumbabeach lodge.co.tz; ⌂ www.fumbabeachlodge.com 2⁻ ▨

Thoughtfully designed, carefully built & attentively managed, Fumba is a model lodge. The whitewashed cottages are solid, clean & tastefully decorated & food & service are faultless. Edwin (the owner/manager) is also keen to make the property more inclusive. Currently, reception is level from the parking area, & then there are 2 steps down to the sandy pathways running through the grounds. The restaurant has 1 step to eat indoors, but is otherwise level next to the stylish infinity pool. Accommodation is a choice of deluxe rooms or luxury suites. All are up at least 1 step & entrances are generally wide or even dbl, sliding doors. Deluxe rooms have step-in showers while some suites have roll-in showers outside or even colossal outdoor bathrooms with roll-in shower, bath & toilet all under the stars. **$$$$**

WHERE TO EAT

When staying on the coast, most people eat in their hotel or resort. If you want to have a greater culinary choice then include a night or two in Stone Town. As with accommodation, eating places are often up steps to catch the cooler air; similarly, as with elsewhere in Tanzania, no restaurants have access or toilet facilities designed specifically for disability. But don't let these issues put you off. Staff are usually willing to help people into buildings or up stairs. If that's not ideal then it may be possible to set a table on the ground floor.

There is a large range of restaurants. This is a small selection of some of the more accessible options around Stone Town:

Mercury's Restaurant Mizingani Rd; ☎ 024 223 3076; ⊘ 10.00–22.00. Only pizzas available after 22.00. Up 2 steps on the ocean front, Mercury's (named after Freddie, Zanzibar's favourite son) offers pizzas, seafood & live music. **$$$**

Al Shabani Restaurant Off Malawi Rd. This small eatery is recommended by the locals as it serves excellent & inexpensive Swahili dishes. **$$**

Amore Mio Shangani Rd; ☎ 024 223 3666; ⊘ afternoons & evenings. Owned & run by an Italian, Amore Mio is up 2 steps & has an airy sea-view location. Unsurprisingly, pastas, pizzas, coffees & ice creams are the dishes of choice. **$$**

Forodhani Gardens Mizingani Rd, opposite the Old Fort; ⊘ evenings. The open-air layout here causes few problems for less-mobile people & the stalls offer a sumptuous selection of cheap & freshly cooked Zanzibar specialities. **$**

Stone Town Café Kenyatta Rd; ⊘ during daytime. Up 2 steps then with outside seating, Stone Town Café is a relaxed hangout with drinks & simple snacks.

Zanzibar Coffee House Mkunazini St. ☎ 024 2239 319; ⊘ www.riftvalley-zanzibar.com; ⊘ 09.00–18.00. Up 2 steps from the quiet street, this relatively new place is a great stop for liquid refreshment – fruit juices, milkshakes & coffee – & a tasty cake or sandwich.

OTHER PRACTICALITIES

Upmarket hotels round the island will accept credit cards but money changing should be done in Stone Town, the airport or port. You'll find bureaux de change in all three places, while the NBC Bank on Kenyatta Road has an ATM and will change travellers' cheques, though the latter is a time-consuming task. Postal services are more reliable in Stone Town than outlying areas, internet cafés here are prolific and many coastal resorts now have internet and email.

Medical services

Zanzibar Medical and Diagnostic Centre (*just off Vuga Rd;* ☎ *024 223 1071*) is equipped and staffed to typical Western standards and will be able to deal with most health issues. Local clinics and hospitals are often crowded and less hygienic, but may be fine for small problems and will always be cheaper. People with serious medical emergencies would normally be taken to Mombasa or Dar es Salaam.

WHAT TO SEE AND DO

It would be hard to be bored on Zanzibar. Not only is there an abundance of things to do, but there is something for everyone, from spice tours to forest walks and explorations of historical buildings. Also, because the island is so small, they are all easily reached. The difficult part is dragging yourself from your beach towel to actually go and do them.

In and around Stone Town

The majority of highlights are in and around Stone Town. These are all easily reached using local taxis, and some, depending on your walking/wheeling abilities and where you are staying, might be walkable. The streets are old and tiled, but these are smooth and easily negotiated in a wheelchair. Also, most of the curios are displayed at the shop doorways and haggling for purchases is done on the street, meaning climbing the usual step or two into the building is rarely necessary. The main fruit and vegetable market on the edge of Stone Town is similarly accessible; most stalls are all set on one level with no steps, presumably because they have to be reached with wheelbarrows. Access to the various highlights is as follows:

Old Arab Fort

(� *free*) Surrounded by more recent structures, this Arab fort (built around the beginning of the 18th century) is no longer imposing, but it takes little imagination to see how intimidating it once was. For wheelers, it is still virtually impenetrable with at least a couple of steps at all entrances and several inside. Nowadays, at least, there is a welcoming smile and a helping hand available.

The Palace Museum

(� *US$3 pp*) This captivating museum is worth the effort of entry. It's up six steps to the main hall then there are flights of stairs between the two floors. It is a conservation building, so will not be changed soon, but the men inside will happily carry less able visitors to see the exhibits. A reasonable tip would be polite for this (see *Chapter 3, Interacting with Africans*, page 98).

House of Wonders

(� *US$3 pp*) It's a pity the lift, one of the reasons this building is so-named, no longer works. Like the Palace Museum, there are eight steps to enter the building and a further 'many' between the two storeys. Unlike the museum, the House of Wonders is staffed by women. Sexist though it may sound, they told me that if you need physical help then you might need to find male 'volunteers' and negotiate their entry price!

Anglican Cathedral

(� *US$3 pp*) Again, a multitude of steps is the barrier here. The cathedral was built over the original slave market, and to venture to the fearsome dungeon, not only do you need to be strong of stomach, but fairly agile; there are many steps and passages are narrow.

SCUBA DIVING

Scuba diving is one recreation which gives disabled people complete freedom from their otherwise essential mobility aids. Water provides the buoyancy, and with a bit of practice and help, getting around under the surface is quite possible. I have not found any dive centres in Africa that focus on this market, but most that I spoke to would be prepared to consider organising a trip for a disabled person. There are several well-run centres on the Kenyan coast and on Zanzibar, often based in hotels and resorts.

Experienced divers should take their own specialised equipment as webbed gloves and other diving gear designed for disability are not easily found in Africa. Basic guidance is that weaker swimmers should aim for dive sites with a slight current, as drifting along requires little effort but allows a large area to be easily covered.

Areas with a flow of water so strong that it requires constant checking should be avoided. Also, boat or jetty entry is generally preferable to beach entry, as the latter may require a long trudge – or swim – to reach deep water. Anyone with mobility issues should contact operators in advance to confirm that their needs can be catered to and check their insurance polices for possible exclusion of adventurous sports.

On Zanzibar, the **Rising Sun Dive Centre at Breezes Beach Club and Spa** (see page 211) has had professional training in the techniques required to teach disabled people to dive.

Outside Stone Town

Mtoni Palace Ruins
(*free*) The ruins of the oldest palace on Zanzibar (from the 1840s) have an exploratory path which is just wide enough for a wheelchair, but too rough for most independent pushers.

Marahubi Palace
(*US$3 pp*) Built for the concubines of Sultan Barghash in1882, these ruins don't really have a 'made' path. Despite this, the ground is level and hard and it would be no problem in a wheelchair with help. Even if the ruins prove too difficult, the nearby boat-building works would make a pleasant half-hour's stopover.

Further afield

Spice Tours
Possibly Zanzibar's number-one 'energetic' activity, visiting a spice farm is also quite possible for people with walking difficulties. The priority should be to ask for a relatively level farm and walking/pushing around should be quite possible, especially in dry weather. Even if you prefer to stay in or

near your vehicle, farm staff will readily bring examples of the spices to you and give their explanation one-to-one. For this, again, I'd offer a slightly enhanced fee.

Jozani Forest
(🔊 US$3 pp) Viewing the rare and indigenous red colobus monkeys in Jozani Forest is a must-try for anyone who loves nature. We were lucky enough to find these entertainingly playful primates after only a 50m push into the trees. A good tip is to arrive early in the day, before other people get there. The mangrove walkway is best arrived at in a car; from there, it's a wooden boardwalk through the swamp that is easily wheelchair navigable for about 150m.

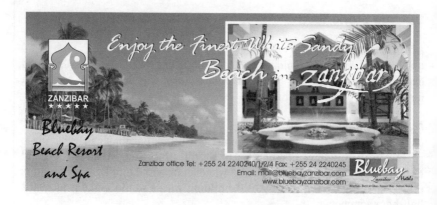

NAMIBIA AT A GLANCE

Location	Southwest Africa with a south Atlantic coastline and borders with South Africa, Angola, Botswana and Zambia
Size	825,418km²
Climate	Subtropical desert; warm winter (Jun–Aug), hot summer (Nov–Mar)
Population	2.1 million (2008 estimate)
Capital and largest city	Windhoek (just under 300,000 in 2008)
Currency	Namibian dollar (N$)
Rate of exchange	£1=N$12.6; US$1=N$8.4; €1=N$11.2; (May 2009)
Language	English (official), Afrikaans, German, several indigenous languages
Religion	Christianity, indigenous beliefs
Time	Apr–Oct GMT +1, Oct–Mar GMT +2
Electricity	220V, delivered at 50Hz; three round pins
Weights and measures	Metric
Public holidays	1 Jan, Independence Day (21 Mar), Good Friday, Easter Monday, Workers' Day (1 May), Cassinga Day (4 May), Africa Day (25 May), Ascension Day, Heroes' Day (26 Aug), Human Rights Day (10 Dec), 25–26 Dec
Tourist board	⚘ www.namibiatourism.com.na
International telephone code	+264
Further information:	For a more in-depth analysis, including background information and mainstream travel information, see Chris McIntyre's Bradt travel guide to Namibia.

6 Namibia

A relatively recent arrival to the world tourism market, Namibia is unique. Its ferocious Atlantic coastline, stark desert landscapes and timeless rocky ranges all speak of a land of extremes, and great swathes of the country are devoid of human settlement. The result is some of the most stunningly beautiful scenery anywhere on the planet.

For the visitor concerned mainly with wildlife, the highlight is Etosha National Park, which is often incorporated into an extended safari through Zambia and Botswana. This is one of Africa's most rewarding reserves, and being predominantly arid (based on the edge of a massive saltpan) is quite unlike any other. In agricultural areas throughout the country there are many guest farms and lodges set in their own, smaller wildlife reserves. These can also provide good game viewing where the subjects, being more used to vehicles, are easily seen and photographed.

For the purposes of this guide, I have covered the areas of the country most visited by safari tourists. These include Windhoek, Swakopmund, north-central Namibia and Etosha then east of the park through the Caprivi Strip. I have also included some accommodation near Sesriem, allowing easy visits to Sossusvlei's enormous sand dunes.

GENERAL INFORMATION

ACCESS SUMMARY

With its distinctly Germanic pedigree, modern Namibia is impressively well structured. The standard of access in accommodation is therefore relatively high and 'wheelchair accessible' signs are often spotted next to supermarkets and public buildings. All the restcamps in Etosha have well-appointed 'disabled' rooms, and many privately owned guesthouses and large hotel chains throughout the country mirror this level of inclusion. Distances between highlights are deceptively long but all the main routes are either smooth tar or well-maintained gravel. Internal flights are always an option.

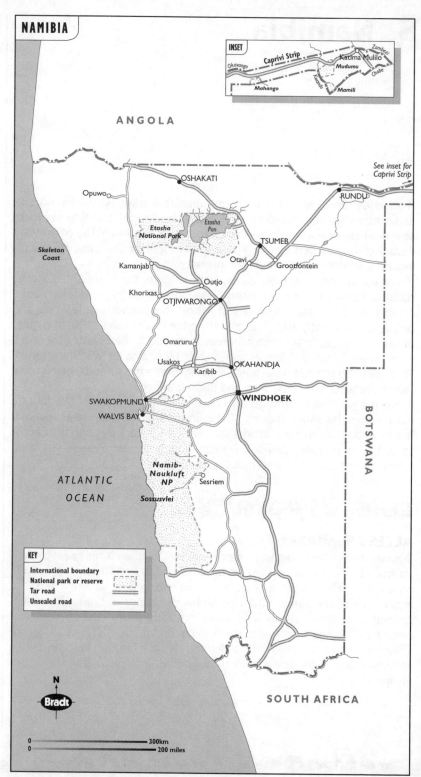

NAMIBIA

ANGOLA

Opuwo

OSHAKATI

RUNDU

See inset for Caprivi Strip

Skeleton Coast

Etosha National Park

Etosha Pan

TSUMEB

Kamanjab

Otavi

Grootfontein

Khorixas

Outjo

OTJIWARONGO

Omaruru

Usakos

Karibib

OKAHANDJA

SWAKOPMUND

WINDHOEK

WALVIS BAY

BOTSWANA

ATLANTIC OCEAN

Namib-Naukluft NP

Sesriem

Sossusvlei

INSET

Caprivi Strip

Okavango

Katima Mulilo

Zambezi

Mudumu

Chobe

Mahango

Kwando

Mamili

KEY

International boundary	—·—·—
National park or reserve	¦ ¦ ¦
Tar road	———
Unsealed road	———

N

Bradt

SOUTH AFRICA

0 ——— 300km
0 ——— 200 miles

LOCAL OPERATORS

For local operators catering to people with mobility issues, plus some mainstream operators that have shown a genuine interest in this market, see *Chapter 1, Specialised operators in Africa,* pages 20–23.

WINDHOEK AND SURROUNDING AREA

Windhoek, unlike many African capitals, is airy, clean and well organised. If it were not for the street stalls selling everything from fruit to curios, it could be any cosmopolitan conurbation in the world. Set at 1,650m, the climate is generally pleasing, although it can be hot in the summer months, and whilst it is the largest city in Namibia (with just under 300,000 people) it is never crowded and frenetic. Known to the Nama and Herero people for centuries because of its thermal springs, the Windhoek area has been a significant centre of business and trade since the mid 19th century. The German colonisers increased its importance, using it as their main base in the country and constructing many beautiful buildings, then, during the era of South African rule, Windhoek was rigidly run and maintained.

The town centre is extremely suited to wheelchair wanders; pavements are smooth, kerb cuts are common and there are pedestrian-only malls with step-free shop entries and the occasional (though well-hidden) accessible public toilet. Despite the secure feel to the place, it is wise never to let your guard down; the great majority of Windhoek's population is relatively poor and casual theft and pickpocketing are common occurrences.

GETTING THERE AND AWAY

By road

Windhoek is located relatively centrally in Namibia – Swakopmund is 356km to the west and Etosha's Okaukuejo is 435km to the north. Scheduled buses (see ⁀ www.townhoppers.iway.na, ⁀ www.ekonolux.com & ⁀ www.intercape.co.za) leave the city centre running to all areas, and connect with Johannesburg and Cape Town, but none of these have made any allowance to disabled travellers; see *Public transport*, page 89. Cars and 4x4 safari vehicles can be hired in the city (see page 25).

By rail

No particularly useful rail services in Namibia have disability access (see pages 91–2 for more information).

By air

Hosea Kutako International Airport (44km east of Windhoek) is the most commonly used hub, dealing with all European and some international flights. It has step-free access throughout and there are male- and female-accessible toilets in the main building and the departure lounge, all with

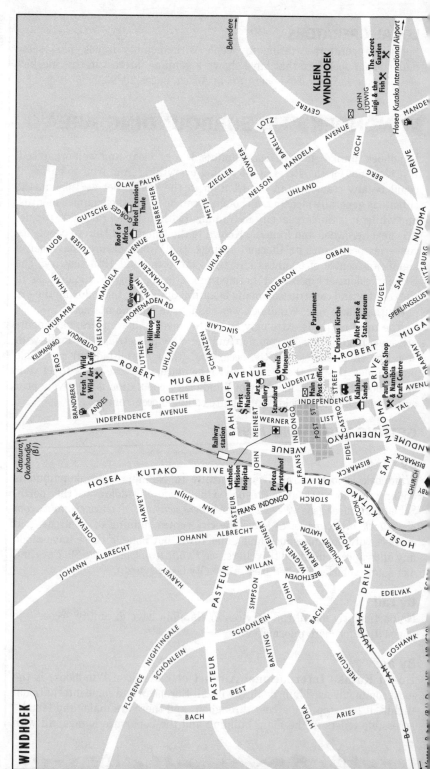

KLEIN
WINDHOEK

The Secret
Garden
Luigi & the
Fish
JOHN
LUDWIG

Hosea Kutako International Airport

GEVERS

MANDE

MANDEL

KOCH

BERG

DRIVE

NUJOMA

Belvedere

LOTZ

BARELLA

MANDELA

AVENUE

NELSON

BOWKER

UHLAND

ZIEGLER

METJE

VON

UHLAND

ECKENBRECHER

OLAV PALME

GUTSCHE

GORGES

Hotel Pension
Thule

Roof of
Africa

AVENUE

SCHANZEN

MANDELA

NELSON

KUISEB

AUOB

KHAN

OMURAMBA

KILIMANJARO

EROS

OUTENIQUA

Olive Grove

PROMENADEN RD

NGAMI

The Hilltop
House

LUTHER

UHLAND

ROBERT

SCHANZEN

SINCLAIR

ANDERSON

ORBAN

Parliament

Christus Kirche

Alte Feste &
State Museum

HUGEL

SAM

NUJOMA

SPERLINGSLUST

WITZBURG

ROBERT

MUGA

MUGABE

GOETHE

AVENUE

BAHNHOF

LOVE

Owela
Museum

Art
Gallery

First
National

Standard

LUDERITZ

Main
Post office

Post office

INDEPENDENCE

STREET

POST ST

Kalahari
Sands

Paul's Coffee Shop

& Namibia
Craft Centre

DRABKAY

DRIVE

AVENU

TAL

INDEPENDENCE AVENUE

BRANDBERG

ANDES

Fresh 'n Wild
& Wild Art Café

Katutura,
Okahandja, (B1)

Railway
station

MEINERT

JOHN

WERNER

INDONGO

FRANS

AVENUE

LIST

FIDEL CASTRO

BISMARCK

SAM

NDUME

NDEMUFAYO

NUJOMA

KUTAKO

HOSEA

CHURCH

ARBY

B-6

Catholic
Mission Hospital

Protea
Furstenhof

DRIVE

STORCH

PUCCINI

MOZART

HAYDN

SCHUBERT

BRAHMS

WAGNER

BEETHOVEN

JOHN

BACH

SAM

NUJOMA

DRIVE

EDELVAK

GOSHAWK

MERCURY

HOSEA KUTAKO DRIVE

HARVEY

VAN RHIJN

PASTEUR

FRANS INDONGO

JOHANN ALBRECHT

MEINERT

WILLAN

SIMPSON

SCHÖNLEIN

BANTING

OLIEVAAR

JOHANN ALBRECHT

HARVEY

PASTEUR

FLORENCE NIGHTINGALE

SCHÖNLEIN

PASTEUR

BEST

BACH

HYDRA

ARIES

Werner Beans (B1) & Kleine AB (C30)

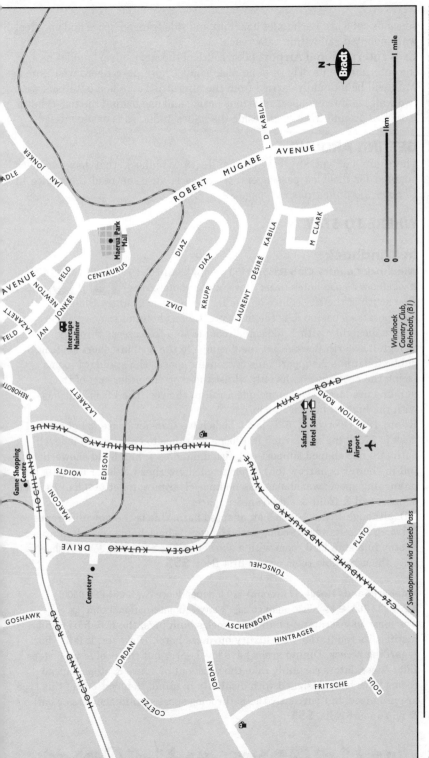

spacious cubicles. Each toilet has front and side transfer space and one steel wall-mounted rail within easy reach.

Eros International Airport (4km south of the city centre) handles most of the internal flights. There is no aisle chair (those passengers who cannot walk will be manually carried from the aircraft). There is a bathroom with two wall-mounted support rails (one beside and one behind the toilet) but it is tucked around the corner beside the ladies' toilet, so is easily missed.

GETTING AROUND

There are not yet any taxi companies in Windhoek that have vehicles adapted for disabled passengers. If access is an issue read the advice in *Chapter 3, Public transport*, page 89.

WHERE TO STAY

In Windhoek

Windhoek Country Club Resort (150 rooms) ☎ 061 205 5911; f 061 252 797; e windhoek@legacyhotels.co.za; ⏱ www.legacyhotels.co.za [icons]
Just south of the city centre on the B1 bypass, the Country Club incorporates a casino & is the most prestigious hotel in the city. It caters well to disability with 1 dedicated room & step-free access throughout, though it's worth noting that the 2 ramps to the pool are short & steep. 1 public toilet has 2 support rails & transfer space. The standard rooms facing the pool have baths only whilst those on the other side of the building are larger & also include a roll-in shower. The lift is spacious with the highest button 124cm.
Room 101: Doorway (76) is level; beds have transfer space & light switch; desk is 77cm; highest switch is 100cm; entrance to ensuite (70) is level; bath (48) has shaped support rail, fitted handles & handheld showerhead; roll-in shower is narrow (65) & has fixed showerhead & lever tap (90), but no turning space; washbasin has no knee clearance; toilet (44) has 1 (rear) support rail & front & side transfer space.
NB: although Room 101 has an adapted bath, this is the only difference between it & standard rooms with showers; wheelchair users often prefer to stay in a standard room with a shower on the reception level rather than the accessible room on the first floor. **$$$**

Kalahari Sands Hotel (173 rooms) 129 Independence Av; ☎ 061 280 0000; f 061 222 260; e ksands@sunint.co.za; ⏱ www.suninternational.com [icon]
The most 'sky-scraping' of all Windhoek's buildings, the Kalahari Sands justifies its reputation as a luxury business hotel. However, it falls short regarding access. Dining areas have level entry but the pool is up 6 steps. Lifts & escalators certainly take the work out of stairs & steps, but no rooms have been designed with disability in mind. Renovations of this type are promised, but currently the bathrooms sport step-in showers or baths & no support rails. **$$$**

Hotel Pension Thule (25 rooms) 1 Gorges St; ☎ 061 371 950; **f** 061 371 967; **e** res.thule@mweb.com.na; 🖱 www.thule-namibia.com ③➕ 🖼
A showy building high above Windhoek, the Thule has some of the city's more easy-to-reach rooms. Sadly, though, the restaurant is up about 20 steps & the pool is down 19. From your vehicle, a ramp leads to the entrance. Reception is up 1 step from here & several rooms are down a shallow incline. Floor surfaces are tiles & seamless crazy paving.
Room 1: Door (78) has threshold (2); bed (56) has transfer space & light switch; highest switch is 140cm; door to ensuite (78) is level & bathroom is very spacious; bath (46) has 1 fitted handle, transfer space & end-fitted lever taps; roll-in shower has fold-down seat (47), handheld showerhead & a lever tap (110); washbasin (73) has a lever tap; toilet has front & side transfer space. **$$$**

The Hilltop House (6 rooms) 12 Lessing St; ☎ 061 249 116; **e** hilltop@iafrica.com.na; 🖱 www.thehilltophouse.com 🖵
As the name would suggest, the Hilltop has exquisite views over the city, & contrary to expectation, it may suit less agile travellers. The owner/manager is also keen to include everyone so will do his best to accommodate you. The terrace is up a step from the parking area, then from here the pool has level access & is entered via 3 corner steps. Food is normally served upstairs but can be brought to pool level or to the rooms. 3 rooms are on the ground floor (terrace level), of which 2 are most suitable.
Rooms 4 & 5: Room 4 has no step at its main entrance (77) but 1 at the bathroom doorway (76), whilst Room 5 has 2 steps at the wide (dbl door) main entrance & its doorway into the ensuite (76) is level; paths are loose pebbles & smooth, hard tiles; both rooms have a step-in shower (16), toilet (43) with transfer space & a washbasin (>80). There are plans to further adapt Room 5. **$$$**

Olive Grove Guesthouse (11 rooms) 20 Promenaden Rd, Klein Windhoek; ☎ 061 239 199; **f** 061 234 971; **e** info@olivegrove-namibia.com; 🖱 www.olivegrove-namibia.com 🖵
The Olive Grove is of a high standard & efficiently run, but still manages to feel relaxed & homely – a fine balance to achieve. After mounting the 4 steps to the terrace, the restaurant, reception & 1 room (number 3) are up 1 step. Other rooms have steps to bathrooms, are up a flight of stairs or are down at car-park level. The plunge pool & sun loungers are raised 6 steps from the terrace.
Room 3: Door (72) up 1 step; bed (56) has light switch, phone & transfer space; desk (74); highest switch is 147cm; door to ensuite (75) is level; the stylish bath (41) has side-mounted round taps & a handheld showerhead; toilet (41) has front transfer space; washbasin has no knee space. **$$$**

Safari Court Hotel (215 rooms) Corner of Auas & Aviation rds; ☎ 061 296 8000; **f** 061 235 652; **e** safari@safarihotelsnamibia.com; 🖱 www.safarihotel.com.na 🄌

This is the more exclusive but less accessible of the 2 'Safari' hotels (they are next to one another). Once you've rolled up the gently curved ramp at the entrance, all public areas are step-free or accessed using the spacious lift. The dining tables are 69cm & guests can use the large pool at the Safari Court. The rooms either have baths (52) with fitted handles or step-in showers (15). Doorways vary from 69cm to 79cm & beds (60) have transfer space, phone & light switch. **$$$**

Hotel Safari (199 rooms) Corner of Auas & Aviation rds; ☎ 061 296 8000; f 061 235 300; e safari@safarihotelsnamibia.com; ⊕ www.safarihotel.com.na ▢▢ ▢ ▢
The comfortable Hotel Safari has 2 rooms with adaptations to suit disabled guests. Flooring inside is polished stone with carpets in the rooms, whilst outdoors to the pool (entered using steps) is crazy paving. There are 2 restaurants: the à la carte option is up 2 steps & the other (with both buffet & à la carte) has 1 step, for which a removable ramp is available. The public toilet has level access & though there are no rails, there is front & side transfer space around the toilet.
Room 50: A business-class room where the doorway is level & wide; beds have transfer space, light switch & phone; bathroom doorway is level; roll-in shower has fold-down seat, shaped support rail, lever tap & handheld showerhead; washbasin has lever taps & low mirror; toilet has side & rear support rails & front & side transfer space. The only disadvantage here is that the room is situated next to the parking area, so the rumble of wheeled suitcases is heard from early morning.
Room 33: a budget room; apparently the bathroom is similar to that in Room 50. **$$**

Protea Furstenhof (33 rooms) 4 Frans Indongo St; ☎ 061 237 380; f 061 237 855; e furstenhof@proteahotels.com; ⊕ www.proteahotels.com ▢▢
The Furstenhof is now part of the Protea group, but is still quite individual & has also not yet joined most other hotels in this chain in having at least 1 adapted room. A steep ramp greets you at the entrance but then the reception & dining room are on 1 level. The basic swimming pool is up 8 steps & is entered using 3 with no handrail. Access routes are tiled with some short-pile carpets & there is a lift with doorway (135); highest control is 150cm. All rooms are similar regarding access.
Room 109: This is close to public areas. Doorway (79) is level; sgl beds (52) have transfer space, light switch & phone; desk is 71cm; door to ensuite (70) is level but bathroom is small; curved, corner bath (58); step-in shower (27) & washbasin (64) have round taps. **$$**

Roof of Africa (27 rooms) 124–126 Nelson Mandela Av, Klein Windhoek; ☎ 061 254 708; f 061 248 048; e info@roofofafrica.com; ⊕ www.roofofafrica.com ▢▢
The abundance of timber in the large main building gives this ex-backpackers' lodge a slightly 'Wild-West' feel. It has no features pertaining specifically to disability, but there are ground-floor rooms. The entrance

has a shallow ramp, then there are level brick & tile paths leading past the shady pool to the rooms. There are steps to enter the pool. Although the main seating area is upstairs, the restaurant & bar are on the ground floor & tables are 72cm.

Standard rooms: Doorway (75) is up 2 steps; bed (67) has light switch & phone; desk is 67cm; door to ensuite (78) is level; step-in shower (26) has fixed showerhead & lever taps (93); toilet (44) has front transfer space only. Luxury rooms are similar regarding access. **$$**

Guesthouse Tamboti (15 rooms) 9 Kerby St; ☎ 061 235 515; f 061 259 855; e tamboti@mweb.com.na; www.tamboti-namibia.com
This cosy guesthouse has a reputation as being the most wheelchair-accessible accommodation in Windhoek. While there are spacious rooms with level entry, the Tamboti's management is quick to say that they don't aim specifically at this market – there are no access features like handrails – so don't expect everything to roll into place. The building is set down a slope, with a cemented courtyard & close-fitting brick paths. The most accessible rooms are Room 1 (with a bath) & Room 10 (with a shower). From Room 1, the dining room is up 14 steps or a long uphill push past the pretty swimming pool (which itself is entered using a ladder). Room 10 is at street level, so is closer to these areas.

Room 1: Doorway (110) has threshold (5); bed (58) has transfer space, light switch & phone; desk is 71cm; door to ensuite (78) is level; bath (49) has fitted handles & transfer space; washbasin (65) has low mirror & round taps; toilet (44) has front & side transfer space.

Room 10: Doorway (120) is level; doorway into the ensuite is 70cm; roll-in shower (76) has a bench seat (not in the washing area), a handheld showerhead & round taps. **$**

Around Windhoek

GocheGanas Reserve (16 chalets) ☎ 061 224 909; f 061 224 924; e reservations@gocheganas.com; www.gocheganas.com
At 29km southeast of Windhoek, this large reserve (with rhino, among other animals) has luxurious accommodation. Public areas (including a spa) are step-free & 4 rooms close to reception are particularly accessible. Their ablutions have roll-in showers with seats & support rails, & a toilet with support rails. **$$$$$**

Midgard Lodge (46 rooms) ☎ 062 503 888; f 064 404 942; e centralres.nsh@olfitra.com.na; www.namibsunhotels.com.na
An expansive complex with horseriding facilities & tennis courts, the Midgard caters more to the business/conference market than individual tourist bookings. Despite this, & the fact that it's a little out of the way (85km or 1½hrs' drive northeast of the capital) it's exceedingly accessible. From your vehicle, it's level wheeling past reception (which is up 2 steps), restaurant & teardrop-shaped pool to the accommodation. Underfoot it's

stone & cement but for the size of the place there's a lack of seating for slow walkers. There are 2 pools, both entered with steps only & dining tables are 72cm.

Rooms 204 & 205: These have level showers. Doorway (81) is ramped; beds (51) have light switch, phone & space for transfers; desk is 69cm; highest switch is 155cm; doorway into ensuite (79) is level; bath (42) has fitted handles, transfer space & end-mounted round taps; roll-in shower has fixed showerhead & round taps; toilet (44) has front & side transfer space. **$$$**

Camelthorn Chalets (5 rooms) ☏ 061 264 336; **f** 061 264 555; **e** info@eddahof.com ☝ www.eddahof.com 📱 🖼
Approximately 10km north of the city, this hospitable little homestead is decorated with a skilfully painted mural, which comically depicts an African hunting scene. Reception, living, TV & dining areas are up a short ramp from well-laid crazy paving, with doorways 75cm & tables 71cm. The swimming pool & sun-lounging area are up 2 steps. Some rooms have roll-in showers & owner/manageress Martina wants to make it even more inclusive.
Elephant Room: Doorway (76) has shallow ramp; bed (49) has light switch & transfer space; door to ensuite (69) is level; roll-in shower has removable seat, handheld showerhead & round taps; washbasin (76) has round taps; toilet (37) has side & front transfer space.
Zebra Room: Doorway (78) has shallow ramp; beds (49 & 54) has light switch & transfer space; door to ensuite (71) is level; roll-in shower has removable seat, handheld showerhead & round taps (129); washbasin (68) has round taps; toilet (37) has side & front transfer space. **$$**

Airport Lodge (6 rooms) ☏ 061 231 491/243 192; **f** 061 236 709; **e** reservations@airportlodgenamibia.com; ☝ www.airportlodgenamibia.com 📱
A cosy but slightly rambling lodge between Windhoek & Hosea Kutako International Airport, this won't suit wheeled visitors as well as the Trans Kalahari Inn (see following entry). Reception & the swimming pool are up a couple of steps & the track to the accommodation is rough gravel, though it can be driven. There's a rudimentary red-brick path between the rooms & the restaurant & the latter has level access.
Room 4: Doorway (76) has 3 steps but there is a steep, makeshift plyboard ramp available for 2 of these; bed (47) has light switch & transfer space; door to ensuite (76) is level; step-in shower (14); the toilet has front transfer space only. **$$**

Trans Kalahari Inn ☏/**f** 061 222 877; **e** grimm@transkalahari.com; ☝ www.transkalahari.com 📱 🖼
This small, mainly German hotel & campground is spotlessly clean & well located between Hosea Kutako International Airport & Windhoek. Fairly isolated in an evocative rocky landscape, it's a super place to stop if you just want to rest after a long flight; however, if you need more stimulation then drive on into the city. It's set on a slope, but the reception &

restaurant – tables (69) – are step-free. The indoor pool is down 4 steps then has stepped entry with handrails. With tiles inside & crazy paving outdoors, the ground surface will suit most wheelers.

3 rooms: These are close to reception with bigger bathrooms. 1 of these (number 1) has almost no step (<5) at entry; doorway is 78cm; dbl bed (48) has transfer space & light controls; desk is 66cm; doorway into ensuite is 73cm; roll-in shower (73) has round taps (109) & fixed showerhead; washbasin (82) has mirror (95); toilet (42) has front access only. **$$**

WHERE TO EAT

Apart from malls, I know of no eating places in Windhoek with purpose-built 'disabled' toilets. The following selection is some of those that are currently most popular and accessible:

Luigi & the Fish 90 Sam Nujoma Drive; 𝄇 061 256 399; ⊘ 12.00–24.00 Mon–Sat. With succulent kingklip & infamous platters of prawns, as well as all the usual meat & veggie options, this is a reliable evening out. Live music, step-free rear entrance & supervised parking complete the picture. **$$$$$**

Fresh 'n' Wild Corner of Liliencron St & Robert Mugabe Av; 𝄇 061 240 346; ⊘07.00–17.00 Mon–Fri, 08.00–13.00 Sat–Sun. With tables outdoors this does tasty daytime food, including lasagne & stir-fries. After 17.00, people tend to drift on to their wine bar (Wild Art Café), which, although it is a short walk away & has about 30 steps, has potential wheelchair access from the back, It stays open until 22.00. **$$$**

Paul's Coffee Shop 40 Tal St; 𝄇 061 307 176; **e** paulscoffeeshop@africaonline. com.na; ⊘ 09.00–17.00 Mon–Fri, 08.00–14.00 Sat. Paul's is part of the Namibia Craft Centre (𝄇 *061 242 2222*), a super place to locate souvenirs & presents. Many of the traders here are members of NACOBTA (Namibia Community Based Tourism Association, ⊕ www.nacobta.com.na), which aims to develop tourism & improve living standards in rural Namibia. This is reason enough to visit, but Paul's Coffee Shop makes it even more attractive as it serves fresh, good quality b/fasts, snacks & lunches, & aims to employ only people with disabilities (see page 102). As a result of this, access is level & there is a spacious bathroom on site with support rails round the toilet. **$$**

The Secret Garden (previously called Jenny's Place) 78 Sam Nujoma Drive; 𝄇 061 236 792; ⊘07.00–23.00 Mon–Sat, 09.00–17.00 Sun. A great place for b/fasts, midday snacks, thirst quenchers & relaxed evening meals. There's no step & a (steep & narrow) ramp to the toilet. **$$**

Shopping malls (Maerua Mall being one) have food courts plying sandwiches & the usual pizza/burger-type hot meals, & also usually contain an adapted, wheelchair-accessible toilet. **$$**

OTHER PRACTICALITIES

In tune with its status as capital city of one of Africa's most developed countries, Windhoek has all the services a traveller would need.

For money issues, ATMs are prolific and banks are as efficient as those in Europe. Bureaux de change are also easily located, but with the prevalence of ATMs and credit cards being widely accepted very few travellers depend on travellers' cheques or hard currency. The main post office is on Independence Avenue in the city centre and internet cafés are never far away; many lodgings and hotels provide email services and some even have Wi-Fi for people who carry their own computer.

Medical services

The **Windhoek Medi-clinic** (*Heliodoor St, Eros (follow Omuramba Rd north from Mandela Av);* ℓ *061 222 687;* e *hospmngrwindh@mediclinic .co.za;* ⌂ *www.windhoekmc.co.za*) is a modern private hospital, which is clean well equipped, and has staff trained to Western standards. The **Catholic Mission Hospital** (*92 Werner List St (between Franz Indongo & John Meinert sts;* ℓ *061 270 2004;* f *061 270 2039;* e *admin@rchna.org*) has a good local reputation and with a central location, this hospital is more basic but cheaper than the Medi-clinic.

WHAT TO SEE AND DO

For almost all visitors, Windhoek is essentially a place to start or end a safari, to stock up or to wind down. However, it is a beautiful city in its own right with museums and galleries displaying its colonial and pre-colonial history. While not completely seamless, access in public buildings is usually more than just an afterthought and most disabled visitors should cope.

Alte Feste and State Museum

(*Robert Mugabe Av, opposite Christuskirche;* ℓ *061 293 4362;* ⊘ *summer 09.00–18.00 Mon–Fri, winter 09:00–17:00; 10.00–12:30 & 15.00–18.00 Sat–Sun; closed public holidays;* ⌆ *free.*) This is the best museum in Windhoek with comprehensive collections covering prehistoric art, colonial artefacts, the independence struggle & national symbols. It is also the most accessible: a ramp leads from the street, the displays are all on one level & there is an adapted toilet.

Owela Museum

(*Robert Mugabe Av;* ℓ *061 293 4358;* ⊘ *same hours as State Museum except closed 13.00–14.00 daily for lunch;* ⌆*free*) Covers traditional cultures and artefacts, fauna and flora and also has a bird room. From Mugabe Avenue there are three small steps and then a ramp, while the Luderitz Street entry is level and ramped. There are three levels with stairway access only and toilets are standard.

TransNamib Museum

(*Railway Station, off Bahnhoff St:* ✆ *061 298 2624/2168;* ⊘ *08.00–13.00 &*
14.00–17.00 weekdays only; closed public holidays; entry N\$5 or N\$3 for
under 18 years old.) Shows the history of transport in Namibia, particularly
by rail. There are three steps at the entrance and I am told that exhibitions
are upstairs.

National Art Gallery

(*Corner of Robert Mugabe Av & John Meinert St;* ✆ *061 231 160;*
⊘ *08.00–17.00 Tue–Fri, 09.00–14.00 Sat; closed Mon, Sun & public*
holidays; ✆ *N\$20 adults, N\$10 students and N\$5 children.*) A small but
worthwhile exhibition of Namibian art, both historical and contemporary.
The main entrance has 11 steps but a ramp is available on Robert Mugabe
Avenue. There are three levels inside with stairs only and toilets are
standard.

SWAKOPMUND AND WALVIS BAY

These neighbouring towns are perched on the edge of the hot, dry desert,
staring into the chilly, choppy Atlantic Ocean. The result of the extremes
is that they are often shrouded by morning fog. Despite this discouraging
climate, they make up Namibia's main coastal holiday resort and the area
is a buzz of activity most months of the year.

German colonists developed Swakopmund as a seaport in the late 19th
century, because although Walvis Bay (30km to the south) has the deepest
and only naturally protected harbour in Namibia, it was under British
control. However, it was never a success and when South Africa took
control of the colony in 1915, Walvis Bay was designated the main port.
Swakopmund then benefited briefly from the nearby discovery of uranium,
but has built itself primarily as a tourist destination. As a result, it is the
larger and by far the livelier of the two. It has some of the finest examples
of colonial German architecture anywhere in the world, and because the
town is so well run, these are meticulously maintained. It all creates a
solid base for a tourist resort, and if you add the colourfully painted
façades and relaxed manner of the locals, the final result is a thriving
seaside town.

In recent years, encouraged in part by the large numbers of overland
trucks reaching the coast, the craze for adrenalin sports has hit
Swakopmund. It is now possible to set your pulse racing by going
parachuting, sand boarding or quad biking in the dunes. Walvis Bay is
much less showy, but still has attractive buildings and some good
birdwatching opportunities. Although most tourists stay in Swakopmund,
Walvis Bay has a broader choice of accessible hotels.

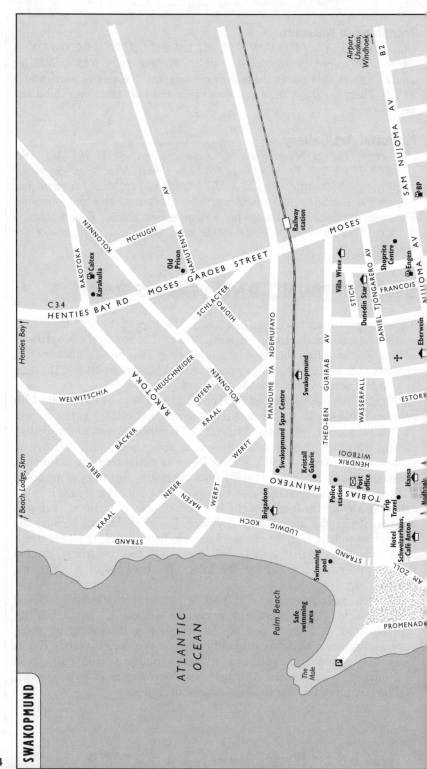

ATLANTIC OCEAN

Palm Beach

Safe swimming area

The Mole

PROMENADE

AM ZOLL

Swimming pool

Brigadoon

Beach Lodge, 5km

Henties Bay

C34

HENTIES BAY RD   MOSES GAROEB STREET

RAKOTOKA

KOLONNEN

MCHUGH

Karakulia

Caltex

Old Prison

HAMUTENYA

Railway station

MOSES

Airport, Usakos, Windhoek

B2

SAM NUJOMA AV

BP

Villa Wiese

STICH

Dunedin Star

DANIEL TJONGARERO AV

FRANCOIS

Shoprite Centre

Engen

NUJOMA AV

Eberwein

ESTORFF

WELWITSCHIA

RAKOTOKA

HEUSCHNEIDER

SCHLACTER

HIDIPO

OFFEN

KOLONNEN

KRAAL

MANDUME YA NDEMUFAYO

Swakopmund Spar Centre

Swakopmund

GURIRAB AV

BÄCKER

WERFT

BERG

KRAAL

NESER

HAFEN

WERFT

HAINYEKO

Kristall Galerie

THEO-BEN

WASSERFALL

HENDRIK WITBOOI

Police station

Post office

TOBIAS

Trip Travel

Hansa

STRAND

LUDWIG KOCH

STRAND

Hotel Schweizerhaus, Café Anton

234

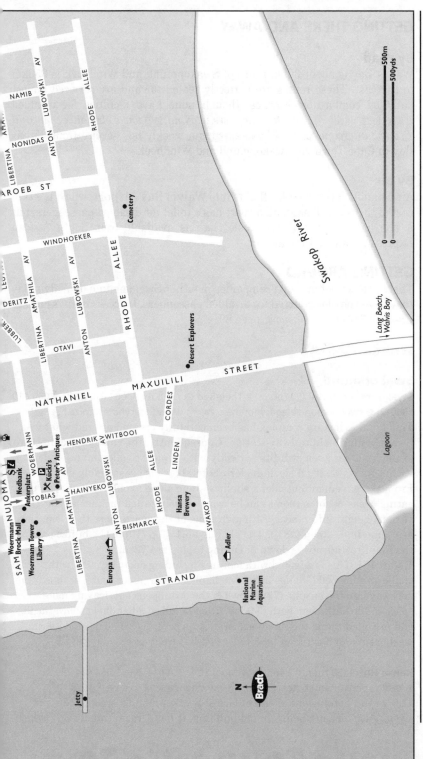

GETTING THERE AND AWAY

By road
Walvis Bay is about 30km south of Swakopmund and Windhoek is 356km to the east. These routes are perfectly sealed tar and are serviced almost daily by comfortable coaches, though none have facilities for disabled travellers (*see* ᐧᐤ *www.townhoppers.iway.na,* ᐧᐤ *www.ekonolux.com and* ᐧᐤ *www.intercape.co.za*). Ekonolux runs a weekly bus service from Walvis Bay to Cape Town via Swakopmund and Windhoek.

By air
Air Namibia has scheduled flights into **Walvis Bay Airport**, which is 11km east of the town. This small airport has a toilet for disabled passengers, but it has no support rails. An aisle chair is available from South African Express Airways at the airport.

GETTING AROUND
There are not yet any taxi companies in either Swakopmund or Walvis Bay that have vehicles adapted for disabled passengers. If access is an issue, see *Chapter 3, Public transport,* page 89.

WHERE TO STAY

Swakopmund
Swakopmund Hotel (90 rooms) 2 Theo-Ben Gurirab Av; ☎ 064 410 5200; **f** 064 410 5360–2; **e** swakopmund@legacyhotels.co.za; ᐧᐤ www.legacyhotels.co.za ⬛ ⬛
This hotel & leisure complex has been carefully created around what was Swakopmund's old railway station. Consequently, the colonial architecture of the building itself still fits perfectly with typical Swakopmund style, yet, within its walls, it's a sleek modern hotel. It is also reasonably accessible. From the pavement outside, a shallow stone slope avoids 4 steps. The pool, eating areas & some rooms can be reached using tiled inclines at the various height differences. Although none of these are more than 1m, they are sometimes steep (>8%). The shop is up 1 step (10) & the buffet part of the main restaurant is down 3. Dining tables are 72cm.
Room 101: This is adapted with features including doorway (105) with shallow ramp; bed (58) has light switch, phone & transfer space; desk is 58cm; doorway into the ensuite (72) is level & the door opens out, leaving more space in the bathroom; bath (54) has fitted handles, a handheld showerhead, end-mounted round taps & an elaborate support rail (18) all around its rim; washbasin (50) has round taps; toilet (44) has front access only. **$$$$**

Hansa Hotel (58 rooms) Hendrik Witbooi St; ☎ 064 414 200; **f** 064 414 299; **e** reservations@hansahotel.com.na; ᐧᐤ www.hansahotel.com.na ⬛ ⬛ ⬛
This grand hotel is one of the pillars of Swakopmund's accommodation scene. Also, despite being an old building, it has 1 room (number 6), which

has been adapted for wheelchair access. The 2 steps at the front door can be avoided by rolling in through the level vehicle entrance then up a stone slope from the courtyard. From reception, the public toilet is down a flight of stairs, but the main dining room has level access. The flooring is cement, tiles & smooth stone outside, & rooms are lightly carpeted.
Room 6: Doorway (150) is up 2 steps (13 & 15), for which a removable ramp is available; entrance to ensuite (75) is level; bath has 1 diagonal support rail (midpoint 15); roll-in shower has fold-down seat, lever tap, handheld showerhead & 1 diagonal support rail; toilet has front & side transfer space. **$$$$**

Beach Lodge (15 rooms) 1 Stint St (5km north of Swakopmund); **℡** 064 414 500; **f** 064 414 501; **e** reservations@beachlodge.com.na; ᐦ www.beachlodge.com.na ①
The maritime theme has almost gone overboard here – stand back & you'll see the whole beach complex take on the shape of a boat, complete with round, porthole windows! There are no rooms specifically designed for disability; however, the floors are smoothly tiled & there is a spacious lift (up 1 step) going to the second-floor restaurant, which has superb cuisine & breathtaking ocean views. The ground-floor rooms all have 2 steps (11 & 9) at their outside doors, though these are long enough to be taken one at a time in a wheelchair.
Ground-floor rooms: Inside doorway (80) is level; bed (52) has phone, light switch & transfer space; highest switch is 117cm; desk is 66cm; patio doorway (>100) has threshold (3); door to ensuite (71) is level; step-in shower (24) has tiled shelf seat; neither toilet (42) nor washbasin would be easy to use from a wheelchair. **$$$**

Hotel Schweizerhaus (24 rooms) 1 Bismarck St; **℡** 064 400 331/2/3; **f** 064 405 850; **e** schweizerhaus@mweb.com.na; ᐦ www.schweizerhaus.net ⓪ ®
The Schweizerhaus is worth considering if you're looking for access. It has level or gently ramped access routes throughout the main public areas & Room 20 (the most accessible) can be reached via the ramp at the back door. Other ground-floor rooms have step-in showers.
Room 20: Doorway (76) is level; bed (48) has transfer space, light switch & phone; door to ensuite (76) is level; bath (54) has transfer space & side-mounted round taps; roll-in shower has a removable seat, fixed showerhead & round taps (110); washbasin (77) has low mirror & round taps; toilet (43) can be approached diagonally only. **$$$**

Villa Wiese (10 rooms) Corner Theo-Ben Gurirab Av & Windhoeker St; **℡** 064 407 105; **f** 064 407 106; **e** enquiry@villawiese.com; ᐦ www.villawiese.com ⓪
This brightly painted backpackers' accommodation has made no deliberate effort to be accessible, but it does have ground-floor rooms. Apart from a shallow storm drain, the bricked courtyard, public areas & access to accommodation should pose no problems for most strong wheelers. It is self-catering, providing b/fast only.

Room 2: As accessible as any – doorway (76) has a threshold (2); bed (54) has light switch & transfer space; highest switch is 135cm; step-in shower is 22cm; washbasin (75) has low mirror; toilet has front transfer space (but then it's not possible to close the door). **$**

Dunedin Star (24 rooms) Corner Theo-Ben Gurirab Av & Windhoeker St; ☎ 064 407 105; **f** 064 407 106; **e** enquiry@villawiese.com; ⏁ www.villawiese.com 🄌
Under the same ownership as the neighbouring Villa Wiese, the Dunedin Star is similarly appointed though slightly less cheery. Bathrooms may suit chair users better. The street entrance is narrow (76), the dining area is up 2 steps (17 & 19) – though a ramp is available – & tables are 65cm. There is a standard public toilet with level entry.
Room 5: The most accessible – doorway (76) is level; bed (55) has light switch & transfer space; highest switch is 133cm; doorway into ensuite (76) is level; step-in shower is 9cm; washbasin (68) has high mirror; toilet has front & side transfer space. **$**

Walvis Bay

Protea Hotel Pelican Bay (50 rooms) The Esplanade; ☎ 064 214 000; **f** 064 200 418; **e** res-pelicanbay@proteahotels.com.na; ⏁ www.proteahotels.com 🄌 🖼 🖳
The Pelican Bay Hotel looks out onto the Walvis Bay Lagoon, an important wetland, & offers spruce accommodation in sea-facing rooms. The staff were particularly upbeat & especially positive towards disability when we visited. From the car park, the entrance, rooms & 2 dining areas are either level or ramped. Ground surfaces are smooth cobbles outside & tiles & short-pile carpets indoors. Dining tables are 70cm & there is a public toilet fitted with support rails near the restaurant.
Room 101: Has been adapted – doorway (76) is level; bed (54) has transfer space, light switch & phone; desk is 71cm; highest switch is 112cm; doorway into ensuite (84) is level; roll-in shower has fold-down seat, star taps (90), handheld showerhead & 2 support rails (1 vertical, 1 shaped); washbasin (61) has lever taps & there are 2 more support rails (83 & 93), 1 beside & 1 in front of the toilet (43). **$$$**

Protea Hotel Walvis Bay (58 rooms) Sam Nujoma Av & 10th Rd; ☎ 064 213 700; **f** 064 213 701; **e** res-walvisbay@proteahotels.com.na; ⏁ www.proteahotels.com
🄌 🖭 🖼 🖳
The first thing you see when you pull up outside the smart, yellow building is the blue 'disabled' parking spot. This gives promise of more to come & it's wholly fulfilled. The atmosphere was less cheerful than at its Pelican Bay cousin, & it has – arguably – a less-inspiring location, but with 5 'accessible' rooms it may be the best choice. There are step-free routes to the rooms & the dining room from reception, wheelchair routes are indicated & floors are carpets, tiles & smooth crazy paving. Dining tables are 72cm & the public toilet has a level doorway (76). The most accessible rooms are of 2 types: 1 'old' & 4 'new'.

Room 102: In the older part of the hotel with a bath. Doorway (77) is level; 2 sgl beds (52) have transfer space, light switch & phone; desk is 69cm; level door to ensuite (76) opens to the bedroom; bath (51) has handheld showerhead, round taps & 2 support rails (17); washbasin (68) has lever taps; toilet (44) has side transfer space & 2 support rails (62), 1 behind & 1 next to it.

Room 318: In the new part of the hotel with a shower; Rooms 317, 319 & 320 are similarly appointed: doorway (87) is level; bed (60) has transfer space, phone & light switch; highest control is 90cm; doorway to ensuite is 87cm; roll-in shower has flip-down seat (44) with front & side transfer space, handheld showerhead, 1 long support rail behind & beside seat (86) & lever tap (109); washbasin is 71cm; toilet (40) has support rails (85) on each side, 1 of which swings up. **$$**

Langholm Hotel (12 rooms) 24 Second St West; ☎ 064 209 230; f 064 209 430; e desk@langholmhotel.com; www.langholmhotel.com 🔳
This crisply painted hotel has a reputation for good food & has won several hospitality awards in recent years. Although it is without custom-designed disability rooms, it may still work for some people. In an unusual solution, the brick pavement rises to meet the main doorway, albeit too steeply for most independent pushers. The dining room has level access & tables are 64cm. From there, the rooms are 1 step (9) down, & some have baths with handheld showerheads while others have step-in showers only.
Rooms 12 & 24: Have level entry. **$$**

Other notable accommodation
The following Swakopmund hotels have not been checked for access but report the following basic information:

Hotel Eberwein Sam Nujoma Av, ☎ 064 414450; f 064 414451; e Enquiry@Hotel-Eberwein.com; www.hotel-eberwein.com.
Has no ground-floor rooms & no lift, so is immediately off-putting unless a flight of stairs is no problem.

Brigadoon 17 Ludwig Koch St; ☎ 064 406064; f 064 464195; e brigadoon@iway.na; www.brigadoonswakopmund.com.
All accommodation is ground floor (up 1 or 2 steps) with baths or showers.

Europa Hof Hotel Bismark Str 39; ☎ 064 405061/2; f 064 402391; www.europahof.com.
Has 8 ground-floor rooms & the restaurant has no steps.

Hotel Adler 3 Strand Street; ☎ 064 405045; f 064 404206; e adler@iafrica.com.na.
Has various ground-floor rooms with baths & 1 step.

WHERE TO EAT
Swakopmund has many eateries and with Namibia's reputation for good-

quality meat plus its coastal location (meaning fresh fish), menus cater well to all tastes. No restaurants have custom-built disability access but most are ground floor.

Kücki's 22 Tobias Hainyeko St; ☎ 064 402 407; ☺ 12.00–15.00 & 18.00–22.30. With high standards, a good atmosphere & excellent food (shellfish & game are often on the menu), Kücki's is a local favourite. Consequently advance booking is advised, especially for wheelchair users who may need more space. **$$$$**

Café Anton (part of the Schweizerhaus Hotel) ☎ 064 402 419; ☺ morning until mid-evening.
This refined coffee shop serves b/fasts, lunches & light evening meals. It has step-free access & the toilet is standard with level doorway at 69cm. **$$$**

OTHER PRACTICALITIES
Most visitors will stay in Swakopmund, but both town centres have plenty of banks with ATMs, shopping centres and internet points.

Medical services
The most recommended first stop is the **Bismarck Medical Centre** (*17–20 Sam Nujoma Drive;* ☎ *064 405 000/1;* f *064 404 650*).

WHAT TO SEE AND DO
Since growing up on a tourism clientele that mainly wanted to relax in the bracing coastal air, this area (and Swakopmund in particular) has evolved to offer much more. Walvis Bay is traditionally the more sedate of the two towns, and the lagoon – with boat trips and superb birding – is the centre of most activities. Swakopmund has an excellent array of old buildings, epitomising the perfection of German colonial architecture, and many of these are now museums and galleries, preserving local history – human and natural – and displaying contemporary art and culture.

Outwith the towns, scenic flights can be organised and the desert has become host to thrilling adventures, like sand boarding and quad biking. Beach- and deep-sea fishing have been popular here for decades, and some of the most recent temptations include kitesurfing and windsurfing.

There are no operators based in the area who make specific efforts to cater to all, but as with any people who live in an unforgiving landscape, Namibians are famous for their drive and ingenuity. If there is a way to make it possible then it will be found here.

SESRIEM AND SOSSUSVLEI

In the southerly region of the ancient and enchanting Namib-Naukluft National Park lies Sossusvlei. This is where the (normally dry) Tsauchab River

above **Early morning cheetah run at the Cheetah Conservation Fund, Namibia** (J&SH) page 243

below **Kayaking at Pelican Point, Walvis Bay** (J&SH) pages 233–40

above left   **Elephant**
   (*Loxodonta african*) (IV)

above right   **African buffalo (*Syncerus***
   ***caffer*)** (IV)

main   **Burchell's zebra**
   (*Equus burchelli*) (IV)

left   **Cheetahs**
   (*Acinonyx jubatus*) (IV)

above	**Lion** (*Panthera leo*) (IV)
right	**Hippo** (*Hippopotamus amphibius*) (IV)
below left	**White rhino** (*Ceratotherium simum*) (IV)
below right	**Leopard** (*Panthera pardus*) (IV)

top left   **Yellow baboon** (*Papio cynocephalus cynocephalus*) (IV)

above   **Red colobus monkey** (*Piliocolobus kirkii*) (IV)

left   **Black-faced impala** (*Aepyceros melampus petersi*) (IV)

below   **Thomson's gazelle** (*Gazella thomsonii*) (IV)

above left **Springbok**
(*Antidorcas marsupialis*) (IV)

above right **White blesbok (*Damaliscus dorcas phillipsi*)** (IV)

right **Black-backed jackal**
(*Canis mesomelas*) (IV)

below **Wild dog (*Lycaon pictus*)** (IV)

Opposite

left, top to bottom:
African fish eagle
(*Haliaeetus vocifer*) (IV)

Red-billed hornbill
(*Tockus erythrorhynchus*) (IV)

Eurasian hoopoe
(*Upupa epops*) (IV)

Allen's gallinule
(*Porphyrio alleni*) (IV)

right, top to bottom
Eastern paradise-whydah
(*Vidua paradisaea*) (IV)

Little bee-eater
(*Merops pusillus*) (IV)

Lilac-breasted roller
(*Coracias caudata*) (IV)

This page
top left
Pale chanting goshawk
(*Melierax canorus*) (IV)

top right
Lesser flamingo
(*Phoenicopterus minor*) (IV)

middle right
Ostrich (*Struthio camelus*) (IV)

right
Secretary bird
(*Sagittarius serpentarius*) (IV)

far right
Pied kingfisher
(*Ceryle rudis*) (IV)

above	**Nile crocodile** (*Crocodylus niloticus*) (IV)
top left	**Red-headed rock agama** (*Agama agama*) (IV)
above left	**Yellow headed dwarf gecko** (*Lygodactylus luteopicturatus*) (IV)
left	**Flap-necked chameleon** (*Chamaeleo dilepis*) (IV)
below	**Nile monitor lizard** (*Varanus niloticus*) (IV)

finally gives up its westward quest to reach the ocean, and creates a slightly fertile pan enclosed by towering ochre sand dunes. These are no ordinary dunes; wind patterns continually shift their layout, forming an ocean-like series of gullies and crests, some of which peak at over 300m high. It's a photographer's paradise, especially in the early morning when the contrast between the lit and shaded sides of the snaking dune ridges is at its most stark.

GETTING THERE AND AWAY
It is only 320km from Windhoek, but depending on the route taken it will take at least four hours and most of the journey will be on good-quality graded gravel. Private flights can also be arranged but there are no facilities designed to aid access. (For access issues in small airfields, see page 92.)

WHERE TO STAY
Sossusvlei Lodge (45 rooms) ☎ +27 (0)21 930 4564; f +27 (0)21 930 4574; e reservations@sossusvleilodge.com; ⌂ www.sossusvleilodge.com 🔲 🔲 🔲
Placed neatly at the entrance gate to the park, Sossusvlei Lodge has 3 adapted rooms, 1 of which is Room 103. Access routes throughout are brick, slate or packed sand. Swimming pool & dining room have level entry & there is an accessible public toilet with 2 support rails (side & rear) & front & side transfer space.
Room 103: The main doorway has a small threshold; beds have transfer space; en-suite bathroom has roll-in shower with tiled seat in washing area & fixed showerhead; toilet has front & side transfer space. **$$$$**

Sossusvlei Desert Camp (20 tents) ☎ +27 (0)21 930 4564; f +27 (0)21 930 4574; e reservations@desertcamp.com ⌂ www.desertcamp.com 🔲 🔲 🔲
With an enchanting desert setting just 5km from Sesriem, Sossusvlei Desert Camp is the cheaper 'accessible' option in the area. It has 2 adapted rooms, 1 of which is Room 11. Pathways are a mix of sand & cement.
Room 11: Has shallow ramped entry from the sand access route; 2 sgl beds have transfer space; en-suite bathroom has level entry, roll-in shower with handheld showerhead & star taps (high); toilet has 2 support rails (side & rear) & has front & side transfer space. **$$**

OTHER PRACTICALITIES
Windhoek is the closest centre with facilities like post offices, fuel, banking and supermarkets.

Medical services
Camps and lodges have basic first aid facilities but people with serious medical issues will be taken to Windhoek.

WHAT TO SEE AND DO
The highlight of the area is a visit to Sossusvlei (N$80 per adult). From Sesriem it is possible to drive the 60km to within about 5km of Sossusvlei,

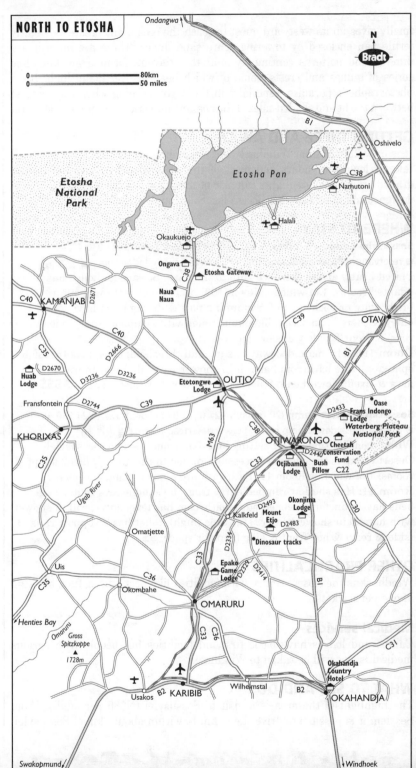

Ondangwa

N

Bradt

0 ——————— 80km
0 ——————— 50 miles

B1

Oshivelo

Etosha Pan

C38

Etosha
National
Park

Namutoni

Halali

Okaukuejo

Ongava ☐ ▲ Etosha Gateway

C38

Naua
Naua

C40 KAMANJAB

D2667

OTAVI

C40

C35

C39

B1

D2666

D3236

D2670

Huab
Lodge

D3236

Etotongwe
Lodge OUTJO

Fransfontein

D2744

C39

D2433 Oase
Frans Indongo
Lodge
Waterberg Plateau
National Park

KHORIXAS

C35

M63

C38

OTJIWARONGO

Cheetah
Conservation
Fund

Ugab River

C33

Otjibamba
Lodge

Bush
Pillow

C22

D2440

C30

D2493 Okonjima
Lodge

Omatjette

Kalkfeld

Mount
Etjo

D2483

C33

D2334

Dinosaur tracks

Uis

C36

Epako
Game
Lodge

D2229

D2414

B1

C35

Okombahe

Henties Bay

Omaruru
Gross
Spitzkoppe
1728m

OMARURU

C36

C33

C31

Okahandja
Country
Hotel

Usakos

B2 KARIBIB

Wilhelmstal

B2

OKAHANDJA

Swakopmund

Windhoek

down a track through an ever-narrowing cleft between the dunes. The last 5km must be walked or a pre-arranged 4x4 shuttle can be used (N$80 per adult). Between Sesriem and Sossusvlei there are various points of interest and beauty, where more energetic and able visitors can partially or fully climb a sand dune.

NORTH TO ETOSHA

This is a huge expanse of territory, which is often driven straight though on the way to Etosha and therefore completely ignored. It has been well fenced and the hilly landscape used for agriculture since the days of the pioneering settlers, but many of these farming families now run guesthouses or have even given up cattle in favour of developing game ranches. The standard of accommodation on these properties can be very high, but always seems to retain that crucial taste of rural hospitality, which is something Namibians excel at. Instead of driving through it, take a few days – if you can afford it, much longer – to absorb this area. These lodges offer some quality game-viewing opportunities and several of them are exceedingly accessible.

GETTING THERE AND AWAY

The main roads through this area are tar sealed. The final kilometres to the properties themselves may be gravel, but all properties covered in this section are reached using well-graded and virtually all-weather roads. Arrival by small aircraft is also possible, but local airstrips are small. (For access issues in small airfields, see page 92.)

WHERE TO STAY

Cheetah Conservation Fund (1 room) ℂ 067 306 225; f 067 306 247; e info@cheetah.org; www.cheetah.org
Dr Laurie Marker started this organisation in 1990 to protect the cheetah & its natural habitats through research & education. It has blossomed, now raising funds in several countries worldwide & has a fascinating (and extremely accessible) visitors' centre 44km from Otjiwarongo. The ample grounds are smoothly paved with interlocking bricks. Reception, the impressive education centre & the standard public toilets have no steps. The café & curio shop are up a steep ramp with tables at 73cm & if they're deemed suitable then visitors' own vehicles may be used for game drives. There is now luxurious accommodation (with kitchenette) at the 2-roomed Babson House, which is 5mins' walk on a smooth, wide path.
Babson House: Doorway (>100) is ramped (8%) then up 1 step (8); bed has light switch & transfer space; desk is 70cm; highest switch is 140cm; doorway to ensuite is 74cm; step-in shower is 14cm; washbasin has no knee clearance; toilet (44) has front, but no side transfer space. **$$$$$**

Huab Lodge (8 bungalows) Bookings through Reservation Destination ☎ 061 224 217; **f** 061 224 712; reservations@resdes.com.na; 🖱 www.huab.com 🔲 🖾 🖳

About 1½hrs' drive from both Khorixas & Kamanjab, Huab Lodge is in 8,000ha of wilderness that has been reclaimed from surrounding farmland. It is the fulfilment of a dream for Jan & Suzi van de Reep, whose aspiration was to give a natural environment to the persecuted desert elephant. If you want to absorb yourself in the beauty of Namibia, this is the ideal location, & whether your hosts are the owners or the managers (they take turns) you can be sure to be entertained as much – or as little – as you want. Its beautiful setting in low hills doesn't lend itself automatically to disability access, but the lodge has made admirable efforts to cater to more than just fully able guests. From the soft-sand parking area, there's ramped access up to the main *lapa* (a large, thatched area, usually serving as the focal point, entrance or reception area in southern African tourist lodges), which has a level, polished slate floor. Here, the bar/dining area has no steps & the tables are 64cm, & the lounge is an easy place to lose a few hours reading or watching the busy birdlife in the surrounding rock pools. The delightfully simple swimming pool has smooth access down a (steep) stone pathway, which narrows to 73cm in parts. From there, it's about 150m to the thermal spring along a sandy track.

Bungalow 1: The closest to reception (about 30m up a hard sand track. Doorway (86) is level; beds (60) have transfer space & light switch; highest control is 111cm; door to ensuite (86) is level; step-in shower (10) has a fold-down seat (52), star taps, support rail (113) & handheld showerhead; washbasins (70) have star taps; toilet is in its own small room with doorway (86) & small support rails (81 & 99) on either side. **$$$$$**

Mount Etjo Safari Lodge (22 rooms) ☎ 067 290 173/4; **f** 067 290 172; **e** mount.etjo@iafrica.com.na; 🖱 www.mount-etjo.com 🔲 🖾

Situated 63km south of Otjiwarongo, this is one of my personal favourites in Namibia; not only is it relaxed & friendly with good game viewing, but the lodge is level & spacious & the owner genuinely strives to cater to everyone. The game-drive vehicle is a large truck, but if this presents problems then guests can use their own 4x4. Reception is ramped, & from there the smooth, tiled track goes past the breakfast area – tables are 61cm – towards the rooms & the unpretentious swimming pool. The pool is set in a lawn & is up 1 step. The huge – & busy – waterhole is a short stroll across the lawn. The dining *lapa* is also reached without steps & although the bench seats are fixed to the floor, meaning wheelchairs must take the end space, tables are 74cm. The standard public toilet has level access. Most rooms have 1-step entries & step-in showers but several are level with roll-in showers.

Room 8: Doorway (77) has threshold (4); beds (53) have light switch & transfer space; desk is 63cm; highest switch is 121cm; entry to ensuite is >100cm; roll-in shower has handheld showerhead, star taps (100) & removable seat; washbasins have no knee space; toilet (40) is in a separate room with doorway of 76cm & has front transfer space only. **$$$$**

Okonjima Lodge (4 camps) ☎ 067 687 032–4; **f** 067 687 051;
e info@okonjima.com; ⟨🖰⟩ www.okonjima.com 2️⃣ 🖼️AR 🖱️

At 47km south of Otjiwarongo, Okonjima is one of Namibia's most recognised & respected names, & deservedly so. As well as being a hospitable lodge in its own right, the Africat Foundation, which aims to conserve Namibia's large predators, is based here. Consequently, most activities revolve around the big cats – leopard tracking is a highlight – & game drives are done in the lodge's 4x4 vehicles. The lion *lapa* is in the main compound & is up a steep ramp, while the small, floodlit hide is a few hundred metres' walk on a dirt track. Short bush walks & relaxed conversations with the staff may sound tame, but can be hugely informative.

There are 4 main accommodation types & although, at the time of writing, nothing was adapted, 1 'fully accessible chalet' was being built at **Main Camp** & 1 at **Bush Camp**. These will have level or lightly sloped entry, roll-in showers & support rails for showers & toilets. These were being started in 2008 – I saw the beginnings of one – & should be completed by 2009. The restaurant area is up 2 steps & is a short walk from the new chalets, but a golf car is available to ferry anybody for whom this may be difficult. Of the other options, the highly exclusive **Okonjima Villa** has step-in showers & baths & **Omboroko Campsite** has step-in showers & is located in soft sand. **$$$**

Epako Game Lodge (23 rooms) ☎ 064 570 551; **f** 064 570 553;
e epako@iafrica.com.na; ⟨🖰⟩ www.epako.com 0️⃣ 🖼️

At 22km north of Omaruru, with French/Dutch ownership, Epako is a luxurious & very well-run lodge. The cuisine has a good reputation & game drives are possible on 11,000ha of bush, with elephant, white rhino & cheetah amongst other attractions. The dining room – with tables at 71cm – is level from reception, there is ramped access to the game-viewing area, & the path to the swimming pool has 2 steps. Access routes are smooth brick & cement. The only 2 rooms that are step-free from reception are described below, & other rooms have several steps or a steep ramp.
Rooms 19 & 20: Doorway (77) has a small ramp; bed (51) has transfer space, light switch & phone; desk is 58cm; highest switch is 138cm; en-suite doorway (76) is level; bath is 53cm; roll-in shower (78) has fixed showerhead & round taps; toilet (43) has front & side transfer space. **$$$**

Frans Indongo Lodge (6 rooms & 8 chalets) ☎ 067 687 012; **f** 067 687 014;
e info@indongolodge.com; ⟨🖰⟩ www.indongolodge.com 0️⃣ 🖼️AR 🖱️

With friendly German management, this tidy, efficiently run lodge is an ideal base 43km from Otjiwarongo. Although it is designed to mirror a protective Ovambo corral, with stake-fenced enclosure, it is surprisingly accessible & most travellers with mobility issues will be delighted with the facilities here. Access routes are generally seamless brick & board walkways, with the only stepped areas being the swimming pool (down 3) &

the observation tower (up 4 flights of 7). Relaxed game viewing is possible from the lounge area, which is step-free. The cuisine is good, if not exciting, & game drives are possible. 1 room has been designed for disabled visitors.
Room 7: There's a bizarre drainage ditch (2cm deep, 20cm wide) outside the level doorway (>100); bed has transfer space, phone & light switch; desk is 63cm; highest control is 141cm; door to ensuite (76) is level; roll-in shower (74) has 2 support rails (1 vertical & 1 shaped), handheld showerhead & lever taps (100); washbasin (69) has lever taps & low mirror; toilet (40) has 2 support rails (80).
Other rooms have narrower doorways (75), baths with fitted handles & handheld showerheads & step-in showers (20). **$$**

Okahandja Country Hotel (22 rooms & 2 family units) ☎ 062 504 299; **f** 062 502 551; **e** okalodge@africaonline.com.na; ⏚ www.okahandjalodge.com 🖲 🖼 🖳
With clean, thatched buildings & well-manicured lawns set in established woodland 2km from Okahandja, there's a solid, organised feel to this lodge. The site is virtually level & access routes are good crazy paving, with gentle slopes taking out the occasional difference in height. The swimming pool has 4 entry steps & dining tables are 73cm.
Room 24: Has been adapted – doorway (76) is level; bed (52) has transfer space, light switch & phone; desk is 70cm; doorway into ensuite is level; step-in shower (10) has a fold-down seat (52), 2 vertical support rails (midpoints 75), a handheld showerhead & round taps (110); washbasin (76) has round taps; toilet (43) has 2 support rails (1 on each side) & front transfer space only. **$$**

Otjibamba Lodge (20 rooms) ☎ 067 303 133; **f** 067 304 561; **e** info@otjibamba.com; ⏚ www.otjibamba.com 🖳
Just south of Otjiwarongo, Otjibamba is a useful roadhouse with a reputation as a pleasant place for a 'meal & sundowner' stopover. It also has a peaceful little game park with various herbivores including blesbok & nyala (the walking trail here has no seating but the dam & *lapa* are just a 10min stroll away). Reception is down 5 steps but can be reached taking a short – but bumpy – bypass, & rough brick & cobble pathways divide the reasonably level site. The dining area – where tables are 71cm – has level access then the pool & 20 rooms are down a step from here.
Accommodation: 10 rooms have baths & 10 have baths & showers; the bathrooms in the latter are noticeably less spacious. All rooms have 1 step at the front door but some (Rooms 1–4, with baths only) have near-level rear verandas & can be entered more easily this way. Doorways are generally 75cm, beds 56cm & baths 60cm. **$$**

Etotongwe Lodge (21 rooms) Luiperd St, Outjo; ☎ 067 313 333; **f** 067 313 644; **e** comms@etotongwelodge.com; ⏚ www.etotongwelodge.com 🖲
This clean & comfortable lodge (just outside Outjo on the C38 heading

north towards Etosha) is built on a slope. Consequently it is not level, but it is owned & managed by a gentleman who uses an electric wheelchair so most rooms have ramped entries & pathways are free of steps if not very smooth. Reception is also (steeply) ramped but from there, the dining area – where tables are 73cm – & pool have level access with the latter having roll-in entry.

Rooms 1 & 2: The most accessible – doorway (76) is up 2 cement ramps; bed (52) has light switch & transfer space; door to ensuite (75) is level; step-in shower is 8cm; washbasin (70) has round taps; toilet has side transfer space. **$$**

Bush Pillow (7 rooms) 47 Son Rd, Otjiwarongo; ✆ 067 303 885; **f** 067 301 264; **e** info@bushpillow.hypermart.net; ✆ www.bushpillow.hypermart.net [1]
With its own idiosyncrasies – typical of small, family-run guesthouses – Bush Pillow is a homely spot to rest your head in Otjiwarongo. Everything is ground floor but it's a bit of an obstacle course for wheelchairs. From the car park, there's a wooden railway sleeper then a pathway of hexagonal paving laid like stepping stones to save materials. The smart pool & the dining room – tables are 62cm – have small thresholds. Of the rooms, numbers 1 & 2 are easiest to use.

Room 1: Doorway (75) is level; bed (52) has light switch & transfer space; highest switch is 135cm; doorway to ensuite (72) is level; bath (42) has a step next to it, blocking wheelchair approach; washbasin has no knee clearance but toilet (44) has front & side transfer space.

Room 2: Same as Room 1, though ensuite has a sliding door (77); step-in shower has 2 steps (18 & 37); washbasin has no knee clearance & there's narrow access (58) to the toilet. **$**

OTHER PRACTICALITIES

All the main towns on this route, including Okahandja, Omaruru and Otjiwarongo, have good supermarkets, banking facilities, fuel and post offices.

Medical services

The excellent **Medi-clinic** in Otjiwarongo (*24hr emergency* ✆ *067 303 734;* **e** *hospmngrotjiw@mediclinic.co.za;* ✆ *www.otjiwarongomc.co.za*) is the best hospital in the northern region.

WHAT TO SEE AND DO

If you want to take your time and explore, there is plenty to see in this area. The main highlights are at the guestfarms and lodges themselves (described above) with **game viewing** at Mount Etjo, Africat at Okonjima and the **Cheetah Conservation Fund** near Okonjima. Otjiwarongo is also home to a **Crocodile Ranch**, while **Waterberg Plateau National Park** (a 250m-high sandstone plateau with game viewing and hiking trails) is about 100km to the east.

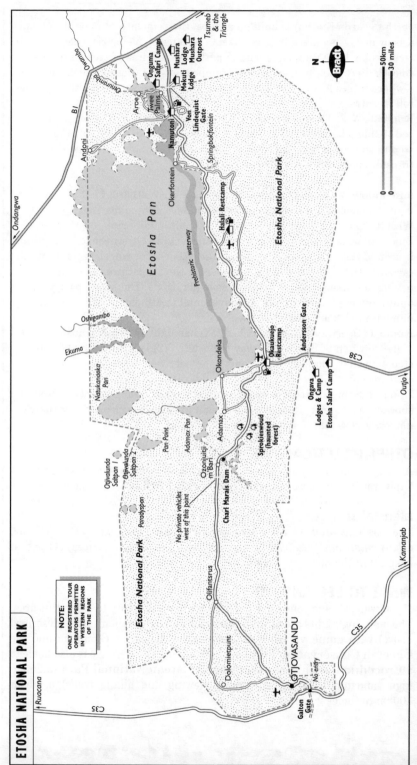

ETOSHA NATIONAL PARK

248

NOTE:
ONLY REGISTERED TOUR
OPERATORS PERMITTED
IN WESTERN REGIONS
OF THE PARK

Bradt

0   50km
0   30 miles

N

Tsumeb & the Triangle

Onguma Safari Camps
Mushara Lodge
Mushara Outpost
Mokuti Lodge

Tsumeb Palms
Aroe
Von Lindequist Gate
Namutoni
Okerfontein
Springbokfontein

Ondangwa
Andoni

Oshivelo
B1
Ondangwa

Etosha Pan

Prehistoric waterway

Halali Restcamp

Etosha National Park

Oshigambo
Ekuma

Okondeka

Natukanaoka Pan

Okaukuejo Restcamp
Anderson Gate
C38
Outjo

Ongwa Lodges & Camp
Etosha Safari Camp

Pan Point
Ojivalunda Saltpan 1
Otjivalunda Saltpan 2
Adamax Pan
Paradyspan

Adamax
Spokieswoud (haunted forest)
Ozonjuitji m'Bari
Chari Marais Dam

No private vehicles
west of this point

Etosha National Park

Olifantsrus

Kamanjab

Dolomiepunt

Ruacana
C35

OTJOVASANDU
Galton Gate
No entry
C35

ETOSHA NATIONAL PARK

Dominated by the shimmering white Etosha saltpan, this huge park is Namibia's most visited game-viewing area. Several rare and endangered species, including black rhino, black-faced impala and the Damara dik dik are present here, but seeing the usual suspects – lion, elephant et al – in this unusually stark habitat is worth it alone.

When Etosha was first declared a protected area in 1907 it was the largest game reserve in the world, but subsequent reductions in size to the current 22,000km² reserve were made in the mid 20th century. The saltpan occupies about one-quarter of this area, and although it is mostly dry, with irate-looking mini-twisters and hazy horizons, good rains in the feeder areas north and east of the park mean water sometimes gathers in the pan in the early months of the year. The park surrounding the pan is generally flat, with a mix of open plains, mopane (drought-resistant) woodland and tropical-looking makalani palms that host the majority of the wildlife. This area is pitted and watered by several permanent springs, which burst through the rock structures forming pools. The well-designed road network weaves around these waterholes, and as a result Etosha provides superb game viewing, especially in the late dry season when animals are drawn from cover to drink.

Not only are Etosha's roads perfectly navigable in a standard 2wd car, but there is extremely accessible accommodation in two of the three restcamps within the park and some reasonably inclusive lodges on its extremities.

Park fees Etosha is managed by Namibia Wildlife Resorts (⌂ www.nwr.com.na). Park fees are paid on entry at the park gates and are N$80 per adult per day (children <16 are free).

GETTING THERE AND AWAY

By road
Okaukuejo Restcamp lies just inside the park from Andersson Gate, and is 120km north of Outjo and 435km north of Windhoek. Fort Namutoni (the most easterly of the park's camps) is at Von Lindequist Gate and is 106km northwest of Tsumeb. Main roads leading to the park are smooth tar.

By air
There are private airstrips at Okaukuejo, Namutoni and Mokuti (outside the park) but no scheduled flights run to these.

WHERE TO STAY

South of Etosha
Ongava Lodges & Camps Book through Expert Africa (UK); ☎ +44 (0)20 8232 9777; f +44 (0)20 8758 4718; e info@expertafrica.com; ⌂ www.expertafrica.com

Ongava reserve flanks Etosha's southern border. As a result, these properties have plenty of game-viewing opportunities of their own, or can be used as your base from which to explore the national park. The main Ongava Lodge & Little Ongava are spread around a steep hillside with more than 40 steps to reach them, but the Tented Camp & Andersson's Camp provide less arduous options.

The Tented Camp (6 tents): Has sandy tracks – narrow (65) in places – that run >100m from the parking, past the tents to the main *boma*. Reception & the game-viewing veranda have level access. The dining table (70) is up 1 step whilst the swimming pool is down 1 & entered using 3 & no handrail. The spacious tents are built & furnished in the same way: entry is up several steps on smooth timber decks with dbl doors; beds (64) have transfer space & light switches plus emergency horn; huge en-suite bathroom areas have inside & outside roll-in showers with star taps (110); toilets (37) has front transfer space.

Andersson's Camp (20 rooms): Called the 'adventure' option, but is the easiest to get around. An extremely accessible public toilet (with 2 support rails) is next to the waterhole viewing & dining areas, which are all on 1 level with tables 61cm. The swimming pool is a 'dam' type, with 7 steps up to it & ladder entry. All rooms are similarly appointed, though room 1 is closest to reception along a hard pathway: doorway is 76cm; sgl beds (58) have light switch & transfer space, plus an emergency horn; ensuite has access is wide & leads to a sunken metal 'bush' bathtub (7) with wooden plank seat, round taps & fixed showerhead; toilet (44) is in a narrow space with door (74), so front transfer only would be possible. The veranda with bush views has level access. **$$$$$**

Etosha Safari Camp (27 tents) ☎ 061 230 066; **f** 061 251 863; **e** etosha@gondwana-collection.com; ⏚ www.gondwana-collection.com ⌂
Only 10km south of Andersson Gate, this is another camp with a good location from which to launch Etosha trips. Currently, it's functional, not chic, but it was recently taken over by Gondwana & developments are expected. Metal-framed tents on cement pads are dotted around the dazzling white, rocky terrain. These are best reached in your vehicle, as the pebble-stone paths are not wheelchair friendly. The pool is up 7 steps & has ladder entry.
Tents vary, but the most accessible have doorway (78) up 1 step (17); bed (58) has light switch & transfer space; desk is 74cm; highest switch is 144cm; bathroom door (84) is level; spacious shower is over a curved threshold (10) & has fixed showerhead & star taps (116); washbasin has no knee clearance; toilet (36) has front & side transfer space. **$$$$$**

Inside Etosha

Namutoni Restcamp (72 bungalows) Namibia Wildlife Resorts; ☎ 061 285 7200; **f** 061 224 900; **e** reservations@nwr.com.na; ⏚ www.nwr.com.na ⌂
Set just inside the park at the eastern end, Namutoni is the most

distinctive of the 3 restcamps. The imposing, whitewashed main building was once a German fort & the whole place feels more individual but less streamlined than Okaukuejo & Halali. It has no rooms designed for disability, but access is still reasonable. From the car park, reception has a shallow ramp. The public toilet here is up a step. Inside the fort, the various shops & restaurants are all up 1 step. There is a flight of stairs to the 'sunset viewpoint'. A long wooden boardwalk (with a steep ramp) leads to the natural-looking swimming pool & the most accessible newer rooms.
New rooms: Some have level access, wide doorways (>80), & baths, step-in or step-down showers. Some toilets have front & side transfer space, but there are no support rails. **$$$$**

Okaukuejo Restcamp (108 rooms) Namibia Wildlife Resorts; ☎ 061 285 7200; **f** 061 224 900; **e** reservations@nwr.com.na; ⌂ www.nwr.com.na 🅿 ♿ 🚽
Okaukuejo is the largest camp in the park. With 7 different room types, including 2 specifically designed for disabled visitors, it should have something for everyone. All main public areas – including restaurants, the swimming pool & standard public toilet – are on 1 level. The curio shop & general shop are up 2 steps. Access routes are smoothly interlocking bricks & seamless tarmac. The alluring floodlit waterhole draws a wide variety of animals & is difficult to leave once you're there. It has level access, plenty of seating & easy viewing, even from a seated position. Rooms D23 & D24 are adapted & identical; the former is closer to reception & the latter is near the waterhole.
Room D23: Ramped dbl-door entry has threshold (1); sgl beds (62) have light switch, transfer space & extra wide mosquito nets; dbl doors into the ensuite are level; roll-in shower has fold-down seat (46), shaped support rail (80), lever tap (118) & handheld showerhead; washbasin (60) has star taps; toilet (41) has a fixed support rail around both sides & behind it, effectively blocking side transfers. **$$$**

Halali Restcamp (70 rooms) Namibia Wildlife Resorts; ☎ 061 285 7200; **f** 061 224 900; **e** reservations@nwr.com.na; ⌂ www.nwr.com.na 🅿 ♿ 🚽
This camp is set approximately halfway between its siblings, & is the smallest & newest. It boasts 4 adapted rooms & as in Okaukuejo, public areas are extremely inclusive. After the kerb from the car park & a low threshold (4), reception, the shop, the swimming pool & the restaurant are on 1 level with no steps. Tables inside & outside are 65cm & 71cm respectively. The public toilets are level, but only that for ladies has a support rail. The 4 'disabled' rooms are identical: the Impala, Oryx, Kudu & Zebra. They are several mins' walk away on rough paths, so it might be prudent to stay in your vehicle if possible.
Room Oryx: Cement car pad then slight ramp up to doorway (87); bed (60) has transfer space & light switch; highest switch is 134cm; ensuite has wide entry; roll-in shower has fold-down seat (43), shaped support rail (midpoint 90), lever tap & handheld showerhead; washbasin has no knee

clearance & toilet (41) has a fixed support rail around both sides & behind it, effectively blocking side transfers. **$$$**

East of Etosha
Mokuti Lodge (106 rooms and suites) ☎ +264 67 229084; **f** +264 67 229091; **e** reservations.mokuti@kempinski.com; 🖱 www.kempinski-mokuti.com [0₊] [▨ᴬᴿ] [⬇]
After undergoing an extensive upgrade & refurbishment, this establishment is now part of the renowned Kempinski group. It is situated on 4,300ha of farmland just 2km from Etosha, & as such is another ideal base for exploring the park. It has a distinct 'hotel' air about it, with tennis courts as well as a spa, gym & swimming pools, but the main *lapa* & rooms are thatched, lodge-like structures & there is a reptile park, all of which help to retain some natural flavour. A shallow slope leads to reception & the public toilet has level access. All public areas, including the gym/spa & the restaurants can be reached without steps. Both swimming pools have steps to enter & 1 also has a handrail. There are 2 deluxe rooms equipped for disabled guests.
Rooms 215 & 216: Standard twin rooms – doorways (77) have threshold (2); beds have transfer space, light switch & phone; highest switch is 121cm; en-suite door (71) is level & opens to bedroom; roll-in shower has seat (50), lever tap, 1 support rail & fixed showerhead; washbasin (69) has lever tap; toilet has front transfer space & 1 support rail. **$$$$$**

Mushara Outpost (8 rooms) ☎ 061 240 020; **f** 061 304 290; **e** enquiry@mushara-lodge.com; 🖱 www.mushara-lodge.com [3⁺]
Mushara's newest sibling – 2km south of Mushara Lodge (see following entry) – has an equally upbeat feel to it. Designed to look like a traditional farmstead from the outside, with a high, corrugated tin roof, the majestic entrance, soaring ceilings & grand fixtures inside contrast completely. A flawless, well-lit brick path leads to the accommodation, but unfortunately, the 2 or 3 steps around the main building, restaurant & pool prevent there being level access throughout. Dining tables are 72cm. The glass, wood & canvas 'tents' are also unique. They are all similar inside & all have ramped boardwalk access. Numbers 7 & 8 have the shallowest ramps (<8%) while numbers 2 & 3 are closest to reception. The spacious bird hide is about 200m from reception; up 1 step & has ample seating & wheelchair space.
Room 6: Wide, sliding doorway has threshold (5); bed (71) has transfer space, phone & light switch; highest switch is 120cm; doorway into ensuite (100) is level; step-in shower (13); washbasin has no knee clearance; toilet has no transfer space. **$$$$**

Mushara Lodge (15 rooms, 2 villas) ☎ 061 240 020; **f** 061 304 290; **e** enquiry@mushara-lodge.com; 🖱 www.mushara-lodge.com [0₊]
As a safari lodge, Mushara is without a blemish. The food is first-rate,

there is tasteful accommodation to suit various budgets & at 8km from Etosha's Von Lindequist gate it has a useful location. What sets this lodge apart from its peers is its workforce. The policy of hiring locals & training on site works here; staff morale is extremely high & consequently, service is excellent. Regarding access, Mushara has no custom-designed 'disabled' rooms, but will suit some people. The reception/bar is 2 steps up from the car park, & then the restaurant, swimming pool (entered via 5 steps & handrail) & rooms can be reached step-free from here. The curio shop & public toilets are up a further 3 steps. Pathways are smooth brick throughout. Several rooms, including the family unit, have comparable bathrooms; of these, Room 1 is closest to the restaurant but up 1 step, while Room 11 has level access.

Room 11: Doorway (76) is level; beds have light switch & transfer space; doorway into ensuite (77) is level; bath (53) has transfer space, lever tap & handheld showerhead; step-in shower (16) has narrow entrance (50); washbasin (67) has lever tap; toilet (43) has no transfer space. A connecting door leads next door, so this room would suit family or an assistant. Sgl room number 12 has more space next to the toilet & the 2 lavishly furnished villas have wider doorways (>80) & a roll-in outside shower with handheld showerhead. **$$$**; villas **$$$$$**

Onguma Safari Camps ☎ 061 232 009; **f** 061 222 574; **e** onguma@visionsofafrica.com.na; www.onguma.com 2

Onguma Game Reserve is 20,000ha of protected land & wildlife in a similar habitat to that of eastern Etosha. There is good game viewing – including predators – within the reserve & it is an ideal point from which to visit the park. The ranch has various accommodation options – Bush Camp, Tented Camp, Tree Top Camp & The Fort – but deliberately channels less mobile visitors & families with young children to the Bush Camp. The reasons given are that it is the only one that is fenced, so is safer, & the others have many more steps & soft-sand pathways. If the other options really appeal more, then I'm sure the policy is flexible.

Bush Camp (6 rooms): This 'camp' resembles a tidy farmyard with low, stonewalled, thatched buildings set in well-kept lawns. The site is level, with smooth, brick pathways, but the dining area – with tables 74cm – & all the rooms are up 1 step. The bar is up 9 steps, the game lookout tower 12 but the swimming pool & campfire *boma* have level access. There are 6 twin rooms, a honeymoon room & 2 family rooms. The twin rooms are all up 2 steps & have step-in showers (19) in small bathrooms. The honeymoon room is up 3 steps but is much more spacious throughout with a standalone bathtub, a step-in shower (5) & a toilet with front transfer space only. 1 of the family rooms (number 8) has a step-in shower; the second (number 9) has a bath (55) with fitted handles & an extended seating area the end of the tub. Room 9 also has a washbasin (72) with star taps & a low mirror, but the toilet has front transfer space only. **$$$**

OTHER PRACTICALITIES

The three restcamps inside Etosha – Okaukuejo, Halali and Namutoni – have well-stocked shops and fuel (although this isn't guaranteed). Okaukuejo has an internet café but the towns surrounding the park would need to be visited for any banking and postal requirements.

Medical services

Lodges have basic medical rooms with a doctor or nurse. The excellent **Medi-clinic** in Otjiwarongo (*24hr emergency* ℓ *067 303 734; ⌂ www.otjiwarongomc.co.za*) is the best hospital in the northern region.

THE TRIANGLE, RUNDU AND THE CAPRIVI STRIP

The northeast of Namibia and the Caprivi Strip is most commonly used as a route to and from Zambia and Botswana. As such, it is a long, but comfortable journey.

East of Etosha, around Tsumeb, Otavi and Grootfontein (the 'triangle') is traditionally one of the most affluent areas in Namibia. As well as farming (the rainfall is enough here to create fertile growing conditions) there was a strong mining industry through the 20th century, particularly around Tsumeb. Copper, lead, silver, zinc and cadmium were in abundance, as well as various rare minerals and precious stones. The mines have now all but closed, but despite this, the area still has an upbeat feel to it. Its proximity to Etosha ensures a steady stream of visitors and there is some excellent – and accessible – accommodation as a result.

Travellers heading east will feel like they are back in 'real' Africa when they arrive in Rundu. The Okavango River (actually called the Kavango in Namibia) and relatively high rainfall give this area a lush, tropical feel, more like northern Botswana and southern Zambia than anywhere else in Namibia. The road crosses the river at Divundu before heading further east into the Caprivi Strip – a sliver of Namibian land squeezed between Angola and Botswana – towards Katima Mulilo. The Caprivi Strip also receives a high annual rainfall, and as a result is verdant and well populated, both by wildlife and by people. This area, initially because of its strategic importance as a through-route to the Zambezi River and eastern trade routes, and more recently, because of its proximity to Angola, has always had huge political importance in the region.

GETTING THERE AND AWAY

A ribbon of tar stretches almost 1,000km from Etosha to Katima Mulilo via the 'triangle', Rundu and the Caprivi Strip. Although the road quality is excellent, it is worth breaking this trip into several days. Intercape Mainliner (⌂ *www.intercape.co.za*) covers this route as part of their thrice-weekly Windhoek–Victoria Falls run, but their service does not include facilities for less mobile passengers (see *Chapter 3*, *Public transport*, page 89). There are provincial airports at Rundu and Katima Mulilo, but neither has adapted bathrooms or aisle chairs. (For access issues in small airfields, see page 92.)

WHERE TO STAY

The Triangle

!Uris Safari Lodge (14 rooms) 20km west of Tsumeb; ☎ 067 687 060/1; f 067 687 062; e manager@uris-safari-lodge-namibia.com; ⌂ www.urissafarilodge.com 🔲 🗺
One of the lodge's directors worked in the region's once-prosperous mining business, & !Uris succeeds admirably in its attempt to preserve some of the industry's history. The sleek steel pillars supporting the building were once water pipes, rescued after the mine closed in the early 1990s, & there's a fascinating collage of photographs near the bar depicting the industry at its peak. The imported Indian timber doors at the 'church' conference centre & other Asian artefacts only add to the lodge's charisma. From the car park, there is a step-free approach to the entrance. The main *lapa*, housing reception, bar & restaurant is on 4 levels, with polished cement floors subtly linked by gradients, some of which are >8%. The swimming pool is up 4 steps. Although there are no support rails in the public toilet next to reception, 1 is very spacious with level doorways (78). Dining tables are 62cm & the buffet is on the same level. The rooms are all similarly kitted out & are reached using cobbles, which are neither bone jarring nor smooth. Rooms 1–4 are closest to reception.
Room 1: Doorway (79) is level, but door has round handles; bed (59) has transfer space, light switch & phone; doorway into ensuite (79) is level; step-in shower (3) has glass doorway (52), fixed showerhead & tiled seat (43); washbasin has no knee clearance & toilet (43) has front transfer space only. **$$$**

Makalani Hotel (28 rooms) 34 4th Rd, Tsumeb; ☎ 067 221 051; f 067 221 575; e makalani@mweb.com.na; ⌂ www.makalanihotel.com 🔲 🗺 💺
If access is your main concern then look no further than this jolly little hotel in the middle of town. It has a reputation for reliability, the rooms are spick & span & 1 is adapted for disability. Apart from the swimming pool, which is down 3 steps, public areas are step-free using smooth access routes of bricks & floor tiles; any height differences are taken out by small ramps. The dining tables are 77cm & 1 spacious public toilet is ramped with a wide doorway (85) – it is denoted 'ladies' but is obviously designed for disabled access. Standard ground-floor rooms are up 1 step with step-in showers & upstairs rooms have baths.
NB: Bradt's *Namibia* guide states that the beds are 'hard' – this is potentially important if you are prone to pressure wounds.
Room 22: Has been adapted – doorway (75) is level; sgl beds (60) have transfer space, phone & light switch; highest switch is 102cm; desk is

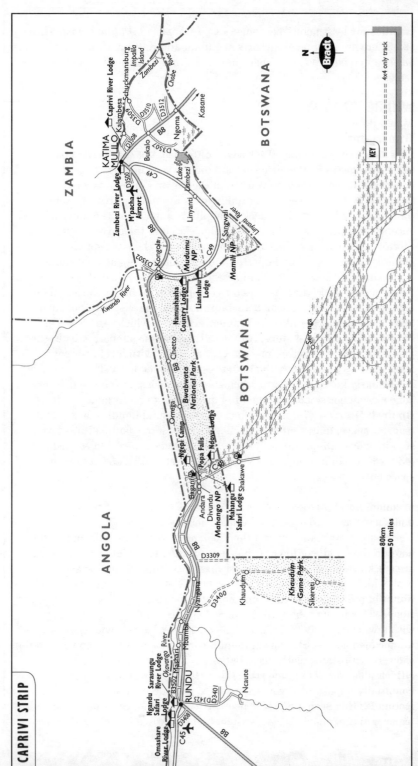

CAPRIVI STRIP

66cm; doorway into ensuite (86) is level; roll-in shower has fold-down seat (49), 2 support rails (86), handheld showerhead & lever taps (110); washbasin (68) has lever taps & a low mirror; toilet (43) has front & side transfer space & side & rear support rails (90). The only blemish is the shaver socket, which is >140cm. **$$**

Minen Hotel (49 rooms) Post St, Tsumeb; ↆ 067 221 071; f 067 221 750; e contact@minen-hotel.com; ⌂ www.minen-hotel.com ①
The Minen proudly displays 'disability access' on its website, but there is none. It is a comfortable hotel with pleasant gardens but it's not as warm & welcoming as the Makalani. From the parking area, reception is up 5 steps, then the swimming pool is down 1 & the rooms are down 1 then along about 150m on concrete paths. The restaurant inside is level with reception & all tables are 73cm.
Room 1: The most accessible – doorway (78) is up 1 step but the bathroom, which consists of bath, sink & toilet, is too cramped to use in a wheelchair. **$$**

Zum Potjie Restcamp (5 bungalows) Postfach 202, Otavi; ↆ 067 234 300; e info@zumpotjie.com; ⌂ www.zumpotjie.com ②
This functional little lodge, about 8km north of Otavi, has reasonable wheelchair access without incorporating any specific disability features. There are a couple of steps leading into reception & the restaurant area, pathways are sand, slate or cement & some rooms – apparently – are accessible without using steps. Bathrooms contain step-in showers, there are no baths, & toilets have – again, apparently – enough space for approach in a wheelchair. **$**

Rundu
Ngandu Safari Lodge (28 rooms) Usivi Rd, Rundu; ↆ 066 256 723; e ngandu@mweb.com.na ③⁺
Ngandu is on the way out of town to Sarasungu. The lodge isn't unclean, but some rooms have a distinct air of damp. For mobility-impaired travellers Rundu has better options as all accommodation here is up several steps, bathrooms are small with step-in showers, & the ramped access at the restaurant is giddily steep. **$$**

Omashare River Lodge (20 rooms) ↆ 066 256 101; f 066 256 111; e omashare@iway.na ①
The green tin roofs & green tiled floors of this pretty lodge sit well with the lush Kavango backdrop. It's in the centre of Rundu, but with a rear view over the river & down into Angola, it has the best of both worlds. From the street, a small ramped bridge then a steep tiled ramp next to 3 steps takes you to reception & the restaurant, where the tables are 71cm. The accommodation blocks & swimming pool are down small ramps from here, & several rooms have only a small threshold (<5) from the brick paths.

Rooms 1 & 2 are some of these & are the closest to reception. Doorways in general are level (76); beds (50) have light switch & transfer space; step-in showers (10) are small & toilets (41) have front transfer space only. **$$**

Sarasungu River Lodge (14 bungalows) **℄** 066 255 161;
e sarasungu@mweb.com.na; ⌁ www.sarasunguriverlodge.com 🄌 📖
This ever-popular lodge is one that is making an impressively proactive effort to cater to all. It suffers from the Kavango region's ubiquitous problem of soft sand, but its most inclusive rooms can be reached with a vehicle. The restaurant (with tables of 73cm) is up 3 steps or a ramp. The simple, but clean, swimming pool is at ground level & is entered using 3 corner steps. Of the traditional thatched chalets, the closest to reception are up 2 steps (number 8, further away, has none) but these all have standard ablutions. Closer to the river, where the sand gets softer, Rooms 9 & 10 are newer – but much less appealing – brick-built buildings with tin roofs. However, they are airy, spacious & clean inside & have roll-in showers. 2 similarly accessible self-catering units are being built next to these.
Rooms 9 & 10: Doorway (77) is level; beds (57) have transfer space & light switch; highest switch is 136cm; access to ensuite is narrow (65); roll-in shower has fixed showerhead & round taps (90); washbasin (66) has round taps; toilet (40) is only diagonally approachable in a wheelchair. **$$**

Divundu and Popa Falls

Ndovu Lodge (8 tents) 20km south of Divundu; **℄** 066 259 901; **f** 066 259 153;
e ndhovu@iway.na; ⌁ www.ndhovu.com 🄁
In direct competition with neighbouring Mahangu, Ndovu has the edge on accessibility & feels more liberal & welcoming. The lawns, pool & river deck are all on 1 level & are all unpretentious but well maintained. The dining *lapa* also has no step & tables are 70cm. Accommodation is in Meru tents (traditional canvas tents with a ridge pole) erected on brick & concrete platforms, hence up at least 1 step. Some – like tent 3 – have level access to ensuite.
Tent 3: Entrance (tent flap) is up 1 step; sgl beds have transfer space; en-suite entrance (80) is level; shower has a small lip (6) to enter it, fixed showerhead & star taps (117); washbasin (71) has star taps & toilet (38) has front transfer space only. **$$$**

Mahangu Safari Lodge (7 bungalows) 22km south of Divundu; **℄** 061 234 342;
f 066 259 115; **e** eden@mweb.com.na; ⌁ www.mahangu.com.na 🄂
The focus is on game fishing here, with more of a leaning towards this active type of holiday than making an aesthetically pleasing camp in which to lie around & relax. The facilities are correspondingly plain. Reception & all accommodation are up a couple of steps & the chalets are more spacious than the tents. The unappealing swimming pool is at ground level & the riverside dining deck has step-free access from the

lawn with tables of 68cm. The boardwalk to the jetty is also level.
Chalets: Doorway is 76cm; beds have transfer space & light switch; highest switch is 125cm; doorway into ensuite (76) is level; step-in shower is 21cm; washbasin is 71cm; toilet (42) has front transfer space only. **$$$**

Ngepi Camp (9 rooms) ☏ 066 259 903; **f** 066 259 906; **e** ngepi@getalifeplanet.com; ⌂ www.ngepicamp.com

What started out as a riverside campground for overland trucks has mushroomed into a rather cult, laid-back stopover used by a large variety of holidaymakers. It offers a wide range of accommodation, from camping sites to lovely private riverbank treehouses. One of these (number 15) has been made more accessible than the others & there are plans to make future units equally easy to use. Tracks around Ngepi are more footworn than constructed, but the area is level. The sundeck is up 2 steps & when we visited, a jetty was being built that has no steps. Most amenities are within 30m from reception & although the treehouses are further, guests normally use their vehicles.

Treehouse 15: A well-made ramp (approx 20%) leads up to the treehouse, which is a simple reed & thatch structure with 1 side completely open to the river; bed (66) has transfer space; roll-in shower has fixed showerhead & star taps (97); washbasin (a bush-style tin pot) has no knee clearance; toilet has front transfer space only. **$$**

Kwando River area

Lianshulu Lodge (11 rooms) ☏ 061 254 317; **f** 061 254 980; **e** info@lianshulu.com.na; ⌂ www.lianshulu.com.na

Lianshulu is set inside Mudumu National Park, & is harmoniously built within established woodland on the waters of the Kwando River. Privately owned, the lodge is also engaged with the local community, supporting education & involving local people in tourism projects. The largest room, number 3, has been adapted for disability. There are 2 steps (15) to enter the main lapa, then the reception/bar/dining areas are level & under the same high, thatched roof. Riverfront dining is down 2 steps – with tables of 74cm – & there is a viewing tower, which is up 15 steps. Public toilets are level with wide doorways (77); the ladies has wheelchair space but the gents is less roomy. The accommodation & simple swimming pool are the same 2 steps down from reception, then over a short pebble & grass pathway, & the boat jetty is down 10 long stairs.

Room 3: Doorway (106) is level; the 3 sgl beds (64, 64 & 69) have light switches & transfer space; there is an emergency gas hooter; desk is 64cm; entrance to ensuite is wide & level; the huge step-in shower (28) has 3 support rails, lever tap, handheld showerhead & a unique & imaginative shelf seat (45) which crosses the step allowing a safe sliding transfer from a wheelchair into the washing area; 2 washbasins (70 & 82) have star taps; toilet (39) has a floor-mounted support rail (67), which blocks side transfers but leaves plenty of space at the front. **$$$$$**

Namushasha Country Lodge (27 rooms) 24km south of Kongola; ☏ 061 374 750;
e namushasha@ncl.com.na; 🖰 www.namibialodges.com [0.]
Overlooking a much-frequented hippo pool on the Kwando River, Namushasha was rebuilt in 2005 & is a solid, handsome lodge of stone, dark woods & thatch. The cavernous main building, incorporating reception, bar & restaurant (with tables 66cm) is all on 1 level & has no steps from the car park. Seamless crazy paving & tile paths meander less than 50m to the most accessible rooms, numbers 16 & 17, while the swimming pool is down 5 steps & set in a pretty lawn.
Rooms 16 & 17: Doorway (76) is up 1 step (7); sgl beds (61) have transfer space & light switch; highest switch is 134cm; desk is 59cm; door to ensuite (76) is level; sunken shower is down 1 step (43) with a tiled seat (50) in the washing area; washbasin has no knee clearance & toilet (40) has front & side transfer space. **$$$**

Katima Mulilo
Zambezi River Lodge ☏ 066 253 149; **f** 066 253 631;
e gm-zambezi@proteahotels.com.na; 🖰 www.proteahotels.com [2.]
When I visited in 2008, this large Protea hotel was open, but undergoing major refurbishments. There will (apparently) be several adapted rooms once the changes are complete, & the 2 or 3 steps presently blocking free movement around the complex will be razed. Rooms 6 & 7 are currently the easiest to reach & are up 2 steps with step-in showers; Rooms 11–14 are up 1 step. **$$**

Caprivi River Lodge (8 chalets) ☏ 066 253 300; **f** 066 253 158;
e info@capririverlodge.net; 🖰 www.capririverlodge.info [2.]
At 5km east of Katima Mulilo, this riverside lodge is on a level site in verdant surroundings. It's not going to suit all abilities, but being small with few steps, it may appeal to some. From the parking area, there are 2 steps then a ramp to reach the brick pathway, which runs to the rooms. The swimming pool has step-free access & the bar/dining area is up 1 step.
Closest room: Sliding door (100) has threshold (10); beds (52) have light switch but no phone; highest switch is 150cm; doorway to ensuite (75) is level & opens to bedroom; step-in shower (16); washbasin is 65cm; toilet (42) has side transfer space. **$$**

OTHER PRACTICALITIES
All the main towns on this route, including Tsumeb, Grootfontein, Rundu and Katima Mulilo, have good supermarkets, banking facilities, fuel and post offices.

Medical services
Hospitals are found in all three towns: **Tsumeb** (*Hospital St;* ☏ *067 221 001/2*), **Grootfontein** (☏ *067 242 141/2*), **Rundu** (☏ *066 255 000*) and **Katima Mulilo** (☏ *066 251 400/252 083*). Serious problems would be

treated at the excellent **Medi-clinic** in Otjiwarongo (*24hr emergency* ☎ *067 303 734;* 🖰 *www.otjiwarongomc.co.za*), which is the best hospital in the northern region.

WHAT TO SEE AND DO

If you want to take things easy and absorb more of the area, there are various **caves** around Otavi, a worthwhile **museum** in Tsumeb and the world-renowned **Hoba meteorite** lies west of Grootfontein.

Divundu is a lovely area to catch up for a day or more. This is near **Popa Falls**, where the Okavango River stumbles rather than plunges over several shallow falls on its way to Botswana. **Mahango National Park** lies just south of here. Further east, instead of driving straight to Katima Mulilo on the tarred road, it is possible to loop south from Kongola through **Mudumu National Park**. This road is all-weather gravel, so although it is twice the distance, account for three-times the journey time. Namushasha or Lianshulu lodges can be used to properly appreciate the area.

BOTSWANA AT A GLANCE

Location	Landlocked in southern Africa, north of South Africa and also bordering Namibia, Zambia and Zimbabwe
Size	600,370km²
Climate	Semi-arid subtropical; warm winter (Jun–Aug), hot summer and rainy season (Nov–Mar)
Population	1.8 million (2008 estimate)
Capital and largest city	Gaborone (population over 208,000 in 2005)
Currency	Pula (BWP abbreviated to P)
Rate of exchange	£1=P10.6; US$1=P7.1; €1=P9.4 (May 2009)
Language	English (official), Setswana (local) and other local languages
Religion	Christianity, indigenous beliefs
Time	GMT +2
Electricity	220V, delivered at 50Hz; three round pins and British-style plugs with three square pins
Weights and measures	Metric
Public holidays	1–2 Jan, Good Friday, Easter Monday, Labour Day (1 May), Sir Seretse Khama Day (1 Jul), President's Day, Independence day (30 Sep), 1 Nov, 25–26 Dec
Tourist board	⁰ www.botswanatourism.co.bw
International telephone code	+267 (for Zambia, relevant for the final section of this chapter, the international telephone code is +260)
Further information:	For a more in-depth analysis, including background information and mainstream travel information, see Chris McIntyre's Bradt safari guides to Botswana and Zambia.

7 Botswana
(including Victoria Falls)

Championed as one of Africa's rare success stories, with its economy cut carefully around the diamond industry, Botswana also has a distinctive policy of 'low impact' tourism. Broadly speaking, the country aims to attract a higher-paying clientele, so reaping the same gross income from fewer visitors while leaving a shallower human footprint on its wild areas. In practice however, although this means safaris to some regions are relatively expensive, more budget-conscious travellers can still find affordable alternatives.

The country is essentially arid, with its bulk being part of, or buffer zone to, the Kalahari Desert and Makgadikgadi Pans National Park. The importance attached to water here is striking when you realise that *pula*, the name of the national currency, is Setswana for 'rain'. Although tourist lodges are opening in the desert areas, the vast majority of visitors still aim for the northern regions where the Okavango and Kwando rivers pour in through the Caprivi Strip, flooding the sand and creating the lush, game-rich reserves we know as Moremi and Chobe.

Livingstone and the Victoria Falls in Zambia is one of southern Africa's major draws and is less than 100km from Kasane in the northeast of the country. As such it is included in many Botswanan safari itineraries and is the final section of this chapter.

GENERAL INFORMATION

ACCESS SUMMARY

Currently, the only game area that is well serviced by officially accessible accommodation is the northern part of Chobe National Park, and it also has good road and air links and enough mid-range lodgings to be considered by all. The Okavango Delta, including Moremi, has many splendid lodges and tented camps that will suit some travellers, but few that are designed with disability in mind. They are reached either by 4x4 vehicle using soft, sandy tracks or by short flights from Maun and Kasane. One disability-specialised operator runs mobile safaris into all regions of Botswana.

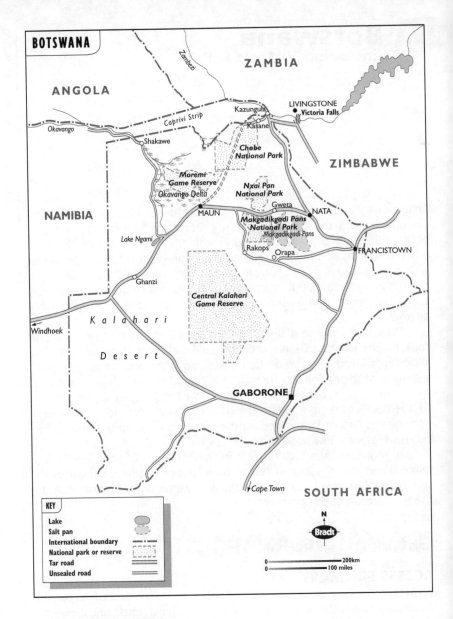

LOCAL OPERATORS

For local operators catering to people with mobility issues, plus some mainstream operators that have shown a genuine interest in this market, see *Chapter 1, Specialised operators in Africa*, pages 20–3.

MAUN

For more than a century, Maun has been the main supply point for all journeys into the lush Okavango Delta and the baking plains of the Kalahari Desert. In the beginning it was the haunt of leathery pioneers and extrovert adventurers and consequently has built up a reputation as a Wild-West frontier town. As exploration increased, and camps became established, so Maun grew, providing equipment, fuel and food to keep them running. The safari industry brought tourists, Maun's appearance softened and with the completion of the asphalt road from Nata in 1990, the town has become easily accessible to anyone.

Nowadays, with a population of around 30,000, Maun is more than just an outpost; it is the safari capital of Botswana and has become a thriving, multi-cultural community. Yes, if you arrive by air then it looks like a brown, sprawling clutter of huts and houses surrounded by oceans of sand, but when you step out of the airport, or if you arrive by road, then it feels more like a normal, well-developed southern-African town.

Despite this, its role is relatively unchanged; it's still mainly just a staging post with the majority of visitors scurrying through, often flying in from abroad and out to the Delta on the same day. But for those with more time, Maun is an experience in itself; there are restaurants and hotels providing decent fare and accommodation, and services and communications that match most of the continent.

GETTING THERE AND AWAY

By road
Nata is 306km to the east of Maun, and Ghanzi (southwest towards the Namibian border at Mamuno) is almost 275km. Heading northwest, the road skirts around the west side of the Okavango Delta, and is 440km to another Namibian border at Shakawe. All of these routes are good tar, giving smooth, comfortable journeys and predictable drive times. Inter-city buses run from Maun to all these regions, departing from the slightly disjointed bus station opposite the large Shoprite in the town centre, but none of these vehicles will have any access designed for disability.

By air
Maun Airport is small but can be busy and has a handy location a few kilometres north of the town centre. It accepts Air Botswana and Air Namibia flights from Johannesburg, Gaborone and Windhoek, as well as co-ordinating the swarm of light aircraft that ferry people in and out of the Okavango Delta. There is a long, shallow ramp at the main entrance and all essential services are on the ground floor. Both the main arrivals hall and the departure lounge have standard toilets with step-free entries, although there is no dedicated 'disabled' bathroom. An aisle chair is available to help those with walking difficulties onto their flight, and the staff here are

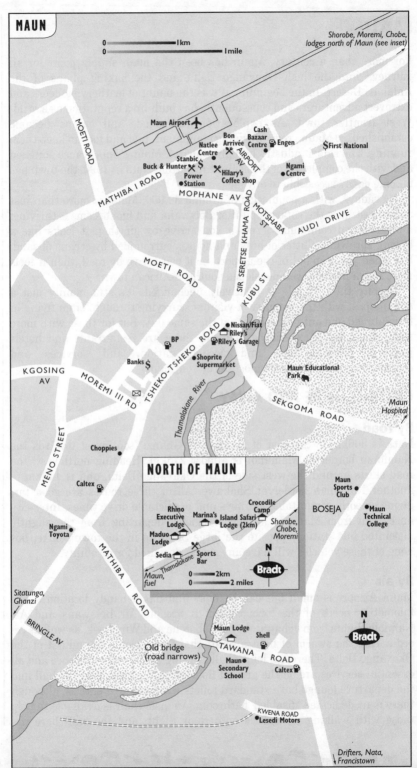

MAUN

0 ———— 1km
0 ———— 1 mile

*Shorobe, Moremi, Chobe,
lodges north of Maun (see inset)*

MOETI ROAD

MATHIBA I ROAD

Maun Airport ✈

Natlee
Centre ●

Bon
Arrivée ✕

Cash
Bazaar
Centre ⊡ Engen

$ First National

Stanbic $
Buck & Hunter ✕ ✕ Hilary's
● Power Coffee Shop
Station

AIRPORT AV

Ngami
Centre ●

MOPHANE AV

SIR SERETSE KHAMA ROAD

MOTSHABA ST

AUDI DRIVE

MOETI ROAD

KUBU ST

● Nissan/Fiat
□ Riley's
🅿 Riley's Garage

⛽ BP

Banks $

TSHEKO-TSHEKO ROAD

● Shoprite
Supermarket

Maun Educational
Park ●🐃

KGOSING
AV

MOREMI III RD ✉

Thamalakane River

SEKGOMA ROAD

*Maun
Hospital* ↗

MENO STREET

● Choppies

⛽ Caltex

Ngami ●
Toyota

MATHIBA I ROAD

NORTH OF MAUN

Rhino
Executive
Lodge 🏠 Marina's 🏠 ● Island Safari
Maduo Lodge (2km)
Lodge 🏠

Crocodile
Camp ●

*Shorobe,
Chobe,
Moremi*

Sedia 🏠 ✕ Sports
Bar

Thamalakane

*Maun,
fuel* ↙

0 —— 2km
0 —— 2 miles

N
Bradt

Maun
Sports ●
Club

BOSEJA

● Maun
Technical
College

*Sitatunga,
Ghanzi* ↙

BRINGLE AV

Maun Lodge ●

TAWANA I ROAD

Shell
⛽

N
Bradt

Old bridge
(road narrows)

● Maun
Secondary
School

Caltex ⛽

KWENA ROAD
● Lesedi Motors

*Drifters, Nata,
Francistown* ↘

uncommonly adept in its use; they fasten all straps and buckles with care ensuring the passenger is comfortable before boarding. I suspect the presence of Endeavour Safaris in Maun has had some bearing on this efficiency.

GETTING AROUND

Maun is flat, making for easy wheelchair pushing, but it is spread out, pavements are often non-existent and high midday temperatures rule this out as a painless means of getting around. Taxis and *kombis* are easily found near the bus station or can be called from your accommodation (ask the reception staff for a reliable company). None of these will be wheelchair accessible; if this is required, then contact Mike or Silvia at Endeavour Safaris (see page 21).

WHERE TO STAY

Crocodile Camp (15 rooms) ☏ 680 0222; **f** 680 1256; **e** sales@crocodilecamp.com; ⌂ www.crocodilecamp.com [2] [R]

Overlooking the Thamalakane 12km north of Maun, Croc Camp has long been a favourite amongst the expat locals, as well as travellers. The camp is set on a steep slope with >40 steps running from the car park down to the bar/restaurant/pool area, & although these steps have been admirably flanked with a smooth concrete ramp, it's a stiff push back up for even the strongest chair user (or their aide!). Once the base area has been reached, the riverside bar has a short, steep ramp (or 3 steps), the dining area is up 2 steps (tables are 71cm) & the standard public toilets are up 3 steps. The appealing little pool is at ground level & is entered using steps only. There are 2 kinds of accommodation: the standard chalets are all up 2 or 3 steps & have step-in showers, but bathrooms are too small for wheelchair users; the newer deluxe chalets are up 7 long, concrete steps up from the bar area, or are step-free from the parking at the top of the hill, though this track is narrow (67), rough & sandy.

Deluxe room: Has the fewest steps – doorway has 2 steps; bed (65) has light switch & transfer space; highest switch is 132cm; roll-in shower has small threshold, star taps (116), fixed showerhead & moulded sitting area (60); toilet (45) has front transfer space only.

Standard rooms: Doorway (76) is up 2 steps; 2 sgl beds (47) have transfer space & light switch; highest switch is 133cm; doorway to ensuite (79) is level but bathroom has no wheelchair space & step-in shower (10). **$$$**

Riley's Hotel (51 rooms) Tsheko-Tsheko Rd; ☏ 686 0204; **f** 686 0580; **e** resrileys@cresta.co.bw; ⌂ www.cresta-hospitality.com [0]

Riley's has been a hotel in Maun for about as long as one was ever needed in this desert outpost, & over the years, has become a local institution. It's now owned & run by the Cresta group, but although a couple of cement & stone ramps are in place to smooth the way between your vehicle, the restaurant & your room, the facilities are getting a little worn & it does not have bathrooms large enough for wheelchairs. Dining tables are 68cm & a ramp (gradient approximately 10%) leads down to the pleasant swimming pool. However, at the time of going to press, the hotel was undergoing a full refurbishment.

Ground-floor rooms: (there are several) Doorway (75) is level; dbl or twin beds (60) have light switch, phone & transfer space; doorway to ensuite (70) is level; bathroom – containing a bath with integral shower – is too small for wheelchair entry. **$$$**

Marina's (8 rondavels) Shorobe Rd; ☎ 680 1231; **e** marinas@dynabyte.bw 3+
8km north of Maun, this homely little lodge is owned & run by Marina (from Botswana) & her husband. Although the ground surface is uneven, the site is small so wheelchairs will suffer, but those guests who can walk a little should be able to cope. The restaurant/bar (up 3 steps) & soft, sandy paths with low walls (around 10cm) connect the fire pit, the swimming pool (up 5 steps) & the thatch-roofed (and cheerily decorated) rondavels. These come in various forms (2 family, 3 twins & 3 dbls), but the dbls & twins have the most spacious bathrooms.

Room 3 (a twin): Doorway (75) is up 2 steps (7 & 10); beds (53) have transfer space & light switch; desk is 69cm; highest switch is 147cm; en-suite is part of room, behind a wall; step-in shower (18) & washbasin (74) have star taps (88); toilet (41) has side transfer space only. **$$**

Sedia Hotel (24 rooms & 6 chalets) Shorobe Rd; ☎ 686 0177; **e** sedia@info.bw;
⌂ www.sedia-hotel.com 1
A few kilometres north of Maun, the Sedia's brightly painted façade is unmissable. The hotel is nestled conveniently between the road & the Thamalakane River – therefore caters to a wide range of business & holiday travellers – & the efficient staff are obviously appreciated by the management. The upshot is a lively, friendly & relaxed atmosphere. The Sedia is also great value. Although there are no 'disabled rooms', there are few steps, a wheelchair & crutches are available on site & there is also talk of making at least 1 fully inclusive chalet during the next phase of renovations. Currently, a steep ramp (approximately 25%) avoids the 8 steps from the car park up to the first floor. The reception, dining area, bar & swimming pool (the largest in Maun) are on this level & the most accessible rooms (numbers 1–12) are up 1 small bevelled step (15). Riverside chalets are a longer walk & have several steps at their entrances. The second floor is up a stairway, but only houses the conference facilities. The standard public toilet has level entry (76) & dining tables are 69cm.

Room 2: Doorway (76) is up 1 step (6), for which a wooden ramp is available; bed (57) has transfer space & light switch; doorway to ensuite (75) is level, & a wheelchair can enter the bathroom, but there is no turning space inside; bath (51) has fitted handles, star taps on one end & a handheld showerhead; washbasin (63) has high mirror & the toilet is out of reach for a wheelchair user. **$$**

Island Safari Lodge (12 rooms) ☎ 686 0300; **f** 686 2932;
e enquiries@africansecrets.net; ⊕ www.africansecrets.net

The Island Safari Lodge's location is quite exquisite. The lodge is spread through mature Okavango woodland on the banks of the Thamalakane River, & being a couple of kilometres from the main road (and 12km north of Maun) it offers a degree of seclusion that others cannot provide. Furthermore, this is the only accommodation in Maun which has bathrooms (2) adapted for wheelchair users. The site is level with good lighting & regular seating, but pathways vary from paving stones to concrete & are bumpy in places. There are 2 swimming pools; the first, near reception with lovely river views, has ramped access; the second, near the campsite, has a sandy access path but does have handrails to assist entry. The traditional bar/dining area is all on 1 level with a shallow ramp from the ground, & tables are 71cm.
Rooms 1 & 2: Have been adapted, & are closest to the main areas. Doorway (74) has cement ramp; beds (59) have transfer space & light switch; highest switch is 121cm; desk is 63cm; doorway into the ensuite (76) has threshold (2); roll-in shower has 2 fixed showerheads, round taps (117), 1 support rail (95) & a seat is available; washbasin (69) has round taps; toilet (41) has 1 rear support rail (94) & has front & side transfer space. Other rooms have step-in showers. **$$**

Maun Lodge (48 rooms) Tawana Rd; ☎ 686 3939; **f** 686 3969;
e maun.lodge@info.bw; ⊕ www.maunlodge.com

There's nothing remarkable about Maun Lodge, either positively or negatively. It is clean, tidy & well organised, & it has a peaceful setting on the Thamalakane River about 2.5km from the centre of Maun. From the parking area, reception is up 1 step or a small, shallow ramp. The restaurant & conference area are reached by descending a dozen steps, or by skirting around the building then going down a smooth but steep bricked slope. From there, the restaurant is up 1 step (a ramp is available), tables are 69cm & there is a standard public toilet with level entry. From reception, the swimming pool is up 1 step then down a steep ramp, has a seating ledge inside it & is entered using 3 steps & no handrail. There are 3 types of room: budget chalets, hotel rooms & riverfront suites. The suites are the least accessible, being down 7 steps then up 2 from the conference centre; the dbl chalets have a kerb & loose pebbles to cross, & have step-in showers (27), while some hotel rooms have level entrances & baths.
Hotel Room 2: The closest to reception. Doorway (76) is level; dbl bed (68) has transfer space, light switch & phone; highest switch is 129cm; desk is 62cm; door to ensuite (76) is level; bathroom is small, but has just enough space to turn a normal wheelchair; bath (60) has fixed showerhead & round taps; toilet (42) has front transfer space only. **$$**

Maduo Lodge (22 rooms) Shorobe Rd; ☎ 686 0846; **f** 686 2161;
e maduolodge@info.bw

This motel-like lodge next to Rhino Executive Lodge (see following entry) has bumpy paths to reach the rooms, all of which are up at least 1 step. The dining room, reception & the swimming pool are all up 2 steps. Standard rooms have step-in showers & executive rooms have bathtubs & doorways are all approximately 75cm. **$**

Rhino Executive Lodge (10 rooms) ✆ 686 1469; **f** 686 5120; **e** rhinolodge@botsnet.bw ②

Opposite the Sedia & next to the Maduo, Rhino Lodge might offer a cheaper option in Maun without being fully accessible. It's new, & the simply furnished rooms are clean, but the light construction of the buildings does mean sound carries – earplugs may be a useful purchase. From the gravel parking area there is a shallow cement ramp to the rooms but reception is up 2 steps. There is a slight rise leading to the bar – where tables are 61cm – & a short, bumpy cobbled floor leads to the restaurant, where tables are 64cm. There is no swimming pool. The rooms vary in size & fittings, & bathroom furniture is the same throughout; it's just laid out differently according to the amount of space available.
Rooms in general: Doorways (76) are level; beds (63) have transfer space & light switches; baths (52) have fitted handrails & handheld showerheads.
Room 3 (a twin): The most airy; the bath & toilet both have transfer space but no support rails. Room 9 has no en-suite facilities. **$**

WHERE TO EAT

In tune with Maun's evolution from dusty desert outpost to cosmopolitan town, there are several very decent eateries dotted around town. As yet, none of these have accessible toilets and step-free entry, but they are all ground floor and helping hands are quick to appear. Anyone spending only a night in Maun will probably eat in his or her lodge or hotel, but for those with more time, the following is a taste of what's on offer:

Bon Arrivée Mathiba I Rd; ✆ 680 0330 ; ⊘ 19.00–22.30, until 23.00 Sat–Sun. Directly opposite the airport & with an assorted menu offering everything from milkshakes to steak, this fashionable new café is 1 step from street level. **$$$**

Buck & Hunter Mathiba I Rd; ✆ 680 1001; ⊘ 10.00–22.00. With the best pizzas in town (& probably within 500km in all directions) the Buck & Hunter is a great place for daytime stopovers. There's no step, only a small, wooden curved bridge at the entrance & it's 5mins' walk from the airport. **$$$**

Sports Bar Shorobe Rd; ✆ 686 2676; ⊘ 18.00–22.00 daily. A favourite amongst the local safari community, which is a sure sign it's reliable, the Sports Bar is the most refined restaurant in Maun. It has a good dinner menu with a wide choice of typically European fare & the bar can be busy, especially on w/ends. The entrance is stepped, but an easier route exists around the side of the building. **$$$**

Hilary's Coffee Shop Mathiba I Rd; ✆ 686 1610; ☉ 08.00–16.00 Mon–Fri, 08.30–12.00 Sat–Sun. Hilary's has a varied menu for b/fast, lunch & snacks in between. Wholemeal & health tends to be the theme. Again, up 1 step from street level & a short walk from the airport. **$$**

OTHER PRACTICALITIES

There are banks in the shopping area opposite the Shoprite in the centre of Maun and bureaux de change spread over town. Similarly ubiquitous are the internet cafés, although I saw none with a level entrance.

Medical services

Dr Chris Carey (*Cash Bazaar Centre;* ✆ *686 4084/5013*) runs his own practice in Maun and being a wheelchair user himself, may have a deeper understanding of some disabilities than most practitioners.

The **Delta Medical Centre** (*Tsheko-Tsheko Rd;* ✆ *686 2999;* **e** *delta med@info.bw or* **e** *pak@info.bw*) is a reliable, private medical facility and is a good option if Dr Carey (above) is unavailable.

Maun Hospital (*Letsholathebe II Memorial Hospital; Disaneng Rd, next to Maun Educational Park;* ✆ *686 0444*) opened in late 2008 and replaces the old building on Bringle Avenue. It is one of five being built in Botswana and, at the cost of more that P650 million, with 240 beds and state-of-the-art equipment, it should be reassuring to anyone visiting the region.

WHAT TO SEE AND DO

Maun is mainly used as a stopover so isn't overflowing with highlights. **Mokoro trips** and scenic flights over the Delta can be organised, but if you just want a relaxed walk in relative nature then one recommendation is to visit **Maun Educational Park** (☉ *daily;* ⌷ *free*). Almost 2km from the centre of town, this small piece of woodland has been fenced to protect the last of Maun's natural habitat. There's no seating to speak of, and the occasional step to irritate wheelers, but it is a lovely place to wander around in complete safety and relatively natural surroundings. Paths are earth and gravel but generally hard.

THE KALAHARI SALT PANS

Roughly southeast of the Okavango Delta and bisected by the tarred road running between Maun and Nata lie great shimmering salt pans. These enormous, desolate plains are the remains of a super-lake which once covered central Botswana. In years of exceptional rainfall, when the Delta spills out into its overflow rivers, they briefly hold water again. Other years, the tiny spatter of rain they receive is enough to nourish the hardy grasses round their boundaries and sustain surprisingly large populations of zebra, wildebeest, various smaller antelopes and their usual carnivorous entourage (as well as lions, roaming packs of wild dogs are also occasionally spotted). Nxai Pans National Park (to the north) and Makgadikgadi Pans National Park (south of the road) are recognised game protection areas within these regions. As it happens, the Boteti River (one of the Delta overflows) finally reached Meno a Kwena camp (featured below) in late 2008, for the first time in 13 years.

GETTING THERE AND AWAY

The only camp in this region currently exhibiting a genuine interest in hosting people with limited mobility is Meno a Kwena. It is between one and two hours' drive from Maun, the vast majority of which is tarred or smooth gravelled road.

WHERE TO STAY

Meno a Kwena Tented Camp (7 tents) ☎ 686 0981; f 686 0493;
e reservations@kalaharikavango .com; ⌂ www.kalaharikavango.com 1⃞

Meno a Kwena is perched on a sandy bluff above the Boteti River, adjacent to Makgadikgadi Pans National Park & about 1½hrs' drive south of Maun. This delightfully rustic safari camp is very relaxed & guests have a lot of freedom to choose what they want to do, & when. Although day trips to Nxai Pans or Baines' baobabs are common excursions, the tranquillity of the place entices many to do very little; browsing the fascinating library, relaxing by (or in) the rock plunge pool or watching the action at the riverside waterhole (about 30m below the camp) is a great way to spend the day. When I visited, Meno a Kwena was set on soft sand, which made getting around a real struggle for wheelchair users & a bit of a trudge for slow walkers. However, plans were in place to create hard paths before the end of 2009. If this is important to you then it ought to be double-checked before booking. In any case, because 'sitting around' is so rewarding, the camp is actually quite suited to less mobile people. The main *lapa* (with library & dining area) is on 1 level with a smooth, hard floor & people are always on hand to help when you do wish to move to other areas. Everything is within about 50m of here, & currently, the traditional Meru tents are up only 1 step & each has dbl beds. Their bathrooms are bush-camp style with traditional safari bucket showers & canvas washbasins, but a seat can be provided in the shower & there is the luxury of flush toilets. **$$$$$**

OTHER PRACTICALITIES

All shopping, fuel and money-changing needs should be dealt with before leaving Maun.

Medical services

Any serious medical problems would be dealt with in Maun.

THE OKAVANGO DELTA

The Okavango Delta is Botswana's best-known and most visited wilderness, and although is often described using adjectives like 'pristine' and 'breathtaking', they barely do it justice. After beginning its terminally flawed journey in the highlands of Angola, the Okavango River heads south, briefly following the Namibian border before flowing headlong into the great sandy expanse of the Kalahari Desert. At this point it fans out and becomes an inland delta, covering an area that can (seasonally) reach 16,000km². In doing so, these pure, clean waters irrigate the sand: islands, inlets, lagoons and swamps are formed and these support a huge variety of Africa's flora and fauna. The result is as stunningly beautiful an environment as it is possible to see.

Moremi Game Reserve (named after the local chief who first declared it in 1962) is the protective hub, surrounded by many different wildlife concessions, which provide it with a large buffer zone, preventing encroachment by agriculture or other domestic animals. Camps in the so-called 'Panhandle', near where the river enters Botswana, tend to concentrate more on birding and fishing than on walking wildlife, as they are often permanently surrounded by water.

Elephant, buffalo and lion are commonly seen, as well as a variety of antelope species, Burchell's zebra and giraffe. Rarer animals that may be spotted include wild dog and sitatunga, while sightings of the omnipresent leopard happen whenever that elusive cat feels like it. Rhino are the only notable species 'missing' from the usual collector's items (though white rhino have recently been reintroduced after being poached to extinction). Night game drives are allowed in some areas, giving the opportunity to see some nocturnal species including bushbabies, aardvarks and spring hares. Birdlife abounds here. With over 400 species in Moremi alone, the Delta is utopia for serious birders; in addition, the serene method of game viewing – gliding silently through the water in a mokoro (traditional dugout canoe) – lends itself perfectly to this activity.

Apart from being heavier on the wallet, visiting the Delta differs from visiting most other wild areas in Africa for two reasons. Firstly, the majority of trips are fly-in, using light aircraft from Maun and Kasane. Secondly, some lodges and camps are surrounded by water; game viewing in these places is done predominantly from a *mokoro* or small boat. If these present no problem then the Delta is everything it's reputed to be and will not disappoint.

Park fees Moremi Game Reserve fees are P120 per adult and P60 per child (<18 years) per day. Fees for people flying into Moremi are usually included in their tour price. Road arrivals need to have booked their accommodation in advance, must show at least a copy of this confirmation at the park gate, and then pay in pula cash.

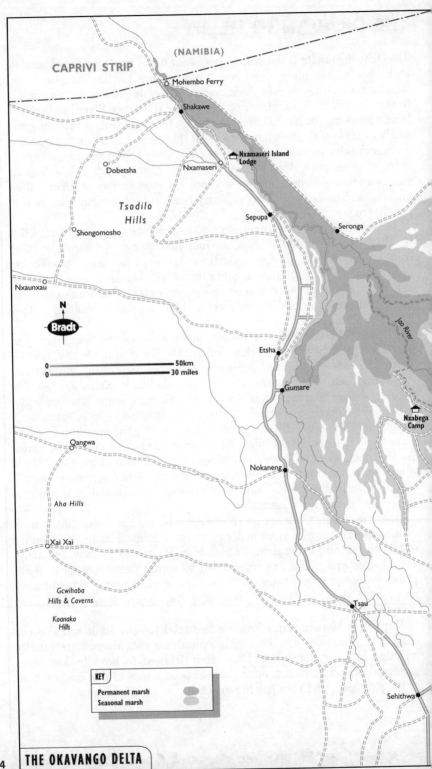

(NAMIBIA)

CAPRIVI STRIP

Mohembo Ferry

Shakawe

Dobetsha

Nxamaseri

Nxamaseri Island
Lodge

*Tsodilo
Hills*

Sepupa

Seronga

Shongomosho

Nxaunxau

N

Bradt

0   50km
0   30 miles

Joo River

Etsha

Gumare

Nxabega
Camp

Qangwa

Nokaneng

Aha Hills

Xai Xai

*Gcwihaba
Hills & Caverns*

*Koanaka
Hills*

Tsau

KEY
Permanent marsh
Seasonal marsh

Sehithwa

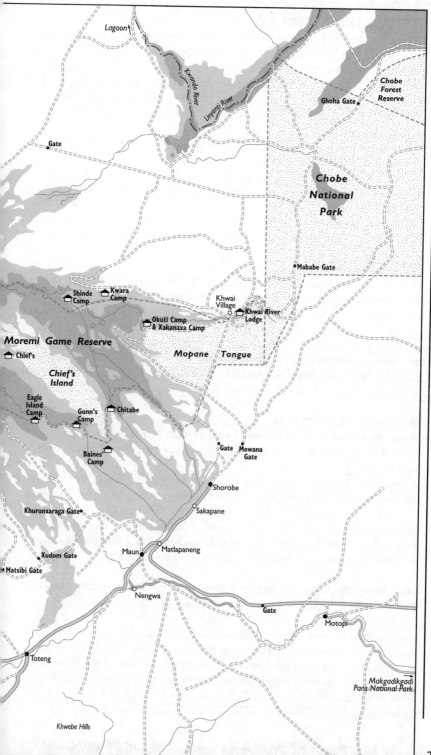

Lagoon

Kwando River

Linyanti River

Gate

Chobe Forest Reserve

Ghoha Gate

Chobe National Park

Mababe Gate

Shinde Camp

Kwara Camp

Khwai Village

Khwai River Lodge

Okuti Camp & Xakanaxa Camp

Moremi Game Reserve

Chief's

Chief's Island

Mopane Tongue

Eagle Island Camp

Gunn's Camp

Chitabe

Baines' Camp

Gate

Mowana Gate

Shorobe

Khurunxaraga Gate

Sakapane

Xudum Gate

Maun

Matlapaneng

Matsibi Gate

Nengwa

Gate

Motopi

Toteng

Makgadikgadi Pans National Park

Khwebe Hills

GETTING THERE AND AWAY

The lodges and camps in and around Moremi are usually reached by air. Some accept unannounced drive-in arrivals, but others – especially the more exclusive places – certainly don't. For those who do drive in, most lodges in Moremi are between 100km and 200km from Maun, but the roads are often little more than tracks in the sand and journeys usually take between four and six hours. Endeavour Safaris in Maun has wheelchair-adapted 4x4 vehicles – see page 21.

Flights from Maun take between 20 and 30 minutes and those from Kasane are between 60 and 90 minutes, depending on the location of the lodge. Facilities at those airports are described on pages 265 and 283 respectively and the usual routine at small airstrips in the Delta is described on page 92. All aircraft are light aircraft, and if you need space then it may be worthwhile trying to organise everything around using one of the larger 12-seater Cessna 'caravans' than the smallest craft.

WHERE TO STAY

There is currently no accommodation in the Okavango Delta with support rails and other, more specific, features designed for disability access. That said, many will be workable, owing to their spacious, level build, and the ever-present 'help is available' attitude of the staff. The following list is a selection of some of the most accessible options, both inside Moremi and in the concession areas that enclose it. Travellers on a tight budget may feel excluded here and might want to consider a mobile safari; see Endeavour Safaris in *Chapter 1, Specialised operators in Africa,* page 21.

Moremi Game Reserve

Khwai River Lodge (15 luxury tents) Contact Orient Express Safaris (South Africa) ☏ +27 (0)21 483 1600; e reservations@orient-express-safaris.com; ⌂ www.orient-express.com [3⚤]

Khwai River Lodge is spread out along the bank of the river, with the furthest of the extremely luxurious tents being a long walk from the main building. Firm, wide access routes run through the complex, but several steps must be mounted to reach the raised, timber platforms that all living quarters use. The honeymoon suite is furnished with a decadent bathtub, while all of the other rooms have step-in showers. **$$$$$**

Okuti Camp (10 chalets) Contact Ker & Downey ☏ 686 0375/0570/1226; f 686 1282; e safari@kerdowney.bw; ⌂ www.kerdowney.com [0⚤] [⚤]

Okuti has recently been rebuilt & opened again in 2007. The camp has been laid out on vast wooden boardwalks, which emphasise the sweeping plains in the surrounding landscape, & the cavernous chalets have 'hut style' thatched roofs which span lofty arcs from one side of the floor to the other. The dining area, swimming pool & rooms have level access – apparently the jetty does too – & huge outside bathrooms have a roll-in shower with fixed showerhead & star taps. Toilet access is currently unknown. 1 of the family rooms may be most suitable & if a bath is required then the honeymoon suite is the only option. **$$$$$**

Xakanaxa Camp (13 tents) Contact Moremi Safaris (South Africa) ☏ +27 (0)11 463 3999; **f** +27 (0)86 517 7388; **e** info@moremi-safaris.com; ⏢ www.xakanaxa-camp.com

Set in a shady woodland site, which is also level, Xakanaxa is one of the Delta's older camps. Despite this, it caters well for wheelchairs. Pathways are packed sand, but these get watered for wheelchair arrivals, making them more solid. In any case, most of the action happens on the raised, timber-frame buildings, & these – including the reception/lounge/dining area – are reached using long, shallow wooden ramps. The kidney-shaped swimming pool is sweetly set, flush with the timber decking, & there is easy wheelchair space at the end of the long dining table.

Room 7: Can be ramped (100cm wide), the bathroom door (80) is level & has a roll-in shower (120) with fixed showerhead, round taps & a bench seat. Apparently a portable toilet seat with side rails exists, which may help some, but otherwise, the toilet has front transfer space only. **$$$$$**

Private concessions around Moremi

Baines' Camp (5 rooms) Contact Sanctuary Lodges (South Africa) ☏ +27 (0)11 438 4650; **f** 27 (0)11 787 7658; **e** southernafrica@sanctuary lodges.com; ⏢ www.sanctuarylodges.com

Baines' Camp, in an area just south of Moremi, is Sanctuary's most accessible lodge in Botswana. It does not have any custom-designed disability features but will suit some independent people or those with help. Most visitors will fly in, then there is a short drive (45–60mins) to the camp. The parking area is wide, level & hard underfoot, as are pathways leading to the lodge & the jetty; the latter has 2 steps *en route*. There is seating around the inside of the attractive pool & the public toilet has both side & front transfer space. The route to the lounge & dining room is level, & stunning views onto the surrounding plains are possible from here, also from a seated position. 2 steps drop down towards the fire pit,

The 5 rooms are similar: Doorway (85) is level; dbl or twin beds (68) have transfer space & light switches; dbl door (level) leads to a balcony & beds are wheeled, meaning it's possible to sleep under the stars; step-in shower (17) has glass doorway (73); washbasins have no knee clearance; toilets have front transfer space only. **$$$$$**

Eagle Island Camp (12 luxury tents) Contact Orient Express Safaris (South Africa) ☏ +27 (0)21 483 1600; **e** reservations@orient-express-safaris.com; ⏢ www.orient-express.com

Built along the same lines as its sister camp, Khwai River Lodge, Eagle Island offers similar access. There are hard, well-lit paths between the tents, all of which are raised with several steps (some as many as 9) on stilted, wooden decks. Ablutions are step-in showers, except in the new exclusive private suite, which has a bath. **$$$$$**

Shinde Camp (8 tents) Contact Ker & Downey 📞 686 0375/0570/1226; **f** 686 1282; **e** safari@kerdowney.bw; 🖰 www.kerdowney.com 2️⃣
Shinde lies just north of Moremi, in a lush, verdant game-rich area of the Delta. With this great location, plus its reputation of providing quality safari service – both guiding & in the camp itself – this is an excellent choice for able-bodied visitors. Those with mobility issues may find it more challenging. The access routes from the parking area are sandy paths, & once you reach the main building, the various levels are ramped, but steeply. However, although most of the 8 tents are up 2 or more steps, there were plans to create 2 with level entry in mid 2008. **$$$$$**

Kwara Camp (8 tents) Contact Kwando Safaris 📞 686 1449; **f** 686 1457; **e** reservations@kwando.co.za; 🖰 www.kwando.co.za 3️⃣
Kwara is the most accessible of Kwando's Delta properties, but the covered tents are still on raised wooden decks (up 2 steps) & sandy paths connect the various units. There are about 4 steps from the arrival area to the bar, then 3 down to the dining room & about 4 again to the outside area. 2 steps lead to the jetty, standard rooms have a step-in shower & the honeymoon suite also has a bath. **$$$$$**

Gunn's Camp (7 tents, 1 chalet) Plot 244, Airport Rd, Maun; 📞 686 0023; **f** 686 0040; **e** sales@gunnscamp.com; 🖰 www.gunnscamp.com 0️⃣ 🖼️
Gunn's Camp is a handsome 2-storey dark wood & thatch construction towering over a river on Moremi's boundary. The first floor houses a bar, lounge & dining room, which may dissuade some people, but the lodge employees will cheerily – & safely – carry you up the ladder. A wooden walkway leads to the main building & packed-earth paths run to the accommodation. The deluxe Meru tents now have real doorways; 4 have roll-in showers while 2 of these have step-free – albeit bumpy – access from their approach route. Various other satellite bush camps have Meru & dome-style tents, but these are all entered using steps. **$$$$$**

Nxabega Camp (9 tents) Contact Conservation Corporation Africa (South Africa) 📞 +27 (0)11 809 4300; **f** +27 (0)11 809 4400; **e** safaris@ccafrica.com; 🖰 www.ccafrica.com 3️⃣ 🖼️
CC Africa, in accordance with their philosophy on conservation in Botswana, tries to avoid building solid paths. Nxabega, therefore, has sandy access paths around the buildings. The bar/dining area & all accommodation at Nxabega are up several steps from these paths, but some rooms have spacious roll-in showers with a standard plastic seat available. **$$$$$**

The Panhandle
Nxamaseri Island Lodge (6 chalets) 📞 687 8015; **f** 687 8016;

e info@nxamaseri.com; 🖰 www.nxamaseri.com 2

Being located in the Panhandle, where there are limited amounts of big game, Nxamaseri concentrates on fishing & birding. It's one of the oldest lodges in the Delta, & its site – on the water's edge, backed by dense Tarzanesque jungle – was obviously chosen with care. A track through deep sand leads all the way to the lodge, but is only open for short periods of the year, when water levels are low. At all other times it is an island & a boat will meet you near the village of Nxamaseri on the western riverbank. The lodge is surprisingly accessible: once you have navigated the 4 steps from the jetty, the dining & bar areas are up 2 steps. From here, Rooms 2–6 (twin rooms) are down 2 steps then along a boardwalk on 1 level – it's not effortless pushing, but with a little help, most chair users will cope. Rooms 1 & 7 (a dbl & a treehouse that is not yet fully finished) are down 2 steps in the opposite direction.

Room 2: The closest to reception: doorway (78) is level, but the boardwalk is craftily constructed around a tree limb, reducing the entrance width to 73cm; bed (50) has light switch & transfer space; door to ensuite (87) is level; step-in shower (24) has fixed showerhead & a simple seat is available; washbasin has no wheelchair access; toilet (38) has front transfer space only. The other rooms are similarly attired, though the toilet in Room 1 (the dbl) has side transfer space & its shower entry is lower (9). Room 6 has a relatively large outside seating deck, but is further from reception. Room 7 (the treehouse) is reached via a vertiginous boardwalk, raised with 3 large steps through the trees; it's not for the faint-hearted. **$$$$$**

Other notable accommodation
Chitabe Camp is a well-established camp located just outside Moremi and is run by Wilderness Safaris. At the time of writing, Wilderness were adopting a policy of making properties more accessible, and at Chitabe there are now apparently new chalets with shallow ramps and wooden boardwalks instead of stepped access (for bookings, contact Expert Africa, see page 18).

OTHER PRACTICALITIES
Once in the Okavango Delta, you will usually be limited to conveniences and facilities that are available in your lodge. Most will accept credit cards but it is more economical to change money in Maun. The same applies to shopping; basic curio outlets exist but other goods are not available. Some lodges may have internet and email access available to clients.

Medical services
Most lodges will have a basic medical room, but people with serious medical emergencies would be evacuated by air to Maun or even Johannesburg.

WHAT TO SEE AND DO
What is available depends on the water level and on the location of the camp or lodge. *Mokoro* (dugout canoe) **trips** are possible virtually everywhere, and

DISEASE CONTROL POINTS IN BOTSWANA

One thing that is unique to Botswana is the regular disease control points on the highways. Botswana's beef industry is a major earner and strenuous efforts are made to limit the spread of disease. At these checkpoints, the vehicle must drive through a shallow bath of murky-looking disinfected water and all foot passengers must walk across a mat impregnated with decontaminant. Anyone unable to walk will be excused this ritual, but their shoes must be removed and the soles pressed onto the mat. Bizarrely, however, although I suggested at every control point to let my wheelchair be rolled across this mat, the officers present insisted only my shoes must be done – even though they rarely touch the ground.

As well as disinfecting, there are also food restrictions of which you need to take note. Red meat (uncooked beef) may not be taken through these internal control points, adding complications for campers. Travellers entering Botswana by road have stricter legislations: no animal products (including fresh meat, dairy, skin and bone goods) are allowed to be brought into the country – this also includes packets of dried meat (*biltong*).

---

are highly recommended. This is a unique way to experience Africa, gliding silently through reed waterways, barely disturbing the myriad bird and animal life, and, with a little trust, is one that can be enjoyed by most people (people with mobility problems, *see Chapter 3, By boat*, page 93). Experienced 'polers' will know all the channels and can name every bird, plant and animal you point out, plus all of those that you didn't see. **Motorboat excursions** are also commonly done, and when the motor is cut, they offer a similarly serene experience to that in a *mokoro*. Many boats have wide, flat bottoms, allowing wheelchair users to stay in their chairs inside the boat. Many camps are situated on enough dry land to offer **Game driving** while those on permanent islands concentrate more on **fishing** and **birding** safaris. Finally, near Baines' Camp, just south of Moremi, a fascinating project has been started called 'Grey Matters', where it is possible to interact with and learn about elephants (*see ⊕ www.livingwithelephants.org for details*).

If all of these are too much work or not possible to do for some reason, then spending the time sitting in camp, possibly armed with binoculars, can be just as rewarding as actively seeking the game. The quiet, wilderness setting of most of the lodges in the Delta means birdlife is especially prolific and wild animals often wander very close by.

NATA

For the vast majority of travellers, this small town will be little more than a stopover between Maun and Kasane. The Sua Pan and Nata Bird Sanctuary are close by, if you wish to spend more time here.

WHERE TO STAY

Nata Lodge (20 chalets) ☎ 621 1210/1260; **f** 621 1265; **e** natalodge@inet.co.bw;
🖰 www.natalodge.com

This was the most used accommodation in Nata & was fittingly clean,
friendly & functional. It was destroyed by fire in 2008, but at the time of
writing the rebuild was well underway & it aims to open again on 1 Aug
2009. The bar, outside dining area & swimming pool will all be on 1 level;
there will be public toilets with disability access & there are plans to have
2 step-free chalets. **$$**

CHOBE NATIONAL PARK AND KASANE

Chobe National Park protects a huge swathe of Botswana – some 10,600km²
of woodland, swamp and desert – stretching from Kasane in the northeast
to Savuti in the west. Geographically, it is part of the Kalahari Desert, and
as such is essentially arid, but the northern edge of the park is continuously
watered by the perennial Chobe and Linyanti river systems and seasonal
waters flow in other areas.

The west of the park borders Moremi Game Reserve and there are no
fences to speak of, meaning that Chobe, Moremi and the Okavango Delta
make up one ecosystem, with animals migrating freely through it. The
result is an environment that supports a great variation of flora and fauna;
some of Africa's largest herds of elephant and buffalo are found here and the
predators exist in proportionately large numbers. Lion and hyena are often
seen, while leopard and cheetah are sometimes spotted. There are roaming
packs of wild dogs, although as with anywhere in Africa, sightings of these
are rare and should be cherished. The flats near the Chobe River are
especially good places to see puku and red lechwe, a couple of similar,
marsh-loving antelope.

Having been a mecca for adventurers and big-game hunters for decades,
Chobe was established as a national park in 1968, placing some protection
on its huge numbers of animals. The early years saw some areas being
overcrowded with visitors, but Botswana's policy of 'high cost, low density'
tourism from 1987 quelled the flow substantially, and nowadays, even in the
most-visited riverside areas in the northeastern corner, game viewing is
never uncomfortably busy.

Northern Chobe is serviced by Kasane, a small town strung out along the
bank of the Chobe River. It begins at the most easterly point of the park
near Sedudu Gate and follows the river further east towards Kazungula,
which is the meeting point of four countries. The town depends on the river
and the park for its livelihood and has prospered enormously in the last ten
to 15 years with the booming safari industry.

Park fees: Fees are P120 per adult and P60 per child (<18 years) per
day. At Sedudu Gate near Kasane park entry fees can be paid in pula cash
or with a credit card. Similarly, if booking and paying in advance in Maun

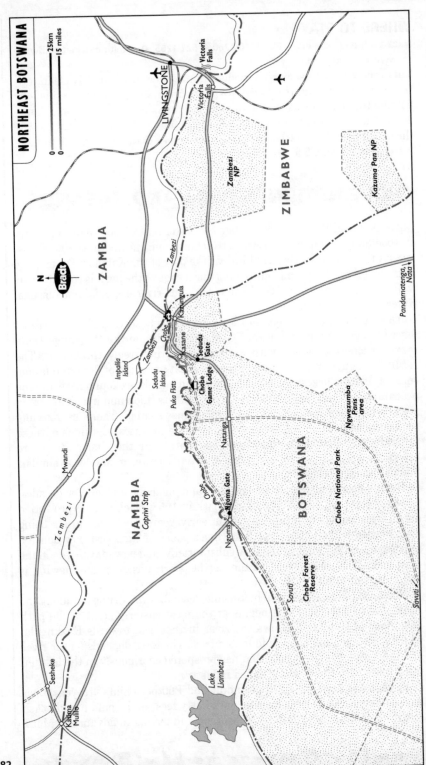

NORTHEAST BOTSWANA

25km
15 miles

282

(Parks and Reservations Office, Kubu St; ☎ 686 1265) then credit card or pula cash can be used but US dollars or GB sterling may also be accepted.

GETTING THERE AND AWAY

By road
The border at Ngoma is approximately 50km west of Kasane, cutting through Chobe National Park, and leading into Namibia and the Caprivi Strip. Kazungula lies about 15km to the east of Kasane and hosts borders with both Zambia (via a ferry over the Zambezi) and Zimbabwe, meaning Livingstone and Victoria Falls are less than 90km away. Looking south, Kasane is about 315km from Nata and just over 500km from Francistown. All of these roads are tarred and good quality, allowing for comfortable journeys in predictable times.

Buses connect Kasane with Francistown, Nata and Maun and the bus station is near the shell station in the centre of town but no services have facilities for disability; see *Chapter 3, Public transport,* page 89.

By air
Kasane International Airport is a quiet, organised little hub, handling Air Botswana flights from Gaborone and chartered flights to lodges and camps in the region. It has ramped access and inside the terminal is level. Both ladies' and gents' toilets have spacious toilets with front and side transfer space for wheelchair users, but no support rails. There is no aisle chair at the airport, but one can be ordered from Gaborone if needed.

Because Kasane is so close to Livingstone in Zambia (and Victoria Falls in Zimbabwe), a lot of fly-in arrivals use these airports then drive to Botswana. It is worth noting that the visa-waiver system that was in place in Zambia – where visa charges were waived if transit passengers spent one night in the country – was scrapped in 2008. Everybody planning to travel through these countries must now pay full-price visas.

GETTING AROUND
Taxis are easily hailed or booked from your hotel in Kasane, but none have specific disability adaptations. If access is an issue read the advice in *Chapter 3, Public transport,* page 89.

WHERE TO STAY
Apart from Liya Guesthouse, all the accommodation covered here takes advantage of the Chobe River and is set on the incline that rises away from it. This, of course, causes inherent problems when trying to make the property accessible, and reams of steps are the traditional solution. However, some lodges – namely Chobe Safari, Marina and Mowana – have dealt with this problem quite well, using slopes and ramps in places.

Chobe Game Lodge (46 rooms & 4 suites) Contact Desert & Delta Safaris (South Africa) ℂ +27 (0)11 706 0861; **f** +27 (0)11 706 0863;
e reservations@desertdelta.com; ☝ www.desertdelta.com 🔲 🛏
About 10km inside the park gate, Chobe Game Lodge has a very traditional atmosphere in a Moorish design – whitewashed walls & ceiling arches abound. From the vehicle drop-off point, reception is up 1 step, then continuing ahead, 10 steps drop directly down to the dining area. Avoiding these, a concrete path runs off behind reception, then edges down the slope to Rooms 301 & 302, which are usually first offered to guests with restricted mobility. This path is steeper than 8% but has no steps. From these rooms, the dining & buffet areas are level & tables are 73cm. The bar & standard public toilets are up 4 steps & a landscaped, natural rock swimming pool was under construction in 2008.
Rooms 301 & 302: The closest to the dining area. Doorway (72) has threshold (6); bed (68) has telephone, light switch & transfer space; desk is 63cm; highest switch is 132cm; doorway into the ensuite (75) is level; bathroom is small, but has wheelchair space; bath (53) has 2 support rails (10 & 54), wall-mounted star taps & a fixed showerhead; washbasin has no knee space; toilet (45) has front access only. **$$$$$**

Chobe Chilwero Lodge (15 cottages) Contact Sanctuary Lodges (South Africa) ℂ +27 (0)11 438 4650; **f** 27 (0)11 787 7658; **e** southernafrica@sanctuarylodges.com; ☝ www.sanctuarylodges.com 3+
With a private entry road, Chilwero is just west of Kasane Town but is remarkably secluded. It is an impressive lodge set on a slope above the Chobe River, with majestic views down onto the floodplains & Sedudu Island. The large, extravagantly furnished timber & thatch rooms are spread amongst established woodland, & standards of food & service match the visual appeal. Unfortunately, little thought has been given to counteracting the sloped setting; a steep cement path does run from the car park to the gardens, but accessing the main body of the lodge in between requires use of at least 6 steps. Dining tables are 63cm & there are several stone steps to the rocky, natural-looking pool. The rooms vary in layout, but all are up at least 2 steps.
Room 8: One of the closest to the main building. Large doorways are up 4 steps; king-sized bed (59) has transfer space, light switches & phone; entrance to the ensuite is level & wide; step-in shower (16) has stone seat (42) which is not in the washing area & star taps not within reach; the standalone bath (61) is up 1 step (16); washbasins have no knee clearance; toilet has front transfer space only. **$$$$$**

Chobe Marina Lodge (66 rooms) ℂ 625 2221; **f** 625 2224;
e res1@chobemarinalodge.com; ☝ www.chobemarinalodge.com 🔲 🔳
Set on the river's edge, this sleek new lodge has made an admirable attempt to facilitate disabled guests. A wheelchair is available at reception & 1 bathroom has a roll-in shower. The solid, wooden walkways are step-

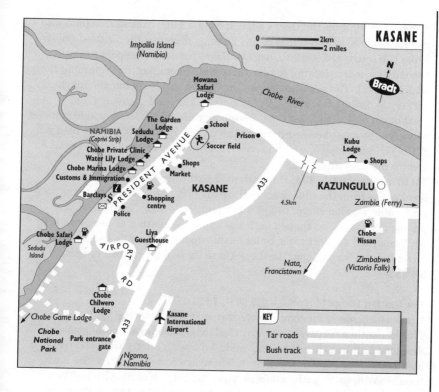

free throughout the public areas & stone & tile access routes have ramps between height differences. 1 public toilet has level doorway (88) & the toilet itself (46) has 70cm free space beside & in front for transfers. The conference room & main dining room are up stairs (2 flights of 11), but food can be brought down to the ground-floor Mokoros Restaurant (usually only used for breakfast & lunch) if that is easier. Tables here are 66cm. A steep ramp leads to the natural rock infinity pool, which merges magically with the river & is entered using steps.

Room 51: Closest to the main lodge, & has the most accessible bathroom. Doorway (88) is up 2 steps (9), but a wooden ramp was available in 2008 & a permanent, step-free solution was planned for early 2009; bed (51) has light switch, transfer space & phone; highest switch is 105cm; desk is 64cm; door to ensuite (87) is level; small roll-in shower (plastic seat is available) has star taps (114), & fixed showerhead; washbasin is not 'roll-under'; toilet (43) has side & front transfer space. Other rooms have baths with fixed showerheads. **$$$$$**

Mowana Safari Lodge (107 rooms) ☎ 625 0300; f 625 0301;
e resmowana@cresta.co.bw; ⌂ www.cresta-hospitality.com 🔲 🛏
With a lot of timber-frame stairways & wooden decking, the Mowana feels relaxed &, in a way, more lodge than hotel-like. It has been thoughtfully

285

designed & built on the river's edge around a huge baobab tree (*mowana* means 'baobab' in Setswana) & has 2 rooms designed for disabled guests. From the courtyard, smooth, bricked floors run step-free past reception, becoming wooden decking & tiles through the complex, but retaining their uniform level. The main restaurant is also on this level but the lunch servery is down a few steps. A public toilet has level doorway (75), washbasin (65) with lever taps, 2 support rails (87) & front & side transfer space. Steps must be used to reach the Savuti Bar, the shop, the boat jetty & the swimming pool, which is entered using steps without a handrail & has an inside seating ledge.

Twin rooms 301 & 304: Have adapted bathrooms & are about 80m on level paths from the dining area. Doorway (79) has 1 step & steep, removable wooden ramp; bed (57) has transfer space, light switch & phone; desk is 72cm; shaped bath has extended seating at head-end & 2 wall-mounted support rails; toilet has 2 support rails. The Cresta website has a helpful 'virtual tour' facility, where these features can be seen. **$$$$$**

The Garden Lodge (8 rooms) ✆ 625 0051; **f** 625 0577;
e gabi@thegardenlodge.com; ◌ www.thegardenlodge.com 🄿
This is another relatively new river lodge in Kasane, & another nicely designed building. It has an airy main *lapa* with a lofty thatched roof & a lush lawn slopes down to the river. There are 5 steps down to the lawn, then smooth, brick paths allow easy pushing if you're on wheels. The swimming pool & dining area are level from reception but all the rooms are up at least 2 steps & have step-in showers. **$$$$**

Kubu Lodge (15 rooms) ✆ 625 0312; **e** kubu@botsnet.bw; ◌ www.kubulodge.net
🄳
Kubu is 9km from Kasane, in the direction of Kazungula. As with all the riverside lodges, it's built on a slope. Unfortunately, however, the stilted – though very attractive – wooden chalets are each up several steep steps, & the path through the lawn from reception is uneven. This is not a place for wheelchairs, but unsteady walkers may be able to cope. There is a level but loosely slabbed pathway between the reception & the excellent restaurant, & the tables are 68cm. The public toilet is up 5 steps from the restaurant & the simple but smart pool is a couple of mins' walk away, again with steps.

Room 4: The closest to reception, but is up 5 steep steps. Doorways are >77cm & the bathroom has a step-in shower (21). **$$$**

Chobe Safari Lodge (71 rooms, 11 rondavels) ✆ 625 0336; **f** 625 0437;
e reservations@chobelodge.co.bw; ◌ www.chobesafarilodge.com 🄾 🖂
This long-established lodge is well positioned on the riverside close to the national park, & has undergone major refurbishments in recent years. There are now several room types, ranging from river rooms, rondavels &

the newer safari rooms. The last are the most wheelchair accessible, with some having no steps. The well-designed main *lapa* has smooth tiles & polished cement floors, with ramped areas connecting the various levels. The restaurant & buffet have no steps & tables are 74cm. The public toilet (45) has a level doorway (76), 2 support rails (98), front & side transfer space, a low mirror & lever taps. A long ramp leads to the attractive swimming pool, which is entered using steps & has seating inside it.

Safari rooms: Several have no step. Doorway (76) has small threshold only; bed (57) has light switch, transfer space & phone; highest switch is 135cm; desk is 69cm; door to ensuite is level; bath (57) has star taps in middle of opposite long side & has transfer space; step-in shower (15) & washbasin have star taps; toilet (40) has front transfer space only.

River rooms: The closest to the bulk of the lodge & some have level entrances, but their bathrooms are too small for a wheelchair. They do have support rails above the bath, so may suit people who can stand but need something to hold.

Rondavels: have a bricked, sometimes narrow pathway then 3 steps to doorways, small bathrooms & step-in showers. **$$$**

Water Lily Lodge (10 rooms) ✆ 625 1775; **e** janala@botsnet.bw; ⌂ www.janalasafaris.com [1]
The whole lodge is housed within 1 large, round building with a central fountain. A cement ramp leads up into the circle from the car park & all rooms & the restaurant are up 1 step (17) from here. Dining tables are 62cm, the standard public toilet is up 1 step & the bean-shaped swimming pool is behind the building, across a short lawn & up 1 step.
Rooms: Doorway (76) is up 1 step (17); beds (56) have light switches (about 60cm above beds) & transfer space; highest switch is 140cm; desk is 67cm; doorway into the ensuite (67) opens into the bathroom, leaving no wheelchair space; step-in shower (17) has fixed showerhead; washbasin is 69cm & toilet is 42cm. **$$**

Liya Guesthouse (6 rooms) ✆ 625 1450; **e** liyaglo@botsnet.bw [1]
The Liya is a relaxed guesthouse in the quiet backstreets of Kasane offering budget accommodation. it is a few kilometres from the river, but consequently closer to the airport. The house is up 1 step (17) & has 5 rooms, with Room 3 having an en-suite bathroom with enough space for a wheelchair. Meals can be provided & the dining table is 70cm.
Room 3: Doorway (76) is level; small dbl bed has transfer space & light switch; doorway into the ensuite (64) is level; bathroom has step-in shower, washbasin (67) has round taps; toilet has front & side transfer space. **$**

Sedudu Lodge (12 rooms) ✆ 625 1748 [3] ▭
Owned & run by Maggie, the Sedudu is basically a large house that has been converted into tourist accommodation. The restaurant is up 5 steps

behind the building, on a level, brick pathway on the way to the river, but the courtyard is lit so tables are often set at ground level. A block of twin rooms has been added outside, but these are small & are all up 3 steps. A campsite is being built for 2009. The best option for mobility-impaired guests is the en-suite inside rooms, which vary slightly in size & style. From the parking area, 2 steps enter the house then a tiled floor leads to the clean, sparsely decorated rooms. A mixture of bathroom facilities – baths & step-in showers – is available, but the first dbl bedroom from the entrance is perhaps the most notable.

First dbl bedroom: Bed (66) has light switch & transfer space; highest switch is 145cm; doorway to ensuite (74) is level; bath (56) has an extended flat end, fitted handles & a handheld showerhead; toilet (42) has front access only. **$**

WHERE TO EAT

There are no restaurants in Kasane that make an effort to be wheelchair accessible, but most are ground floor and help will be available to overcome the odd step. The majority of safari visitors tend to eat in their place of lodging.

The Gallery Africana & Coffee Bar (*Audi Shopping Centre;* ✆ *625 0949;* ⊘ *07.30–16.30 Mon–Fri, 07.30–12.30 Sat;* **$$**) is one independent eatery that may be worth visiting. It provides breakfasts and light lunches and also houses a small art gallery.

OTHER PRACTICALITIES

The centre of Kasane is small, and services are within a kilometre of each other. Barclays Bank is next to the Spar and there are also several bureaux de change in the area, which normally have longer opening hours. Cape to Cairo (opposite the Spar) is one, and it doubles as an internet café. More broadband outlets are also appearing as Kasane continues to grow.

Medical services

Chobe Private Clinic (✆ *625 1555*) and **Chobe Medical Centre** (✆ *625 0888*) are the two best local medical clinics. People with serious medical emergencies would be flown to Johannesburg.

WHAT TO SEE AND DO

The Chobe River and Chobe National Park are the lifeblood of Kasane. Game drives into the park are the main way of seeing the area, but **river cruises** and **motorboat trips** are a very worthwhile alternative approach. Most itineraries should spend at least two nights here allowing time for several game drives and at least one water-based excursion, but consider taking more if you need extra time for daily practicalities. If sitting in a boat appeals more, cruising between quiet pools, watching elephants lumbering down to the river's edge to drink and training binoculars on the tiny water birds that flit between reed fronds, then it might be worth hiring a motorboat privately for an early morning trip. The majority of package trips will already include these activities, but your hotel or lodge will be able to amend or add bookings.

LIVINGSTONE AND THE VICTORIA FALLS

When, in 1855, local people first led David Livingstone to what they called 'Mosi-oa-Tunya' ('the Smoke that Thunders'), the explorer could hardly have imagined that a few generations later this area would become the adrenalin capital of Africa. There's no doubt his heart beat faster marvelling at the largest sheet of falling water in the world – on average, about ten million litres plummet more than a hundred metres every second – but the concept of tourist helicopter flights and bungee jumps would have been beyond his imagination. Nowadays, Victoria Falls (the English name that Livingstone gave this World Heritage Site) is one of the first boxes to be ticked on many southern itineraries, and most visitors spend at least three or four days here.

Livingstone the town was, of course, named after the explorer. It has always been much bigger and more planned than the town of Victoria Falls, its opposite number on the Zimbabwe side of the Zambezi, and with a strategic location on the Zambian/Zimbabwean border (and just an hour's drive from Botswana and Namibia), it has long been a traveller's rest. Its proximity to the falls only heightens its appeal and a wealth of activities to suit all tastes has grown around it.

At Victoria Falls, the whole Zambezi River rolls over a lip of rock almost 2km wide, sending a plume of spray half a kilometre into the air. Although the surrounding Mosi-oa-Tunya National Park is essentially dry bush, this moisture creates a permanent mini-ecosystem in which an impressive array of flora and fauna thrives, providing very decent game viewing. Canoe, elephant-back and walking safaris complement standard game drives; boat trips, ballooning and game fishing further enhance the list of activities, and adrenalin junkies can get wet and worried by negotiating the whitewater rapids in a raft or stay dry but frightened by bungee jumping the 110m from Victoria Falls Bridge. Calmer pursuits like cultural shows and a crocodile farm are available in Livingstone, where the nightlife can be as wild or as refined as you wish. Lastly, but most importantly, viewing the falls is the ultimate highlight and can be done on foot, by microlight, or by helicopter.

GENERAL INFORMATION

Access summary

Zambia's rapidly developing tourism industry has not yet had time to glance back and cater fully to less mobile visitors. Livingstone is a good example; new accommodation is mushrooming in this boomtown, but extremely good access is scarce, especially in lower-budget accommodation. More positively,

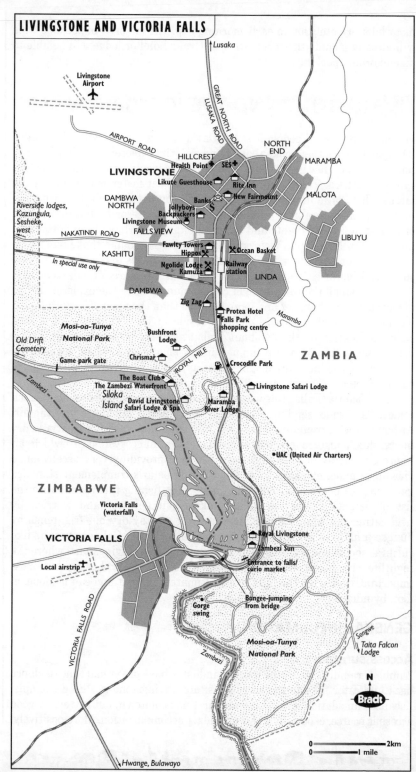

LIVINGSTONE AND VICTORIA FALLS

↑ Lusaka

Livingstone Airport

GREAT NORTH ROAD

LUSAKA ROAD

AIRPORT ROAD

HILLCREST
Health Point ✚ SES ✚
LIVINGSTONE
Likute Guesthouse
Rite Inn
Banks New Fairmount
DAMBWA NORTH
Jollyboys Backpackers
Livingstone Museum
FALLS VIEW

NORTH END
MARAMBA
MALOTA
LIBUYU

Riverside lodges, Kazungula, Sesheke, west

NAKATINDI ROAD
KASHITU
In special use only
DAMBWA

Fawlty Towers
Hippos
Ngolide Lodge
Kamuza
Zig Zag

Ocean Basket
Railway station
LINDA

Maramba

Protea Hotel
Falls Park shopping centre

Mosi-oa-Tunya National Park
Old Drift Cemetery
Game park gate

Bushfront Lodge
Chrismar
ROYAL MILE

Crocodile Park

Zambezi

ZAMBIA

The Boat Club
The Zambezi Waterfront
Siloka Island
David Livingstone Safari Lodge & Spa

Livingstone Safari Lodge
Maramba River Lodge

UAC (United Air Charters)

ZIMBABWE

Victoria Falls (waterfall)

VICTORIA FALLS

Local airstrip ✚

Royal Livingstone
Zambezi Sun
Entrance to falls/ curio market

Bungee-jumping from bridge

Gorge swing

VICTORIA FALLS ROAD

Mosi-oa-Tunya National Park

Zambezi

Songwe
Taita Falcon Lodge

N

Bradt

0 ———————— 2km
0 ———————— 1 mile

↓ Hwange, Bulawayo

several hotels and lodges have made efforts and most people should be able to find suitable rooms at a price they can afford. The town is easily reached with excellent road and air links and the next stage will be that the intense competition will drive the exploitation of niche markets; disability is one so access should improve.

Local operators

For local operators catering to people with mobility issues, plus some mainstream operators who have shown a genuine interest in this market, see *Chapter 1, Specialised operators in Africa*, pages 20–3.

GETTING THERE AND AWAY

By road

Lusaka is 473km from Livingstone on tar-sealed road, which is good in stretches but intermittently pot-holed. Allow six or seven hours for this journey. Kazungula border post, which unites Zambia with Botswana, Zimbabwe and Namibia, is 60km to the west of Livingstone. Here, a car ferry crosses the Zambezi to Botswana. From there, Kasane (next to Chobe National Park) is about 15km further. The Ngoma border (crossing into Namibia) is about 50km further on from Kasane. Zimbabwe's Victoria Falls is a short drive (about 10km) over Victoria Falls Bridge. All these roads are surfaced with smooth tar but at least an hour should be included for each border crossing. Most buses leave Livingstone from the busy area in front of Barclays Bank and none have specialised access for restricted mobility; see *Chapter 3, Public transport*, page 89.

By rail

The little-used passenger train to Lusaka has no access for people with disabilities.

By air

Livingstone International Airport (℡ *021 332 1153/3322;* **m** *0977 790733;* **f** *021 332 4235;* **e** *nacliv@zamnet.zm*) lies about 5km from the town. It currently handles flights from Lusaka and other cities in Africa but will soon be receiving direct European flights. There is a spacious, step-free toilet with ramped access (but no support rails) at departures and arrivals. The airport claims to have an aisle chair on site but one traveller reports being manually carried by several people from their plane, so it might be worth clearly explaining what is needed, then waiting for it to be found; in smaller airports staff are not as used to using this equipment and might not be sure of its whereabouts. (For access issues in small airfields, see page 92.)

GETTING AROUND

Localised areas in Livingstone are easily explored on foot, but anyone wanting to go to the falls, the airport or even from one end of town to the

VICTORIA FALLS

An understanding of how the falls were created – and an appreciation of their immense size – can only really be obtained from the air. There are no towering mountains or cliffs in the region; the colossal Zambezi River flows through a gentle valley, the base layer of which is a sheet of basalt. The water has found a fissure in this rock floor, and over time – many millennia – has forced and worn a chasm into which it now tumbles. This is the current Victoria Falls. Only once you look from above do you see that this has happened seven times already; each time, the new falls is a few hundred metres upstream from the old one. The result is that the fallen water now batters its way through a slalom of deep rock gorges, every one an ancient site of the falls, before relaxing into a series of milder rapids and eventually spilling into Lake Kariba.

other will need transport. There is no accessible public transport in Livingstone, but Hemingways (see *Chapter 1, Specialised operators in Africa,* page 22) have vehicles adapted for wheelchairs. For those who can use them, local taxis are easily arranged from your accommodation or found at their stands on the street.

WHERE TO STAY

In and around Livingstone

Royal Livingstone (173 rooms) Mosi-oa-Tunya Rd; ✆ 021 332 1122;
f 021 332 2128; **e** falls@sunint.co.za; ⌂ www.suninternational.com ⬛ ⬛ ⬛
The Royal Livingstone is fittingly regal, with luxurious furnishings & attentive service. Located 15mins' walk from the falls, & with its own private falls viewpoint (shared only with its sister hotel, the Zambezi Sun (see following entry), it also has the ideal location. Add to this the fact that it is in the national park, so grazing & browsing animals are often seen, plus the bonus that it has 2 extremely accessible rooms, then this hotel may be the one stop that's required for people who struggle to get around. A wheelchair is available from the front desk & the public toilet behind reception has an accessible cubicle with transfer space, 2 support rails, a low mirror & lever taps in the washbasin (65). A golf car can take less ambulant guests to the falls viewpoint. The ground is smooth & level from the car park to reception. 2 steps (avoidable using a ramp) lead to the elegant dining areas where the tables are 70cm high. The large pool is set in a lawn, 20m away, & has stepped entry with a handrail & a seating ledge inside. Rooms 5061 & 5064 are adapted & apparently identical & both face the river.
Room 5061: Doorway (77) is level; dbl bed (56) has transfer space, phone & light switch; highest light switch is 97cm; desk is 58cm; en-suite doorway (77) is level; roll-in shower has seat (48) with front & side

transfer space, handheld showerhead, lever tap (105) & 2 support rails (82 & 73) beside & behind seat; washbasin (66) has lever taps & low mirror; toilet (42) has front & side transfer space & 2 support rails, 1 beside (85) & 1 behind (85). **$$$$$**

Zambezi Sun (212 rooms) Mosi-oa-Tunya Rd; ☎ 021 332 1122; **f** 021 332 2128; **e** falls@sunint.co.za; ⌂ www.suninternational.com
This is the more laid-back of the 2 Sun hotels with the theme reflecting traditional Africa. The ochre walls resemble those of earth-built village compounds, while the interiors are decorated with colourful ethnic murals. The rooms themselves are spacious & 2 have been designed for disabled guests. The Sun shares a private falls viewpoint with the Royal Livingstone, a wheelchair is available from reception & 2 accessible public toilets have level doors (74), 2 support rails & a washbasin (64) with lever taps but high mirror. The restaurant/buffet areas are all level or with shallow ramps & tables are 69cm. There is level access to the pool & it is entered using steps & a handrail. The 2 adapted rooms are identical inside, but Room 3120 faces the pool & Room 3121 faces the gardens. The doorway to Room 3121 is slightly narrower, at 71cm. Standard rooms have baths (49) & step-in showers (10), but no wheelchair space in the bathroom.
Room 3120: Doorway (74) is level; 2 sgl beds (52) have transfer space, phones & light switches; highest switch is 100cm; wardrobe & hangers are lowered; door to ensuite (75) is level; roll-in shower has flip-down seat (51), handheld showerhead, round taps (96) & 2 support rails (82), 1 beside & 1 behind seat; washbasin (70) has lever taps & low mirror; toilet (50) has front & side transfer space & 2 rails, 1 beside & 1 behind it. **$$$$$**

David Livingstone Safari Lodge & Spa (77 rooms) ☎ 031 310 3333; **f** 031 310 6949; **e** ceres@threecities.co.za; ⌂ www.threecities.co.za
Set on the Zambezi, near the Waterfront Hotel, this lofty new lodge had planned to include 2 fully accessible rooms (numbers 136 & 137). Unfortunately, although they are more spacious than the other options in the hotel, their bathrooms stop short of perfect (support rails were 'on order' in 2008). The lodge itself has smooth, bricked & paved pathways, although these are too steep in places, & the pool is reached via a slope then 7 steps; it is also entered using steps. The lunch diner has ramped access & dinner is served on the first-floor restaurant, for which an accessible lift was in place but not yet functional when I visited in 2008. Tables are 72cm.
Rooms 136: Doorways (73) are level, after a steep ramp from reception; bed (57) has light switch, phone & transfer space; desk is 77cm; patio with river view is level; door to ensuite (68) is level; roll-in shower has tiled seat (50), wide doorway (84), fixed showerhead & star taps (125) but is too small to use comfortably in a wheelchair; washbasin has no knee access, star taps & a low mirror; toilet (46) has front transfer space only.

Room 137: the same as Room 136, except has standalone bath (62) making the bathroom less spacious & has connecting door to Room 138, so may suit families or those with assistants. **$$$$**

Chrismar Hotel (60 rooms) Sichango Rd; ☎ 021 332 3141; **e** chrismar@zamnet.zm; ⏻ www.chrismar.co.zm 🄿🖼 🛏

With airy, clean lines & minimal furnishings, there's a pleasing sense of space about the Chrismar. 4 rooms are already designed to be accessible to wheelchairs, & with a further 40 being built more detailed inclusion is planned. From the car park, access through the hotel is level or gently ramped using polished stone indoors & crazy paving outside. Dining tables are 74cm & the restaurant & buffet are step-free. The pool (with floating bar) is up 1 step with 6 to enter it & the public toilet is level but has no specific disability access.

Rooms 54–57: Although these 4 rooms are almost the furthest from the main complex, doorways (89) are ramped; bedroom doors (76) are level; beds (53) have light switches, transfer space & phones; highest switch is 122cm; desk is 81cm; door to ensuite (67) is level; bath has extended flat area at both ends, & has fitted handles; step-in shower (15) has lever tap but fixed showerhead & narrow door (58); washbasin has no knee space but has lever taps; toilet (40) has front transfer space only. There are connecting doors between Rooms 54 & 55 & between Rooms 56 & 57, making them suitable for families or anyone travelling with a personal assistant. **$$$**

The Zambezi Waterfront (21 rooms, 30 tents) Off Sichango Rd, near the Boat Club; contact Safari Par Excellence; ☎ 021 332 0606/7; **f** 021 332 0609; **e** waterfront@safpar.com; ⏻ www.safpar.net 🄵

One of the stalwarts of the Livingstone tourist scene, the Waterfront offers affordable, dependable food & accommodation & is the hub of much of Livingstone's nightlife. Reception is up 1 step from the level parking area. From there, the bar, dining & small pool are up a short ramp. The main pool is at ground level <50m from reception & with 2 steps to enter it. There are no fully accessible rooms, although the ground-floor twins may suit some visitors. The executive & family rooms are all upstairs & the 2-person dome tents are set on cement platforms (up 1 step) & share ablutions.

Ground-floor standard twin rooms: Doorways (75) have 1 small step; beds (60) have transfer space & light switch; door to ensuite 67) is level; bathroom has just enough wheelchair turning space with door closed; step-in shower is 25cm; toilet (42) has front transfer space only. **$$$**

Protea Hotel Livingstone (80 rooms) Mosi-oa-Tunya Rd; ☎ 021 332 4630; **e** reservations@phliving stone.co.zm; ⏻ www.proteahotels.com 🄿

With a handy location next to the mall in the centre of town, Livingstone's Protea is a perfectly functional hotel. It opened in 2008, & is therefore still spick & span & thoroughly modern, but it lacks that touch of character necessary to make a stay more memorable. Public areas, including reception, pool (with stepped entry but no handrail) & restaurant (tables are 72cm) are all on 1 level. The public toilet opposite reception is also level, although it has no access features & has a narrow doorway (58). There are plans to make 1 ground-floor room more inclusive, but currently they are all similarly furnished.

Rooms: Doorway (76) is level; bed (52) has light switch, phone & transfer space; desk is 58cm; doorway into the ensuite (66) has threshold (2); step-in shower is 9cm; washbasin has no knee access & toilet (43) has front transfer space only. **$$$**

The Bushfront Lodge (13 rooms) Zambia reservations; ☎ 021 332 2446; f 021 332 0609; e bushfront@safpar.com; ⏚ www.safpar.net [2] [▨]

With modest but clean thatched chalets, spread around a lightly wooded site 5km from the falls, Bushfront Lodge gives a good-value option without going budget. It's not easy wheeling everywhere, but a maximum of 2 steps must be mounted to reach most areas. Reception, the heart-shaped pool & simple diner – where tables are 58cm – are on 1 level, 2 steps up from ground level. The standard public toilet is 1 step up from the pool level. Brick pathways are level, but narrow in places & incomplete – they peter into hard-earth tracks in parts. Room 9 is the closest to reception & is typical of the 10 standard rooms. The family room (number 14) may suit larger groups.

Room 9: Doorway (77) is up 1 step; dbl bed (60) has light switch & transfer space; cement floor has woven mat; door into the ensuite (84) is level; large step-in shower (10) has stone seat (52) & daringly mimics Victoria Falls, by being stone-built with plants set in crevices & the water falls from a rock ledge above head-height; washbasin has no knee space; toilet (42) has side transfer space only.

Room 14: dbl door is up 1 step (14); 3 beds (65) have transfer space & light switch; door to ensuite (77) is level; standard, tiled bathroom has bath (55) with narrow (65) transfer space, fitted handles & handheld showerhead; step-in shower (15) has narrow glass door. **$$$**

Livingstone Safari Lodge (11 chalets) m 095 583 2168/097 740 3881; e livingstone-lodge@microlink.zm; ⏚ www.livingstonebushlodge.com [0]

Despite the rather sprawling appearance of this lodge, it is surprisingly accessible. There are no disability gadgets in the bathrooms, but access routes are generally smooth & hard, if a little steep, & the charismatic Dutch owner – who bears a striking resemblance to the eminent Scottish explorer – has tried to make inclusion part of the design. Doorways are wider than normal & paths between rooms & the reception/bar area are reasonably hard with built-in ramps avoiding steps. The pretty pool is also a long walk on a gravel path & has ladder & water slide (!) entry. Anyone with mobility problems & arriving in their own vehicle should use it to get around.

Room Zoet: Doorway (80) has a brick ramp; bed (51) has a light switch & transfer space; highest switch is 125cm; door to ensuite (77) has threshold (1); shower tray is set into floor, although a wooden trellis is apparently available that would make this roll-in; bath (51) has transfer space & round taps set in the centre of the long side; washbasin (71) has round taps; toilet (36) has front transfer space only. **$$**

Ngolide Lodge (16 rooms) 110 Mosi-oa-Tunya Rd; ☎/f 021 332 1091/2; e ngolide@zamnet.zm; ⏚ www.ngolidelodge.com [1]
The Ngolide has a useful location at the edge of the town centre, & is a compact, secure little compound. The solid walls draped with a high thatched roof give a cool, shady, but slightly sombre feel to the lodge, although the rooms are airy & open. An ocean of rocks greets visitors attempting to enter via the front door, then there are 2 steps down to reception. Wheelchair users are advised to skirt round behind the building, where entry is level & smooth. The ground surface inside is still rough & the highly rated Indian restaurant is up 1 step with tables 65cm.
Rooms: Doorways (76) all up 1 step (10); beds (60) have phone, light switch & just enough transfer space; doorway into the ensuite is 76cm; step-in shower is 10cm; toilet has no wheelchair access. **$$**

Rite Inn (9 rooms) 301 Mose St; ☎ 021 332 3264; e riteinv@zamnet.zm [1]
Just around the corner from the Likute Guesthouse (see below), Rite Inn (owned by Mr Rite) is a more accessible option. It is compact & surrounded by high walls, but these – painted peach with tidy white trim – only serve to brighten the place. It has a cluster of steps (4) at the entrance, but once these are overcome then the restaurant is up 1 small step (10) & has a nifty sliding door with threshold (2). Tables are 75cm & the uncluttered bar is up another step (20). The inviting pool is entered using 4 steps & has a handy seating ledge on each side.
Room 10: The largest room, with a jacuzzi, has a level entrance. Room 1 (a dbl) has 1 step (5) & other rooms have larger steps. Doorways are generally around 75cm, bathrooms contain step-in showers & toilets have front transfer space only. **$$**

Maramba River Lodge (25 tents & chalets); ☎ 021 332 4198; f 021 332 3130; e maramba@zamnet.zm; ⏚ www.maramba-zambia.com [2]
Only 4km from Victoria Falls, & a similar distance from the centre of town, Maramba is close to all that's essential in Livingstone. Despite this, its woodland setting on a bluff above the dense flow of the Maramba River makes it feel like it could be deep in the bush. The safari-style tents & natural rock swimming pool only add to the natural ambiance. Of the wide range of accommodation on offer, the luxury tents are most suited to disability. The restaurant has level access, tables are 76cm & the

bar/lounge is up 1 step. The pool is up 2 steps then down 3 & access throughout is via bumpy paths.

Luxury tents: Doorway (81) is up 2 steps; beds (50) have light switches & transfer space; highest switch is 156cm; door to ensuite (76) is level; step-in shower is 25cm; washbasin has no knee clearance; toilet (45) has front transfer space only. The chalets & family rooms are similarly appointed, with narrower doorways. **$$**

New Fairmount Hotel (104 rooms) Mosi-oa-Tunya Rd; ✆ 021 332 0723; **f** 021 332 1490; **e** nfhc@zamnet.zm; ⌂ www.newfairmounthotel.com
This large hotel, with dazzling white walls & a labyrinthine, medina-like interior does make some effort to facilitate wheeled visitors. Once the 4 steps from the pavement are mounted, smooth cement access routes run through arched corridors & the various levels are connected by short, steep ramps. The standard public toilet at reception has a level doorway (64). A ramp is available to help scale the 3 steps to the main restaurant & tables are 66cm. The swimming pool can be reached without steps (& is entered using 4) but has no seating or handrail.

Executive dbls & sgls: Those in '2' block & '3' block often have level entries; standard rooms are all up 3 steps. Doorways are generally around 70–75cm but all bathrooms have baths with hand-held showerheads in baths – there are no roll-in or step-in showers. **$$**

Likute Guesthouse (14 rooms) 62 Likute Way; ✆ 021 332 3661
If steps put you off, then the Likute is one to be avoided. It's a clean, friendly little guesthouse but the obstacle course begins at the entrance with 2 flights of 3 steps split by a drop of 2. The rooms share a level concrete veranda which is 4 steps up from the ground, then all doorways are up 1 from there. Most rooms have showers; 1 has a bath although this one has different levels in the room. There's no swimming pool & the bar is up 3 steps from the courtyard. **$$**

Zig Zag (12 rooms) ✆ 021 332 2814; **e** info@zigzagzambia.com; ⌂ www.zigzagzambia.com
Close to the railway crossing in the centre of town, this funky little B&B has made a conscious effort to include wheelchair users. Although the ablutions won't suit everyone, it is the most accessible of the cheaper accommodation in Livingstone. From the parking area there's a narrow cement ramp (76) to the row of rooms. The swimming pool – with stepped entry & a seating ledge – is about 30m from reception, over pebbles, a loose brick path then lawn. The popular restaurant has level entry & tables are >65cm.

Rooms: Doorway is level; 2 sgl beds (53) have transfer space & light switch; highest switch is 100cm; doorway into ensuite (78) is level; step-in shower (8) has round taps (89) & fixed showerhead; washbasin (74) has reasonably low mirror; toilet (37) has side transfer space only. **$$**

Jollyboys Backpackers 34 Kanyata Rd; ✆/f 021 332 4229; **e** jollybs@zamnet.zm;
🖰 www.backpackzambia.com 3️⃣

Built high above the town, & with a cleverly designed stairway leading to
a commanding falls-view lookout, Jollyboys retains its position among the
best budget options in Livingstone. Its steep setting doesn't sound
appealing to those with mobility problems, but the topmost entrance is on
the same level as reception & rooms. From there, the rocky swimming pool
& bar/dining area is down a steep ramp & 3 steps. Dining tables are 70cm.
As well as camping & standard backpackers' dorms with shared ablutions,
Jollyboys has several dbl & twin rooms with private en-suite bathrooms.
These generally have level entry doorways (70), step-in showers & toilets
with front transfer space only. **$**

Fawlty Towers Lodge & International Backpackers 216 Mosi-oa-Tunya Rd; ✆
021 332 3432; **e** ahorizon@zamnet.zm; 🖰 www.adventure-africa.com 1️⃣

For those on wheels, or with walking problems, the biggest plus with
Fawlty Towers is its level setting. The first negative is the bed of pebble
stones that must be crossed in the car park. Once that's done, 1 step takes
you up to reception then 1 step down leads to the large courtyard, where
the funky swimming pool has level access & is entered using 2 steps.
B/fast is normally served upstairs, but can easily be brought down if
necessary; other meals are normally taken at neighbouring – & ground-
floor – Hippo's (see *Where to eat*, page 300), where the tables are 74cm. As
well as the standard backpackers' dorms sharing ablutions, there are both
dbl & sgl rooms downstairs, surrounding the courtyard. These are reached
using the rough brick paths or crossing the smooth lawn, then climbing 1
small step (14) to the walkway that runs around, joining room doorways.
Rooms: 1 dbl & 1 twin both have level entry from the walkway. Doorway
is 76cm; bed (50) has transfer space & light switch; highest switch is
145cm; door to ensuite (82) opens to the room, making the small bathroom
more spacious; step-in shower (8) has star taps (82) & fixed showerhead,
but there's a gap of only 54cm between the washbasin (74) & the wall to
get there; toilet (43) has front transfer space only. **$**

Outside Livingstone
Taita Falcon Lodge (7 chalets) ✆/f 021 332 1850; **e** taita-falcon@zamnet.zm;
🖰 www.taitafalcon.com 1️⃣ 🖊️

This pleasant lodge is a 45min drive from Livingstone, & has a gasp-
inducing location peering over the edge of the gorge onto Zambezi
whitewater 100m below. There are 7 chalets (each can be made dbl, twin or
trpl), of which numbers 3 & 4 are closest to the restaurant & parking area.
All entrances into chalets & restaurant are via sliding doors. Pathways
throughout are hard & level, 2 steps approach the simple swimming pool &
the public toilet area is large with both front & side transfer space.
Chalet 3: Has a ramp into the spacious shower whereas all other rooms
have a small step (usually a natural stone border) into theirs; toilets can

be reached in wheelchairs but have front transfer space only. **$$$$$**

Thorntree River Lodge (9 chalets) Contact Safari Par Excellence; ☎ 021 332 0606/7; **f** 021 332 0609; **e** zaminfo@safpar.com; ✆ www.thorntreelodge.net 🔲
Thorntree Lodge is about 15km upstream from the falls & just within Mosi-oa-Tunya National Park. The stone-build chalets are sturdy & rustic, with immaculately thatched roofs & lie in neatly manicured lawns next to the Zambezi. Inside, they are spacious & well appointed, & although none are designed for disability, some may suit particular mobility needs. Pathways around the lodge are smooth & level, being made from tile & hard-packed calcrete, & there is only the occasional sgl step around the dining/bar area. Tables are 74cm. A drainage trench (about 15cm wide & 10cm deep) is the only hindrance on the way to the attractive, stone swimming pool, which has stepped entry with no handrail.
Camelthorn Room 6: The closest to reception. Veranda is up 1 step then dbl sliding door has threshold (2); the woven reed-mat floor is an earthy, natural touch, & slipping is less likely, but it can make for laborious wheelchair pushing; beds have transfer space & light switches; entrance into the ensuite (>100) is level; huge step-in shower (17) has fixed showerhead & star taps (106); twin washbasins (68) have high mirror & star taps; toilet (40) has front transfer space only. Other rooms are very similar in style & access, though the **Winterthorn Room** has a step down into the room, a corner bath (60) & a cavernous outside step-in shower (16). **$$$$$**

Tongabezi (15 cottages & houses) ☎ 021 332 7468; **f** 021 332 4282; **e** reservations@tongabezi.com; ✆ www.tongabezi.com 🔲
At 15km upstream from the falls, set on a wide, sweeping bend of the Zambezi, Tongabezi offers exceptional luxury in distinctive & stylish accommodation. Not content with just offering lavish riverside cottages, the unique option here is Sindabezi Island, a midstream sandbank where 5 open-fronted chalets look out into the flow of the magnificent river. Tongabezi main camp is set on the riverbank, down a steep slope from the road. On arrival, your vehicle can be driven further than the car park, avoiding the 21 steps to reception & using a gently sloped, hard, footworn path to reach the reception/bar/dining area. Tables are 66cm inside (up 1 step) & 74cm outside. The wooden jetty is down 8 steps from here. Although Sindabezi is 2km downstream, it is reached using a flat-bottomed boat, which has space for a wheelchair. Plenty of help is available around both sites.
None of the rooms have access designed for disability, but all mainland riverside chalets are ground floor & are a short walk with a few steps from reception. Bathrooms all have plenty of space & sumptuous, river-view bathtubs. Room 1, being the nearest, is usually the one recommended if mobility is an issue. On Sindabezi, pathways are deep, soft sand, but distances are short (<50m); outside showers have 1 step into them & toilets, although they are reached using soft, sandy paths, have lots of space around them. **$$$$$**

WHERE TO EAT

No restaurants, unless you use those in the Royal Livingstone & the Zambezi Sun hotels, have toilets designed with disability access. That said, most eating places are on the ground floor & staff will always be delighted to help guests over thresholds or up the one or two entrance steps. A few local favourites are:

Ocean Basket 82 Mosi-oa-Tunya Rd; ☎ 021 332 1274; ⊘ 12.00–22.00 daily. This fish restaurant (part of the large South African chain) has a great name in Livingstone. It is ground floor with tables in or outdoors. **$$$$**

Hippos Behind Fawlty Towers Lodge & International Backpackers; ☎ 021 332 3432; ⊘ 07.00–24.00 daily. This is a regular haunt of the local tourist industry workers, which is always the best vote of confidence. The wide-ranging menu should please all palates & it is entered using a doorway (76) up 1 step (15). Tables are 74cm. **$$**

Kamuza As the Indian restaurant in Ngolide Lodge (see *Where to stay*, page 296), the Kamuza is reputed to have the best Asian food in town. It's up 1 step, tables are 65cm & wheelchair users can avoid the sea of stones by entering from the rear. **$$**

OTHER PRACTICALITIES

The post office and several banks are bunched together in the centre of the older, northern part of town. Numerous bureaux de change are spread around Livingstone and the tourist office is further south, in front of Jollyboys Backpackers on Mosi-oa-Tunya Road. The Falls Park Shopping Centre, next to the new Protea Hotel, is the most accessible in Livingstone. It has several fast-food joints, a Spar supermarket, the Lynx pharmacy and all shops have level entrances while kerb cuts drop from the pavement to street level. Four parking bays are reserved for disabled customers and it is highly unlikely that official proof of disability will be asked for. Other shops and local markets in town are ground floor, but there's no guarantee that underfoot will be smooth and hard or that steps will be circumvented by ramps. As always, willing hands are only a smile away!

Medical services

For medical problems, the best-equipped local service is **Speciality Emergency Services (SES)** (*Corner of Likute Way & Obote Av;* ☎ *021 332 2330; emergency control centre;* ☎ *021 127 3302–7;* **m** *097 774 0307–8/095 577 2132;* **e** *seslivingstone@zamnet.zm;* ◌ *www.ses-zambia.com*).

A cheaper option may be **Health Point (Dr Shanks Chakravarty)** (*2644/401 Mushili Way (off Airport Rd close to Radio Mosi-oa-Tunya);* ☎ *021 332 2170;* **f** *021 332 3005;* **e** *shanks@zamnet.zm*).

People with serious medical emergencies would be evacuated by air to Maun or even Johannesburg.

WHAT TO SEE AND DO
With one of the world's greatest natural phenomena just a few kilometres away, Livingstone has developed a multitude of sideshows to keep travellers a day or two longer. Although recent years have seen a rush of adrenalin-inducing adventures, the traditional, more sedate pursuits still exist. The following selection is given in order (roughly) of increasing adventure level. Some are listed with the operator's contact details, but all the hotels, lodges and camps in the area (plus Safari Par Excellence, see page 23) will be able to make reservations. If you are travelling on an itinerary organised by an operator, you may have booked some of these activities in advance.

Curio markets
As in most tourist towns and there are craft markets where souvenir sellers and woodcarvers gather. Livingstone's best (next to the falls' entrance gate) has a superb selection and has no barriers to wheelchairs.

Livingstone Museum
(⊙ *from 09.00–16.30 daily;* 🎫 *US$5*) Just next to Jollyboys Backpackers, this extremely informative little museum is surprisingly accessible. There's a ramp up to reception, then the first level is step-free. The next display – The Stone Age – is suitably period with sandy floors to plough through, then a rather steep ramp takes you up to Natural History. A disabled toilet (37) for both men and women is next to reception and has front and side transfer space but no support rails.

Crocodile Park
(📞 *021 332 1733;* **e** *gwembesafaris@zamtel.zm;* 🖳 *www.gwembesafaris.com;* ⊙ *08.00–17.00 daily;* 🎫 *US$8*). The Crocodile Park is an absorbing diversion from the falls, and is an excellent – and perfectly safe – way to get photographs of these snappy creatures. For more cold-blooded entertainment, there is a snake display in the same compound with Africa's most dangerous, as well as some that can safely be handled. 2 steps lead up to the reception hut then there are 4 up to the wide (>80) croc-viewing boardwalk. The snake display is also up 2 steps and there is a spacious public toilet on the same level as the rather unadventurous snack bar.

Victoria Falls visits
(*US$10 pp Zambian side;* 🎫 *US$20 pp Zimbabwean side plus visa costs*) The undisputed – and unmissable – main attraction in the area is still Victoria Falls itself, and the most 'hands-on' way to experience this incredible sight is on foot. A visit near the end of the rains (March/April) will mean the flow is at its most powerful. If you follow the paths as far as they go at this time, you'll be soaked with spray, deafened by noise and will return absolutely exhilarated. Bring a rain jacket if you have one (or they can be hired at the falls' entrance), although this is no guarantee of keeping you dry. A ziplock waterproof bag (or similar) is recommended to thoroughly

protect any electrical/camera equipment. A dry-season, low-water visit should be an altogether calmer affair. The falls can be viewed from both the Zambian and Zimbabwean sides, and both are different yet equally memorable. Crossing to the Zimbabwean side will mean buying a visa to enter that country, the cost of which will vary depending on your nationality.

People with walking difficulties or wheelchair users will not be able to explore the maze of viewing paths completely, as some involve many steps. However, tracks are generally wide and hard (cement) and very rewarding views can be reached on level ground, or with no more than two steps; for example, the 'boiling pot' viewpoint on the Zambian side is up one step only. If you want to go further, then offers of help will be forthcoming. I waited for my friends at the top of one flight of stairs and was asked by countless passers-by if I wanted to be carried down.

Be warned, not only are there few seating areas, but guard rails – where they are present – are not always as strong as you would like and, depending on the season, the ground surface can be wet and potentially slippery. Less mobile visitors should take extra care.

River cruises

(☞ US$40–55) A serene cruise on the Zambezi is a superb way to watch the sunset and indulge in a little relaxed game viewing at the same time. Several different boats go out on the river, and standards of finesse vary according to price. The boats themselves are all entered in similar fashion – up two steps from a floating jetty – but crew will help wheelchair users to board. Once aboard, the second (and third in the case of *The African Queen*) decks are reached using stairs. Those less adept at climbing can have a perfectly satisfactory cruise on the bottom deck. Toilets on all boats are standard with narrow entrances (between 55cm and 60cm wide) so are only for those who can walk or stagger to some degree, and tables are all between 70cm and 75cm high. *The African Queen* and *African Princess* (departing, aptly, from a pier on the Royal Mile) are maybe most suited to disabled sailors, as their dock has an accessible toilet (see below). Other Zambian boats are the *Lady Livingstone* (leaving from the David Livingstone Lodge), the *MV Makumbi* (leaving from The Waterfront Hotel) and the less salubrious *Taonga*.

The African Queen and **African Princess**: a ramp bypasses the two steps from the parking area up to the main area. From here, the shop/restaurant is up one step (10) and spacious public toilets – with support rails (82) – have level access doorways (76). The floating jetty is down a total of about 20 shallow steps then there are two more up into the vessels.

Fishing excursions

(*Angle Zambia;* ☎ *332 7489;* **e** *anglezam@microlink.zm;* ⬧ *www. zambezifishing.com;* ☞ *US$120 half day; US$250 full day inc lunch*) Angle

Zambia is one of the most experienced fishing operators in the area. They use flat-bottomed aluminium boats where seats can be removed giving space for a wheelchair and their guides have done courses with Sun International about how to handle disable people. (See pages 93–4 for guidance on entering boats.)

Microlight flights
(*US$100 pp for 15mins; US$200 for 30mins*) Depending on the time you choose, you'll either do a trip over the falls or incorporate a game flight upriver. This is nothing short of exhilarating, but getting into the all-in-one jumpsuit may be the big stumbling block for people with stiff joints or high spasticity.

Helicopter flights
(*Usually in the region of US$200 for 15/30mins*) The two Zambian-based helicopter flights companies – United Air Charters and Batoka Sky – offer similar services, although UAC has a larger 6-seater 'Squirrel' helicopter, which is apparently easier to enter.

Batoka Sky (℡ 021 332 0058; e reservations@livingstonesadventures.co.zm; www.batokasky.com) operates from Maramba aerodrome; from the car park to the helipad is approximately 20m on level, cobbled ground; public toilets are wheelchair accessible with doorways of 71cm, two support rails (82) and toilet (42) has side and front transfer space.

United Air Charters (℡ 021 332 3095; e uac@microlink.zm; www.uaczam.com) is based in a sublime setting a few kilometres out of town on Baobab Ridge, with views over the falls area. A steep ramp leads to the viewing deck, cafeteria and helipad and public toilets here are also accessible with level doorways (76), two support rails (80) and toilet (42) with side and front transfer space.

Light aircraft flights
(*around US$140 pp; min 2 people*) Short flights (25–40mins) can be arranged from Livingstone Airport in small fixed-wing Cessna 206 aircraft. See *Livingstone Airport* (page 291) for facilities there.

Jet boats
(*US$100 pp inc gondola lift*) This relatively new method of adrenalin induction takes place in the Batoka Gorge, downstream from the wildest whitewater. A maximum of 11 people can be taken each time on the thrilling 30-minute trip, skidding over the surface, broadsiding past sheer rock faces and spinning out on flat water. Help may be needed to clamber onto the boat, but once squeezed inside all that is required is to hold on. Anyone unable to do this should enlist a couple of friends for help. Theoretically, this thrill should be possible for virtually anybody as, despite appearances, it is perfectly safe. The gondola (cable car) at rapid 25 is the usual method of

gorge entry, but various combinations can be used, including connecting with helicopter flights and rafting trips.

Whitewater rafting

(*A half-day trip is around US$120; full days are US$135*) Renowned as having some of the best whitewater rafting in the world, a day plummeting down the Zambezi is as exciting as it gets. The guides are highly trained and can usually give as breathtaking or as sedate a ride as their clients demand, but there is never a guarantee that the boat won't capsize, spilling its occupants into the river. Having said that, everyone wears life vests and highly disabled people have been taken before. The usual policy, apart from making sure the person is able to hold onto the boat him or herself, is for at least one, preferably two, able-bodied 'buddies' to accompany anyone who is less able. In the event of a roll over, these people would ensure the disabled person gets back to the boat. A device called an 'aquabac' has also been used by one client, giving more spinal support in the raft, but this would need to be taken from home (an 'aquabac' can be supplied by Equal Adventure in the UK (see *Chapter 1*, page 38).

The biggest problem with rafting for people with walking difficulties is its location; rafters normally traipse down steep, wooded pathways into the gorge, and trudge slowly up similar tracks at the end of the trip. This can be overcome by taking a helicopter flight and joining the raft at rapid 10, then leaving the gorge using the funicular railway at rapid 23 or the cable car at rapid 25. None of these options are intrinsically wheelchair accessible, so will require a little compromise, but it has been done before. Perhaps more importantly, this will be substantially more expensive. The only advice I can offer is that if you were planning a helicopter flight anyway, then it might be worth combining the two. Rafting here, if it appeals, is simply not to be missed.

Elephant riding

(*US$140 for a half day, plus US$10 park fees*) This very popular (book early!) activity involves a safari in Mosi-oa-Tunya National Park, both in bush and riverside regions, then a chance to help feed the elephants and learn about their welfare. It is also one where extra efforts have been made to cater for less-mobile clients. The normal sitting position is astride the elephant, but a new double-bench seat has been made that allows a side-saddle position. This will definitely suit some people as it results in much less sacral pressure, but is not a guaranteed solution for every disability. The 'stirrup' is a wooden beam hung on ropes and the rider is held in place by a waist belt.

Other, more active options

The activities described above are relatively sedentary, where the difficult part is getting into the vehicle or boat. For people who are more physically capable (not to say daring!) there are possibilities to do bungee jumping, abseiling, high wiring, gorge swinging, canoeing, horseriding and quad biking.

Segways

Finally, for the ultimate in modern game-drive technology, 'segways' (self-balancing, personal electric vehicles that are reminiscent of lawnmowers) can be hired at the Sun International complex; monkeys, baboons and various surprised herbivores can now be approached on two wheels!

SOUTH AFRICA AT A GLANCE

Location	Southern Africa, at the southern tip of the continent, bordered by Namibia, Botswana, Zimbabwe and Mozambique
Size	1,219,912km²
Climate	Extremely varied but with generally hot summers (Dec–Apr) and mild winters (May–Nov). Most of the interior is semi-arid, the east coast subtropical, and Johannesburg mostly dry and sunny, Cape Town is similar to Mediterranean Europe.
Population	48.8 million (2008 estimate)
Capital	Pretoria (administrative capital, population 2.4 million in 2007); Cape Town (legislative capital, population 3.5 million in 2007); Bloemfontein (judicial capital, population 370,000 in 2001)
Largest city	Johannesburg (3.9 million in 2007)
Currency	South African rand (R)
Rate of exchange	£1=R12.6; US$1=R8.4; €1=R11.2 (May 2009)
Language	There are 11 official languages including English (the accepted language of commerce and science)
Religion	Christianity, indigenous religions
Time	GMT +2
Electricity	220V, delivered at 50Hz; three round pins
Weights and measures	Metric
Public holidays	1 Jan, Human Rights Day (21 Mar), Good Friday, Easter Monday, Freedom Day (27 Apr), Workers' Day (1 May), Youth Day (16 Jun), National Women's Day (9 Aug), Heritage Day (24 Sep), Day of Reconciliation (16 Dec), 25–26 Dec
Tourist board	⌐ www.southafrica.net
International telephone code	+27
Further information:	For more information about any of the properties listed here, plus an extensive library of inclusive accommodation throughout South Africa, visit Karin Coetzee's website ⌐ www.disabledtravel.co.za.

8 South Africa

South Africa is the most economically well oiled of the countries featured here. Fertile farmland is efficiently tilled, mineral wealth is hauled from the ground and parts of middle-class suburbia resemble those in Europe. Cynics may be forgiven for thinking it's a little too tame for a safari, but huge chunks of wild land still exist. Kruger National Park is admired worldwide while places like Addo Elephant National Park are an example of how modest beginnings and room for expansion can allow nature to return to its eclectic best. This area of the country is also unaffected by malaria, so if you are unable to take prophylactics then Addo might be an ideal game-watching destination.

Many private game reserves – MalaMala being one – are responsibly managed and city visits give a taste of the country's diverse heritage. Johannesburg is touched on as a point of arrival and departure and Cape Town treated as a highlight in itself; it is generally accepted as being one of the most beautiful cities in the world.

GENERAL INFORMATION

ACCESS SUMMARY

South Africa has had the framework for easy travel in place for decades. On top of that, disability access is relatively good. There are no accessible public transport systems worth mentioning, but road networks are solid and airports usually have efficient passenger-assistance units. Inclusive bathrooms are an expectation, not a luxury, and nationwide standards of access are recognised, if not yet completely adhered to.

The 2010 FIFA World Cup has given the country the impetus to improve tourism facilities. In 2009 disability access movements were fighting for their share of this funding, with access guides to Johannesburg, Durban and Cape Town being some of their top priorities. See ⌐ www.access-africa.co.uk to obtain more information about these.

For safari visitors, Kruger National Park in particular is an ideal destination. Many of the restcamps here have been designed to cater for all, while 'drop-in' facilities throughout the park – including picnic areas and viewpoints – often have step-free access and sometimes have adapted

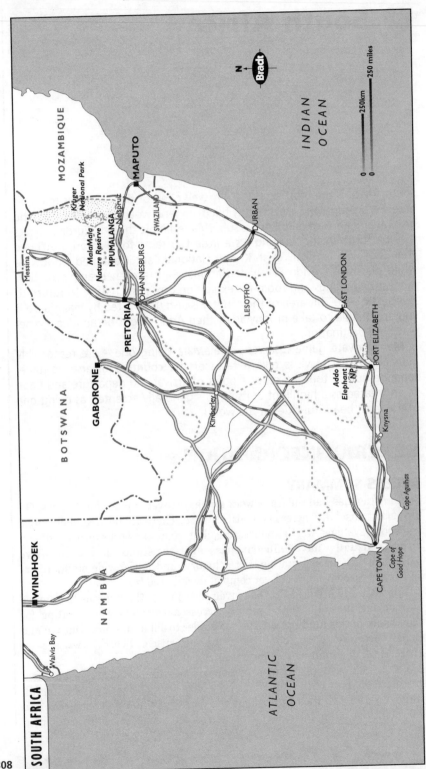

SOUTH AFRICA

ATLANTIC
OCEAN

INDIAN
OCEAN

NAMIBIA

■WINDHOEK

Walvis Bay

BOTSWANA

■GABORONE

Messina

MalaMala
Nature Reserve

MPUMALANGA

Kruger
National Park

MOZAMBIQUE

■PRETORIA

JOHANNESBURG

Nelspruit

■MAPUTO

SWAZILAND

Kimberley

LESOTHO

DURBAN

EAST LONDON

Addo
Elephant
NP

PORT ELIZABETH

Knysna

CAPE TOWN

Cape of
Good Hope

Cape Agulhas

N

Bradt

0   250km
0   250 miles

ablutions. The park is managed by South African National Parks (SANParks) and their comprehensive website gives regularly updated details about access; see below for contact details.

LOCAL OPERATORS

For local operators catering to people with mobility issues, plus some mainstream operators that have shown a genuine interest in this market, see *Chapter 1, Specialised operators in Africa,* pages 20–3.

SOUTH AFRICAN NATIONAL PARKS – BOOKING AND FEES

Kruger National Park and Addo Elephant National Park are run by South African National Parks (*PO Box 787; Pretoria 0001;* ↆ *012 428 9111;* **f** *012 343 0905;* **e** *reservations@sanparks.org;* ⵏ *www.sanparks.org*).

It is wise to reserve accommodation in advance, especially if visiting in high season, and this is easily done online, by email, fax, telephone or by old-fashioned 'snail mail'. However, anyone who wishes to reserve adapted accommodation should do this directly through SANParks' reservations department (details above).

A 'wild card' system is in place as a loyalty scheme to benefit frequent visitors and those staying longer in the areas covered by SANParks. South African nationals and members of the SADC are the primary beneficiaries of this system, but an International 'wild card' is also available for overseas visitors. For those visiting Kruger alone on a typical safari, paying normal conservation fees is as cheap and simple a method.

JOHANNESBURG

The most populous city in South Africa, Johannesburg is a meeting place of many cultures, creating a fast, brash and thrilling atmosphere not unlike that of London or New York. Possibly the major visible difference is that because of South Africa's previous policy of racial segregation, shanty towns of extreme poverty are only a nervous walk away from lavish whitewashed homes. The city, therefore, has a reputation as one fraught with crime and danger.

While (statistically) there is truth in this, most tourist visitors (especially those just passing through) can greatly limit their chances of experiencing such hazards by taking care and precautions – see *Chapter 3, Security,* page 105, for advice about staying safe in African cities.

GETTING THERE AND AWAY

By road

Motorways are as smooth and efficient (and sometimes as maddeningly mobbed) as anywhere in the 'developed' world, but those in South Africa quickly lead out to open wild country while still retaining a solid, asphalt surface. Bus and coach services link the airport and city (leaving from the main bus station in the city centre) with the rest of South Africa, but none cater specifically to limited mobility; see *Chapter 3, Public transport*, page 89. Car hire is possible at several points around Johannesburg and vehicles with hand controls can be arranged with advance booking (see page 24).

By rail
Apart from a handful of exclusive services (see page 92) none of South Africa's rail services make extra allowances for people with limited mobility.

By air
As southern Africa's largest metropolis, Johannesburg has daily air links with countries across the globe. It also serves as a hub for flights within South Africa connecting international arrivals with provincial towns and outlying game reserves. Consequently, **Oliver Tambo International Airport** (✆ *011 921 6911;* **f** *011 921 6422;* ⊕ *www.airports.co.za*) has all the required passenger conveniences – shops, banks, Wi-Fi and food outlets – and has an efficient and well-equipped disability support service with wheelchairs, aisle chairs and fully accessible toilets. Shuttle services link the airport with sights and hotels around the city (all between 30 minutes and 60 minutes away) and self-drive or chauffeur-drive adapted vehicles are available (see page 24).

GETTING AROUND
Taxis and other minibus transport services are easily organised from the airport or your hotels; for operators with wheelchair-adapted vehicles, see pages 20–3.

WHERE TO STAY
Most quality hotels in and around Johannesburg contain some adapted rooms. However, the more budget conscious you are, the more limited your options will be. The following is a selection of hotels offering fully adapted rooms, both near the airport and in the city:

North of the centre
City Lodge Morningside (160 rooms) Corner of Hill & Rivonia rds, Sandton; ✆ 011 884 9500; **f** 011 884 9440; **e** clmside.resv@citylodge.co.za; ⊕ www.citylodge.co.za ⬚ ⬚ ⬚
Just north of the centre of Sandton, the City Lodge is 30mins' drive from Oliver Tambo International Airport. Public areas are step-free except the lounge, swimming pool & garden. A ramp is available for pool access. **Ground-floor rooms:** 4 rooms are adapted – roll-in showers have lever taps, fold-down seats & vertical support rail, but not in reach of the seat; washbasin (65) has lever taps, low mirror & shelf; toilet has front transfer space & 2 support rails. **$$**

Near Oliver Tambo International Airport

Intercontinental Johannesburg O R Tambo Airport (138 rooms) ☎ 011 961 5400/1; e airportsun@southernsun.com; ⌂ www.southernsun.com 📱 🛏 🖼 🖥
This international business hotel is a short walk (<100m) from Terminal 3 of the airport, making it an ideal option, especially after a long flight. All public areas within the building, including the pool & spa, have step-free (or lift) access & 1 room has been adapted for disabled guests.
Room 120: Bed (56) has transfer space, light controls & phone; bath (53) has extended surface for easy transfer & 1 support rail; roll-in shower has handheld showerhead, lever tap, fold-down seat (46) & shaped support rail (82); washbasin (67) has round taps; toilet has side transfer space & 2 support rails (side & rear). **$$$$**

Road, Town & City Lodges, O R Tambo International Airport (92, 135 & 219 rooms respectively) Near junction R24 (airport) ☎ 011 392 2268;
e rlairport.dm@citylodge.co.za, e tlairport.resv@citylodge.co.za &
e clairport.resv@citylodge.co.za respectively; ⌂ www.citylodge.co.za 📱 🖼 🖥
These 3 sister hotels are located in Germiston, near OR Tambo International Airport, & each has a shuttle bus for the 10min trip. The hotels are appointed to various degrees of luxury but each has 1 room with level entry & a roll-in shower & toilet with support rails. Minimum doorway widths are 75cm. **$$**

Near the city centre

Parktonian (300 rooms) 120 De Korte St, Braamfontein; ☎ 011 403 5740; f 011 403 2401; e reservations@parktonian.co.za; ⌂ www.proteahotels.com 📱 🛏 🖼 🖥
As well as having a disabled parking bay & smooth, level access throughout, the Parktonian has 4 rooms (2 twins & 2 dbls) designed for disability. Located virtually in the centre of the city, it is about 25km from the airport.
Adapted rooms: Beds have light switches, phones & transfer space; roll-in shower has fold-down seat, round taps & handheld showerhead; washbasin has leg space & low mirror; toilet has angled transfer space & 2 support rails (side & rear). **$$$$**

OTHER PRACTICALITIES

As would be expected in any major city, Johannesburg is well furnished with all the services essential to travellers. Credit cards are widely accepted, ATMs are found in shopping malls and filling stations as well as banks, and the last are abundant and efficient. Post offices are competent, internet cafés are easily found and Wi-Fi is common in hotels, malls and restaurants.

Medical services

South African health services are of an extremely high standard in comparison with most of the rest of the continent. **Medi-clinic** centres (⌂ *www.mediclinic.co.za*) are reputed to be among the best and are dotted around the city.

WHAT TO SEE AND DO

For the purposes of this book, Johannesburg is taken only as an arrival and departure point. However, it is also a very worthwhile tourist destination in its own right. Anyone with a day or so to kill can explore a plethora of museums, galleries and libraries, and the choice of restaurants justifies the size of the city.

See Bradt's *Johannesburg* for detailed analysis of these highlights. The booklet *Access Gauteng*, which looks at the city from a disability perspective, can be ordered from The QuadPara Association of South Africa (*PO Box 2368, Pinetown 3600;* \ *031 767 0348;* f *031 767 0584;* e *pcqasa@iafrica.com*).

Remember that although effective access legislation is not yet effective to most 'Western' standards, many modern malls, restaurants and public buildings are accessible, at least to some degree.

CAPE TOWN

Nobody who visits the Cape area can fail to be blown away by its natural beauty. The peninsula is a rocky finger about 50km long that dares to tickle the south Atlantic, and is at the mercy of its fickle wind and weather patterns. The famously flat-topped Table Mountain sits on the first knuckle of the finger, and the protected bay running off its northern slopes is home to the gently sprawling city of Cape Town.

The 'Mother City' is one of contrasts. Its hugely diverse population can create an atmosphere as sophisticated and cosmopolitan as Johannesburg, or as relaxed and rural as country towns; the legacy of old divisions are still very obvious, with desperate shanty towns bordering some of the most exclusive beaches in the country; and perfectly placed between mountain and ocean it ranks with the most scenic cities in the world. The Cape is the most visited area in South Africa and has good disability access making it easily seen by all.

GETTING THERE AND AWAY

By road

All three trunk routes that terminate in Cape Town follow the South African norm of being good-quality, tar-sealed highways. Vehicles of all types can easily be hired by those who wish to drive independently, and hand-controlled hire cars are also available, with prior bookings (see page 24). Inter-city coaches leave from the main bus/train station in the city centre; see *Chapter 3, Public transport*, page 89, for advice on using public transport as a disabled person.

By rail

Apart from a handful of exclusive services (see page 92) none of South Africa's rail services make extra allowances for people with limited mobility.

By air

Cape Town International Airport (✆ *021 937 1275;* **f** *021 936 2937;* 🖰 *www.airports.co.za*) has all the logistics and equipment (including aisle chairs, wheelchairs and accessible toilets fitted with support rails) that passengers with mobility problems may need and is consistently voted 'Africa's leading airport' at the World Travel Awards. This reputation was discoloured slightly in mid 2008, when refurbishments meant that wheelchair users had no easy access to the terminal, but this should only be a temporary hindrance. It is just over 20km from the city centre and although shuttle buses and taxis ply this route, none have made allowances for disability. Anyone who needs more than a standard vehicle should contact a specialised operator (see *Chapter 1, Specialised operators in Africa*, pages 20–3).

GETTING AROUND

Taxis and other minibus transport services are easily organised from the airport or your hotels; see pags 20–3 for operators with wheelchair-adapted vehicles.

WHERE TO STAY

In the city

Cape Sun Hotel (368 rooms) Strand St; ✆ 021 488 5100; **f** 021 423 8875; **e** capesun@southernsun.com; 🖰 www.southernsun.com 🔲 🔲 🔲 🔲
The Cape Sun towers above the city centre, giving super views onto Table Mountain & the harbour, yet is still within easy walking distance from shops, restaurants & nightlife. All public areas except the pool & fitness room are fully accessible from the underground or street parking & 1 room has disability adaptations.
Adapted room: Bed (56) has phone, light switches & transfer space; roll-in shower has 2 support rails, lever tap, handheld showerhead, but no seat, although a shower commode chair is available; washbasin (73) has lever tap; toilet (44) has front & side transfer space & side & rear support rails (82 & 99). **$$$**

City Lodge V & A Waterfront (207 rooms) Cnr Dock & Alfred rds; ✆ 021 419 9450; **f** 021 419 0460; **e** clva.resv@citylodge.co.za; 🖰 www.citylodge.co.za
🔲 🔲 🔲 🔲
Functional & conveniently located at the entrance to the Waterfront area (so still close to the CBD (Central Business District), this City Lodge has 4 adapted ground-floor rooms. The hotel is accessed via a long ramp from the disabled parking bay & the lounge, bar & restaurant all have step-free access (the latter uses a small, open lift). There are steps leading to the pool & fitness centre.
2 rooms with adapted baths: Beds have transfer space, light switch & phone; bath has transfer space, horizontal support rail & lever tap, & a

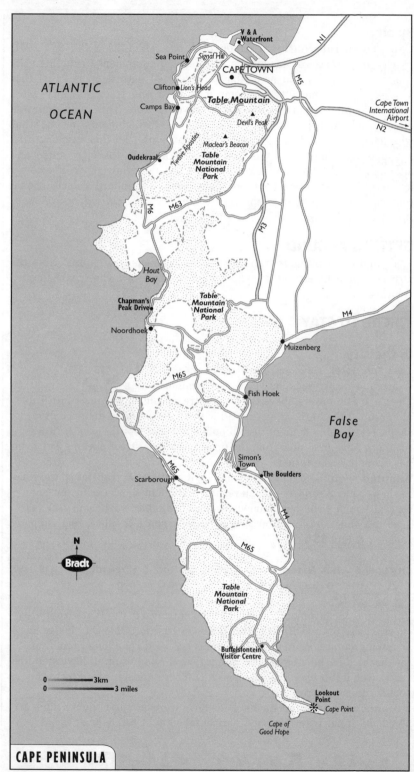

ATLANTIC
OCEAN

False
Bay

N1

V & A
Waterfront

Sea Point   Signal Hill
                                   CAPE TOWN
Clifton Lion's Head   M5
                        Table Mountain
Camps Bay
                            ▲ Devil's Peak   Cape Town
                                               International
                      Maclear's Beacon ▲   Airport
Oudekraal   N2
                        Table
                        Mountain
                        National
                        Park

            M6 M63

                                        M3

        Hout
        Bay
                        Table
Chapman's   Mountain
Peak Drive   National
                        Park   M4
Noordhoek

                                              Muizenberg

              M65

                                Fish Hoek

                                        Simon's
                                        Town
                                              The Boulders
Scarborough

                                        M4

              M65

N
Bradt

                        Table
                        Mountain
                        National
                        Park

                        Buffelsfontein
                        Visitor Centre

0 ——————3km   Lookout
0 ——————3 miles   Point
                                       ☀ Cape Point
                        Cape of
                        Good Hope

CAPE PENINSULA

swivel chair is available; washbasin (61) has lever tap & low mirror; toilet has side & rear support rails, but limited transfer space.
2 rooms with roll-in showers: Beds have transfer space, light switch & phone; roll-in shower (door 76cm) has lever tap, handheld showerhead, shaped support rail & fold-down seat; washbasin (61) has lever tap & low mirror; toilet has side & rear support rails, but limited transfer space. **$$$**

Hedge House (4 rooms) 12 Argyle Rd, Sunnybrae, Newlands; ☎ 021 689 6431; f 021 689 1286; e hedge@mweb.co.za; ⏁ www.hedgehouse.co.za 🔲 🖼️
This B&B option is nestled under the hulk of Table Mountain in Cape Town's southern suburbs. The dining room has 1 small step & to reach the pool, a larger step must be mounted, but 1 suite has level entry & an adapted bathroom.
Adapted suite: Entry is via the paved parking area; bed (56) has transfer space; bath (48) is set within a tiled wall (43) & has fitted handles; roll-in shower has round taps (130) & fixed showerhead; washbasin (74) has round taps; toilet (43) has front transfer space. **$$**

Outside the city
The Bay Hotel (78 rooms) 69 Victoria Rd, Camps Bay; ☎ 021 438 3972; f 021 438 4433; e res@thebay.co.za; ⏁ www.thebayhotel.co.za 🔲 🖼️
About 7km south of the centre of Cape Town, Camps Bay has one of the best-known beaches in the Cape area. The Bay Hotel is a luxurious & sophisticated resort, & 2 of its 'club classic' north-facing rooms (with views onto the 'Lion's Head') have features for disabled guests.
Rooms 352 & 452: Doors (95) are level; bath has shaped support rail & lever tap; roll-in shower has fold-down seat, handheld showerhead & lever tap; washbasin has round taps & low mirror; toilet has front & side transfer space & fold-away side support rail. **$$$$**

A Tuscan Villa (6 rooms) No 15 & 17, 3rd Av, Fish Hoek; ☎ 021 782 7907; f 021 782 7909; e info@atuscanvilla.co.za; ⏁ www.atuscanvilla.co.za 🔲 🖼️
The quaint village of Fish Hoek (translated from Afrikaans as 'fish corner') is situated about halfway down the peninsula, about 30mins' drive south from Cape Town & a similar time north of Cape Point. A Tuscan Villa is a cosy guesthouse with 1 room designed to be accessible. From the parking area through to the dining & lounge rooms is free of steps, & although there's no restaurant on site, the owners host *braai* & pizza evenings & several recommended eating places are within 10mins' walk.
Boulders Room: Standard doorways are level; cupboard has lowered hang rail; beds (57) can be adjusted down or up by 7cm; private patio has level entry; roll-in shower has fold-down seat (51), 2 support rails (79), lever tap & a handheld showerhead; washbasin (67) has knee access & lever taps; toilet (49) has side transfer space & side & rear support rails (76 & 77). **$$**

Blue Tangerine (6 rooms) 3 Bodrum Cl, Noordhoek; ☎ 021 785 3156; f 021 785 3176;

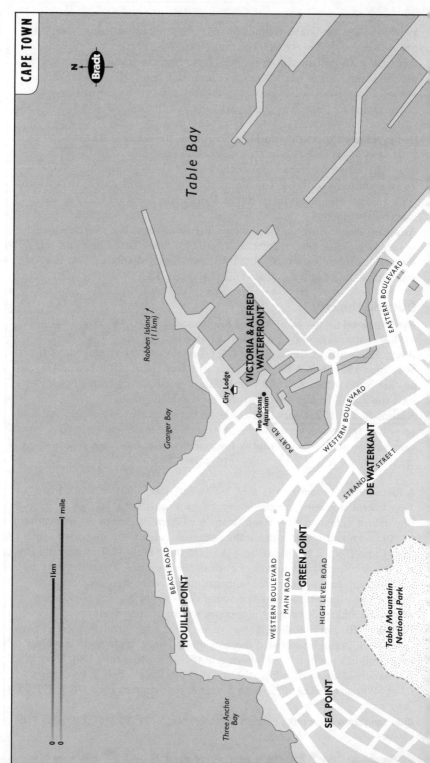

N

Brad't

Table Bay

Robben Island
(11km)

Granger Bay

City Lodge

VICTORIA & ALFRED
WATERFRONT

Two Oceans
Aquarium

PORT RD

WESTERN BOULEVARD

DE WATERKANT

EASTERN BOULEVARD

STRAND STREET

MOUILLE POINT

BEACH ROAD

Three Anchor
Bay

WESTERN BOULEVARD

MAIN ROAD

GREEN POINT

HIGH LEVEL ROAD

SEA POINT

Table Mountain
National Park

0   1km

0   1 mile

316

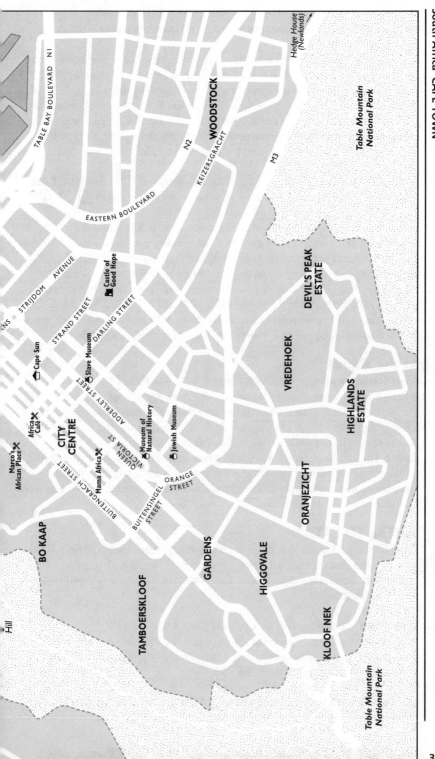

TABLE BAY BOULEVARD N1

WOODSTOCK

KEIZERSGRACHT

N2

M3

EASTERN BOULEVARD

Hedge House
(Newlands)

Table Mountain
National Park

STRIJDOM AVENUE

Castle of
Good Hope

STRAND STREET

DARLING STREET

Cape Sun

Slave Museum

ADDERLEY STREET

DEVIL'S PEAK
ESTATE

VREDEHOEK

Africa
Café

CITY
CENTRE

Marco's
African Place

Mama Africa

Museum of
Natural History

QUEEN
VICTORIA ST

Jewish Museum

HIGHLANDS
ESTATE

BUITENGRACH STREET

BUITENSINGEL
STREET

ORANGE
STREET

ORANJEZICHT

BO KAAP

GARDENS

HIGGOVALE

Hill

TAMBOERSKLOOF

KLOOF NEK

Table Mountain
National Park

m 0726 341 778; **e** info@bluetangerine.co.za; ⌂ www.bluetangerine.co.za

With expansive gardens & stunning sea views, this attractive guesthouse
was taken over by Alfie & Sabine from Epic Enabled (see page 21) in 2008.
It immediately had 1 'wheelchair' room (Fountain Room) with wide level
doorways & a roll-in shower with support rails & bench seat, but further
inclusion was planned for early 2009 including swimming pool access &
more accessible rooms. The purpose is to complement their accessible
safari business so I have no doubt it will be done. **$$**

Mnandi Lodge B&B (4 rooms) 13 Spray Rd, Bloubergrant; ℂ 021 554 1184; **f** 086
670 0141; **e** info@mnandilodge.co.za; ⌂ www.mnandilodge.co.zav
This B&B is set a few hundred metres back from the seafront in a
residential suburb about 12km north of the city. It has wheelchair access
throughout the building, the garden & swimming pool & has made 1 room
especially suitable for guests with mobility limitations.
Room 4: Paved pathway leads to level doorway (>85); bed (55) has
transfer space; roll-in shower has lever tap, fold-down seat, horizontal
support rail & handheld showerhead; washbasin (75) has lever tap & an
accessible shelf (on wheels) is available; toilet (42) has side transfer space
& 1 horizontal support rail, though this is not within reach. **$$**

At the airport
Road Lodge Airport Cape Town (90 rooms) ℂ 021 934 7303; **f** 021 934 7473;
e rlctia.dm@citylodge.co.za; ⌂ www.citylodge.co.za
Perfectly situated within the airport grounds, this road lodge is an easy &
affordable place to rest after a long flight. As well as having seamless
access through its public areas, it has 1 inclusive room.
Room 16: Roll-in showers have fold-down seat, horizontal, wrap-around
support rail support, handheld showerhead & a lever tap, but limited
transfer space; washbasin has leg space & lever tap; toilet has side & front
transfer space & side & rear support rails. **$**

WHERE TO EAT
Cape Town is known for having good-quality restaurants. The following
town centre restaurants all have adapted bathrooms and there are lots of
reasonably accessible eateries on the Waterfront, where accessible toilets
are also easily found.

Africa Café 108 Shortmarket St; ℂ 021 422 0221; **f** 021 422 0482;
e africafe@iafrica.com; ⌂ www.africacafe.co.za; ⊘ 18.30 every evening. Take
your pick from the large set menu, which changes seasonally but always
gives a great flavour of Africa. **$$$$$**

Mama Africa 178 Long St; ℂ 021 426 1017; **f** 021 424 9457; **e** mama@mweb.co.za;
⌂ www.mamaafricarest.net; ⊘ 12.00–15.00 & 19.00–23.15. With a varied menu –

containing specialities from all over the continent plus the usual worldwide favourites – this restaurant will suit all tastes. **$$$$**

Marco's African Place 15 Rose Lane, Bo-Kaap; ✆ 021 423 5412; **f** 021 423 9125; **e** marko@marcosafricanplace.co.za; 🖰 www.marcosafricanplace.co.za; ⊘ 12.00–late Tue–Sat, 15.00–late Sun. Marco's regularly hosts live music, especially jazz, & specialises in dishes from the Cape. **$$$**

OTHER PRACTICALITIES
Cash is easily obtained from ATMs and banks in all areas of the city, post offices and internet outlets are equally prolific and an increasing number of public areas (including hotels and restaurants) have Wi-Fi.

Medical services
South African health services are of an extremely high standard in comparison with most of the rest of the continent. **Medi-clinic** centres (🖰 www.mediclinic.co.za) are reputed to be among the best and are dotted around the city.

WHAT TO SEE AND DO
This beautiful area has no shortage of visitor attractions. As with most of South Africa, tourist highlights here have been built or adapted with disabled visitors – at least to some degree – in mind. However, I have been warned that although this is true, be prepared for changes in advertised access on a day-to-day basis. For more information about what to see and do as a disabled person, an organisation called CapeAble (🖰 www.capeable.co.za) is planning to publish a universal access travel companion to the Western Cape and specialised local operators (see pages 20–3) are worth using, as they know most about access. The most common highlights are as follows:

In Cape Town

Table Mountain
(🖰 www.tablemountain.net; ⊘ daily, times vary with season; ⊛ cable car: adult return R145, discounts for students, senior citizens & children) The most recognisable landmark in the area, Table Mountain is also easily accessed. There are lots of walking routes, but for those who are less nimble, a relatively new (opened in 1997) cable car runs to the top. Once there, the restaurant, 2km of paths and most viewpoints are designed to be accessed by wheelchairs. Visitors receive a map of the area on arrival, which shows accessible routes.

Cape Point
(🖰 www.capepoint.co.za; ⊘ 06.00–18.00 Oct–Mar daily; 07.00–18.00 Apr–Sep daily; Cape of Good Hope entry R60 pp with discounts for children). A trip to Cape Point, which is part of Table Mountain National Park, is a popular day out. The lighthouse at the point is reached via many steps but

the funicular railway, shops and eateries have wheelchair access. Chapman's Peak Drive is a 9km section of the western seaboard of the peninsula with thrilling cliff-hugging corners and spectacular ocean views. This was closed in 2008 so check first that it has reopened.

City Sightseeing Tour

(*City Sightseeing Tours;* ☎ *021 511 6000;* **f** *021 511 2288;* ⌂ *www.city sightseeing.co.za;* 🖃 *a 1-day, route-specific ticket costs R120 while a 24hr ticket is valid over 2 days, costs R200 and can be used on both routes*) Running daily, these vehicles all have wheelchair access (double doors on the bottom deck open to an area where chairs can be clamped down), cover two main routes and visitors can hop on and off at any point.

Robben Island

(⌂ *www.robben-island.org.za;* ☉ *daily, times vary with season;* 🖃 *adult R150*) Most notorious as being a prison for anti-apartheid critics, including Nelson Mandela, Robben Island is now open to the public. A vehicle with wheelchair access – but no tie-downs – exists on the island and ramps are available for boarding the transfer catamaran, though wheelchairs are often manually carried aboard. Chair users should book in advance.

Other highlights

Other highlights within Cape Town include the **Two Oceans Aquarium** (*Dock Rd, V & A Waterfront;* ⌂ *www.aquarium.co.za*) and the **Natural History** (*25 Queen Victoria St, Gardens;* ⌂ *www.iziko.org.za/sam;* ☉ *from 10.00 daily*) and **Jewish museums** (*Hatfield St;* ⌂ *www.sajewish museum.co.za;* ☉ *from 10.00 Sun–Fri*), which are both normally fully accessible. **The Castle of Good Hope** (*behind the bus & train station;* ⌂ *www.castleofgoodhope.co.za*) and the **Slave Museum** (*Adderley St & Bureau St*) are less accessible, but can still be visited in a wheelchair. Local operators bring their own ramps.

Outwith Cape Town

Wine tours

Wine tours run through Stellenbosch, Paarl and Franschhoek, where the wine-growing industry is big business. John Platter's South African Wine Guide is an annual publication that not only describes the wines, but also gives good information about access in the wineries themselves. It can be bought in most bookstores for between £8 and £12, or ordered online from ⌂ www.platterwineguide.com for R499.

Whale watching

Hermanus is a small town about 115km southeast of Cape Town and according to *Time* magazine has the best land-based whale watching in the world. It is also the hometown of Karin Coetzee (*of* ⌂ *www.disabled*

travel.co.za) who helped research this chapter, and as such is possibly the most wheelchair-friendly town in the country. Between 5km and 10km of the whale-viewing cliff paths are wheelchair friendly and have regular seating. Accessible toilets, restaurants and accommodation are easy to find in the town. They even have a beach wheelchair.

Other Highlights
Scuba diving, shark cage diving and bungee jumping may interest some visitors, depending on their ability to walk, swim and conquer vertigo.

Other highlights in the Western Cape include Cango Caves, 29km from Oudtshoorn (⌘ *www.cangocaves.co.za*), where the visitors' centre is wheelchair friendly but the caves aren't, and various ostrich farms. No visit to Oudtshoorn is complete without going to **Cango Wildlife Ranch** (⌘ *www.cango.co.za*) which is extremely accessible and gives opportunities to get really close to various animals (cheetahs can even be petted).

Further afield
Heading further east, the **Garden Route** is one of South Africa's most visited tourist areas, and includes idyllic coastal towns with equally attractive names like Wilderness, Plettenberg Bay and Knysna. There is no shortage of very accessible accommodation here (see ⌘ *www.disabled travel.co.za*) and the most accessible highlights include **boat-based whale watching** from Plettenberg Bay and the **Small Cat Sanctuary** at Tenikwa (⌘ *www.tenikwa.co.za*). The latter has gravel paths but can provide a helper if given advance warning. Contact Pam at Flamingo Tours (see page 22) for more information and booking.

KRUGER NATIONAL PARK

The claim that Kruger is South Africa's flagship game reserve is difficult to dispute. It is the largest, is host to a hugely impressive array of fauna and flora and has an outstanding infrastructure of roads, lodges and communications. It is also one of the most studied safari ecosystems in the continent, and as such is a model to many others. To the experienced safari hand it may all sound a little too tidy, but before judgements are made it is worth remembering that this is a wilderness the size of Wales. Great swathes of wild Africa thrive between the tiny ribbons of tarmac, and being so well managed, these will only flourish further.

Stretching more than 400km from Zimbabwe in the north to Swaziland in the south, the park is essentially flat, and is bisected by several vast rivers that run roughly west to east. These include stirring names like the Olifants and the Crocodile and provide guaranteed water in times of low rainfall. Rolling grasslands with lonesome granite kopjes stretch out between these perennial waterways, producing a landscape with many different habitats. Great herds of antelope, buffalo and elephant roam the plains and prides of lion prowl their

KRUGER NATIONAL PARK

Pafuri Gate

0 ————————— 30km
0 ————————— 20 miles

Punda Maria Camp

Get-out Point/ Picnic Area

Shingwedzi Camp
Get-out Point

Get-out Point

Get-out Point

Get-out Point

Mopani
Pionneer Dam Birdhide

Picnic area
Shipandani Birdhide

MOZAMBIQUE

Get-out Point
Letaba Restcamp

Phalaborwa

Get-out Point/ Picnic Area

Get-out Point

Get-out Point
Olifants Restcamp

N

Bradt

Ratel Pan Birdhide

Satara Restcamp

Tamboti Satellite Camp

Get-out Point

Sweni Birdhide

Orpen Gate

Get-out Point/ Picnic Area

Get-out Point

Get-out Point

Paul Kruger Gate
Lake Panic Birdhide
Phabeni Gate
Skukuza Restcamp

Get-out Point

Numbi Gate
Pretoriuskop Restcamp

Berg-en-Dal Restcamp

Lower Sabie
Nthandanyathi Birdhide

Get-out Point/ Picnic Area

Crocodile Bridge

Nelspruit

Get-out Point

Malelane Gate

Komatipoort

territories, competing with other large carnivores – hyena, wild dog and cheetah – for their share of the hoofed fodder. Dense, riverine forests provide a refuge for the reticent leopard and birdlife is varied and prolific throughout.

Despite its great size, Kruger is more of a strip than a spread of land, averaging only around 60km wide. The total size is just under 19,000km². The whole length of its eastern flank serves as South Africa's border with Mozambique, rubbing shoulders with that country's Limpopo National Park. With their dividing fence recently removed these reserves now reunite, forming the magnificently named 'Great Limpopo Transfrontier Park', and populations of animals are being carefully redistributed through the area. Kruger's western border is adjacent to several private reserves, and there are no fences to block animal migration here. The resulting ecosystem (including habitats in southern Zimbabwe) creates a huge conservation area of around 100,000km².

Park fees SANParks call their entry fees 'conservation fees', and at Kruger these are R140 per adult and R70 per child (<12 years) per day, or per night for overnight visitors. For booking procedures, see page 309.

GETTING THERE AND AWAY

By road
Tar-sealed roads from Kruger's entry points link the park robustly with the surrounding towns and cities on the South African side. The three main feeder airports: KMIA, Hoedspruit and Phalaborwa, are 52km from Numbi Gate, 68km from Orpen Gate and 3km from Phalaborwa Gate respectively, and Johannesburg is just over 400km from the south of the park. Cars can be hired at all three airports, or shuttle buses run into the park and cars can be hired at Skukuza Restcamp. Two vehicle-hire companies can supply vehicles with hand controls (see page 24) and most major service stations on the main roads heading towards Kruger have adapted toilet facilities.

By air
Three airports lie strategically positioned near Kruger, each servicing a fairly distinct area of the park. **Kruger/Mpumalanga International Airport (KMIA)** is 23km northeast of Nelspruit and supplies the southern region. It has two adapted toilets sporting support rails and an aisle chair available to facilitate access for non-ambulant passengers. Visitors flying into the central region usually use **Hoedspruit Airport**, while **Phalaborwa Airport** is the main air entry point to the northern region. All three ports are short (1–1½-hour) flights from Johannesburg, while KMIA and Hoedspruit are also connected to other South African hubs, including Durban and Cape Town. **Skukuza Airport** (within the park) will reopen for commercial flights sometime in 2009 and has an aisle chair and ramp.

WHERE TO STAY
Of the 14 restcamps within Kruger, the following is a selection of those most suited to visitors with limited mobility:

Southern region

Pretoriuskop Restcamp (131 bungalows, 4 cottages & 2 guesthouses) 8km east of Numbi Gate; contact SANParks, page 309, for reservations 🔲 🔲 🔲

The massive granite dome of Shabeni Hill dominates the landscape around Pretoriuskop, the southerly camp closest to Numbi Gate. Reception has stepped entry, but can be approached using a ramp from the rear & an adapted public ablutions block is tucked in behind this building. The shop & restaurant – where tables are >65cm – have smooth, level access, & a second accessible toilet block exists behind the dining room. A rougher track leads to the attractive, open swimming pool, which has no steps or ladder for entry. 2 bungalows have facilities for disabilities, though these are among the furthest from the main camp & up a slight slope. Several standard rooms are step-free, but these do not have adapted bathrooms. The perimeter trail has a rough unmade path; strong chair users (or those with strong assistants) will cope with these.

Adapted rooms: Doorway (75) is level; beds (59) have transfer space & light switch; highest switches are <140cm; door to ensuite (76) is level; roll-in shower has seat (52), support rail (80) & lever taps (95); washbasin (66) has lever taps; toilet (45) has front & side transfer space. **$$**

Skukuza Restcamp (200 bungalows, 21 tents & 19 cottages) 12km southeast of Paul Kruger Gate; contact SANParks, page 309, for reservations 🔲 🔲 🔲

Well landscaped on the southern banks of the Sabie River, Skukuza is the largest camp in Kruger & is the park's administrative headquarters. It has a range of accessible accommodation, & apart from the ATM (which is up 1 step) is apparently level throughout. Small ramps take out differences in height & drop curves run from various room doorways & at the main entrance to reception. The Stevenson-Hamilton Memorial Library, the lovely riverside walkway & the main restaurant, cafeteria & shop (there is an adapted toilet adjacent to these amenities) are all quite navigable by wheelchair. A small step leads into the conference area & the doctor's rooms are steeply ramped. There's another adapted toilet at the second restaurant in the charming Selati Train Station, but 1 step must be mounted to enter the carriage bar. The new Skukuza Wetland Boardwalk (just outside the camp) gives a stunning – & fully accessible – 260m window into some of the indigenous habitat of the region, & a bird hide nearby is similarly accessible. 8 bungalows (6 with roll-in showers & 2 with baths with grab rails) & a more luxurious river rondavel have accessible features. Also, 1 of the 6-bed guest cottages & 2 of the 8-bed guesthouses have twin rooms with en-suite roll-in showers & baths.

Bungalows 1, 2, 110 & 111, 130 & 131: Shallow ramp to doorway; bed (59) has transfer space & light switch; highest switch <140cm; ensuite (76) is level; roll-in shower has seat (not close enough to controls), handheld showerhead, lever tap (105) & support rail (80); the washbasin (65) has lever taps & support rail; toilet (47) has support rail & front & side transfer space.

Bungalows 178 & 179: Have baths with grab rails as opposed to roll-in showers with fold-down seats.

River Rondavel 88: Doorway is level; beds (54) have light switch & transfer space; highest switch is <140cm; doorway into ensuite (76) is level; roll-in shower has handheld showerhead, lever tap (100) but no seat; washbasin (68) has lever taps; toilet (45) has front transfer space only. **$$**

Berg-en-Dal Restcamp (69 bungalows, 23 cottages & 2 houses) 13km northwest of Malelane Gate; contact SANParks, page 309, for reservations 🖼 🖼 🖼 🖼
Located in the far south of Kruger, Berg-en-Dal (meaning 'hill & dale' in Afrikaans) is set in rugged terrain. Sweet, grassy plains fall between the rock kopjes, drawing plenty of game & a bonus of the setting is its more bearable climate, even when other areas are baking in the heat. The site is relatively flat, & bricked paths & ramps join main buildings, but the riverside walk is not seamlessly smooth. The restaurant (where most tables are >65cm) & the picturesque swimming pool (with stepped entry) have level access. The beginning of the 'Rhino Trail' is passable in a wheelchair & Berg-en-Dal's unique feature is its walking trail with guide ropes designed for people with visual impairments. There are 2 adapted 6-bed family chalets, each with 1 adapted bathroom & 1 new (Jul 2008) 3-bed bungalow with roll-in shower.

Cottage 83: Doorway is ramped; bed (56) has transfer space; highest switch is <140cm; ensuite (76) is level; roll-in shower (78) has fold-down plastic seat (48), handheld showerhead & 2 support rails (102); washbasin (70) has lever taps; toilet (41) has support rail (next to & behind toilet) & front & side transfer space.

Cottage 84: Similar to Cottage 83, except the toilet support rails are less useful (fixed left & right behind toilet) & instead of a shower, it has a bath (45) with 1 vertical support rail & a wall-mounted lever tap. In both rooms, toilets have no cistern or backrest. **$$**

Crocodile Bridge (20 bungalows & 8 tents) 8km north of Komatipoort; contact SANParks, page 309, for reservations 🖼 🖼 🖼
Despite its proximity to the border of the park, the area around Crocodile Bridge is home to a large proportion of Kruger's rhino, as well as many other sought-after species, including lion & kudu. It is the smallest camp in the park, but is one of the best run & sports 2 chalets that are kitted out for disability. Main public areas are level, with reasonably smooth pathways, but there is no restaurant or swimming pool here. Note also that the shop is small, so it may be worthwhile stocking up on supplies before arrival.

Bungalows 17 & 18: Doorway (75) is ramped; beds (62) have light switch & transfer space; door to ensuite (76) is level; highest switch is <140cm; roll-in shower has seat (but too far from tap & showerhead), 2 horizontal support rails (76), star taps (85) & handheld showerhead; washbasin (76) has lever tap & low shelf & mirror; toilet (50) has front & side transfer space & 2 support rails (side, 97 & rear, 90).

1 twin safari tent: this is also ramped, & has access to adapted communal ablutions that are similar to those in Rooms 17 & 18. **$$**

Lower Sabie (93 rooms, 24 tents, 2 cottages & 1 guesthouse) 35km north of Crocodile Bridge; contact SANParks, page 309, for reservations ⬛ ⬛ ⬛ ⬛
Lower Sabie lies in lovely woodland next to the perennial Sabie River. This permanent water, plus the sweet grass of the surrounding savanna, guarantees grazers & their usual wake of predatory followers in all seasons. On top of this, this is one of the most accessible camps in the park with more than 7 adapted units. A fairly steep ramp leads to reception from the car park, but then the main building, including restaurant, shop & deck are all level. Most tables are >65cm & an attractive – & step-free – river-viewing walkway extends from the main deck. A rough path then a stretch of lawn accesses the swimming pool.
Rondavel 31: Has an adapted bath. Doorway is level; beds (60) have light switches & transfer space; access to ensuite (71) is level; bath (53) has fitted handles & shaped support rail; washbasin (67) has lever taps; toilet (49) has front & side transfer space & 2 support rails (side & rear).
2 riverside bungalows (15 & 16) have roll-in showers: Doorway is level; beds (58) have light switches & transfer space; highest switch is <140cm; ensuite door (80) is level; roll-in shower has fold-down plastic seat (53), shaped hand rail (70), handheld showerhead & lever tap (87); washbasin (67) has lever taps; toilet (50) has 2 support rails (90) & front & side transfer space.
Twin riverside safari tents: 3 are ramped & have very small roll-in showers with foldaway metal seats.
Keartland Guest House: Has 1 bathroom with a roll-in shower with flip-up seat, lever taps & handheld showerhead, & a toilet with 2 support rails (side & rear) & front & side transfer space.
Moffat House: The former Moffat House has now been split into 2 separate bungalows, 1 of which is ramped & has 1 adapted bathroom with a step-in shower with seating & support rails & a toilet with 2 support rails (side & rear) & front & side transfer space.
Northern Campsite: Has 1 communal ablutions block with roll-in shower with seat & support rail, & a toilet with 2 support rails (side & rear) & front & side transfer space.
Southern Campsite: Similar, but has a step-in, instead of a roll-in, shower. **$$**

Central region

Satara Restcamp (152 bungalows & 10 cottages) 48km east of Orpen Gate; contact SANParks, page 309, for reservations ⬛ ⬛ ⬛
Set in fertile grassland plains, Satara's game viewing ranks as highly as any in the park, with the big cats & their hoofed prey especially prevalent. The camp is large, but feels less crowded than Skukuza as the accommodation is more spread out through the flat, tree-studded lawns. From the car park, reception is level & the dining area (with all tables

>65cm) also has step-free level entry. A short stretch of grass must be crossed to reach the pool, which has stepped entry. The day visitors' site has level access to an adapted toilet & a sandy path to the picnic area. 4 bungalows (D57, C67, A1 & A2) have been adapted, & are very similarly attired. Some other cottages are ramped & have baths but no adaptations.
Bungalow C67: Doorway (76) has a small incline to veranda; beds (49) have light switch & transfer space; doorway to ensuite (76) is level; roll-in shower has seat (46), horizontal support rail, handheld showerhead & lever tap; washbasin (66) has round taps & low mirror; toilet (46) has front & side transfer space & 1 shaped support rail. **$$**

Tamboti Satellite Camp (40 tents) 4km from Orpen Gate; contact SANParks, page 309, for reservations 🅿 🖼 🛏
Situated on the banks of the Timbavati River so close to Orpen, Tamboti is a very popular tented camp. It is self-catering only & visitors sign in on entry to Orpen Gate.
Safari tents: 3 here have adapted facilities. 2 of these (1 twin & 1 4-bed) have access to a communal ablution block with roll-in shower & toilet with grab rails & basin with lever taps. The third is a 3-bed unit with en-suite bathroom. Here the toilet has grab rails & the shower has no steps or curves, but does not have a fold-down seat. **$$**

Northern region

Olifants Restcamp (111 bungalows, 2 guesthouses) 83km east of Phalaborwa Gate (32km from Letaba); contact SANParks, page 309, for reservations 🅿 🍴 🖼 🛏
Olifants has a stunning position on a rocky promontory high above the Olifants River. Although this situation sounds ominous for less mobile visitors, all the main buildings are ramped & there is wheelchair access from the restaurant block to the breathtaking river viewpoint. Most dining tables are >65cm & there is an adapted toilet at reception. 2 huts currently have accessible features.
Rondavel 107: Has roll-in shower; sliding door has threshold (3); beds (56) have transfer space but light switches are too high; highest switches are <140cm; doorway into ensuite (76) is level; roll-in shower has support rail (80), no seat & round taps; washbasin has no knee space; toilet (40) has 2 support rails (side & rear) & has front & side transfer space.
Rondavel 76: Has adapted, sunken bath; doorway is level; beds (51) have light switches & transfer space; highest switches are <140cm; doorways into ensuites (76) are level; bath (41) has extended sitting area, fitted handles, lever taps & a wall-mounted support rail (10); washbasin (72) has high mirror; toilet (45) has 1 side support rail (68) & has front & side transfer space. **$$**

Letaba Restcamp (86 bungalows, 10 cottages & 2 guesthouses) 51km east of Phalaborwa Gate & 32km north of Olifants; contact SANParks, page 309, for reservations 🅿 🍴 🖼 🛏

Sweetly laid out on a wide bend of the Letaba River, this flat-lawned camp is shaded by mature woodland. Although no rooms have river views, there is excellent game viewing onto the sandy riverbed from the main restaurant. The shop & café have level access & the restaurant has a step-free side entrance (most tables are >65cm). The camp's unique feature – an elephant museum & display – is also accessible, & adapted ablutions can be found here & near the restaurant. A bricked pathway runs around the camp perimeter, but it is stepped in places, rendering it not completely wheelchair friendly. The swimming pool has a level approach, but the final stretch is over grass. 4 rondavels (7, 71, D37 & D38) are adapted, whilst the 10 cottages & 2 guesthouses have ramped access though no specialised bathroom furniture.

Rondavel 7 & 71: Have roll-in shower; doorway has a sharp ramp; beds (56) have transfer space & light switch; doorway to ensuite (76) is level; roll-in shower is narrow but has seat, handheld showerhead & lever tap (106); washbasin (68) has lever taps; toilet (49) has 2 support rails (side & rear) & front & side transfer space.

Rondavels D37 & D38: Have adapted baths; doorway has sharp ramp; beds (46) have transfer space & light switch; doorway into ensuite (73) is level; bath (52) has round taps, a very small, extended seating area, fitted handles & a support rail (8); washbasin (65) has lever taps but high mirror; toilet (42) has 2 support rails (side & rear) & has front & side transfer space. **$$**

Mopani Restcamp (57 bungalows, 45 cottages & 1 guesthouse) 47km north of Letaba & 74km northeast of Phalaborwa Gate; contact SANParks, page 309, for reservations 🄿 🖼 🗗

Mopani, situated in mopane scrubland next to the large Pioneer Dam, is Kruger's newest camp; consequently, very good access was built into the design. The sweeping, thatch-roofed reception has level access, then the restaurant, shop, day visitors' area & café are step-free with smooth bricked paths & attractive, wooden boardwalks. The bar is up 1 step but most restaurant tables are >65cm & adapted public ablutions are within easy reach of public areas. The lookout platform – with dam vistas – is ramped access but the swimming pool has no accessible access point. 2 of the small bungalows have been adapted & are similarly appointed; 1 is near the swimming pool & has quite steep access, while the other is in the flat area of the camp.

Bungalows 17 & 66: Doorway (76) is level; beds (48) have light switches & transfer space; highest switch is <140cm; entry to the ensuite (73) is level; roll-in shower has a seat (not in washing area) with 1 horizontal support rail (80) not within reach of seat & round taps (132); washbasin (64) has lever taps; toilet (44) has 1 side support rail (80) & front & side transfer space. **$$**

Other notable accommodation

Further north in the park, **Punda Maria Camp** (contact SANParks, page

309, for reservations) has an accessible twin safari tent and six-bed family cottage (although two of these beds are up stairs in a loft). Both these units have roll-in showers and grab rails with the toilets. **Shingwedzi Camp** (contact SANParks, page 309, for reservations) has four ramped accessible units with baths and toilets equipped with grab rails. These units each have five beds, but two beds are up stairs in a loft.

WHERE TO EAT

People who wish to leave cooking and washing-up tasks at home will find efficiently run restaurants in most restcamps, and the more inclusive of these (listed above) normally have step-free entry, accessible tables and adapted toilets. For those on tighter budgets, or people who prefer complete autonomy, Kruger (like many of South Africa's game parks) has very good self-catering facilities. Most camps and many picnic areas have gas *braais* (barbecues), covered cooking, seating and eating areas, and clean ablution blocks. Furthermore, many of these are designed to be easily accessible with fully equipped toilet areas. Good planning is required if this is your preferred style of travel, as not every camp has comprehensively stocked shops, but most have the basics.

OTHER PRACTICALITIES

The main camps have shops, cafés, restaurants, laundries, post boxes, fuel, first-aid facilities and mobile-phone reception. Skukuza also has an ATM, although you are strongly advised to take enough South African rand with you.

Medical services

Most restcamps in Kruger have basic first-aid facilities and Skukuza has a full-time resident doctor, but people with medical emergencies would be airlifted to suitable hospital facilities in nearby towns such as Nelspruit, Phalaborwa or Polokwane.

WHAT TO SEE AND DO

Apart from game driving, which is as smooth, comfortable and rewarding here as anywhere in the continent, many Kruger camps offer other methods of enjoying the area. **Bird and animal hides** are often located near a restcamp, or are signposted from game-drive routes, and many have step-free wooden decks and benches (with no backrest but space between them to park a wheelchair. The most accessible bird hides and are marked on the Kruger National Park map (see page 322). **Viewpoints, 'get-out' points** and **lookouts** are often set on level ground and, as with some **picnic spots,** may even have inclusive features like an accessible toilet. Be aware, however, that gates are often difficult to open, as they need to be heavily sprung to keep wild animals out. **Walking trails** are generally deemed too rough for people with mobility problems, though this obviously depends on the extent of the disability.

MALAMALA GAME RESERVE

Several private reserves hug Kruger's western flank, providing the park with a buffer zone from human and domestic animal influence and sharing the populations of game that roam the region. MalaMala is one and is included here because it has some of the most accessible safari accommodation in Africa.

The reserve is 13,500ha of riverine forest, bushveld and grasslands typical of its easterly neighbour, and there are no fences between the two habitats. Similarly, the western border of the reserve runs barrier-free into Sabie Sand Wildtuin. As a result, animal populations move unrestricted through the whole ecosystem. As well as numerous antelope species and smaller game, the 'big five' are regularly seen; wild dog and cheetah are also sometimes encountered on game drives and birdlife is comparable with Kruger itself.

GETTING THERE AND AWAY

MalaMala is less than 400km from Johannesburg but most visitors arrive by air. SAA Airlink operates a daily service to MalaMala's private airfield, where an aisle chair is present to help non-ambulant guests in and out of aircraft. Vehicles for lodge transfers are not adapted but a ramp has been constructed at the main camp to counteract the extra height that 4x4 game vehicles present.

WHERE TO STAY

MalaMala Game Reserve (3 camps) PO Box 55514, Northlands 2116; ✆ 011 442 2267; **f** 011 442 2318; **e** reservations@malamala.com; ⌂ www.malamala.com

MalaMala offers the finest in traditional safari luxury – haute bush cuisine & premium wines are served in refined style & sumptuous surroundings, all with the natural backdrop of wild Africa. The reserve is exclusive – access is restricted only to guests staying at the lodge – so meanderings around the area are a peaceful affair. However, it is also exceedingly inclusive; 2 of the **Main Camp's** suites were designed with advice from South African disability experts & public areas are step-free. Not content with catering for disability indoors, the vehicle has extra (sheepskin) cushions, chest & seatbelts & a hand strap for extra stability, while guides/drivers here are used to dealing with disability & handle guests with care & respect.

Disabled suites 25 & 27: The narrowest doorway in each room is 75cm & 74cm respectively. Ramped entry; desk at appropriate height; elevated deck with bush views; lounge can be converted to sleeping area for a personal assistant; 2 en-suite bathrooms plus an adapted bathroom; roll-in shower with fold-down seat, handheld showerhead & support rail; lowered washbasin & mirror; toilet with side & rear support rails & front & side transfer space. **$$$$$**

OTHER PRACTICALITIES
Credit cards are accepted, internet access is available and souvenir shopping can be done at Main Camp.

Medical services
The doctor's surgery in Kruger's Skukuza (a 40-minute drive from MalaMala) is the first stop. For more serious requirements there is the **Nelspruit Medi-clinic** (⌂ www.nelspruitmc.co.za) and the **Rob Ferreira Government Hospital**, both of which are a two-hour drive away.

ADDO ELEPHANT NATIONAL PARK

Only a trumpet call from the N2 trunk route, Addo is easily reached and worth the visit. From modest beginnings (first gazetted in 1931 as 20km² to protect 11 tuskers), the park has grown in size and stature. Black rhino, lion, leopard and buffalo have been reintroduced, and the ecosystem named the Greater Addo Elephant National Park now covers 3,600km² reaching through the former Zuurberg National Park to the Indian Ocean. The result is a splendid collection of habitats, from bush to marine, which supports the newly coined 'big seven' – with great white sharks and whales making up the numbers.

Despite the competition, the trump card remains the elephant. More than 450 roam the reserve and they are well accustomed to vehicles, meaning viewing these giants is as up close – yet relaxing – an experience here as you can get anywhere. The fringe areas support less common mammals, such as Cape mountain zebra and aardwolf, and there are future plans to complete the circle of carnivores further by adding wild dog and cheetah to the fray. Less rousing, unless entomology is your passion, is the fact that the Addo is one of the last bastions of the flightless species of dung beetle, *Circellium bacchus*. These shiny scarabs have a taste for elephant dung and their activities make them a vital cog in nature's recycling machinery. Addo is also one of the few safari areas in Africa that is malaria-free.

Park fees SANParks call their entry fees 'conservation fees', and at Addo these are R110 per adult and R55 per child (<12 years) per day, or per night for overnight visitors. For booking procedures, see page 309.

GETTING THERE AND AWAY
International airports at Johannesburg and Cape Town connect seamlessly with **Port Elizabeth Airport** (⌂ www.airports.co.za), where there is no guarantee of aisle chairs. Tours are often joined here, or independent travellers can hire cars (including hand-controlled vehicles – see page 24); Addo is approximately 75km on perfectly good tarred roads.

WHERE TO STAY
Kuzuko Bush Lodge (24 chalets) m 0795 217 490; f 011 806 6899; e kuzuko@legacyhotels.co.za; ⌂ www.legacyhotels.co.za

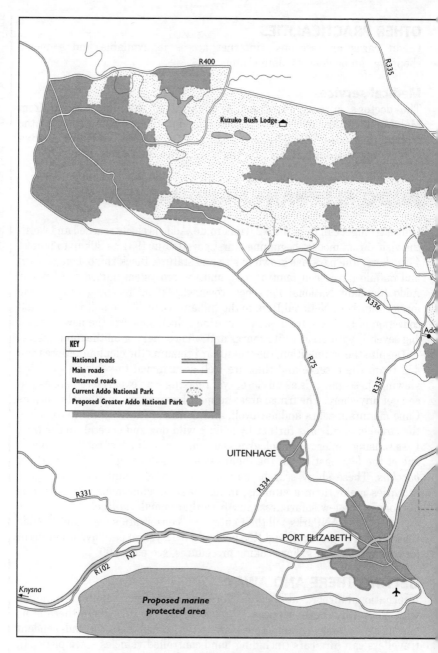

KEY

National roads
Main roads
Untarred roads
Current Addo National Park
Proposed Greater Addo National Park

Towering over a private section of bushveld north of the main area of Addo, Kuzuko is the only independent lodge in the region currently offering inclusive accommodation. The track from reception to the rooms is rough, so it may be preferable to use the lodge's vehicles here (4x4s & a Quantum minibus). Similarly, game drives in private vehicles are not

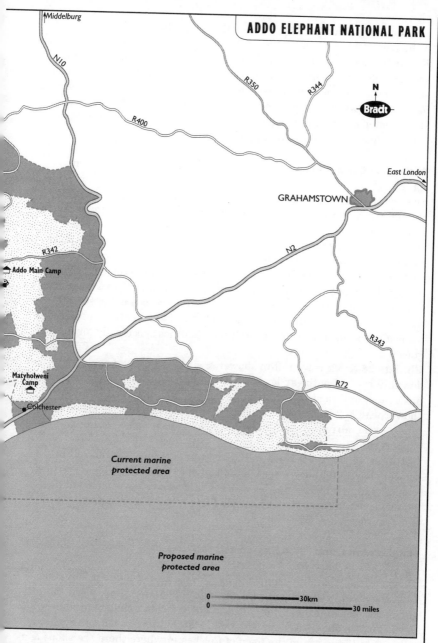

ADDO ELEPHANT NATIONAL PARK

Middelburg

N10

R350

R344

R400

East London

GRAHAMSTOWN

R342

N2

Addo Main Camp

R343

Matyholweni
Camp

R72

Colchester

Current marine
protected area

Proposed marine
protected area

0   30km
0   30 miles

possible, but a built-up step exists near reception to facilitate transfers into the standard lodge 4x4s. A long slope leads from the car park up to reception; from here, there is level access through to the lounge, bar & restaurant areas. Dining tables are 76cm & a public toilet has 2 support rails. The pathway to the swimming pool is steep & rough & the pool is entered using a ladder. 3 of the bungalows have been designed to be inclusive.

Room 1: Doorway (90) is level; beds (56) have transfer space & light switches; desk is 69cm; entrance to ensuite is level; bath (50) has extended surface on 1 side for easy transfer but no support rails; roll-in shower has handheld showerhead, lever taps & a fold-down seat, with 2 vertical & 1 shaped support rails; washbasin (74) has lever taps; toilet (44) has side transfer space & side & rear support rails (82 & 90). **$$$$$**

Addo Main Camp (61 units) Contact SANParks, page 309, for reservations

Sited close to the main gate, Addo's main restcamp has access ramps throughout reception, shop & restaurant areas. An adapted toilet is nearby & the waterhole-viewing area & bird hide are also ramped. The Discovery Trail, where a signposted boardwalk snakes through typical Addo vegetation, is disabled-friendly. People with mobility restrictions can park their vehicle near the start point, there is a guide rope for visually impaired guests & regular benches line the route. 2 chalets & 3 cottages have accessible features. The guesthouses are accessed using steep ramps, but bathrooms here only have standard baths. Several other cottages also have step-free entrances but no ablution facilities specifically for disabled guests.

Chalets 28 & 32: Have roll-in shower & standard bath; a slightly downhill bricked pathway leads to a level patio entrance (main doorway has 1 step); roll-in shower has limited space, fold-down seat, handheld showerhead & 2 horizontal support rails; washbasin has leg space & lever taps, but no mirror or shelf; toilet has side transfer space & side & rear support rails.

Cottages 43, 46 & 51: Have roll-in shower; entrance is level; roll-in showers have a fold-down seat, handheld showerhead & a small vertical support rail; washbasin has leg space & a lever tap but mirror (on flexi-mount) is out of reach; toilet has side (very high) & rear support rail & side transfer space. **$$**

Matyholweni Camp (9 cottages) Contact SANParks, page 309, for reservations

This is a small, satellite camp run by SANParks. Although it is further from the main, well-stocked area around Addo Main Camp, plans for a game-enticing waterhole were afoot in 2008. It has 2 chalets (numbers 2 & 9) with roll-in showers & support rails. Matyholweni is self-catering only, but is only 15mins from the town of Colchester where there are shops & a restaurant. **$$**

OTHER PRACTICALITIES

Credit cards can be used in the park, fuel is available at the main restcamp and there are ATMs in the town of Addo, 15km away. Around 1¹/₂ hours' drive away, Port Elizabeth has all conveniences normally found in large towns.

Medical services

The following two hospitals in Port Elizabeth are among the best in the region and are within 80km of Addo: **St George's Hospital** (*40 Park Drive;* ✆ *041 392 6111;* f *041 392 6000*), and **Netcare Greenacres Hospital** (*cnr of Cape & Rochelle rds in Greenacres, just northwest of town;* ✆ *041 390 7000;* f *041 390 7089*).

Appendix

FURTHER INFORMATION

BOOKS

Disability
Carp, Gary *Life on Wheels: The A to Z Guide to Living Fully with Mobility Issues* Demos Health, 2008. Well researched and attractively written, this book isn't focussed on travel but is a thorough guide to life as a person with a mobility disability.

Harrington, Candy *101 Accessible Vacations: Vacation Ideas for Wheelers and Slow Walkers* Demos Medical Publishing, 2007. 101 ideas for accessible holidays, mainly in North America.

Harrington, Candy *Barrier-Free Travel: A Nuts and Bolts Guide for Wheelers and Slow Walkers* Demos Medical Publishing, 2007. This very popular guide is written mainly from the perspective of travellers from the USA but covers all the basics in detail and will have something for everyone. The third edition is expected in 2009.

Radar *There and Back travel guide for disabled people* Radar, 2008. Describes air, rail, road and sea travel options from the UK for people with disabilities.

Steves, Rick *Easy Access Europe: A Guide for Travelers with Limited Mobility* Avalon Travel Publishing, 2006. The foremost paper guide to exploring Europe with restricted mobility.

Various contributors *Accessible Britain* Rough Guides, 2008. 100 of Britain's tourist highlights described with an eye on access.

Health
Wilson-Howarth, Dr Jane and Ellis, Dr Matthew *Your Child Abroad: A Travel Health Guide* Bradt Travel Guides, 2005. A useful resource for those travelling with children.

Wilson-Howarth, Dr Jane *Bugs, Bites & Bowels: The Essential Guide to Travel Health* Cadogan, 2006. Contains information and treatment guidelines for adults.

Field guides
There is a great range of reference material available for while you are actually on safari. The trick is to take what suits your needs – both depth of knowledge of information required and space and weight available for packing, while remembering that basic guidebooks are often present in safari vehicles.

Animals
The following two books from Bradt offer more information than just checklists and make interesting reading even when not on safari.

Briggs, Philip *East African Wildlife* Bradt Travel Guides, 2007. For Kenya and Tanzania, this guide is compact, comprehensive and beautifully illustrated.

Unwin, Mike *Southern African Wildlife: A Visitor's Guide* Bradt Travel Guides, 2005. Equally good for the southern region is this guide.

Estes, Richard D *The Safari Companion* Chelsea Green, 1999. For anyone who wants to achieve a deeper understanding of the animals' lives and habits, this guide also covers all safari regions. It doesn't have glossy colour pictures and will require a little dedicated reading, but goes into fascinating detail about behaviour and interactions. Anyone planning to sit and watch the animals, as opposed to seeing their first 'big five', will find this book invaluable.

Tilde, Stuart, and Southern, Chris *Central and East African Mammals: A Photographic Guide* Ralph Curtis Publishing, 1998. Much smaller than either of the titles above, this guide has correspondingly less information, but is more easily carried. It is still a handy resource for beginners but doesn't offer much more than the vital statistics and basic facts.

Birds
Sinclair, Ian and Ryan, Peter *Birds of Africa South of the Sahara: A Comprehensive Illustrated Field Guide* Struik, 2004. A respected guide covering the whole region.

Sinclair, Hockey and Tarbolton *Birds of Southern Africa* Struik, 2002. A user-friendly guide for the southerly countries, including Livingstone in Zambia.

Stevenson, Terry and Fanshawe, John *Birds of East Africa* Helm, 2003. For birding in Kenya and Tanzania, this guide has clear plates and maps and is easy to navigate.

Plant life

Budding botanists and anyone with a basic interest in the flora will benefit from the following books:

Dharani, Najma *Field Guide to the Common Trees and Shrubs of East Africa* Struik, 2002

Van Wyk, Braam, Palgrav, Keith Coates and Van Wyk, Piet Field *Guide to Trees of Southern Africa* Struik, 1997

Mainstream travel guides

As mentioned at the beginning of each chapter, Bradt publish dedicated mainstream guidebooks to most of the countries covered here. These will provide more background material and more information about the destinations themselves.

Briggs, Philip *Northern Tanzania: The Bradt Safari Guide with Kilimanjaro and Zanzibar* Bradt Travel Guides, 2006

Briggs, Philip *Tanzania* Bradt Travel Guides, 2007

French, Carole with Butler, Reg *Tipping* Bradt Travel Guides, 2009

McIntyre, Chris *Botswana: Okavango Delta, Chobe, Northern Kalahari* Bradt Travel Guides, 2007

McIntyre, Chris *Namibia* Bradt Travel Guides, 2007

McIntyre, Chris & Susan *Zanzibar* Bradt Travel Guides, 2009

McIntyre, Chris *Zambia* Bradt Travel Guides, 2008

Williams, Lizzie *Johannesburg* Bradt Travel Guides, 2006

Pritchard-Jones, Siân & Gibbons, Bob *Africa Overland* Bradt Travel Guides, 2009

Travelogues

Murphy, Dervla *The Ukimwi Road* Flamingo, 1994. A cycle journey from Kenya to Zimbabwe in 1992.

Theroux, Paul *Dark Star* Safari Penguin, 2003. Not Theroux's best travelogue, but still a witty and insightful account of an overland journey from Cairo to Cape Town.

Van der Post, Laurens *The Lost World of the Kalahari* Vintage, 2002. A classic and sometimes mystical description of the author's search for authentic Kalahari bushmen.

Wildlife and conservation

Adamson, Joy *Born Free Trilogy* Pan Books, 2000. The story of the rehabilitation of Elsa the lioness (see Elsamere, page 143).

Gavron, Jeremy *The Last Elephant: An African Quest* HarperCollins Ltd, 1993. The plight of the African elephant is a metaphor for the continent itself in this tenderly written melange of tales.

Owens, Mark and Delia *Cry of the Kalahari* HarperCollins Ltd, 1986. A moving account of seven years of a couple's life studying the animals of the central Kalahari.

Lynch, Peter *Wildlife & Conservation Volunteering: The Complete Guide,* Bradt Travel Guides 2009.

Scott, Jonathon and various authors *Big Cat Diary* Collins, 2006. A range of books derive from the title and all are based on the hugely popular BBC television series of the same name. They provide an insight into the lives of the Maasai Mara's lions, leopards and cheetahs.

History

Meredith, Martin *The State of Africa: A History of Fifty Years of Independence* Free Press, 2006. A readable account of events across Africa leading up to and since the colonial powers were removed. Covering the whole continent, it is surprisingly easy to read for such a complicated subject.

Reader, John *Africa: A Biography of a Continent* Penguin, 1998. This book is widely recognised as the best attempt yet to gather the events that have shaped the continent, from prehistory to modern times, and make it an easy and interesting read.

Fiction and autobiographies

Although not all of the titles below are from the region covered by this book, they do give a flavour of the continent as a whole.

Achebe, Chinua *Things Fall Apart* Penguin Classics, 2006. This Nigerian story is an African classic, read worldwide and used in schools throughout the continent.

Coetzee, J M *Disgrace* Vintage, 2000. Award-winning story reflecting post-apartheid South Africa.

Fuller, Alexandra *Don't Let's Go to the Dogs Tonight* Random House Trade

Paperbacks, 2003. A white upbringing in Rhodesia (now Zimbabwe) during the turbulant civil war.

Kingsolver, Barbara *The Poisonwood Bible* Harper Perennial Modern Classics, 2005. Although it is set in DR Congo, this gives a good portrayal of the struggle of an American missionary and his family in colonial Africa.

Le Carré, John *The Constant Gardener* Scribner, 2005. A gripping tale exposing the testing of new pharmaceutical drugs on Africans (Kenya, in this instance).

McCall-Smith, Alexander *The No 1 Ladies' Detective Agency* Pantheon, 2005. Set in Botswana, this is the first of nine light-hearted and easy-to-read stories.

Coffee-table books
Ginn, Peter, McIlleron W G and le S Milstein, P *The Complete Book of Southern African Birds* Struik, 1996

Iwago, Mitsuaki *Serengeti: Natural Order on the African Plain* Chronicle, 1987

Lanting, Frans *Okavango: Africa's Last Eden* Chronicle, 1995

Mills, Gus and Hes, Lex *The Complete Book of Southern African Mammals* Struik, 1997

Ricciardi, Mirella African *Visions: The Diary of an African Photographer* Weidenfeld & Nicolson, 2000

WEBSITES

Health
🖰 **www.emedicine.com** Information about various medications from the UK
🖰 **www.fitfortravel.scot.nhs.uk** General travel health information for people travelling abroad from the UK
🖰 **www.istm.org** International Society of Travel Medicine, including lists of travel clinics
🖰 **www.nathnac.org** General travel health information with frequent updates for people travelling abroad from the UK
🖰 **www.preventingmalaria.info** Information on malaria prevention and other immunisations
🖰 **www.tripprep.com** General travel health information for travellers worldwide, including lists of travel clinics
🖰 **www.tmvc.com.au** General travel health information for people travelling abroad from Australia and New Zealand, including lists of travel clinics

Disability and travel

 www.able-travel.com Resources, travel tips and country-specific information for travellers with disabilities

 www.direct.gov.uk A UK government resource with directories carrying information for disabled people who wish to travel

 www.globalaccessnews.com A searchable online library of information for travellers with disabilities

 www.miusa.org Mobility International USA encourages international exchange for people with disabilities, and their website carries 'tip sheets' with information that will be useful to all disabled travellers.

 www.spinalistips.se A growing library of tips, advice and equipment to make life with a disability easier

 www.youreable.com A UK-based general resource for disability information, with an active forum

 www.apparelyzed.com A site dedicated to spinal injury, but containing info that other disabilities will also find useful. It also hosts a hugely popular forum.

Flying with a disability

 http://airconsumer.ost.dot.gov The booklet *New Horizons – Information for the Air Traveller with a Disability* can be downloaded from this US-based website

 www.allgohere.com A commercial site carrying general information about access policies on many airlines, as well as their contact details

 www.casa.gov.au/airsafe/disable/index.htm This resource is produced by the Australian government, but will help readers from most countries

 www.dptac.gov.uk/pubs/aviation/access A detailed online guide produced by the UK government's Disabled Persons Transport Advisory Committee

 www.flying-with-disability.org A user-friendly site covering the main points.

DISABILITY ORGANISATIONS IN AFRICA

Kenya

Kenyan Paraplegic Organization (KPO) Lenana Rd, Kilimani, Nairobi; ℃ +254 (0)20 273 3360; f +254 (0)20 272 3884; e talk2us@kenyanparaplegic.org; www.kenyanparaplegic.org

Tanzania

Organisation of People with Disabilities in Zanzibar (UWZ) Creed Rd/Wireless, Zanzibar; ℃ +255 (0)24 223 3719; f +255 (0)24 223 1730; e uwz@zanzinet.com; www.uwz.or.tz

Tanzania Association for the Disabled-Chawata PO Box 1982, Mwanza; m +255 (0)744 771 825; f +255 (0)222 668 830; e malimi2003@yahoo.com

Namibia
National Federation of People with Disabilities in Namibia (NFPDN) PO Box
3659, Windhoek; ☏ +264 (0)61 225 717; e nfpdn@mweb.com.na

Botswana
Botswana Council for the Disabled (BCD) Private Bag 459, Gaborone;
☏ +267 (0)397 3599; f +267 (0)391 1784; e bcd@info.bw

Zambia
Zambia Federation of the Disabled (ZAFOD) Lusaka; ☏ +260 (0)121 2311;
f +260 (0)128 6529; e zafod@zamnet.zm; 🖰 www.safod.org

South Africa
QuadPara Association of South Africa (QASA) PO Box 2368, Pinetown 3600;
☏ +27 (0)31 767 0348; f +27 (0)31 767 0584; e pcqasa@iafrica.com
The National Council for Persons with Physical Disabilities (NCPPDSA) 4
Lancaster Rd, Westdene, Gauteng 2092; ☏ +27 (0)11 726 8040; f +27 (0)11 726 5705;
🖰 www.ncppdsa.org.za

Index

Page entries in **bold** indicate major entries; page numbers in *italics* refer to maps.

Bradt Travel Guides
www.bradtguides.com

Africa

Africa Overland	£15.99
Algeria	£15.99
Benin	£14.99
Botswana: Okavango, Chobe, Northern Kalahari	£15.99
Burkina Faso	£14.99
Cameroon	£15.99
Cape Verde Islands	£14.99
Congo	£15.99
Eritrea	£15.99
Ethiopia	£15.99
Gambia, The	£13.99
Ghana	£15.99
Johannesburg	£6.99
Madagascar	£15.99
Malawi	£13.99
Mali	£13.95
Mauritius, Rodrigues & Réunion	£13.99
Mozambique	£13.99
Namibia	£15.99
Niger	£14.99
Nigeria	£17.99
North Africa: Roman Coast	£15.99
Rwanda	£14.99
São Tomé & Príncipe	£14.99
Seychelles	£14.99
Sierra Leone	£16.99
Sudan	£13.95
Tanzania, Northern	£13.99
Tanzania	£16.99
Uganda	£15.99
Zambia	£17.99
Zanzibar	£14.99

Britain and Europe

Albania	£15.99
Armenia, Nagorno Karabagh	£14.99
Azores	£13.99
Baltic Cities	£14.99
Belarus	£14.99
Belgrade	£6.99
Bosnia & Herzegovina	£13.99
Bratislava	£9.99
Budapest	£9.99
Bulgaria	£13.99
Cork	£6.99
Croatia	£13.99
Cyprus see North Cyprus	
Czech Republic	£13.99
Dresden	£7.99
Dubrovnik	£6.99

Estonia	£13.99
Faroe Islands	£15.99
Georgia	£14.99
Helsinki	£7.99
Hungary	£14.99
Iceland	£14.99
Kosovo	£14.99
Lapland	£13.99
Latvia	£13.99
Lille	£6.99
Lithuania	£14.99
Ljubljana	£7.99
Luxembourg	£13.99
Macedonia	£14.99
Montenegro	£14.99
North Cyprus	£12.99
Paris, Lille & Brussels	£11.95
Riga	£6.99
Serbia	£14.99
Slovakia	£14.99
Slovenia	£13.99
Spitsbergen	£14.99
Switzerland Without a Car	£14.99
Tallinn	£6.99
Transylvania	£14.99
Ukraine	£14.99
Vilnius	£6.99
Zagreb	£6.99

Middle East, Asia and Australasia

China: Yunnan Province	£13.99
Great Wall of China	£13.99
Iran	£14.99
Iraq: Then & Now	£15.99
Israel	£15.99
Kazakhstan	£15.99
Kyrgyzstan	£15.99
Maldives	£15.99
Mongolia	£16.99
North Korea	£14.99
Oman	£13.99
Shangri-La: A Travel Guide to the Himalayan Dream	£14.99
Sri Lanka	£15.99
Syria	£14.99
Tibet	£13.99
Turkmenistan	£14.99
Yemen	£14.99

The Americas and the Caribbean

Amazon, The	£14.99
Argentina	£15.99

Bolivia	£14.99
Cayman Islands	£14.99
Chile	£16.95
Colombia	£16.99
Costa Rica	£13.99
Dominica	£14.99
Falkland Islands	£13.95
Grenada, Carriacou & Petite Martinique	£14.99
Guyana	£14.99
Panama	£13.95
Peru & Bolivia: The Bradt Trekking Guide	£12.95
St Helena	£14.99
Turks & Caicos Islands	£14.99
USA by Rail	£14.99

Wildlife

100 Animals to See Before They Die	£16.99
Antarctica: Guide to the Wildlife	£15.99
Arctic: Guide to the Wildlife	£15.99
Central & Eastern European Wildlife	£15.99
Chinese Wildlife	£16.99
East African Wildlife	£19.99
Galápagos Wildlife	£15.99
Madagascar Wildlife	£16.99
New Zealand Wildlife	£14.99
North Atlantic Wildlife	£16.99
Peruvian Wildlife	£15.99
Southern African Wildlife	£18.95
Sri Lankan Wildlife	£15.99
Wildlife and Conservation Volunteering: The Complete Guide	£13.99

Eccentric Guides

Eccentric Australia	£12.99
Eccentric Britain	£13.99
Eccentric California	£13.99
Eccentric Cambridge	£6.99
Eccentric Edinburgh	£5.95
Eccentric France	£12.95
Eccentric London	£13.99

Others

Your Child Abroad: A Travel Health Guide	£10.95
Something Different for the Weekend	£9.99
Britain from the Rails	£17.99